Godchild

Earl Cain Series 5

Vol. 8

Story & Art by **Kaori Yuki**

Contents

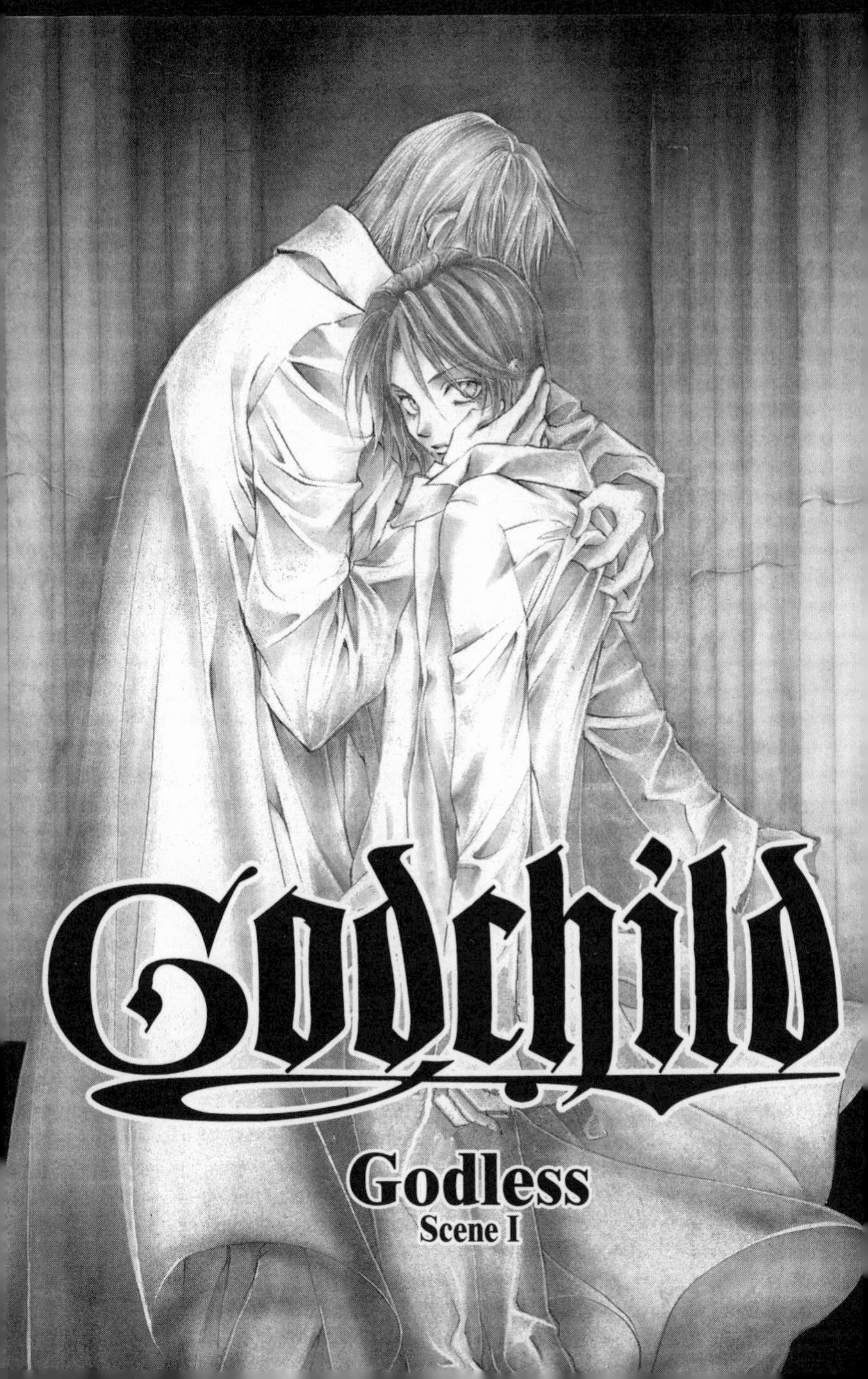
Godchild
Godless
Scene I

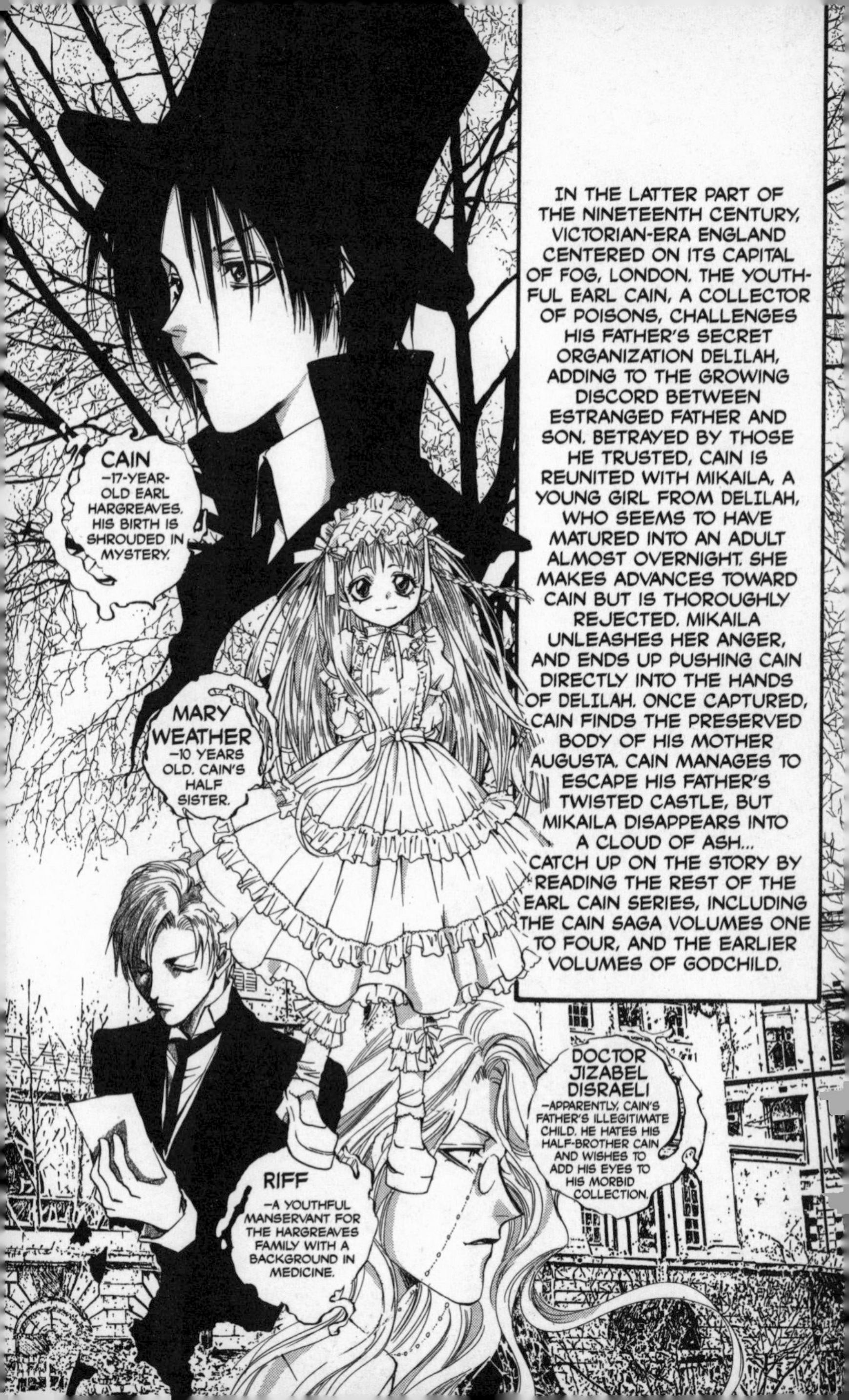
IN THE LATTER PART OF THE NINETEENTH CENTURY, VICTORIAN-ERA ENGLAND CENTERED ON ITS CAPITAL OF FOG, LONDON. THE YOUTHFUL EARL CAIN, A COLLECTOR OF POISONS, CHALLENGES HIS FATHER'S SECRET ORGANIZATION DELILAH, ADDING TO THE GROWING DISCORD BETWEEN ESTRANGED FATHER AND SON. BETRAYED BY THOSE HE TRUSTED, CAIN IS REUNITED WITH MIKAILA, A YOUNG GIRL FROM DELILAH, WHO SEEMS TO HAVE MATURED INTO AN ADULT ALMOST OVERNIGHT. SHE MAKES ADVANCES TOWARD CAIN BUT IS THOROUGHLY REJECTED. MIKAILA UNLEASHES HER ANGER, AND ENDS UP PUSHING CAIN DIRECTLY INTO THE HANDS OF DELILAH. ONCE CAPTURED, CAIN FINDS THE PRESERVED BODY OF HIS MOTHER AUGUSTA. CAIN MANAGES TO ESCAPE HIS FATHER'S TWISTED CASTLE, BUT MIKAILA DISAPPEARS INTO A CLOUD OF ASH... CATCH UP ON THE STORY BY READING THE REST OF THE EARL CAIN SERIES, INCLUDING THE CAIN SAGA VOLUMES ONE TO FOUR, AND THE EARLIER VOLUMES OF GODCHILD.
CAIN —17-YEAR-OLD EARL HARGREAVES. HIS BIRTH IS SHROUDED IN MYSTERY.
MARY WEATHER —10 YEARS OLD. CAIN'S HALF SISTER.
DOCTOR JIZABEL DISRAELI —APPARENTLY, CAIN'S FATHER'S ILLEGITIMATE CHILD. HE HATES HIS HALF-BROTHER CAIN AND WISHES TO ADD HIS EYES TO HIS MORBID COLLECTION.
RIFF —A YOUTHFUL MANSERVANT FOR THE HARGREAVES FAMILY WITH A BACKGROUND IN MEDICINE.

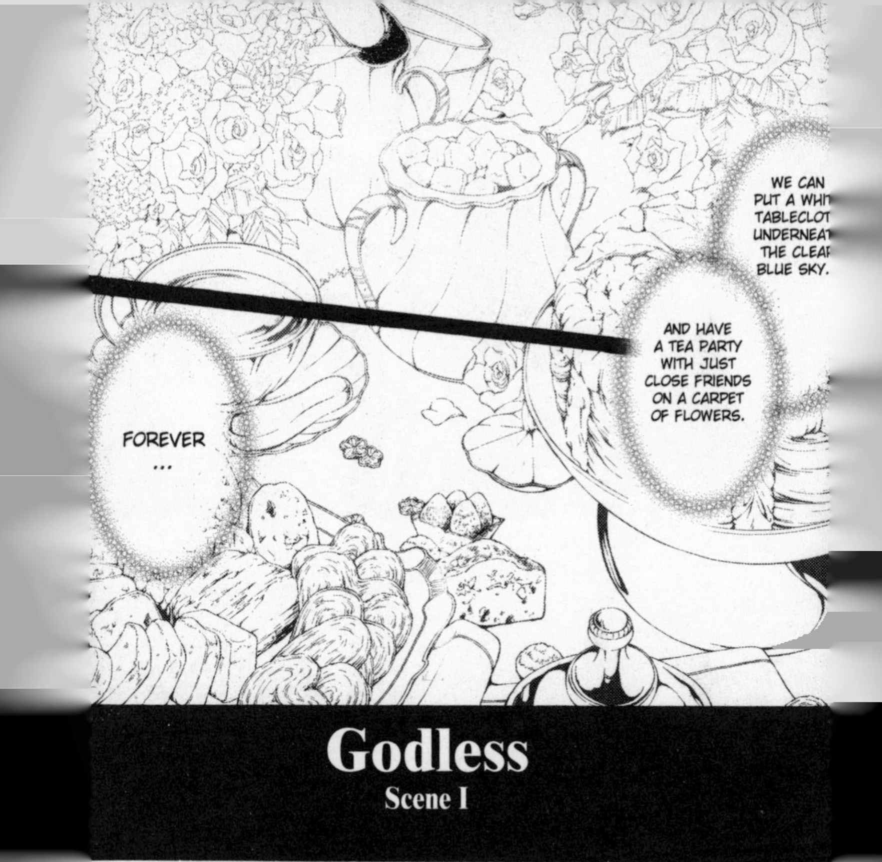
WE CAN PUT A WHIT TABLECLOT UNDERNEAT THE CLEAR BLUE SKY.
AND HAVE A TEA PARTY WITH JUST CLOSE FRIENDS ON A CARPET OF FLOWERS.
FOREVER ...

Godless
Scene I

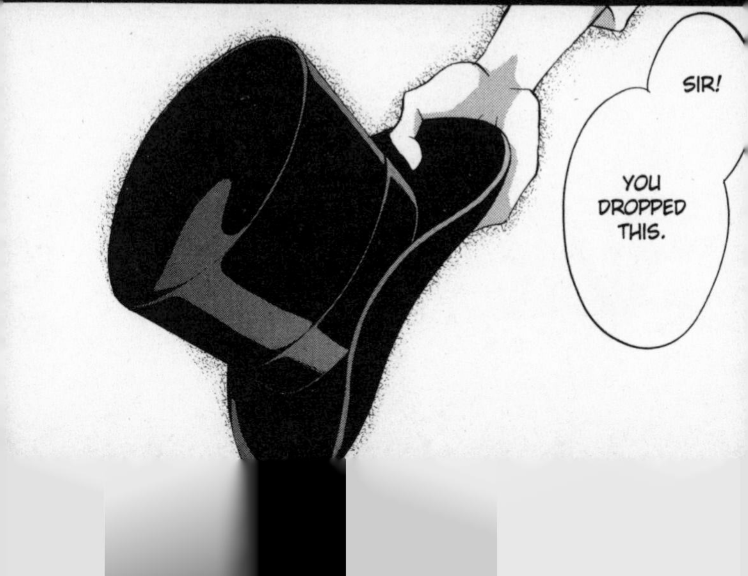
SIR!
YOU DROPPED THIS.

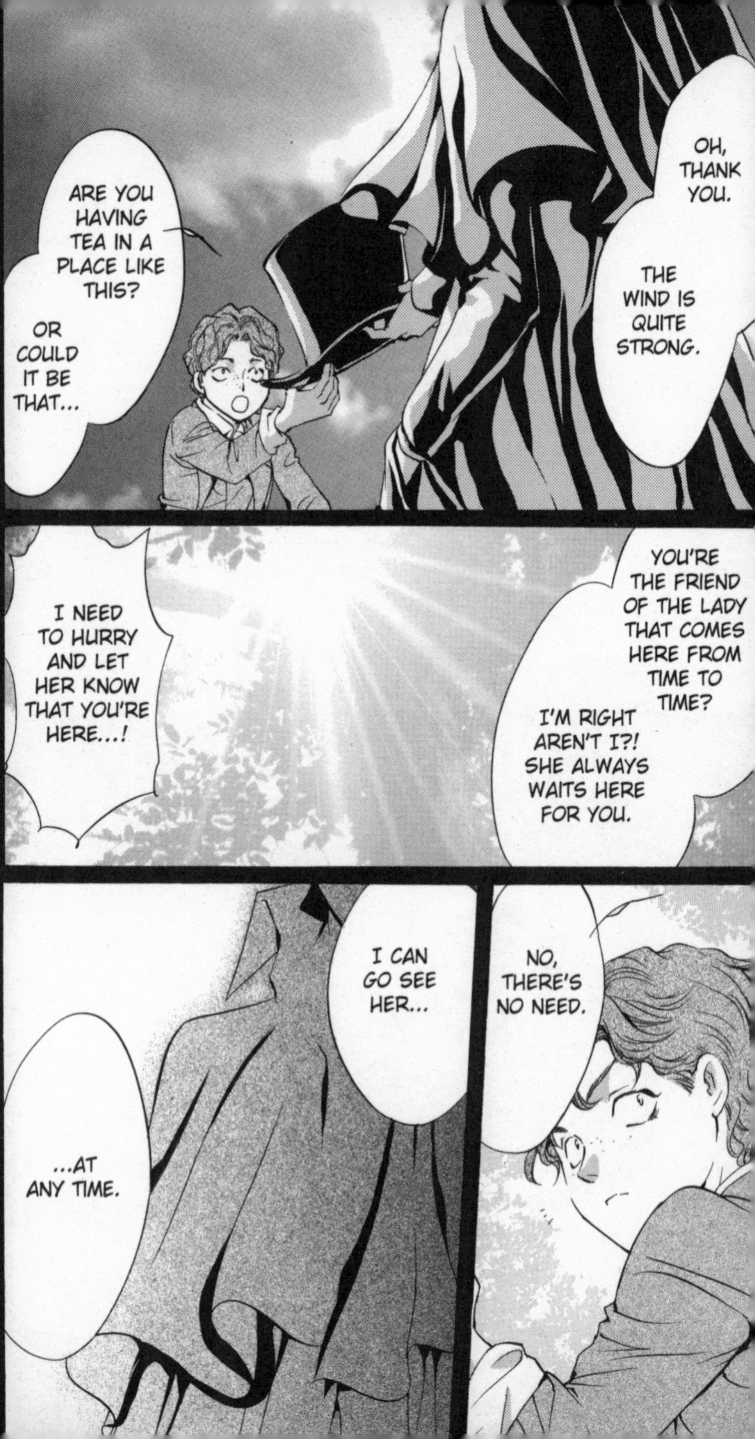
OH, THANK YOU.
THE WIND IS QUITE STRONG.
ARE YOU HAVING TEA IN A PLACE LIKE THIS?
OR COULD IT BE THAT...
YOU'RE THE FRIEND OF THE LADY THAT COMES HERE FROM TIME TO TIME?
I'M RIGHT AREN'T I?! SHE ALWAYS WAITS HERE FOR YOU.
I NEED TO HURRY AND LET HER KNOW THAT YOU'RE HERE...!
NO, THERE'S NO NEED.
I CAN GO SEE HER...
...AT ANY TIME.

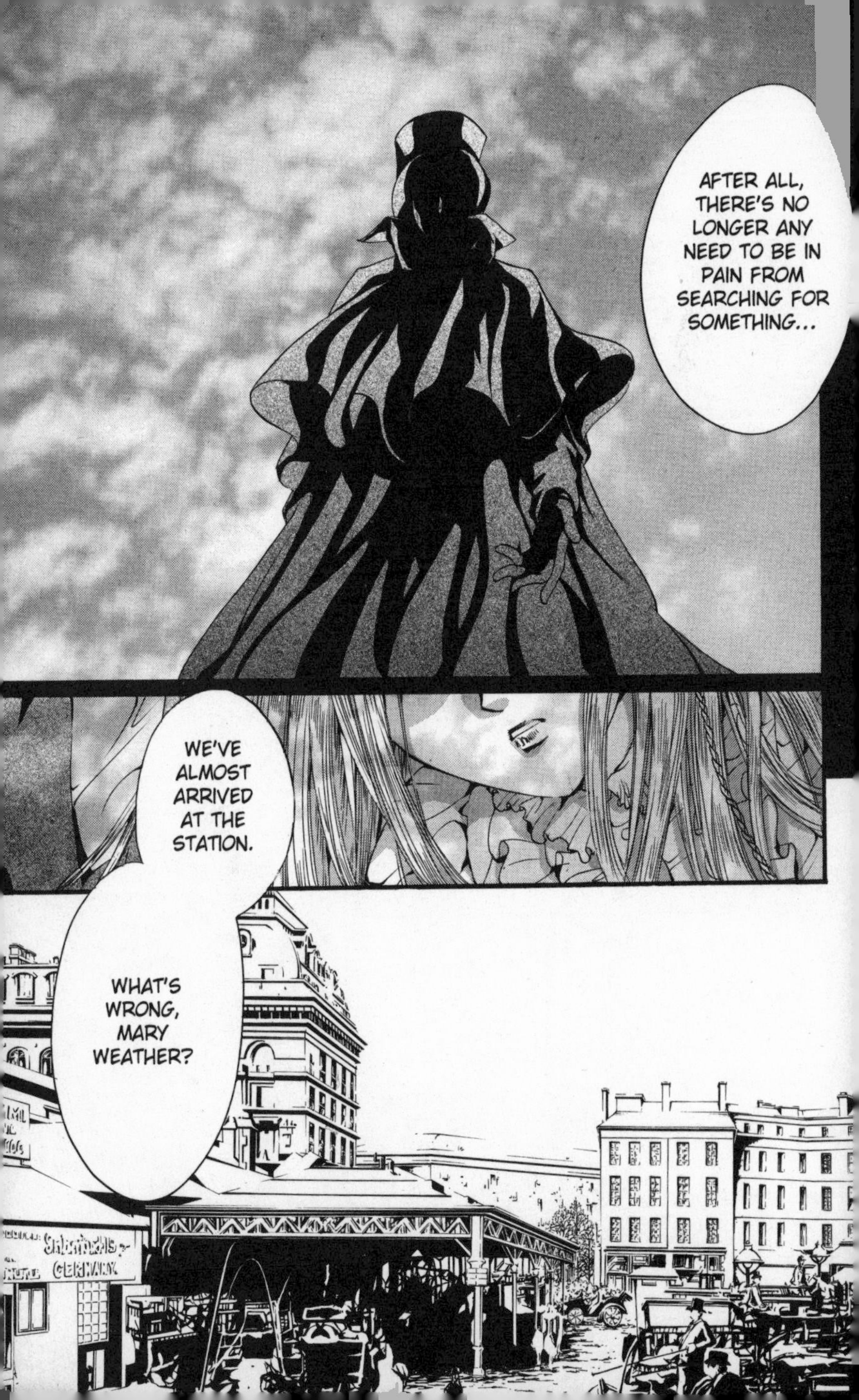
AFTER ALL, THERE'S NO LONGER ANY NEED TO BE IN PAIN FROM SEARCHING FOR SOMETHING...
WE'VE ALMOST ARRIVED AT THE STATION.
WHAT'S WRONG, MARY WEATHER?
GERMANY

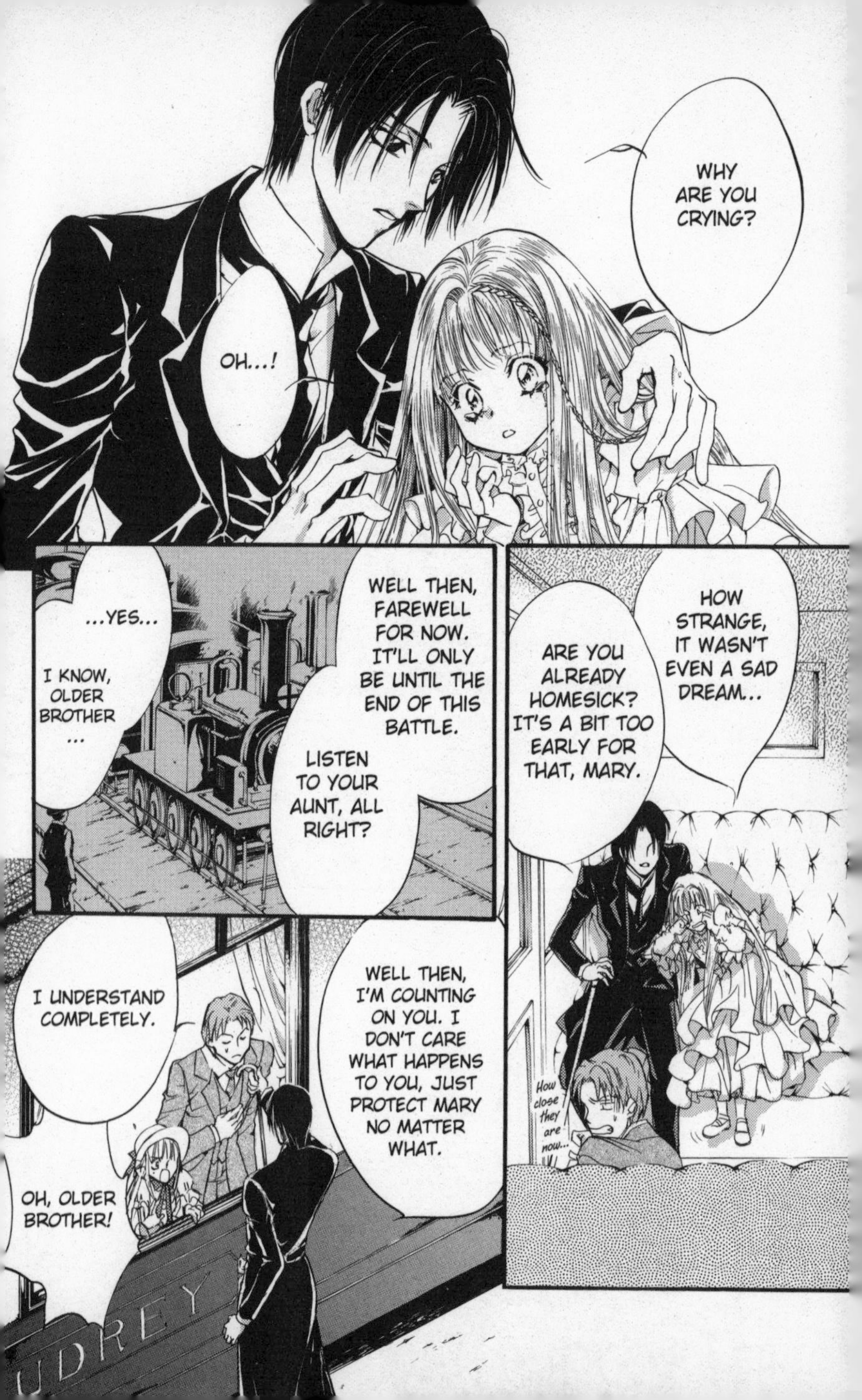
WHY ARE YOU CRYING?
OH...!
HOW STRANGE, IT WASN'T EVEN A SAD DREAM...
ARE YOU ALREADY HOMESICK? IT'S A BIT TOO EARLY FOR THAT, MARY.
How close they are now...
WELL THEN, FAREWELL FOR NOW. IT'LL ONLY BE UNTIL THE END OF THIS BATTLE.
LISTEN TO YOUR AUNT, ALL RIGHT?
...YES...
I KNOW, OLDER BROTHER...
WELL THEN, I'M COUNTING ON YOU. I DON'T CARE WHAT HAPPENS TO YOU, JUST PROTECT MARY NO MATTER WHAT.
I UNDERSTAND COMPLETELY.
OH, OLDER BROTHER!
UDREY

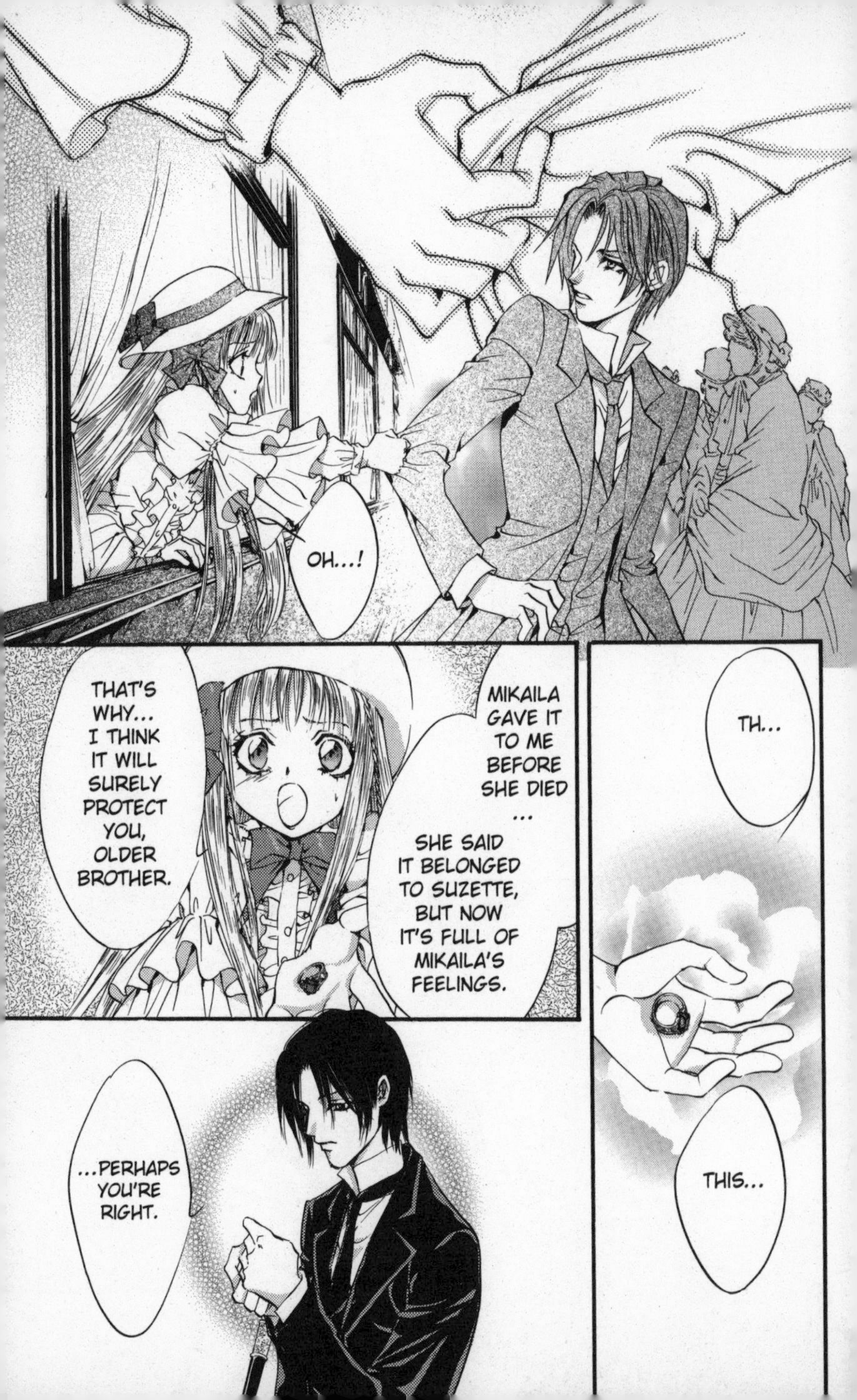
OH...!
TH...
THIS...
MIKAILA GAVE IT TO ME BEFORE SHE DIED ...
SHE SAID IT BELONGED TO SUZETTE, BUT NOW IT'S FULL OF MIKAILA'S FEELINGS.
THAT'S WHY... I THINK IT WILL SURELY PROTECT YOU, OLDER BROTHER.
...PERHAPS YOU'RE RIGHT.

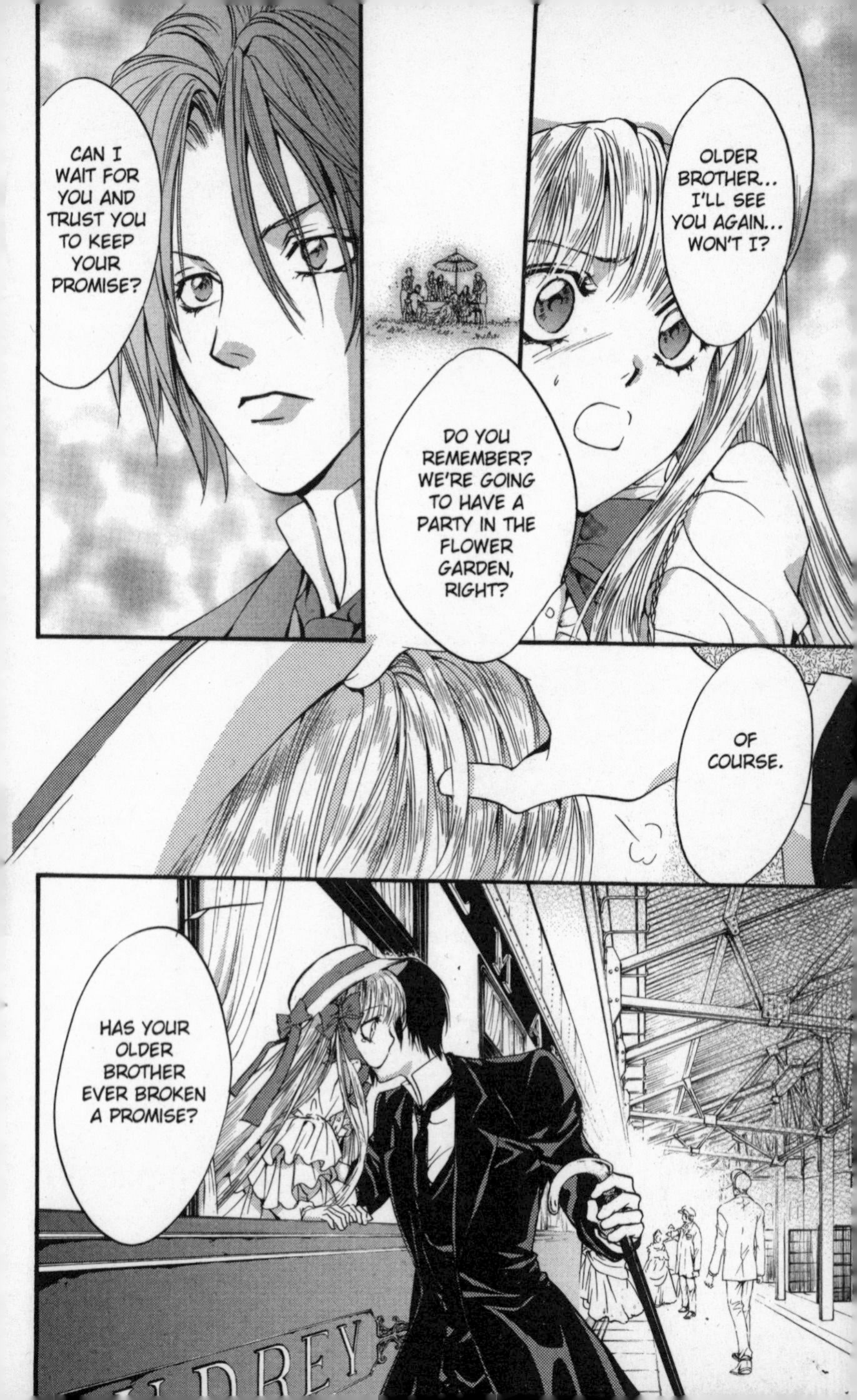
OLDER BROTHER... I'LL SEE YOU AGAIN... WON'T I?
DO YOU REMEMBER? WE'RE GOING TO HAVE A PARTY IN THE FLOWER GARDEN, RIGHT?
CAN I WAIT FOR YOU AND TRUST YOU TO KEEP YOUR PROMISE?
OF COURSE.
HAS YOUR OLDER BROTHER EVER BROKEN A PROMISE?

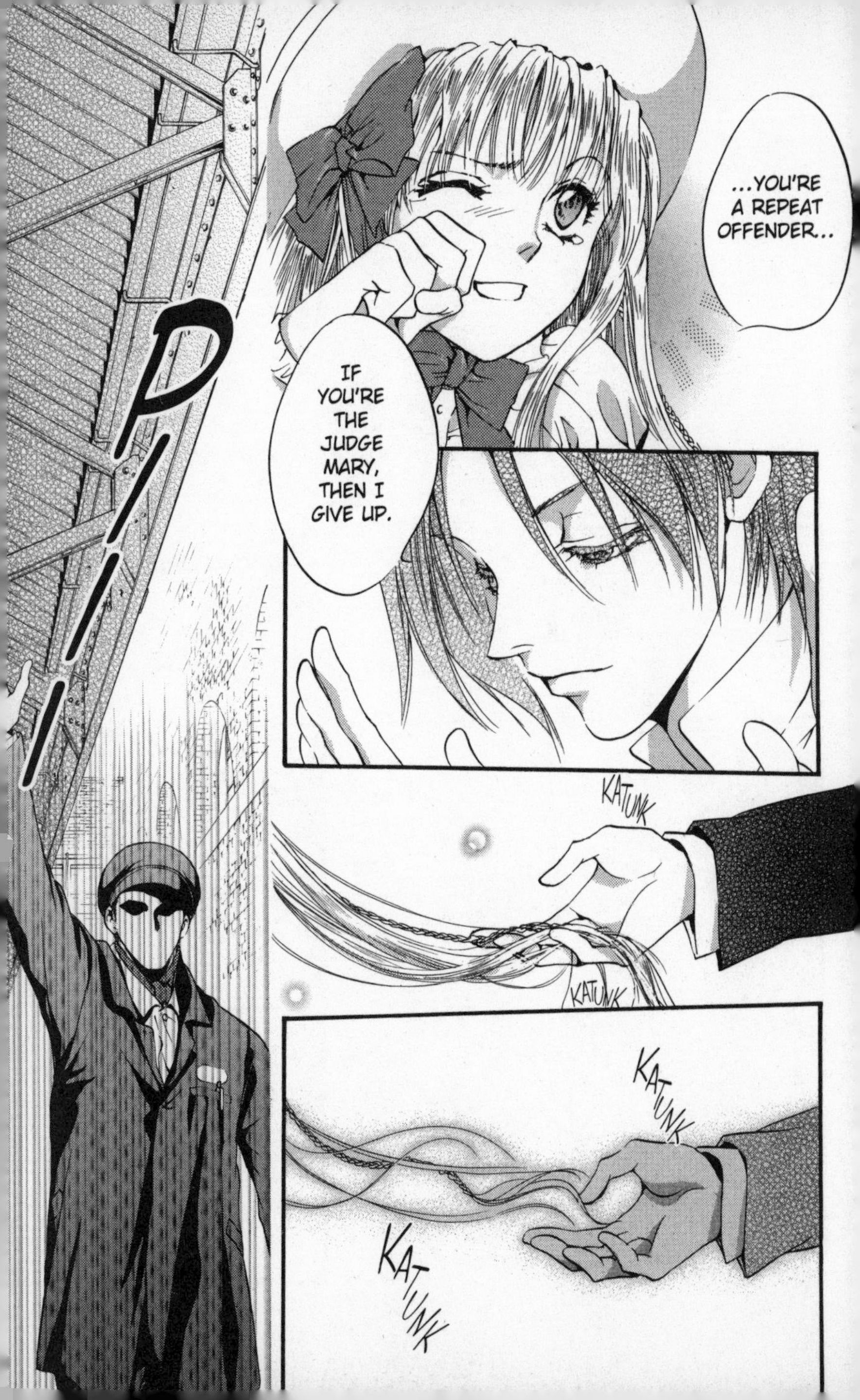
...YOU'RE A REPEAT OFFENDER...
IF YOU'RE THE JUDGE MARY, THEN I GIVE UP.
P-----
KATUNK
KATUNK
KATUNK
KATUNK

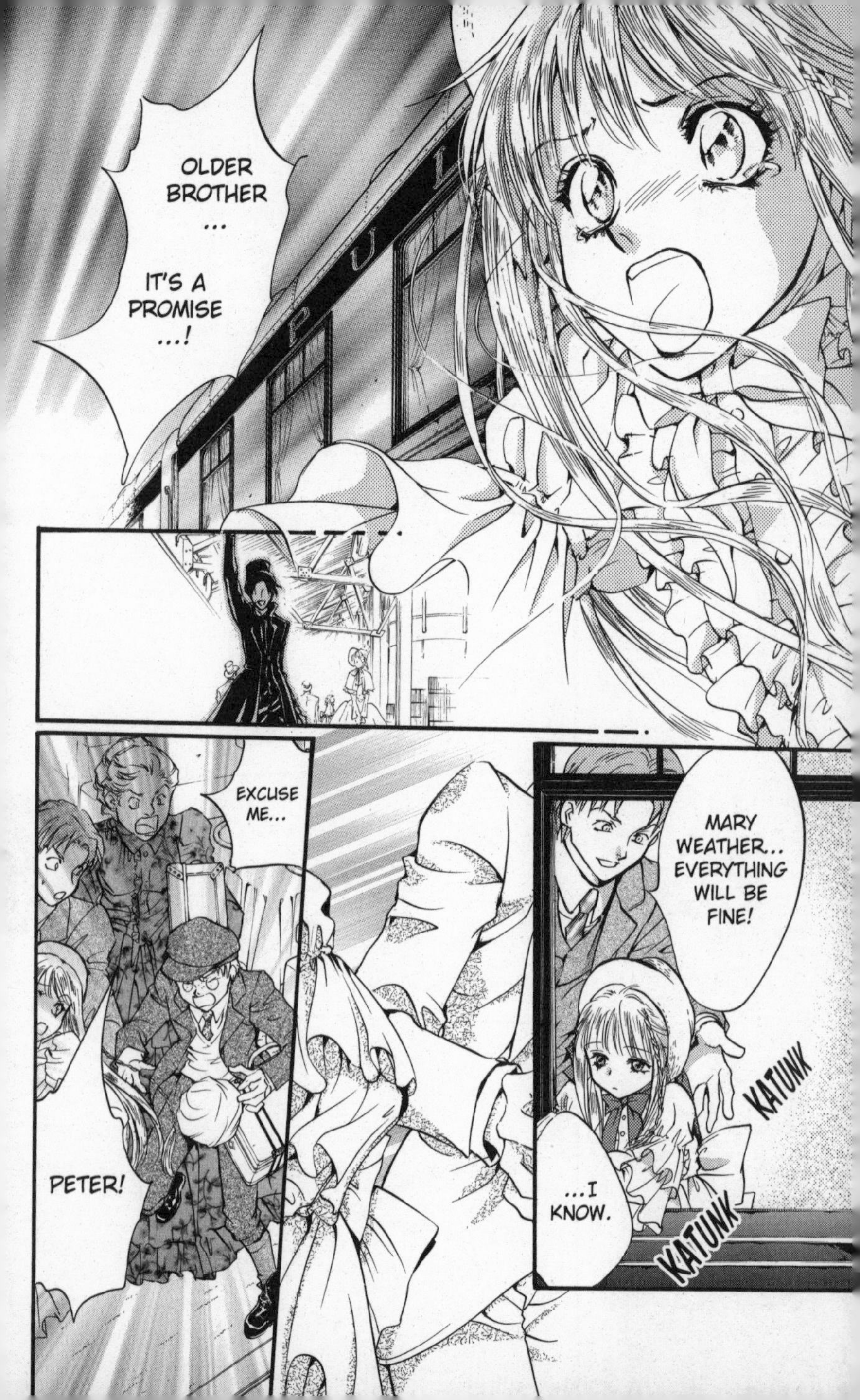
OLDER BROTHER ...
IT'S A PROMISE ...!
MARY WEATHER... EVERYTHING WILL BE FINE!
...I KNOW.
KATUNK
KATUNK
EXCUSE ME...
PETER!

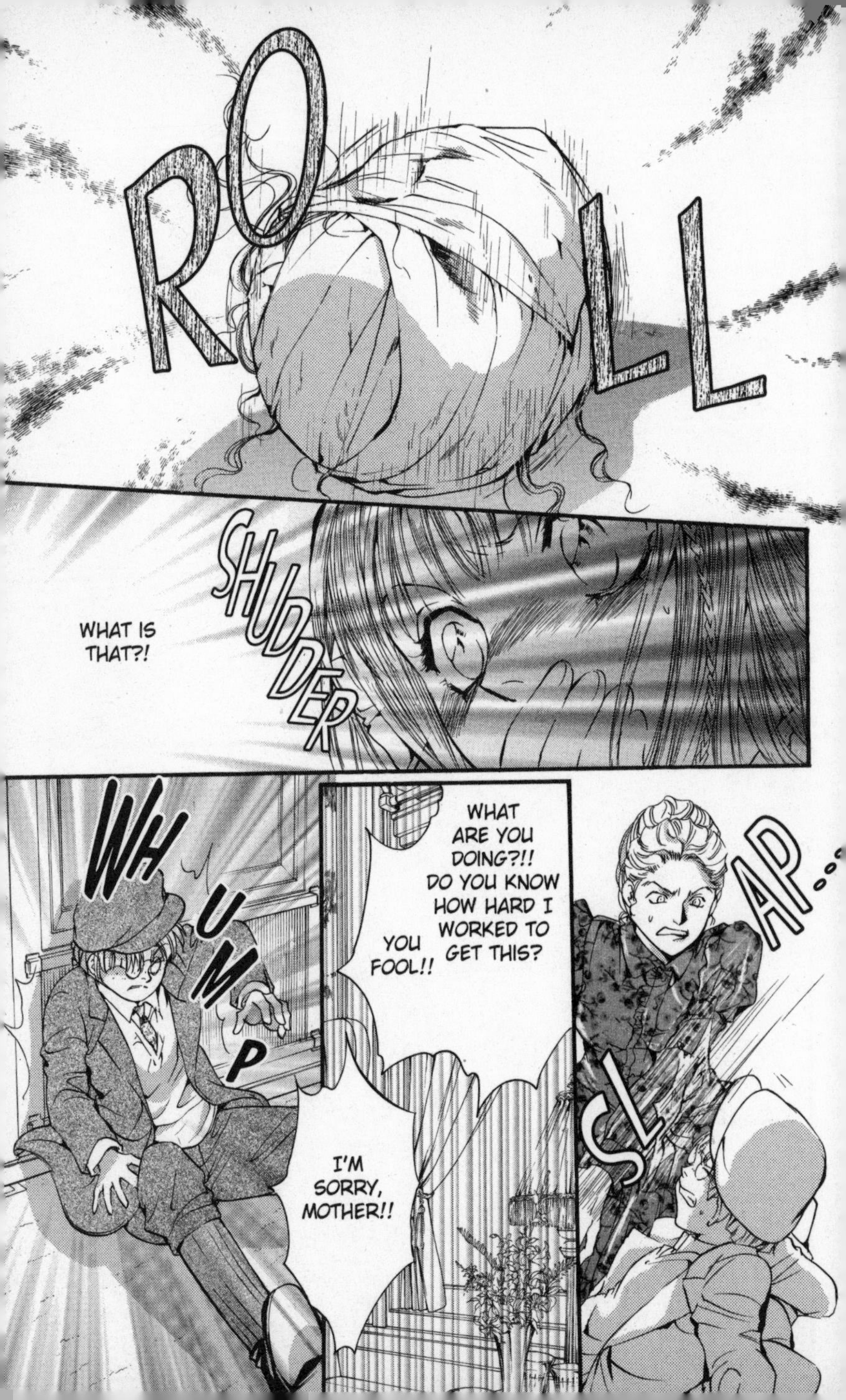
ROLL
SHUDDER
WHAT IS THAT?!
SLAP...
WHAT ARE YOU DOING?!! DO YOU KNOW HOW HARD I WORKED TO GET THIS?
YOU FOOL!!
WHUMP
I'M SORRY, MOTHER!!

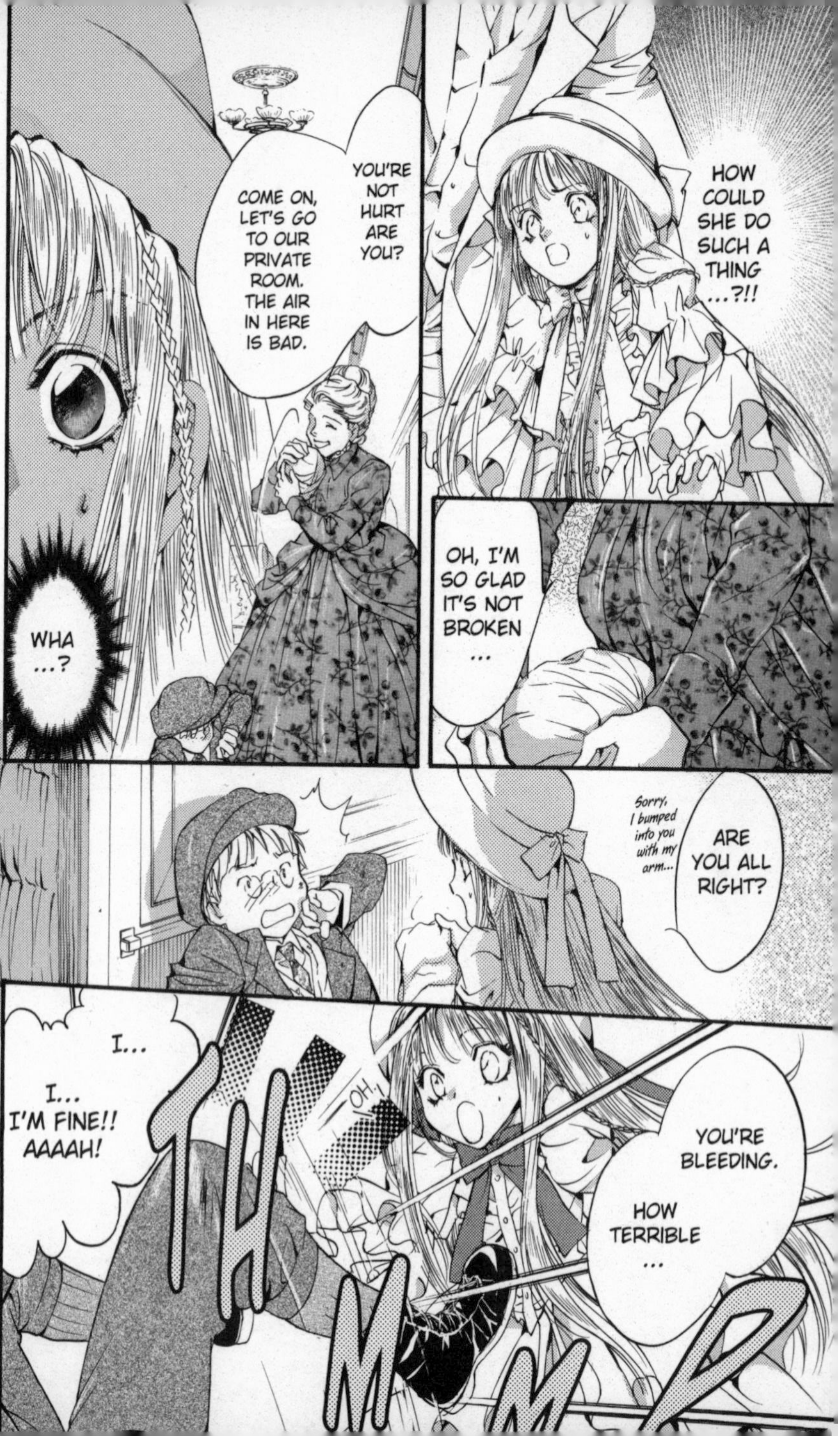
HOW COULD SHE DO SUCH A THING ...?!!
OH, I'M SO GLAD IT'S NOT BROKEN ...
YOU'RE NOT HURT ARE YOU?
COME ON, LET'S GO TO OUR PRIVATE ROOM. THE AIR IN HERE IS BAD.
WHA ...?
ARE YOU ALL RIGHT?
Sorry, I bumped into you with my arm...
YOU'RE BLEEDING.
HOW TERRIBLE ...
OH,
THMMP
I...
I... I'M FINE!! AAAAH!

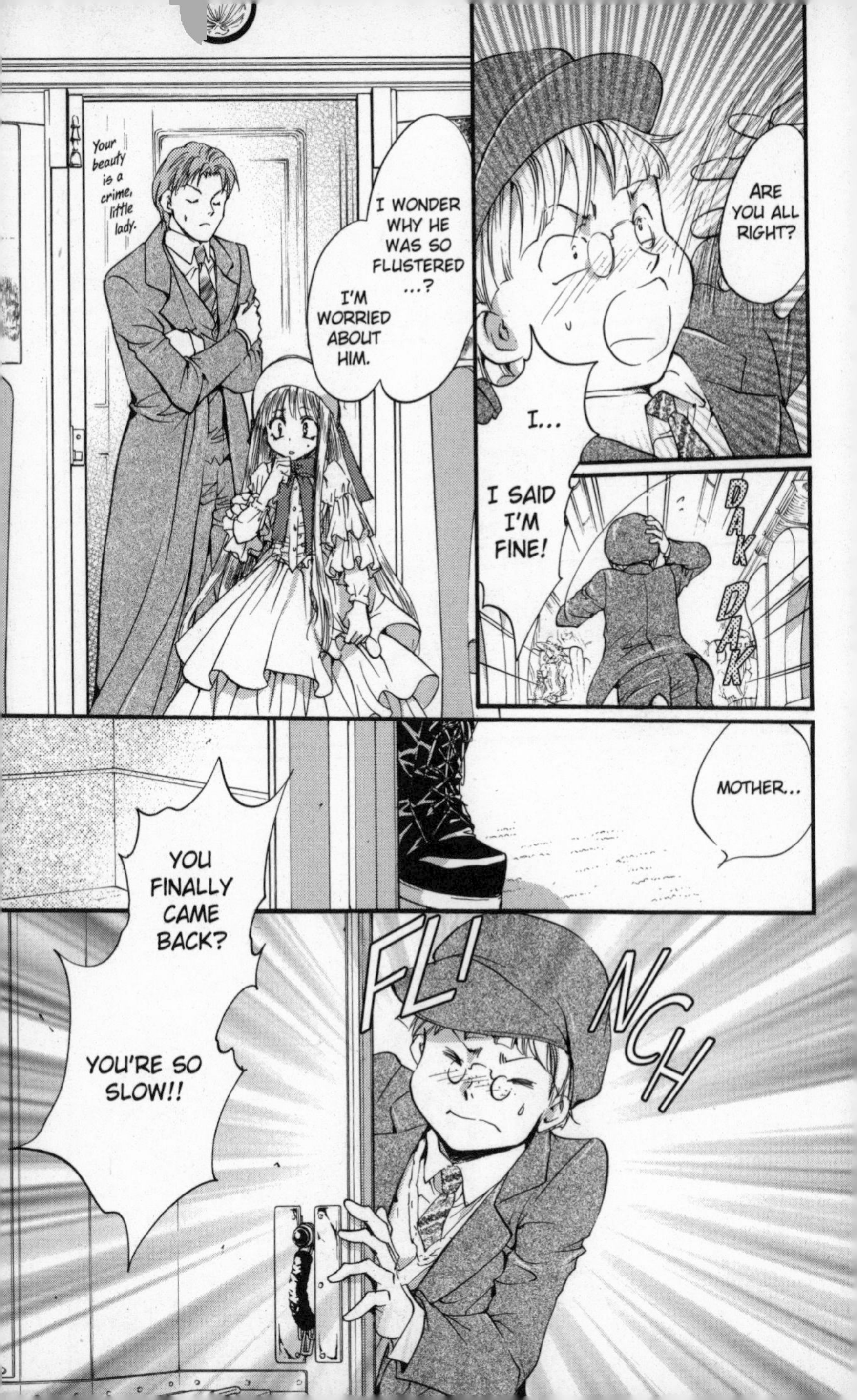
ARE YOU ALL RIGHT?
I...
I SAID I'M FINE!
DAK DAK
I WONDER WHY HE WAS SO FLUSTERED ...?
I'M WORRIED ABOUT HIM.
Your beauty is a crime, little lady.
MOTHER...
YOU FINALLY CAME BACK?
YOU'RE SO SLOW!!
FLINCH

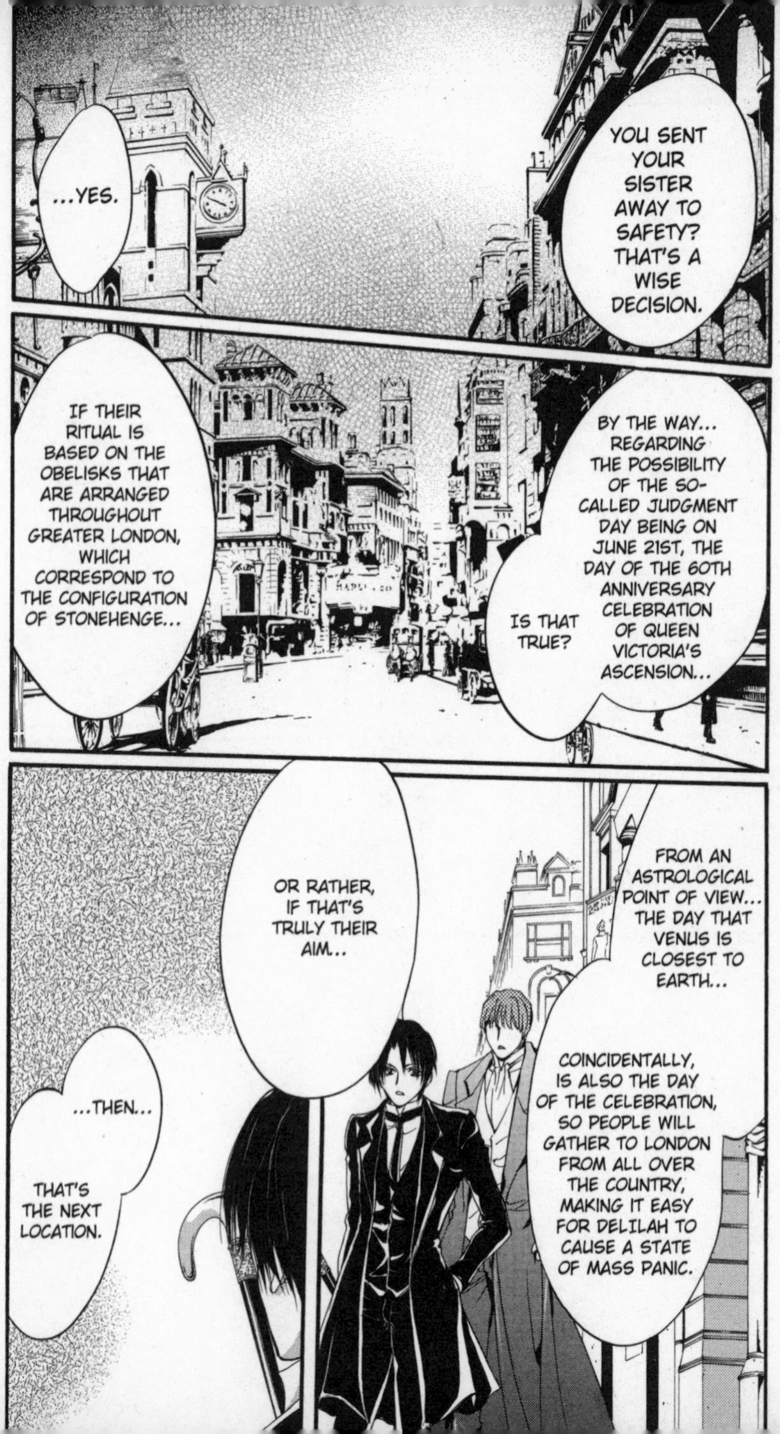
YOU SENT YOUR SISTER AWAY TO SAFETY? THAT'S A WISE DECISION.
...YES.
BY THE WAY... REGARDING THE POSSIBILITY OF THE SO-CALLED JUDGMENT DAY BEING ON JUNE 21ST, THE DAY OF THE 60TH ANNIVERSARY CELEBRATION OF QUEEN VICTORIA'S ASCENSION...
IS THAT TRUE?
IF THEIR RITUAL IS BASED ON THE OBELISKS THAT ARE ARRANGED THROUGHOUT GREATER LONDON, WHICH CORRESPOND TO THE CONFIGURATION OF STONEHENGE...
FROM AN ASTROLOGICAL POINT OF VIEW... THE DAY THAT VENUS IS CLOSEST TO EARTH...
COINCIDENTALLY, IS ALSO THE DAY OF THE CELEBRATION, SO PEOPLE WILL GATHER TO LONDON FROM ALL OVER THE COUNTRY, MAKING IT EASY FOR DELILAH TO CAUSE A STATE OF MASS PANIC.
OR RATHER, IF THAT'S TRULY THEIR AIM...
...THEN...
THAT'S THE NEXT LOCATION.

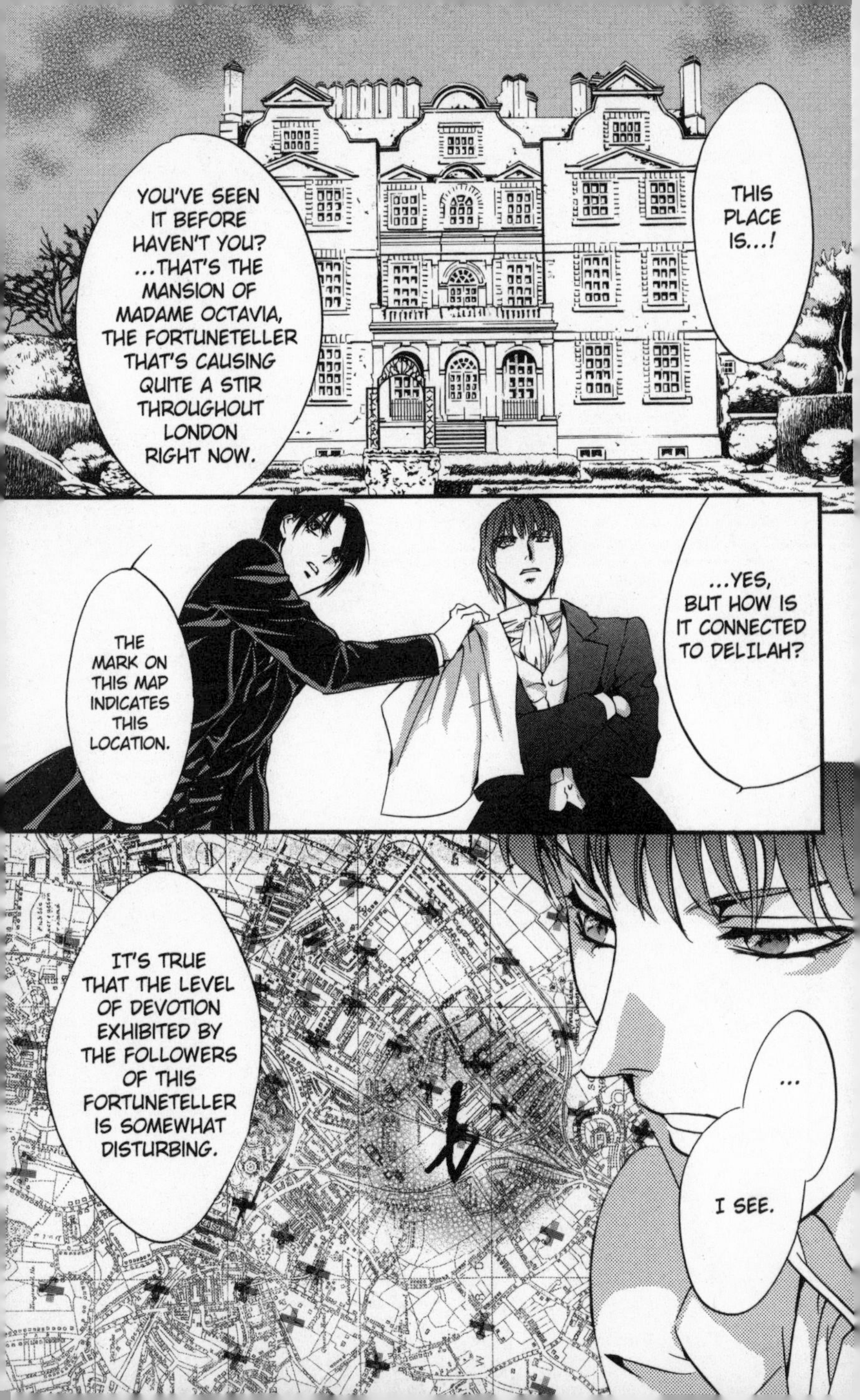
THIS PLACE IS...!
YOU'VE SEEN IT BEFORE HAVEN'T YOU? ...THAT'S THE MANSION OF MADAME OCTAVIA, THE FORTUNETELLER THAT'S CAUSING QUITE A STIR THROUGHOUT LONDON RIGHT NOW.
...YES, BUT HOW IS IT CONNECTED TO DELILAH?
THE MARK ON THIS MAP INDICATES THIS LOCATION.
...
I SEE.
IT'S TRUE THAT THE LEVEL OF DEVOTION EXHIBITED BY THE FOLLOWERS OF THIS FORTUNETELLER IS SOMEWHAT DISTURBING.

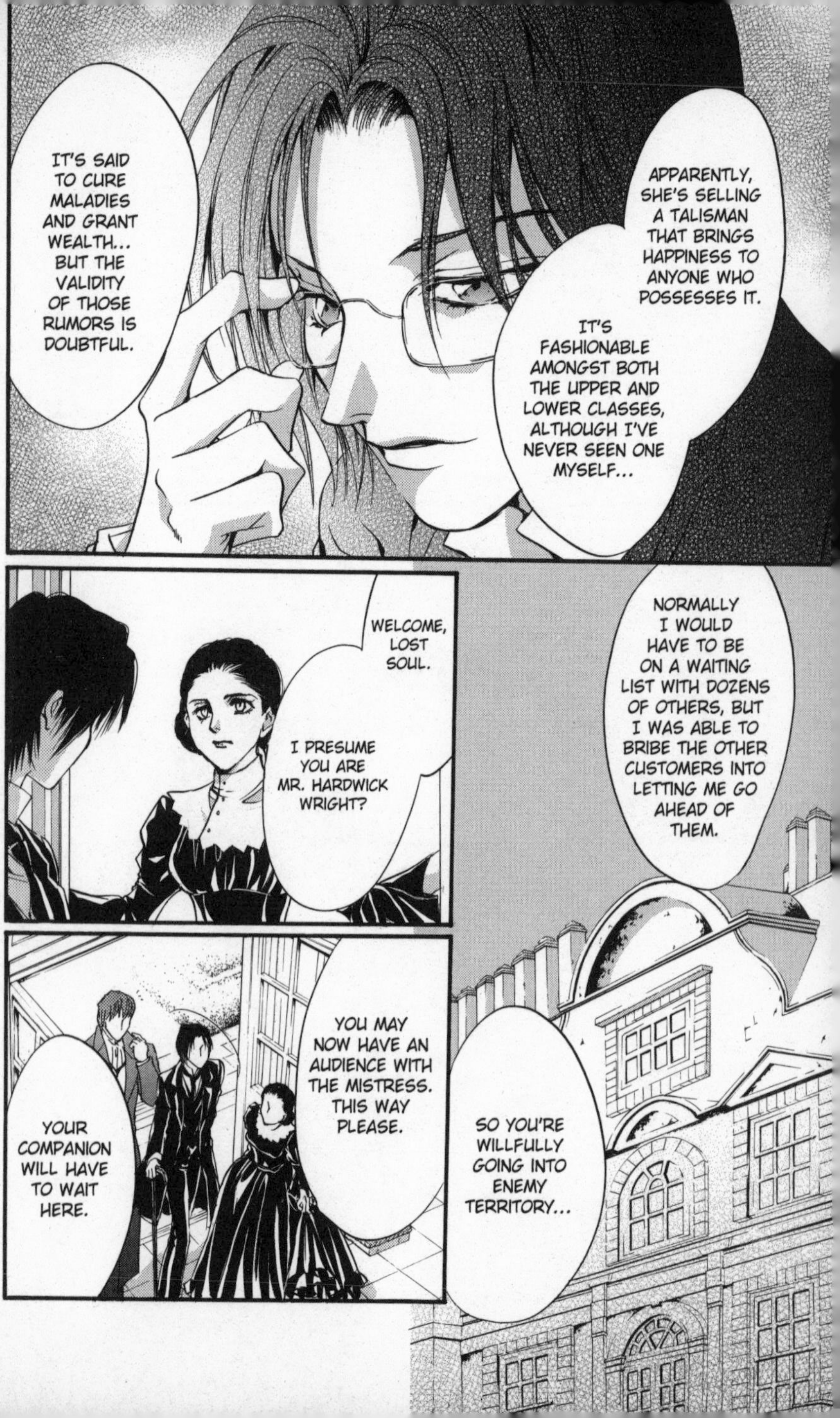
APPARENTLY, SHE'S SELLING A TALISMAN THAT BRINGS HAPPINESS TO ANYONE WHO POSSESSES IT.
IT'S FASHIONABLE AMONGST BOTH THE UPPER AND LOWER CLASSES, ALTHOUGH I'VE NEVER SEEN ONE MYSELF...
IT'S SAID TO CURE MALADIES AND GRANT WEALTH... BUT THE VALIDITY OF THOSE RUMORS IS DOUBTFUL.
NORMALLY I WOULD HAVE TO BE ON A WAITING LIST WITH DOZENS OF OTHERS, BUT I WAS ABLE TO BRIBE THE OTHER CUSTOMERS INTO LETTING ME GO AHEAD OF THEM.
SO YOU'RE WILLFULLY GOING INTO ENEMY TERRITORY...
WELCOME, LOST SOUL.
I PRESUME YOU ARE MR. HARDWICK WRIGHT?
YOU MAY NOW HAVE AN AUDIENCE WITH THE MISTRESS. THIS WAY PLEASE.
YOUR COMPANION WILL HAVE TO WAIT HERE.

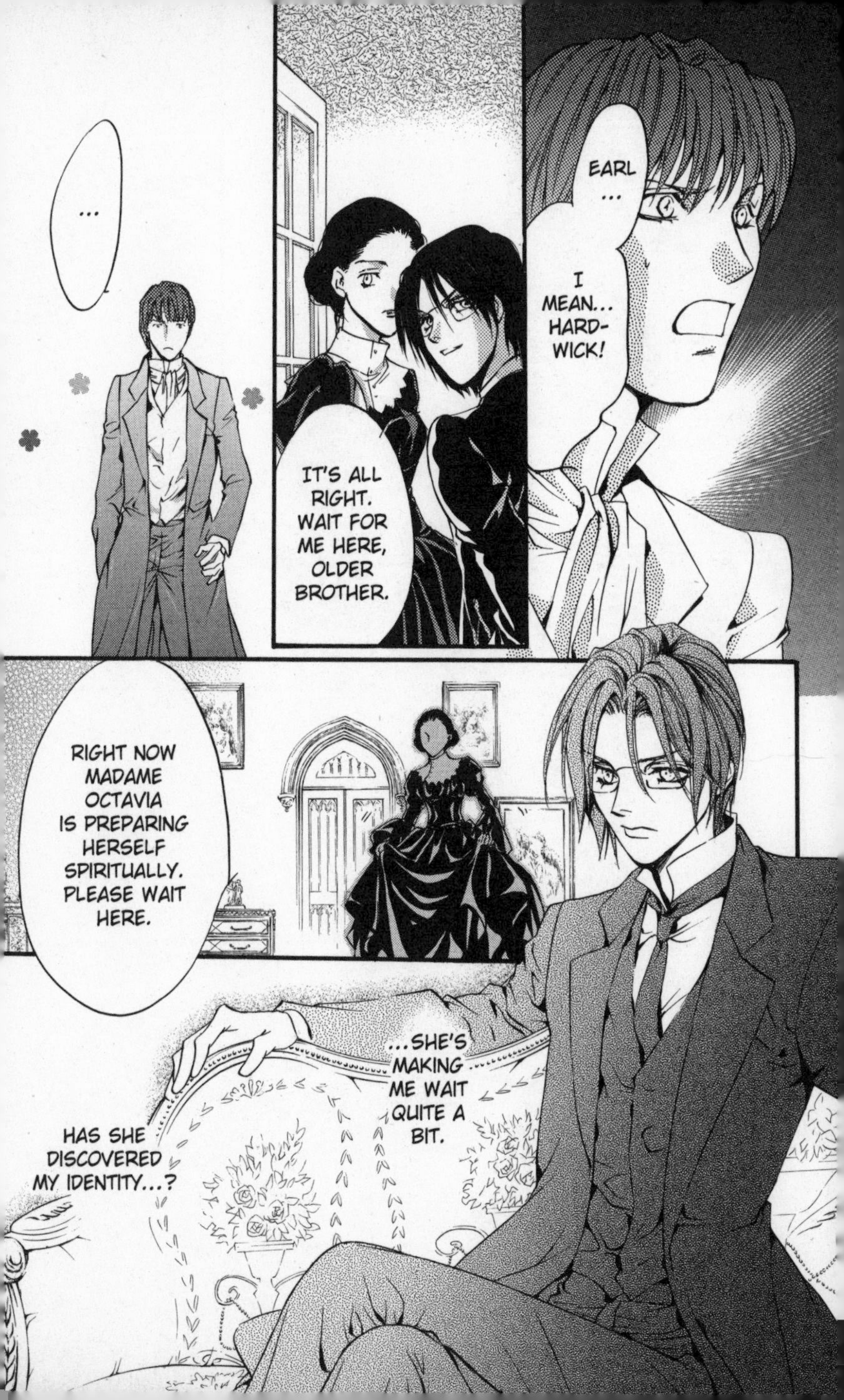
EARL ...
I MEAN... HARD-WICK!
IT'S ALL RIGHT. WAIT FOR ME HERE, OLDER BROTHER.
...
RIGHT NOW MADAME OCTAVIA IS PREPARING HERSELF SPIRITUALLY. PLEASE WAIT HERE.
...SHE'S MAKING ME WAIT QUITE A BIT.
HAS SHE DISCOVERED MY IDENTITY...?

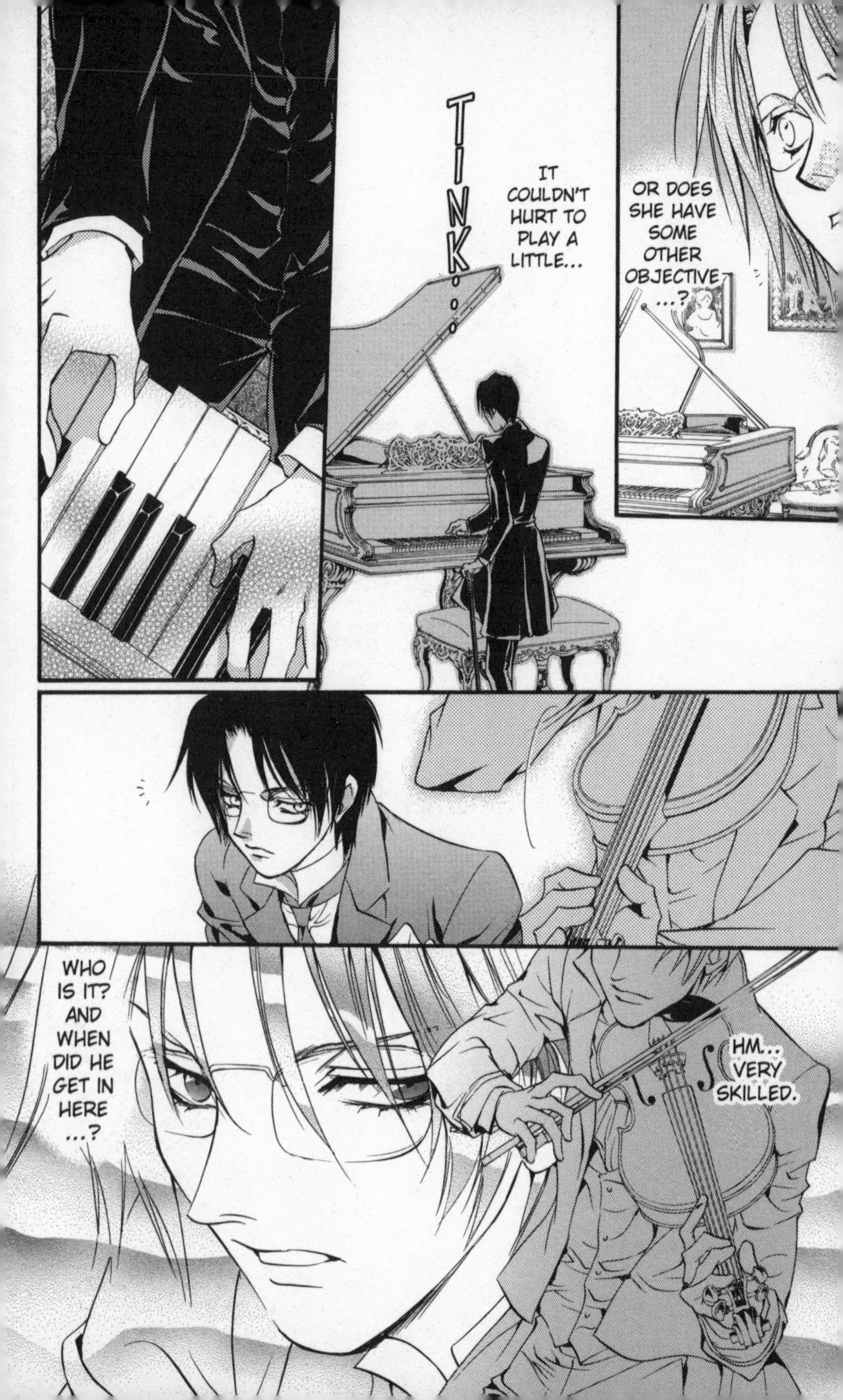

OR DOES SHE HAVE SOME OTHER OBJECTIVE ...?
IT COULDN'T HURT TO PLAY A LITTLE...
TINK...
HM... VERY SKILLED.
WHO IS IT? AND WHEN DID HE GET IN HERE ...?

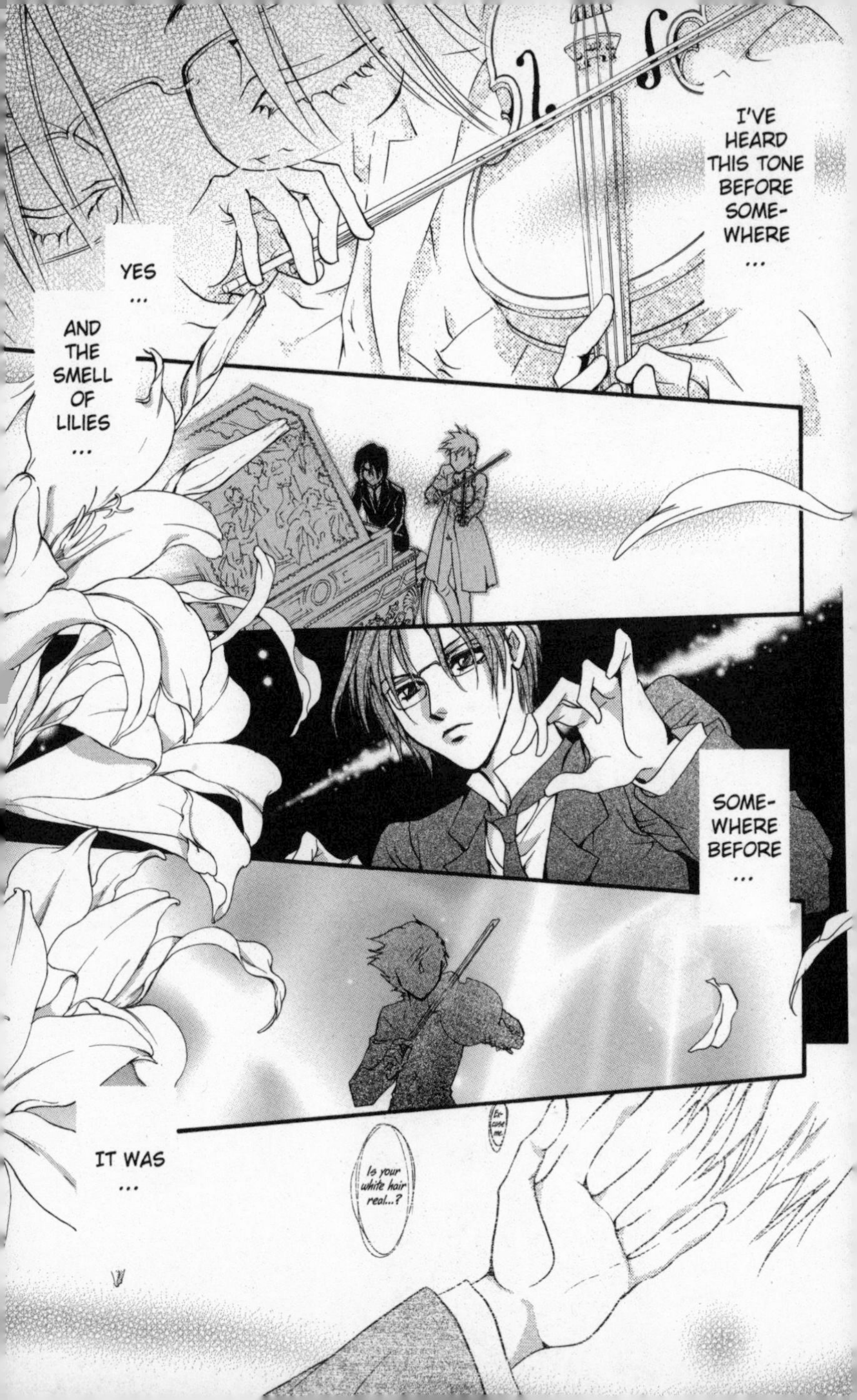
I'VE HEARD THIS TONE BEFORE SOME-WHERE ...
YES ...
AND THE SMELL OF LILIES ...
SOME-WHERE BEFORE ...
Ex-cuse me.
Is your white hair real...?
IT WAS ...

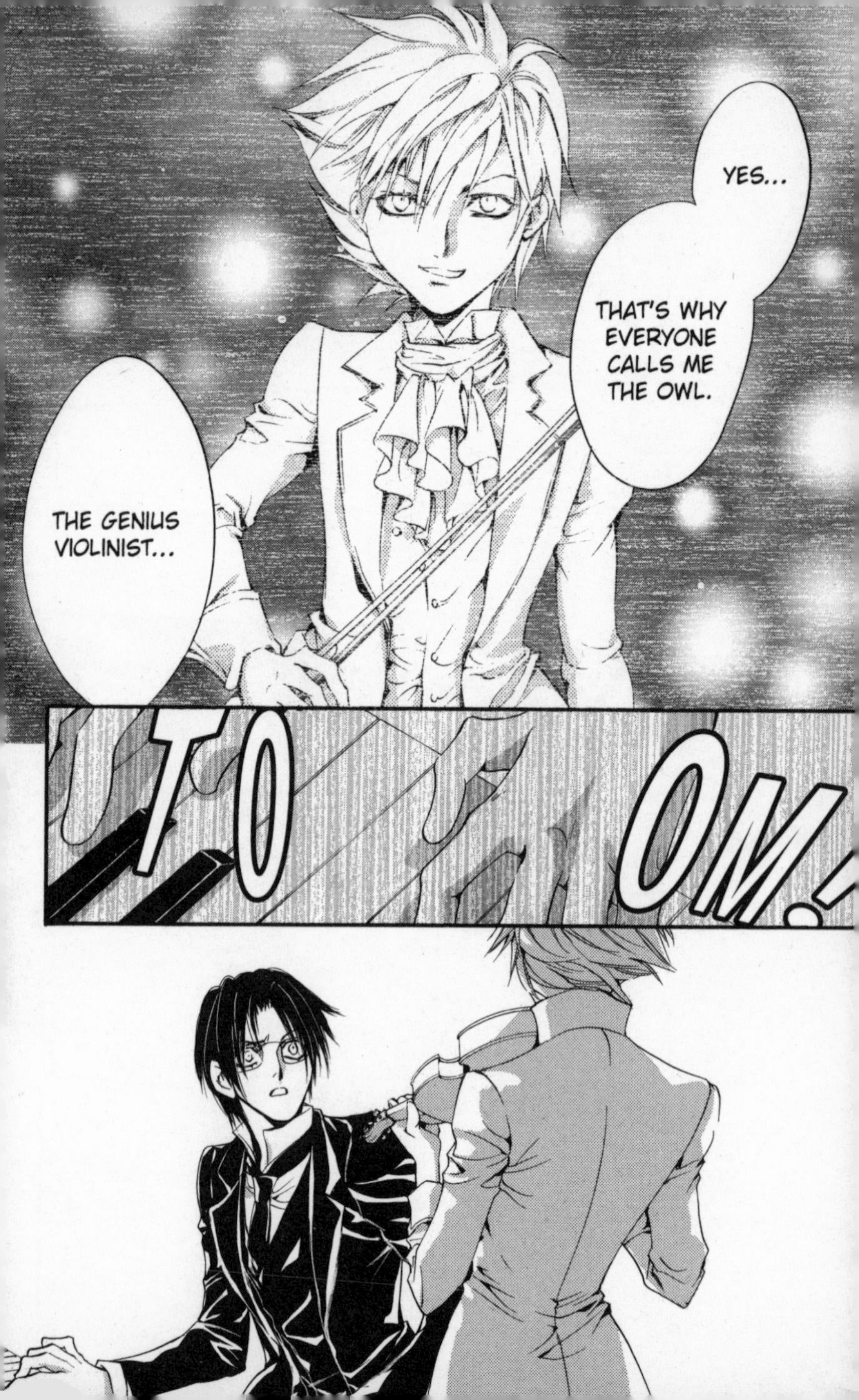
YES...
THAT'S WHY EVERYONE CALLS ME THE OWL.
THE GENIUS VIOLINIST...
TO OM!

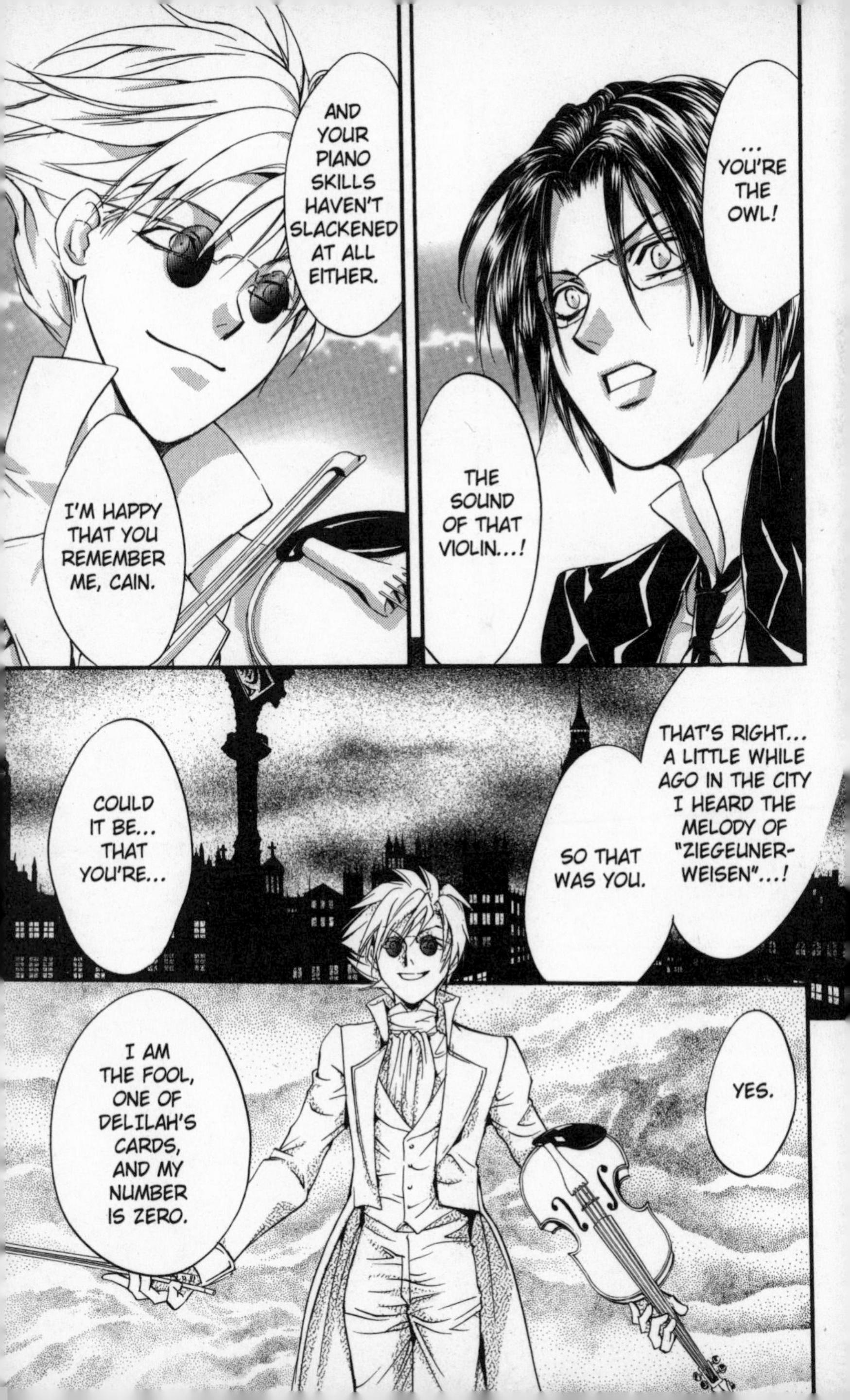
... YOU'RE THE OWL!
THE SOUND OF THAT VIOLIN...!
AND YOUR PIANO SKILLS HAVEN'T SLACKENED AT ALL EITHER.
I'M HAPPY THAT YOU REMEMBER ME, CAIN.
THAT'S RIGHT... A LITTLE WHILE AGO IN THE CITY I HEARD THE MELODY OF "ZIEGEUNER-WEISEN"...!
SO THAT WAS YOU.
COULD IT BE... THAT YOU'RE...
YES.
I AM THE FOOL, ONE OF DELILAH'S CARDS, AND MY NUMBER IS ZERO.

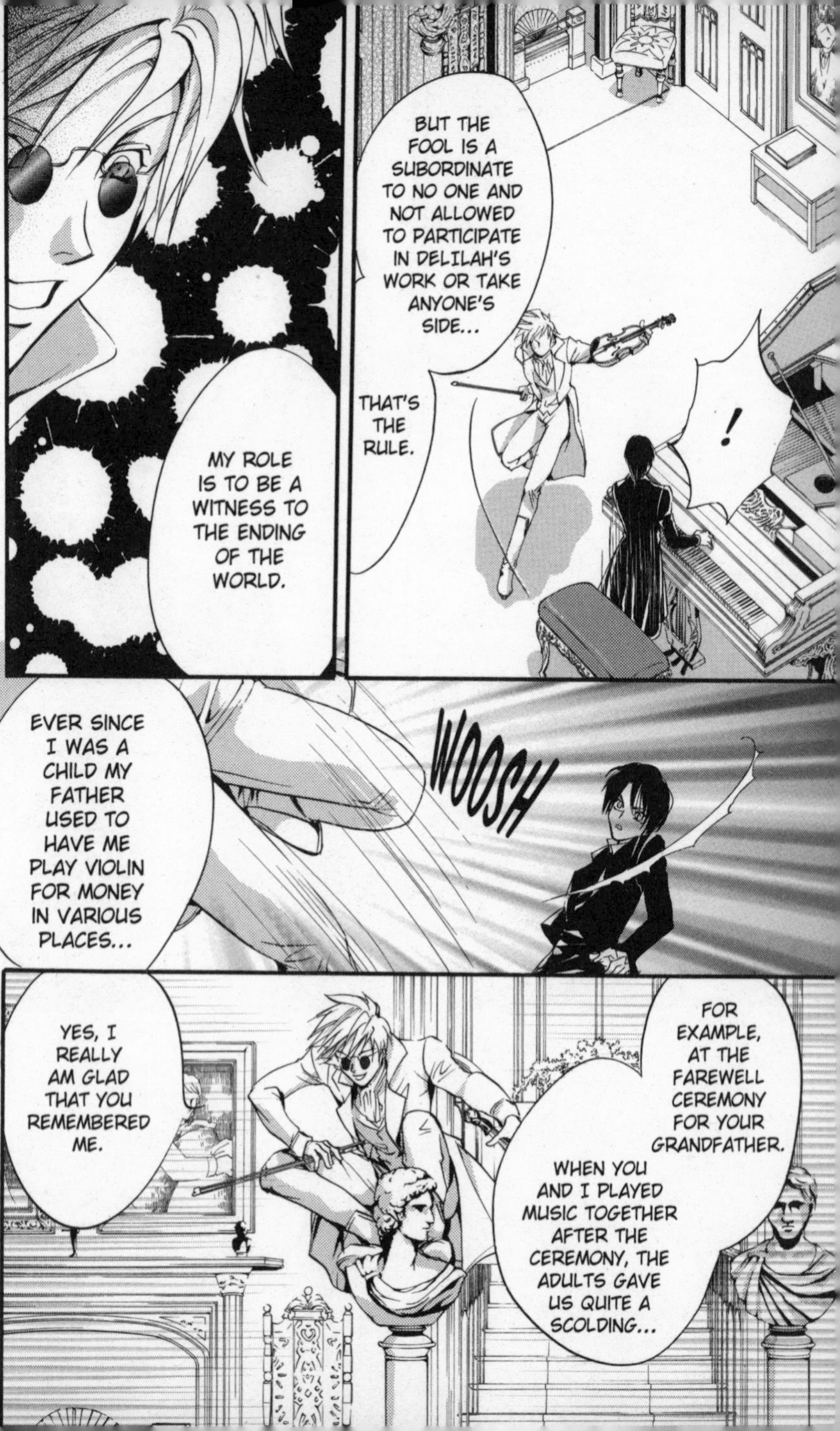
BUT THE FOOL IS A SUBORDINATE TO NO ONE AND NOT ALLOWED TO PARTICIPATE IN DELILAH'S WORK OR TAKE ANYONE'S SIDE...
THAT'S THE RULE.
!
MY ROLE IS TO BE A WITNESS TO THE ENDING OF THE WORLD.
WOOSH
EVER SINCE I WAS A CHILD MY FATHER USED TO HAVE ME PLAY VIOLIN FOR MONEY IN VARIOUS PLACES...
FOR EXAMPLE, AT THE FAREWELL CEREMONY FOR YOUR GRANDFATHER.
WHEN YOU AND I PLAYED MUSIC TOGETHER AFTER THE CEREMONY, THE ADULTS GAVE US QUITE A SCOLDING...
YES, I REALLY AM GLAD THAT YOU REMEMBERED ME.

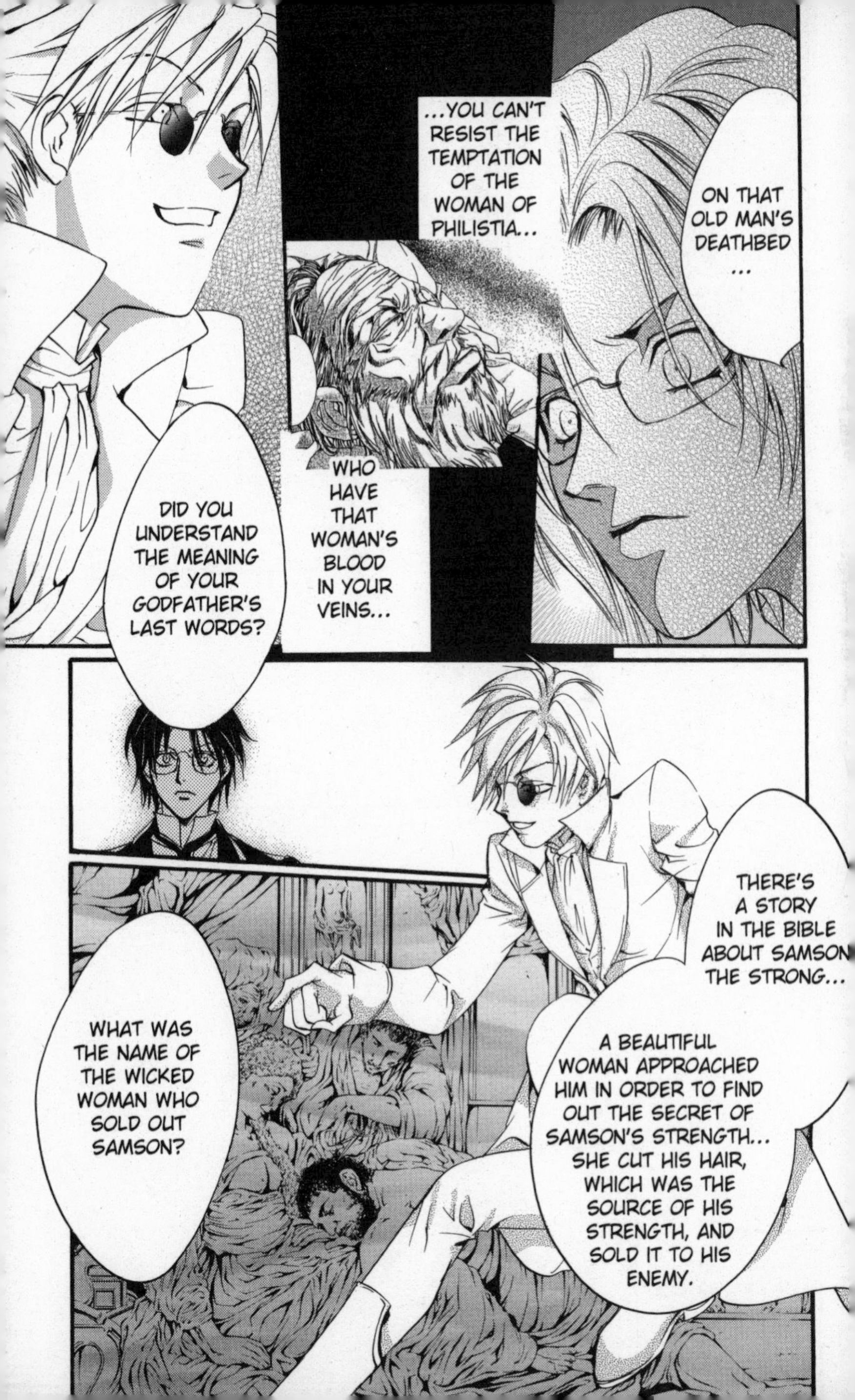
ON THAT OLD MAN'S DEATHBED ...
...YOU CAN'T RESIST THE TEMPTATION OF THE WOMAN OF PHILISTIA...
WHO HAVE THAT WOMAN'S BLOOD IN YOUR VEINS...
DID YOU UNDERSTAND THE MEANING OF YOUR GODFATHER'S LAST WORDS?
THERE'S A STORY IN THE BIBLE ABOUT SAMSON THE STRONG...
A BEAUTIFUL WOMAN APPROACHED HIM IN ORDER TO FIND OUT THE SECRET OF SAMSON'S STRENGTH... SHE CUT HIS HAIR, WHICH WAS THE SOURCE OF HIS STRENGTH, AND SOLD IT TO HIS ENEMY.
WHAT WAS THE NAME OF THE WICKED WOMAN WHO SOLD OUT SAMSON?

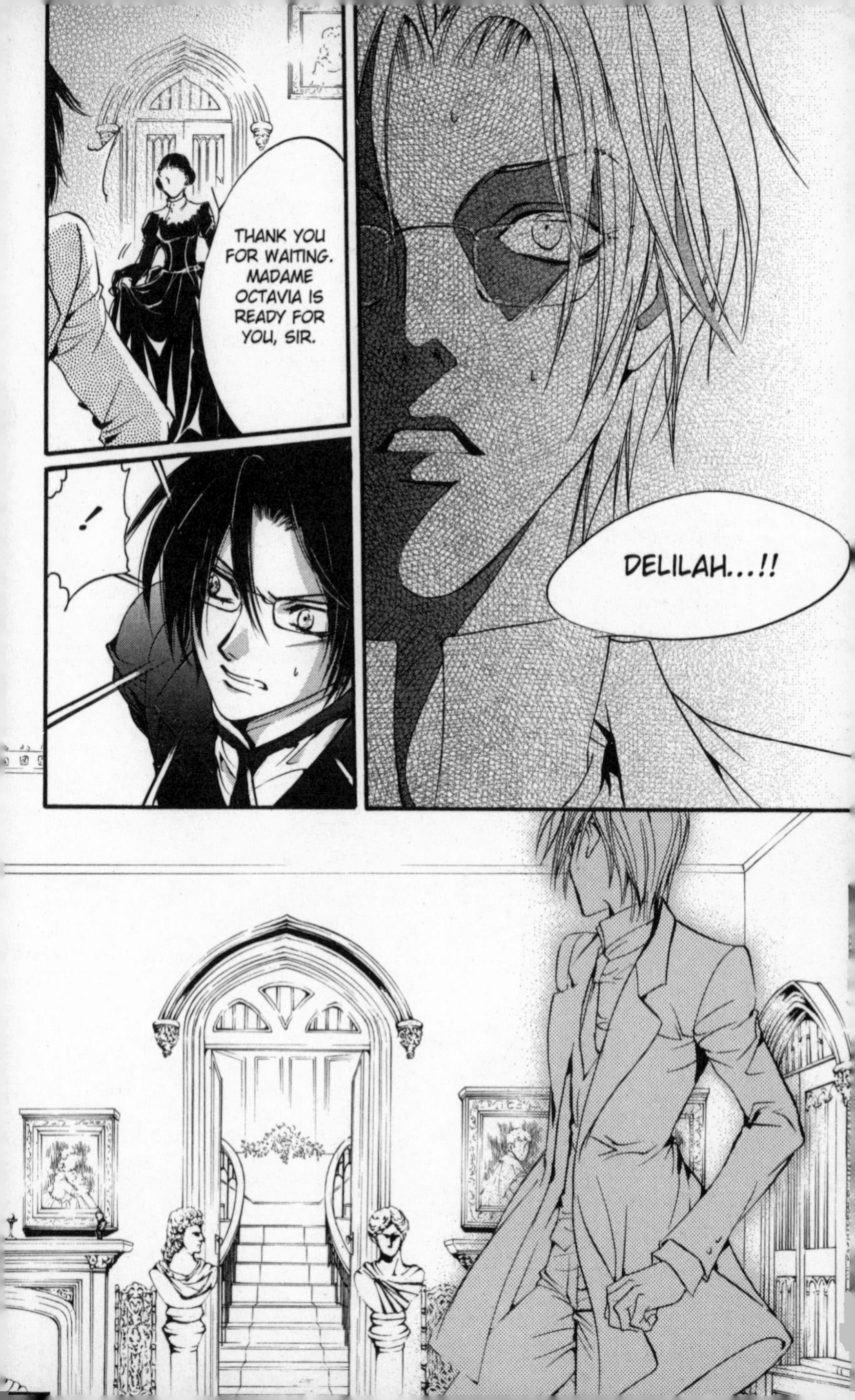
DELILAH...!!
THANK YOU FOR WAITING. MADAME OCTAVIA IS READY FOR YOU, SIR.
!

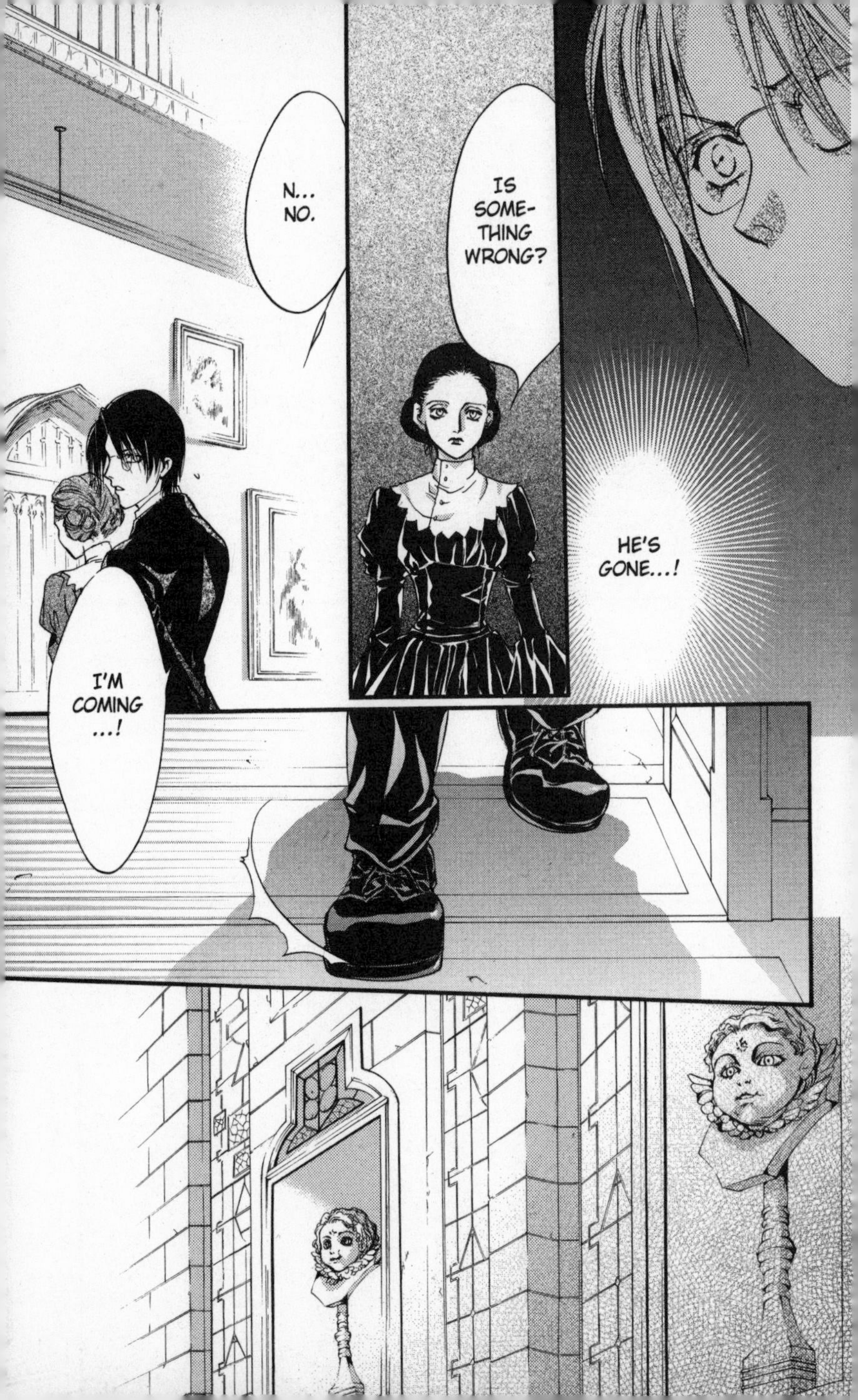
HE'S GONE...!
IS SOME-THING WRONG?
N... NO.
I'M COMING ...!

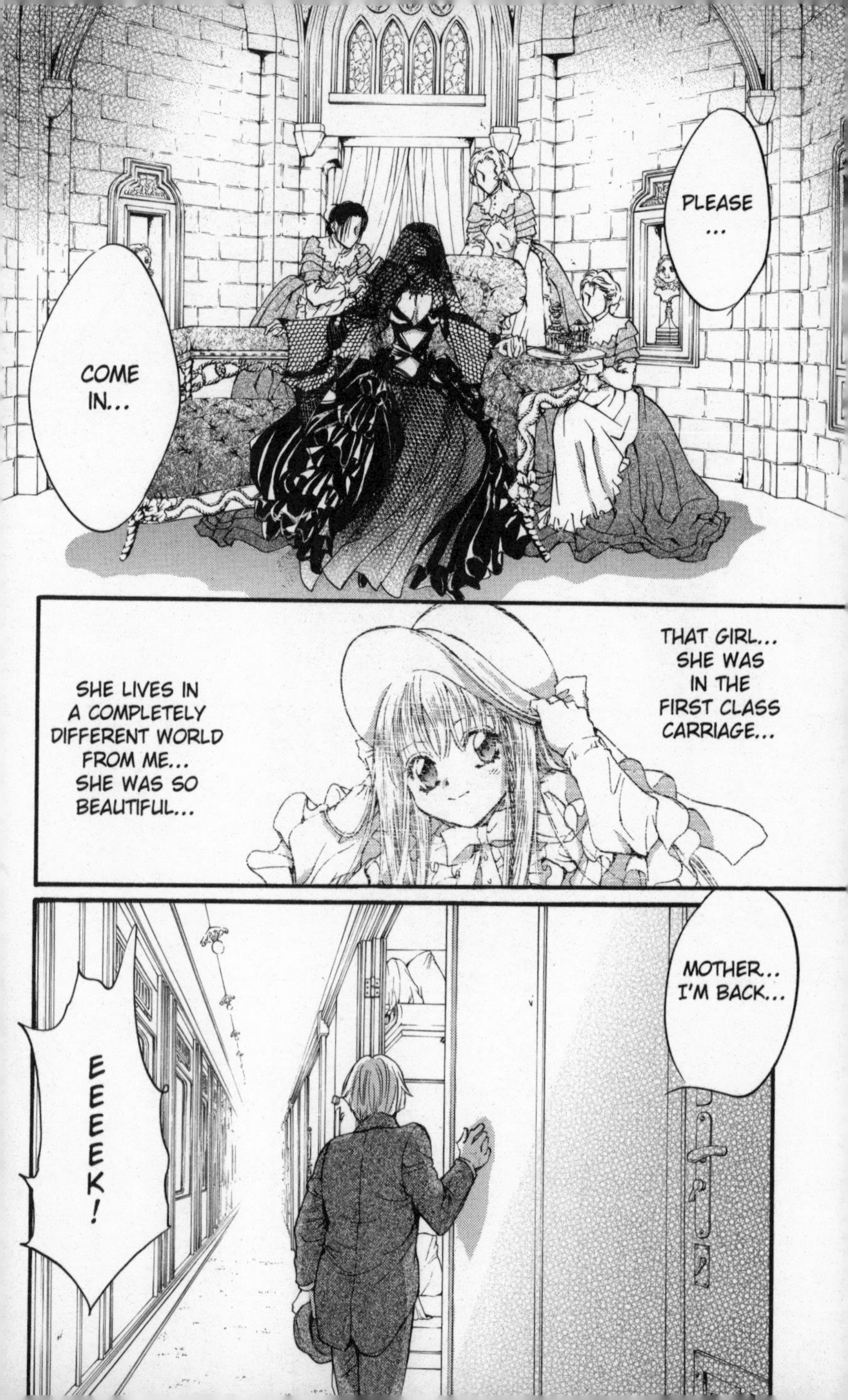
PLEASE ...
COME IN...
THAT GIRL... SHE WAS IN THE FIRST CLASS CARRIAGE...
SHE LIVES IN A COMPLETELY DIFFERENT WORLD FROM ME... SHE WAS SO BEAUTIFUL...
MOTHER... I'M BACK...
EEEEEK!

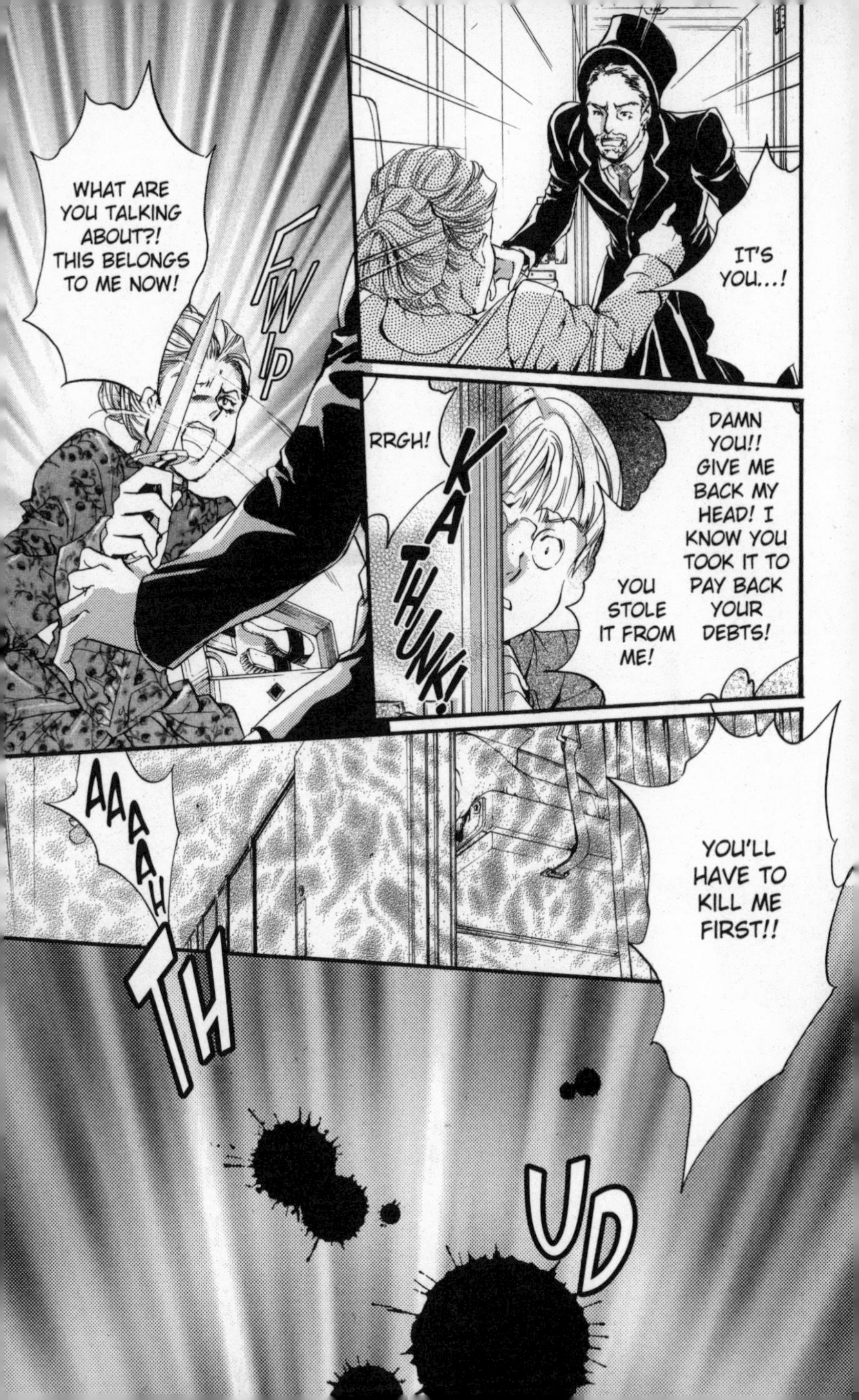
IT'S YOU...!
DAMN YOU!! GIVE ME BACK MY HEAD! I KNOW YOU TOOK IT TO PAY BACK YOUR DEBTS!
YOU STOLE IT FROM ME!
KATHUNK!
RRGH!
WHAT ARE YOU TALKING ABOUT?! THIS BELONGS TO ME NOW!
FWIP
YOU'LL HAVE TO KILL ME FIRST!!
AAAAH
THUD

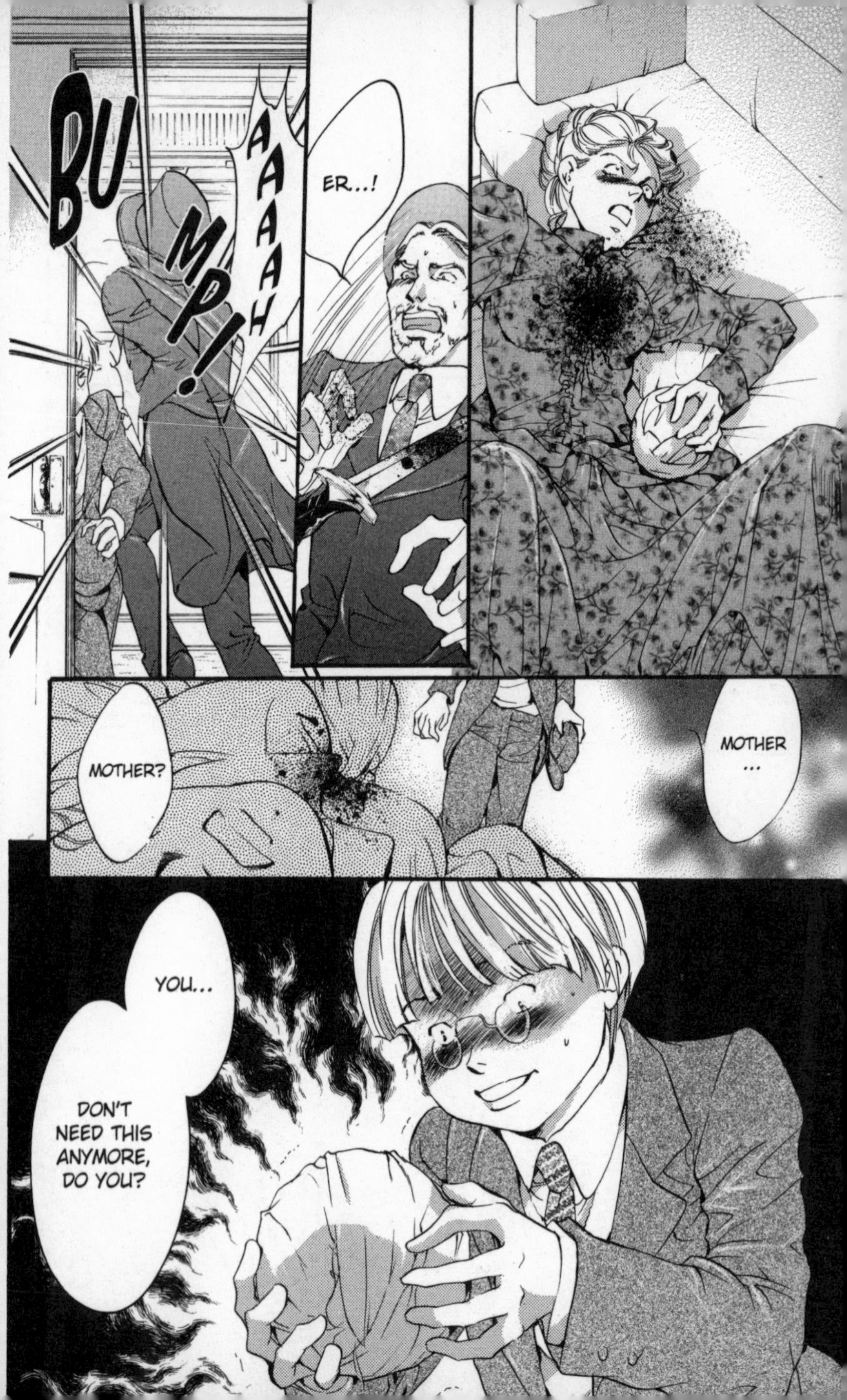
ER...!
AAAAAH
BUMP!
MOTHER
...
MOTHER?
YOU...
DON'T NEED THIS ANYMORE, DO YOU?

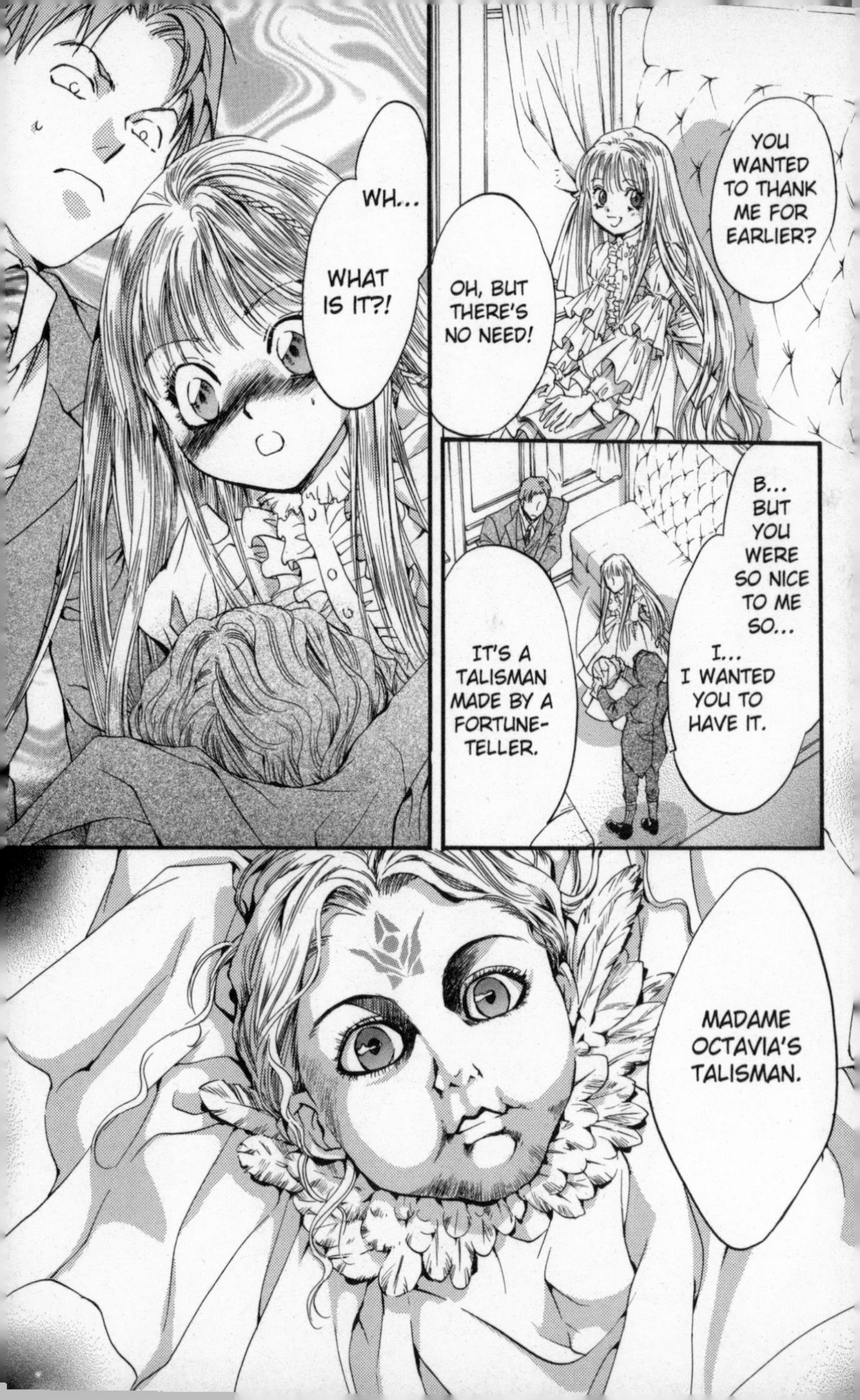
YOU WANTED TO THANK ME FOR EARLIER?
OH, BUT THERE'S NO NEED!
B... BUT YOU WERE SO NICE TO ME SO...
I... I WANTED YOU TO HAVE IT.
IT'S A TALISMAN MADE BY A FORTUNE-TELLER.
WH...
WHAT IS IT?!
MADAME OCTAVIA'S TALISMAN.

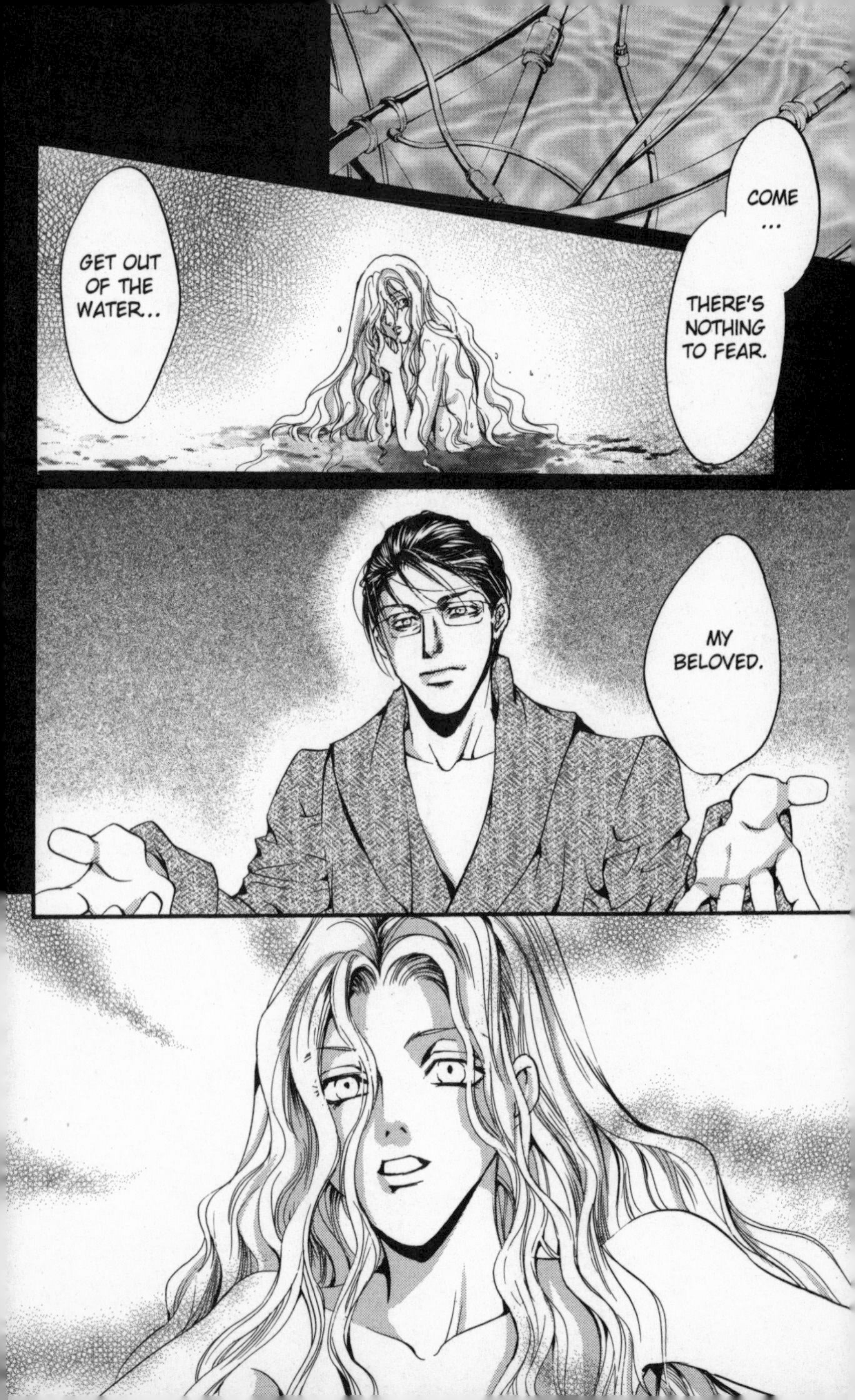
COME ...
THERE'S NOTHING TO FEAR.
GET OUT OF THE WATER...
MY BELOVED.

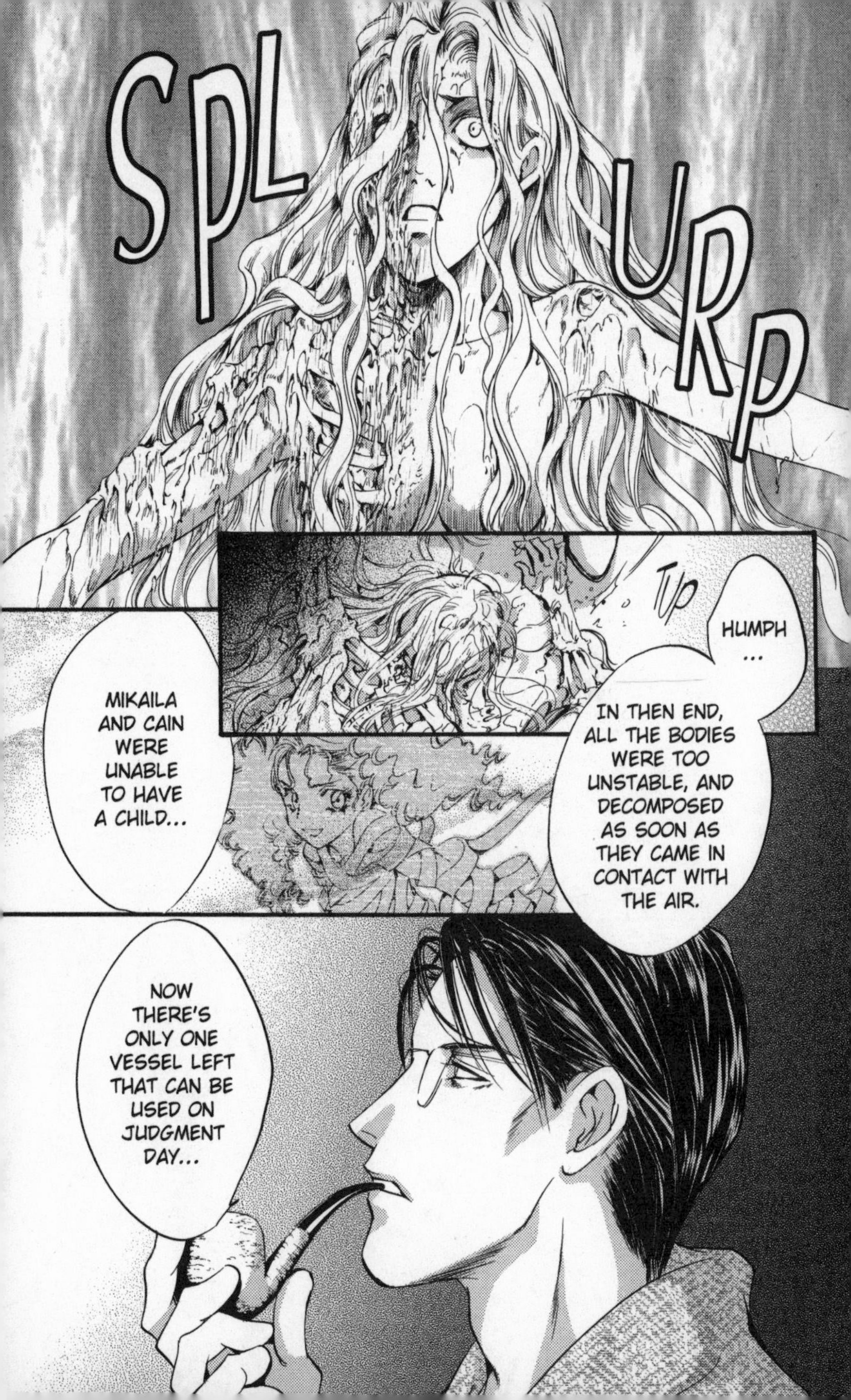
SPLURP
TUP
HUMPH...
IN THEN END, ALL THE BODIES WERE TOO UNSTABLE, AND DECOMPOSED AS SOON AS THEY CAME IN CONTACT WITH THE AIR.
MIKAILA AND CAIN WERE UNABLE TO HAVE A CHILD...
NOW THERE'S ONLY ONE VESSEL LEFT THAT CAN BE USED ON JUDGMENT DAY...

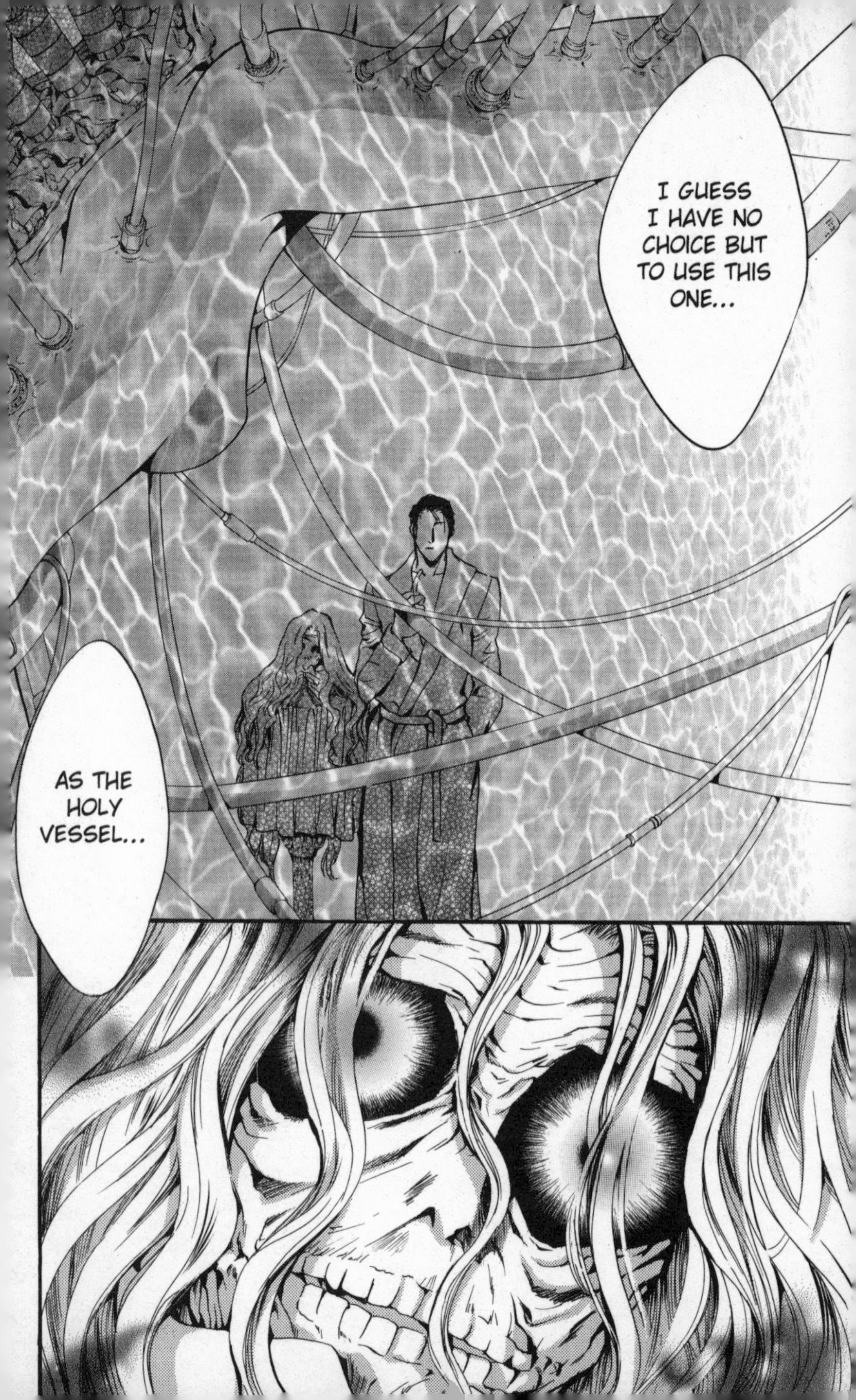
I GUESS I HAVE NO CHOICE BUT TO USE THIS ONE...
AS THE HOLY VESSEL...

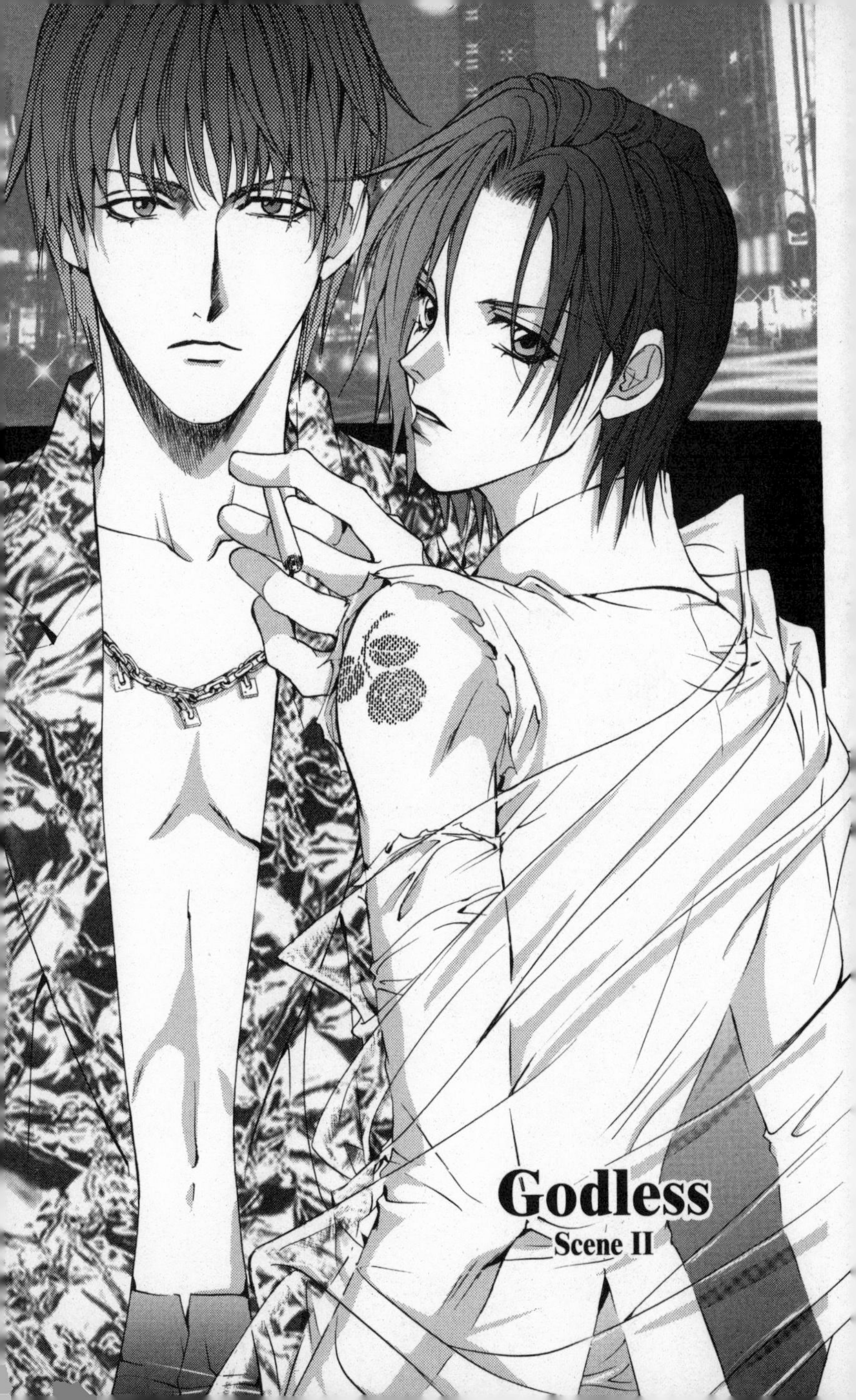
Godless
Scene II

Godless

Scene II

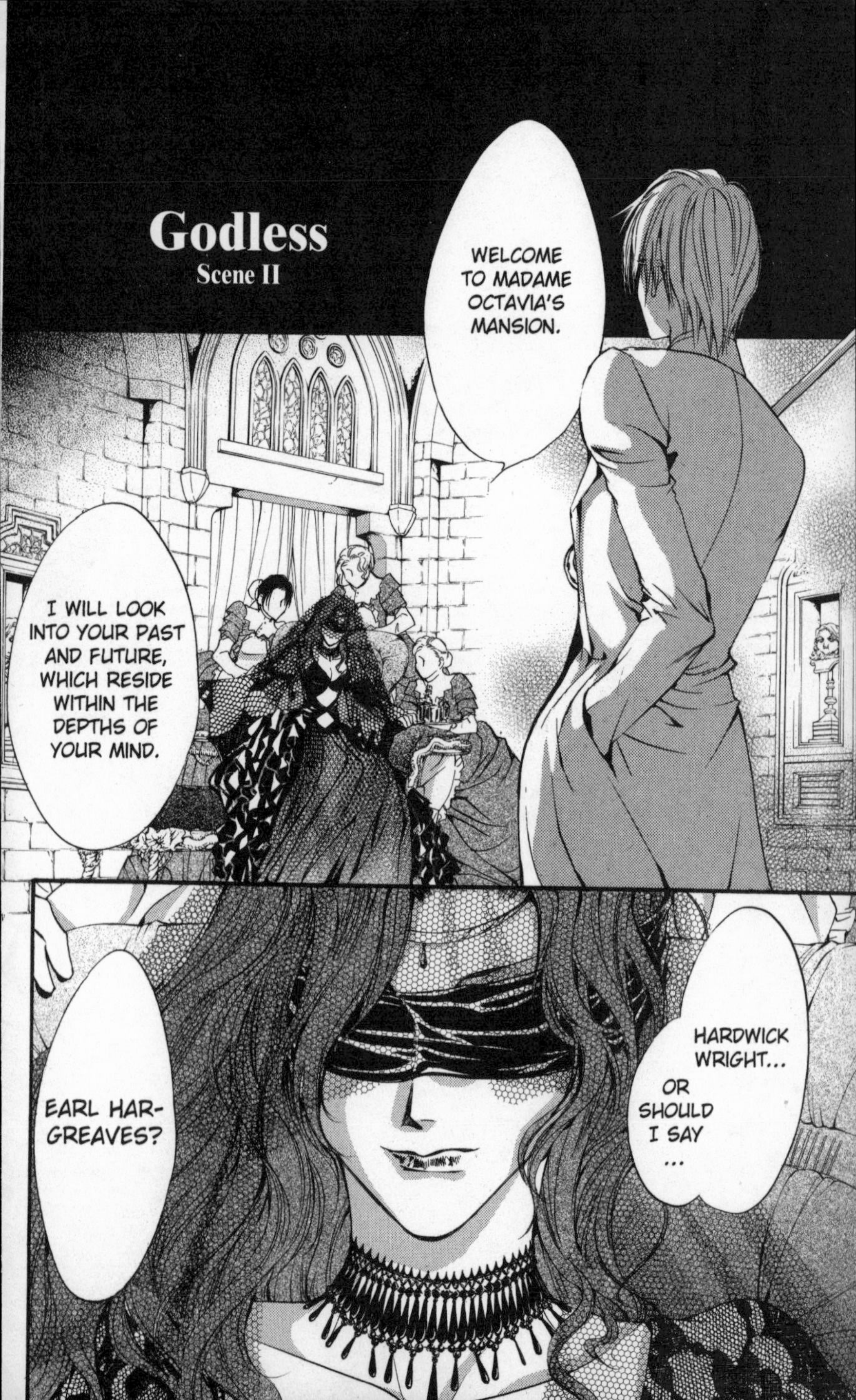
WELCOME TO MADAME OCTAVIA'S MANSION.
I WILL LOOK INTO YOUR PAST AND FUTURE, WHICH RESIDE WITHIN THE DEPTHS OF YOUR MIND.
HARDWICK WRIGHT... OR SHOULD I SAY ...
EARL HAR-GREAVES?

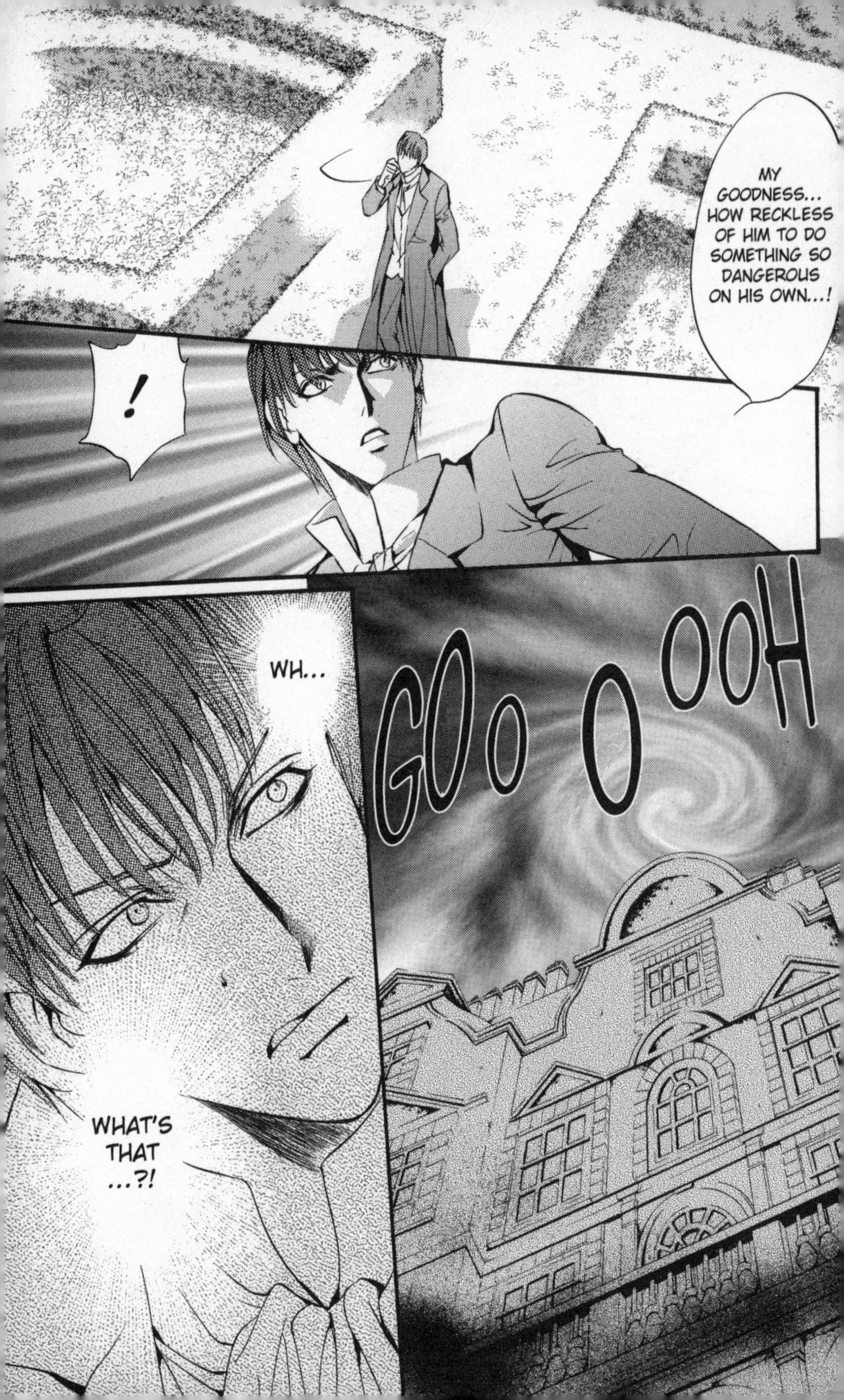
MY GOODNESS... HOW RECKLESS OF HIM TO DO SOMETHING SO DANGEROUS ON HIS OWN...!
!
GOOOOOOH
WH...
WHAT'S THAT ...?!

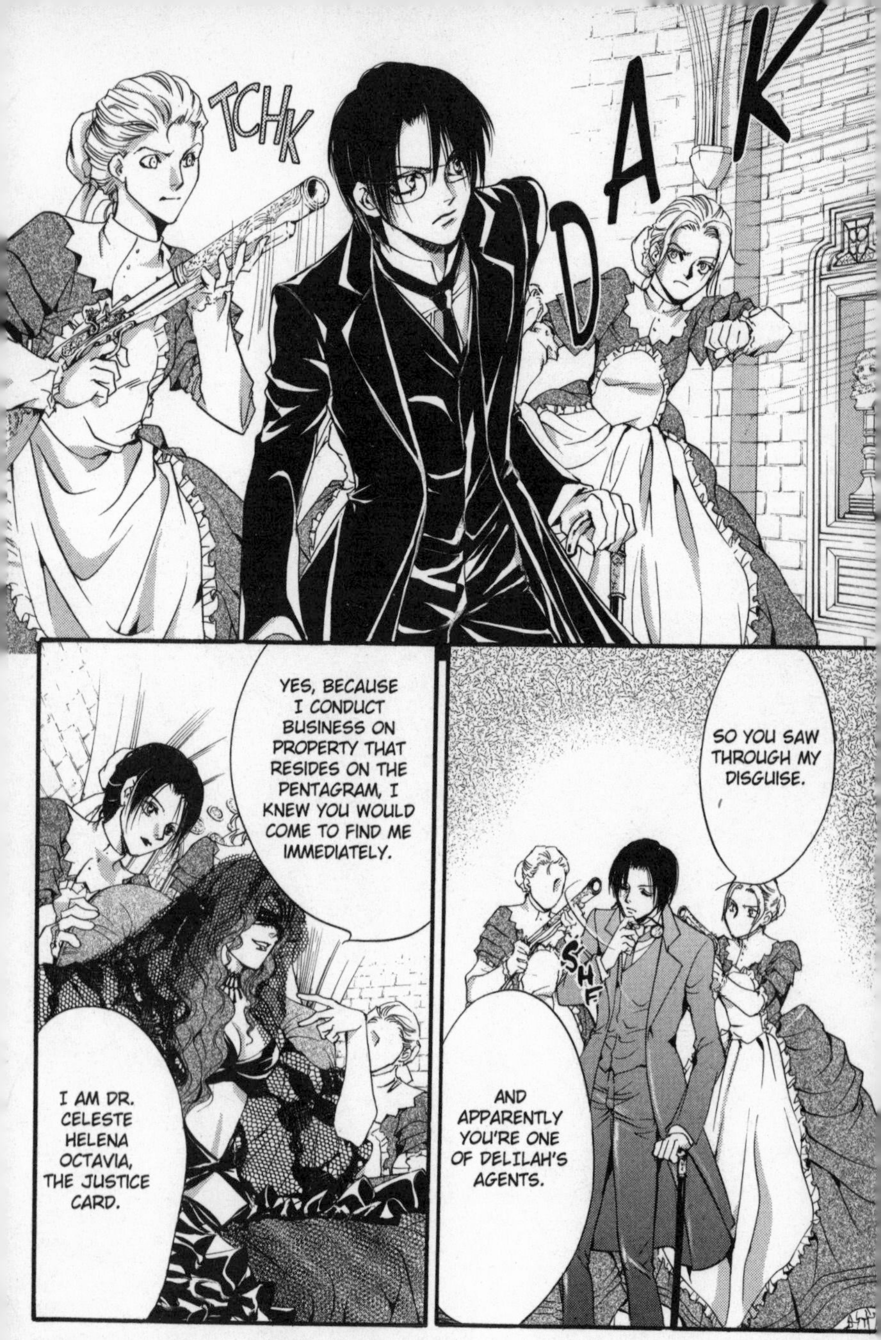
DAK
TCHK
SO YOU SAW THROUGH MY DISGUISE.
SHF
AND APPARENTLY YOU'RE ONE OF DELILAH'S AGENTS.
YES, BECAUSE I CONDUCT BUSINESS ON PROPERTY THAT RESIDES ON THE PENTAGRAM, I KNEW YOU WOULD COME TO FIND ME IMMEDIATELY.
I AM DR. CELESTE HELENA OCTAVIA, THE JUSTICE CARD.

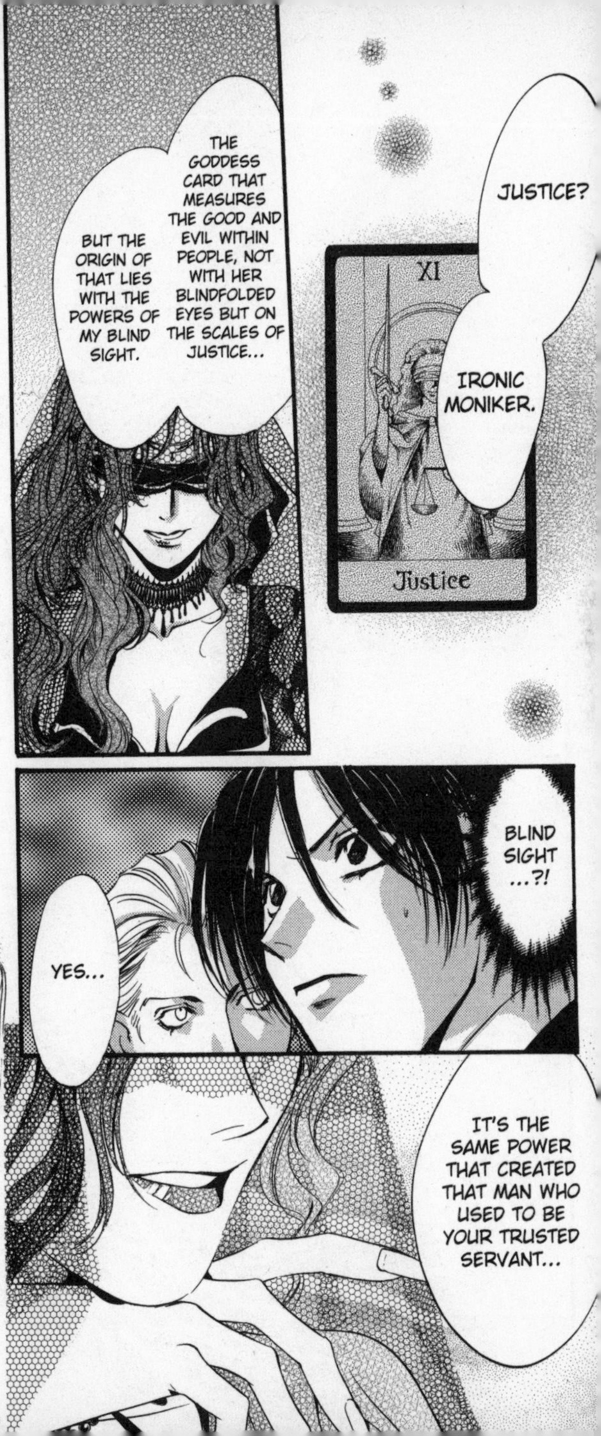
JUSTICE?
IRONIC MONIKER.
XI
Justice
THE GODDESS CARD THAT MEASURES THE GOOD AND EVIL WITHIN PEOPLE, NOT WITH HER BLINDFOLDED EYES BUT ON THE SCALES OF JUSTICE...
BUT THE ORIGIN OF THAT LIES WITH THE POWERS OF MY BLIND SIGHT.
BLIND SIGHT ...?!
YES...
IT'S THE SAME POWER THAT CREATED THAT MAN WHO USED TO BE YOUR TRUSTED SERVANT...

It's finally the last volume.

There are four of these page panels in which I included some of the panels that didn't make it into the story. This is the first of those four.

It was a very tight schedule, but compared to the magazine we've really bulked up the content, so I hope you enjoy it.

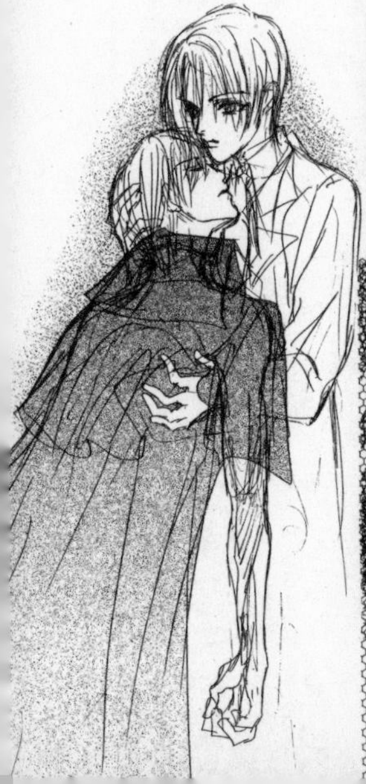

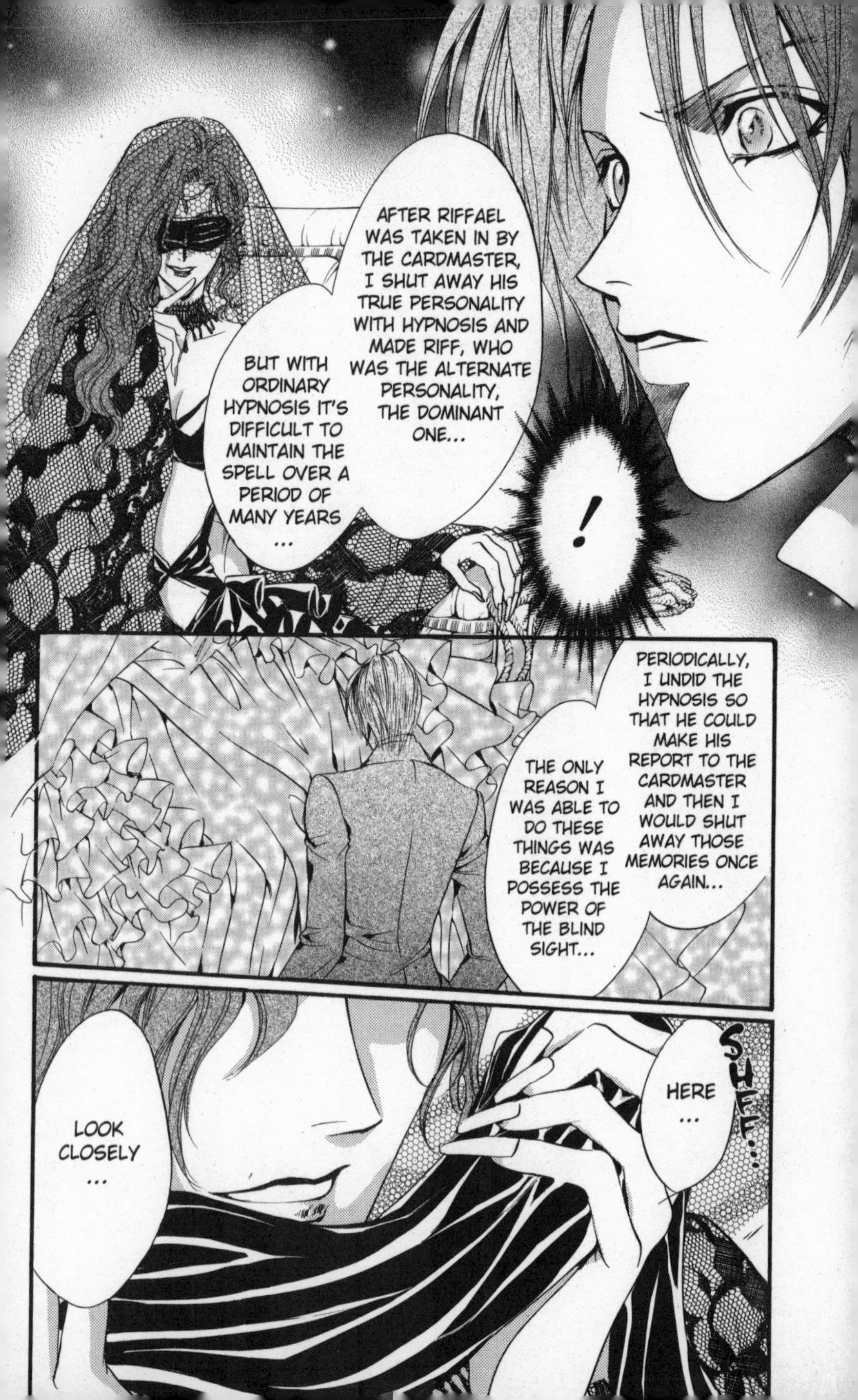
AFTER RIFFAEL WAS TAKEN IN BY THE CARDMASTER, I SHUT AWAY HIS TRUE PERSONALITY WITH HYPNOSIS AND MADE RIFF, WHO WAS THE ALTERNATE PERSONALITY, THE DOMINANT ONE...
BUT WITH ORDINARY HYPNOSIS IT'S DIFFICULT TO MAINTAIN THE SPELL OVER A PERIOD OF MANY YEARS...
!
PERIODICALLY, I UNDID THE HYPNOSIS SO THAT HE COULD MAKE HIS REPORT TO THE CARDMASTER AND THEN I WOULD SHUT AWAY THOSE MEMORIES ONCE AGAIN...
THE ONLY REASON I WAS ABLE TO DO THESE THINGS WAS BECAUSE I POSSESS THE POWER OF THE BLIND SIGHT...
SHFF...
HERE...
LOOK CLOSELY...

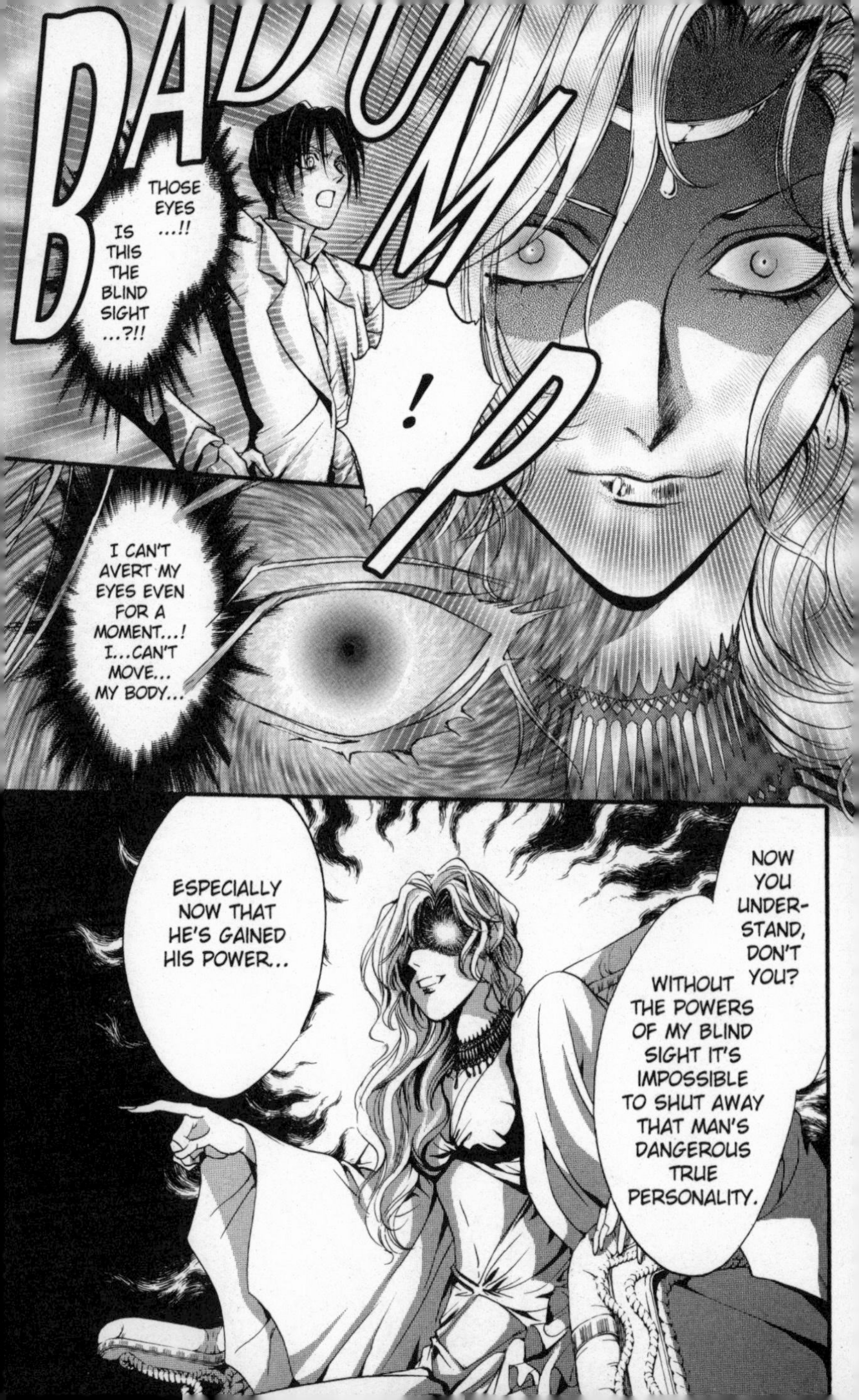
BADUMP
!
THOSE EYES ...!!
IS THIS THE BLIND SIGHT ...?!!
I CAN'T AVERT MY EYES EVEN FOR A MOMENT...! I...CAN'T MOVE... MY BODY...
NOW YOU UNDER-STAND, DON'T YOU?
WITHOUT THE POWERS OF MY BLIND SIGHT IT'S IMPOSSIBLE TO SHUT AWAY THAT MAN'S DANGEROUS TRUE PERSONALITY.
ESPECIALLY NOW THAT HE'S GAINED HIS POWER...

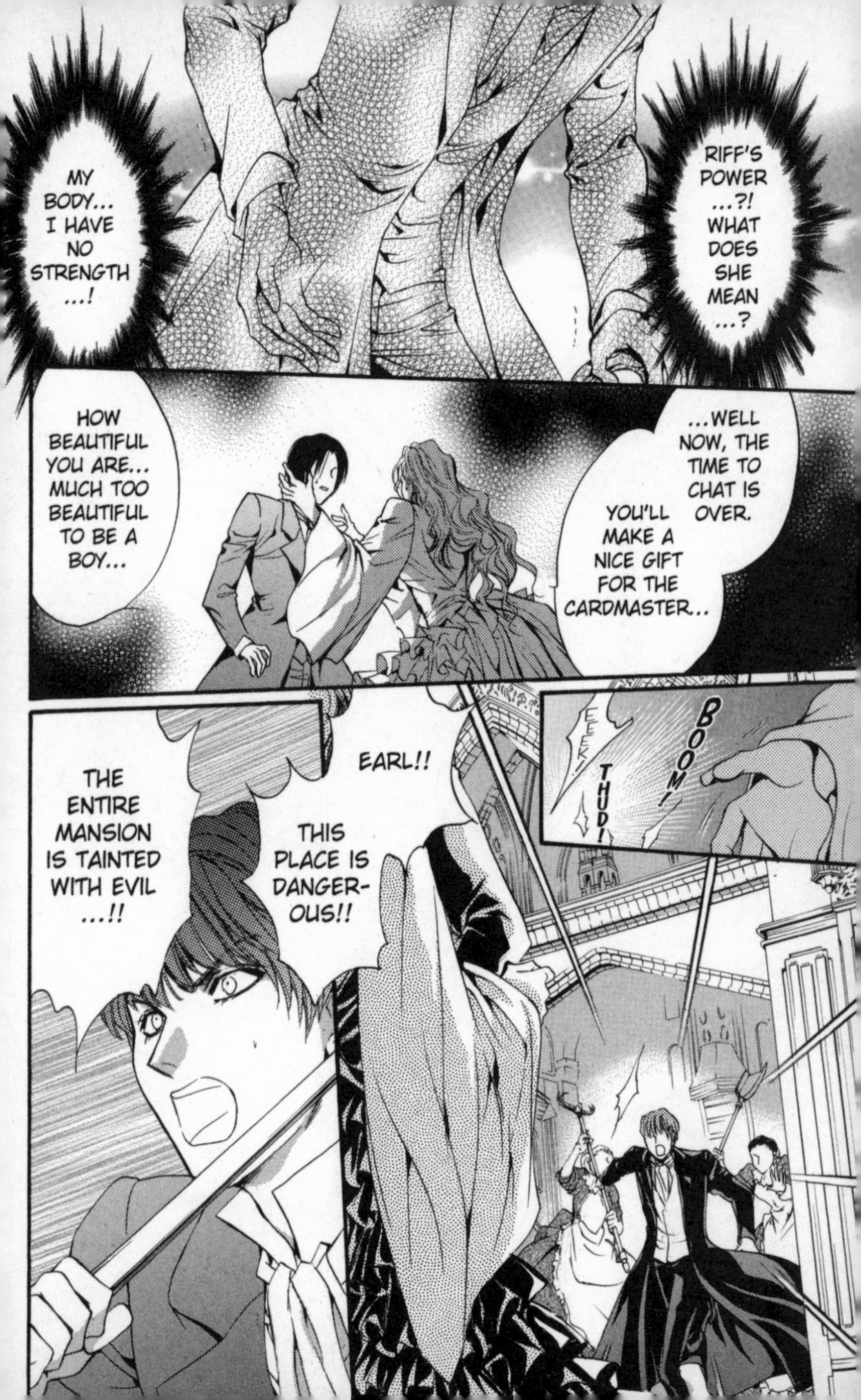
RIFF'S POWER ...?! WHAT DOES SHE MEAN ...?
MY BODY... I HAVE NO STRENGTH ...!
...WELL NOW, THE TIME TO CHAT IS OVER.
YOU'LL MAKE A NICE GIFT FOR THE CARDMASTER...
HOW BEAUTIFUL YOU ARE... MUCH TOO BEAUTIFUL TO BE A BOY...
BOOOM!
EEEK!
THUD!
EARL!!
THIS PLACE IS DANGER-OUS!!
THE ENTIRE MANSION IS TAINTED WITH EVIL ...!!

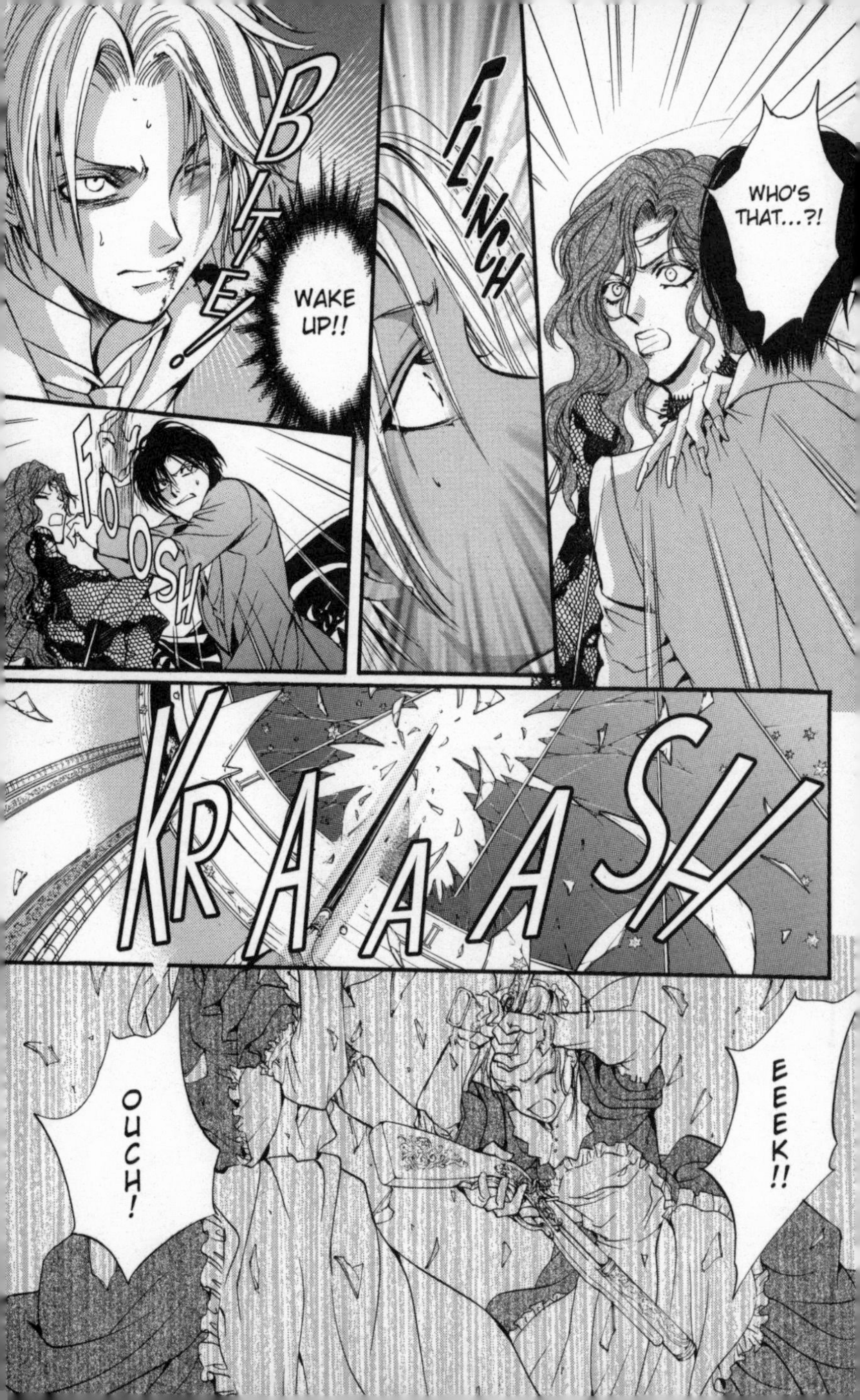
WHO'S THAT...?!
FLINCH
BITE!
WAKE UP!!
FOOSH
KRAAASH
EEEK!!
OUCH!

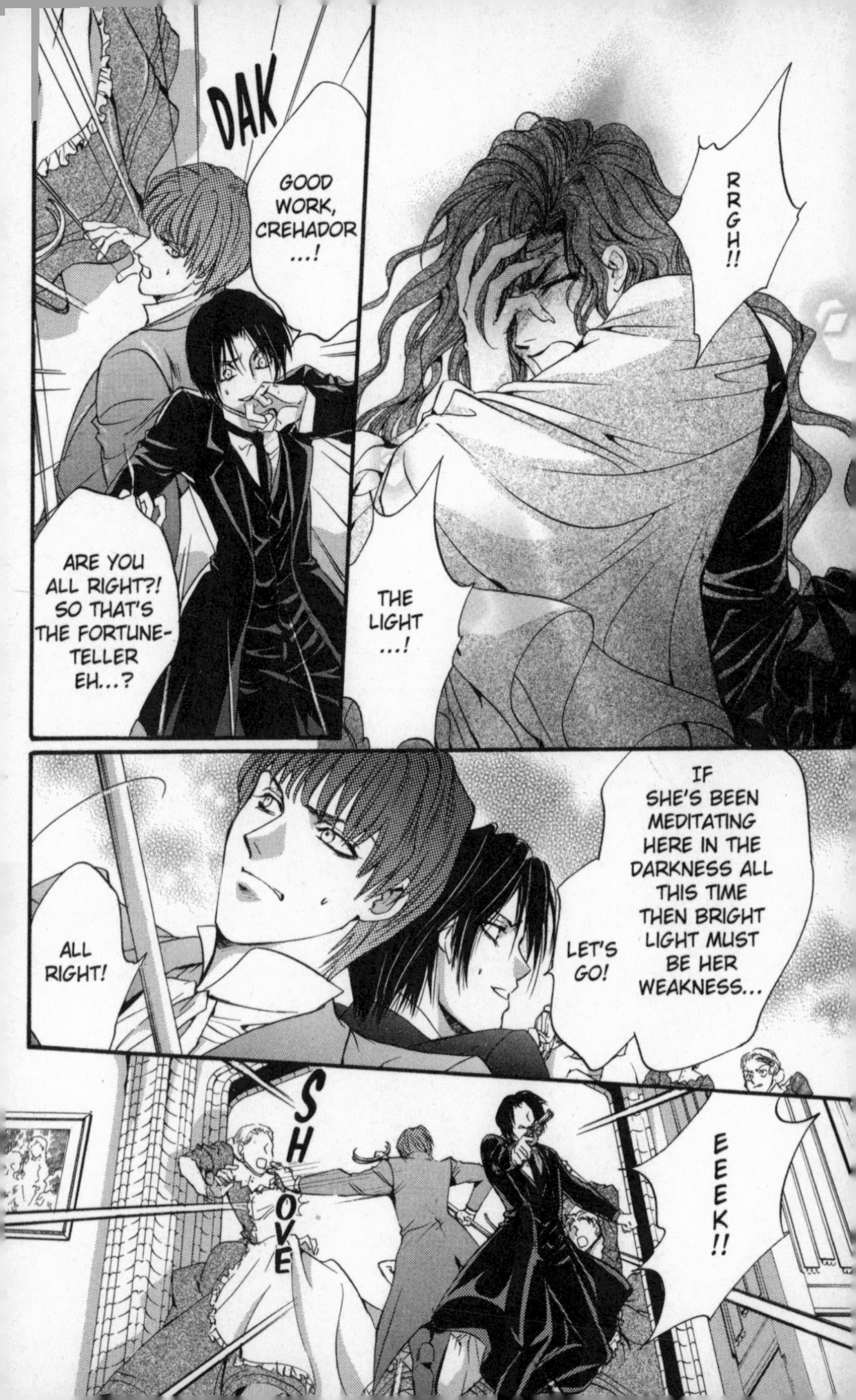
RRGH!!
THE LIGHT ...!
DAK
GOOD WORK, CREHADOR ...!
ARE YOU ALL RIGHT?! SO THAT'S THE FORTUNE-TELLER EH...?
IF SHE'S BEEN MEDITATING HERE IN THE DARKNESS ALL THIS TIME THEN BRIGHT LIGHT MUST BE HER WEAKNESS...
LET'S GO!
ALL RIGHT!
EEEK!!
SHOVE

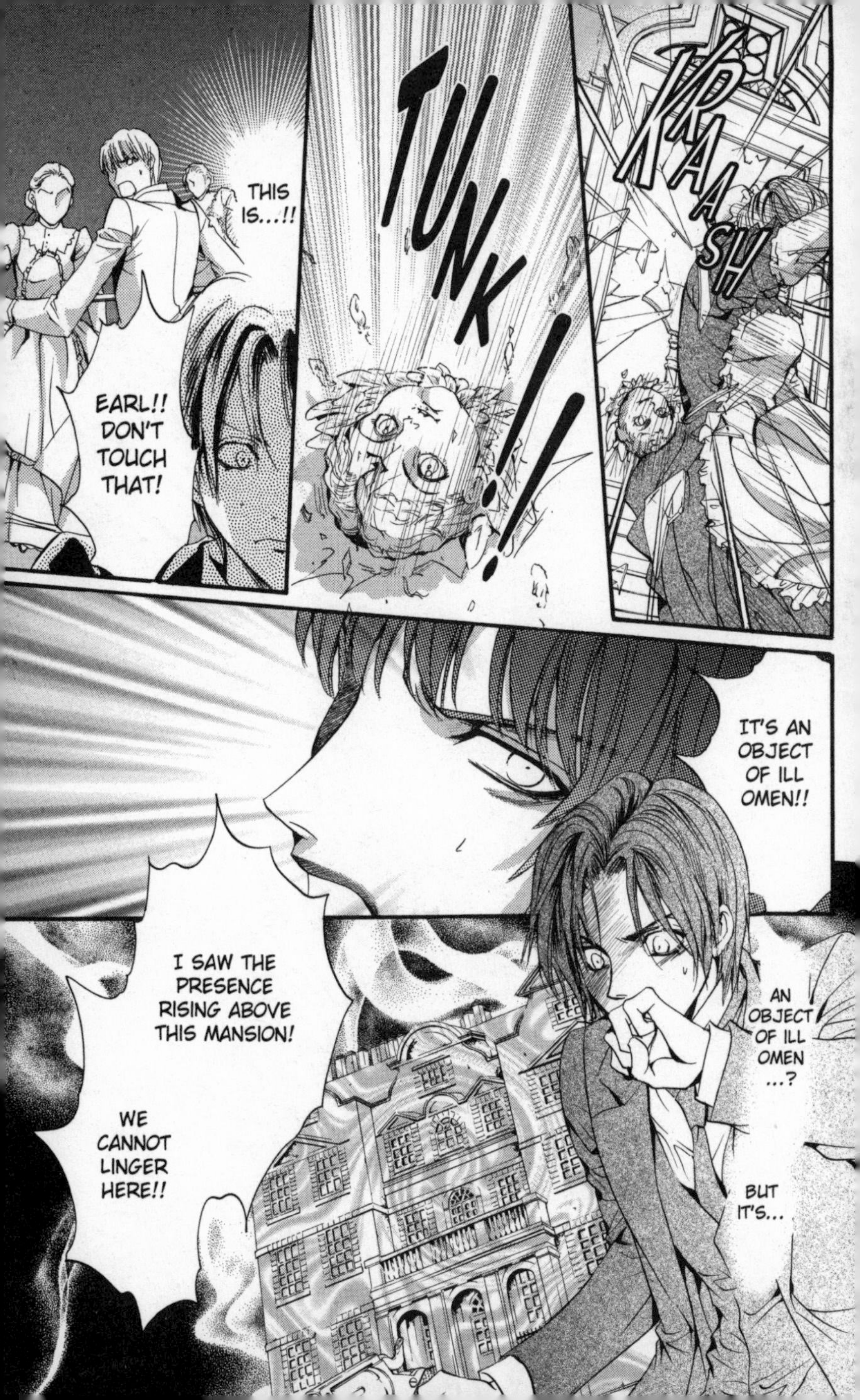
KRAAASH
TUNK!!!
THIS IS...!!
EARL!! DON'T TOUCH THAT!
IT'S AN OBJECT OF ILL OMEN!!
AN OBJECT OF ILL OMEN ...?
BUT IT'S...
I SAW THE PRESENCE RISING ABOVE THIS MANSION!
WE CANNOT LINGER HERE!!

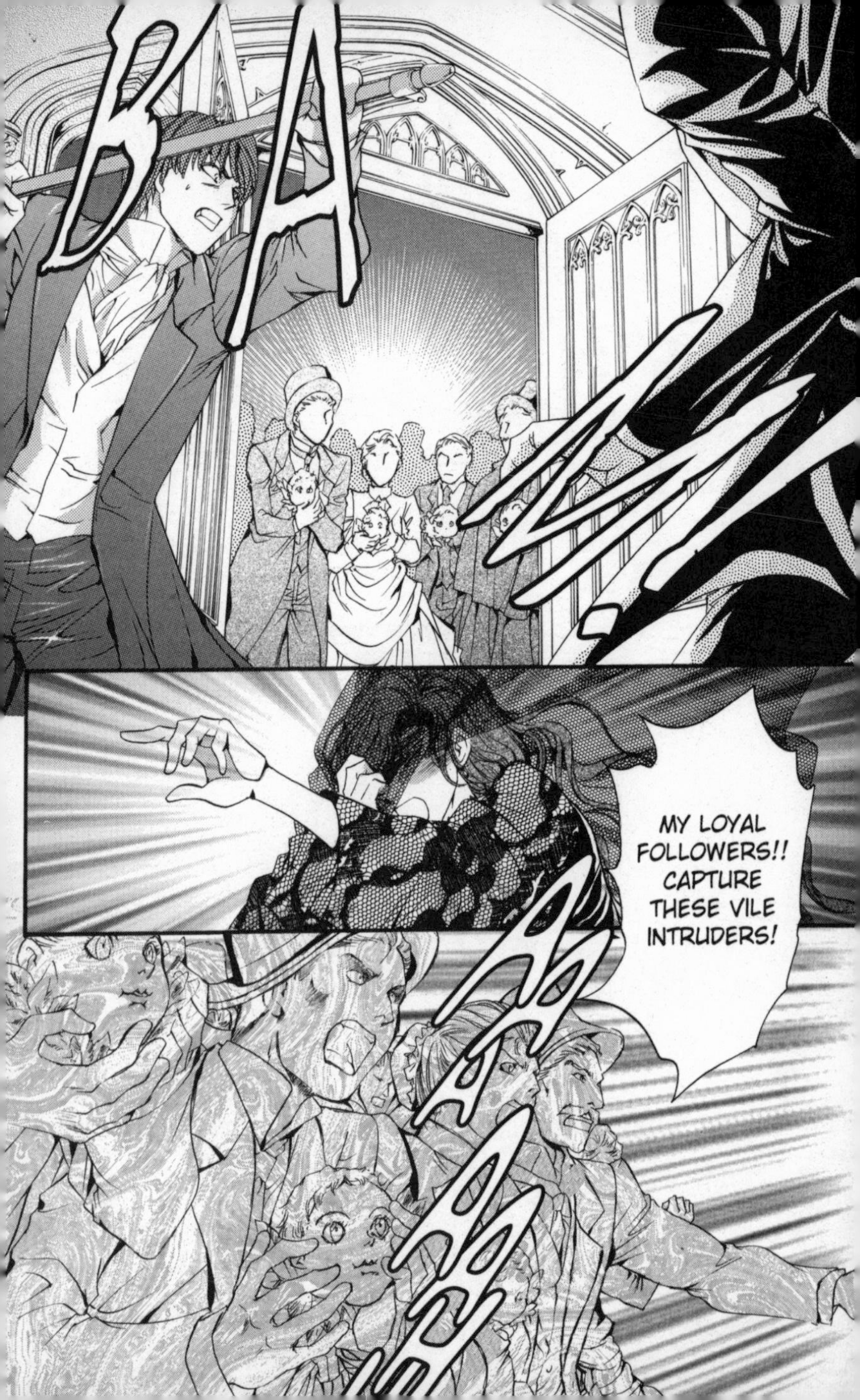
BA
M
MY LOYAL FOLLOWERS!! CAPTURE THESE VILE INTRUDERS!

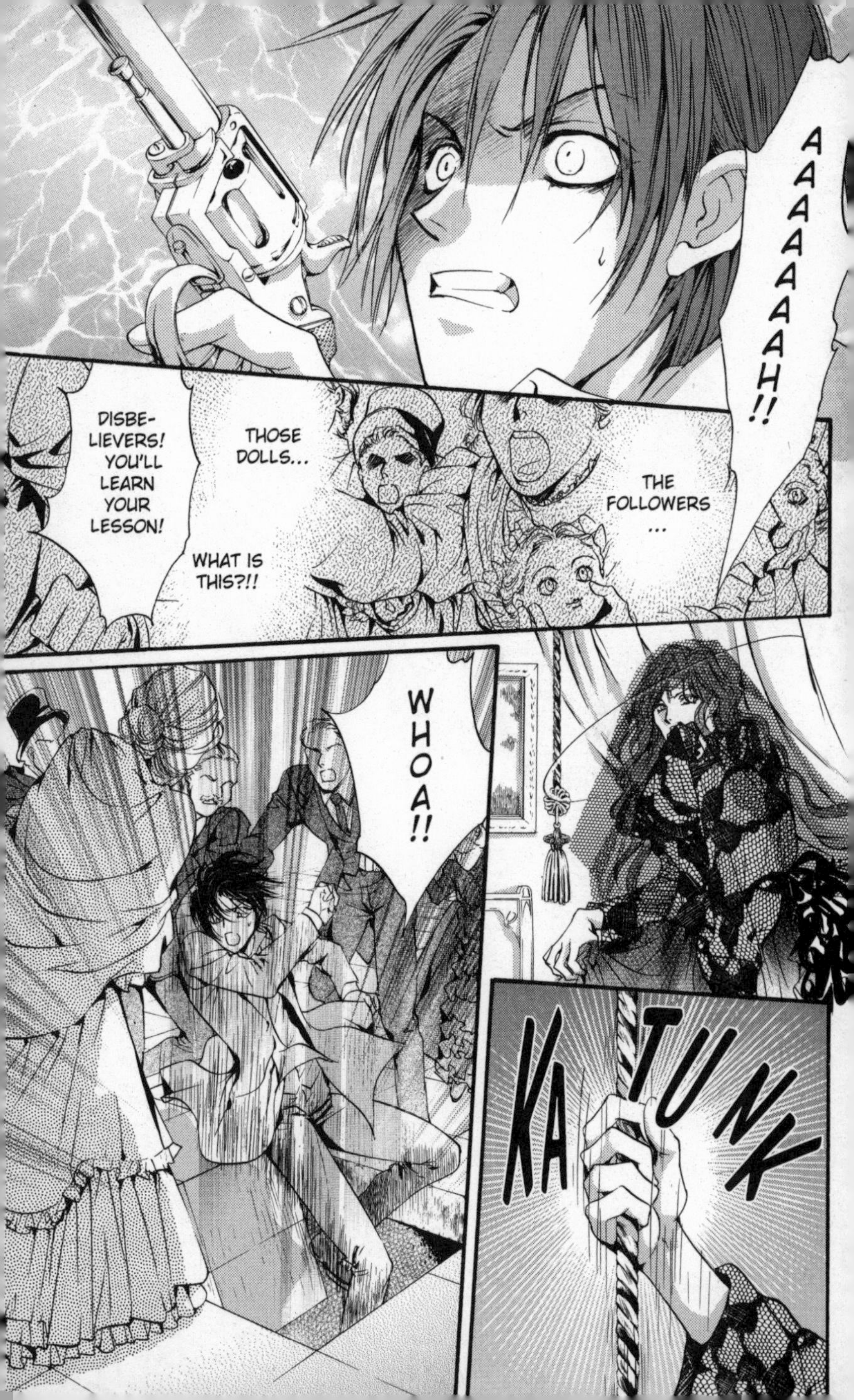
AAAAAAAH!!
THE FOLLOWERS...
THOSE DOLLS...
WHAT IS THIS?!!
DISBELIEVERS! YOU'LL LEARN YOUR LESSON!
KATUNK
WHOA!!

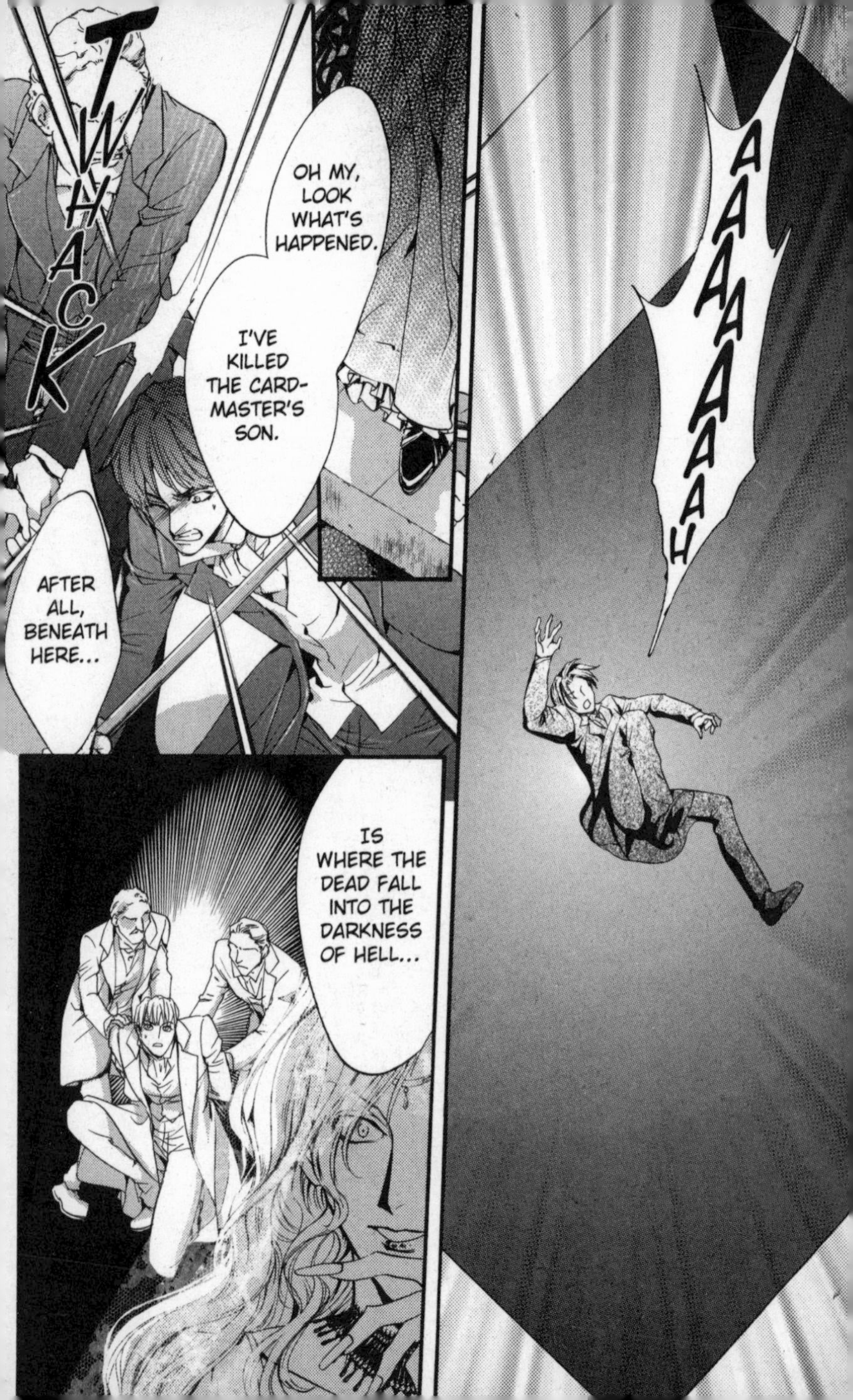
AAAAAAAAH
TWHACK
OH MY, LOOK WHAT'S HAPPENED.
I'VE KILLED THE CARD-MASTER'S SON.
AFTER ALL, BENEATH HERE...
IS WHERE THE DEAD FALL INTO THE DARKNESS OF HELL...

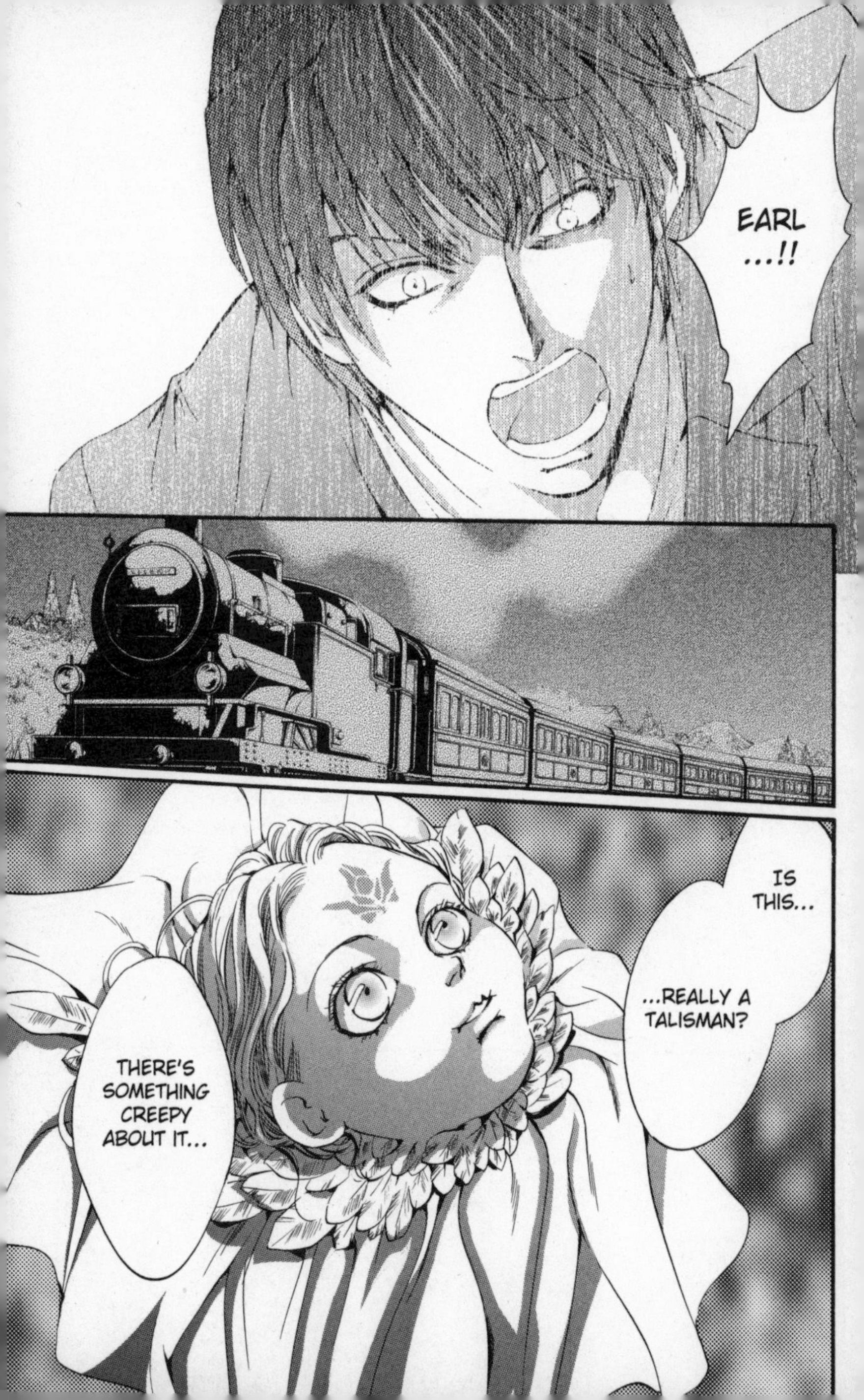
EARL ...!!
IS THIS...
...REALLY A TALISMAN?
THERE'S SOMETHING CREEPY ABOUT IT...

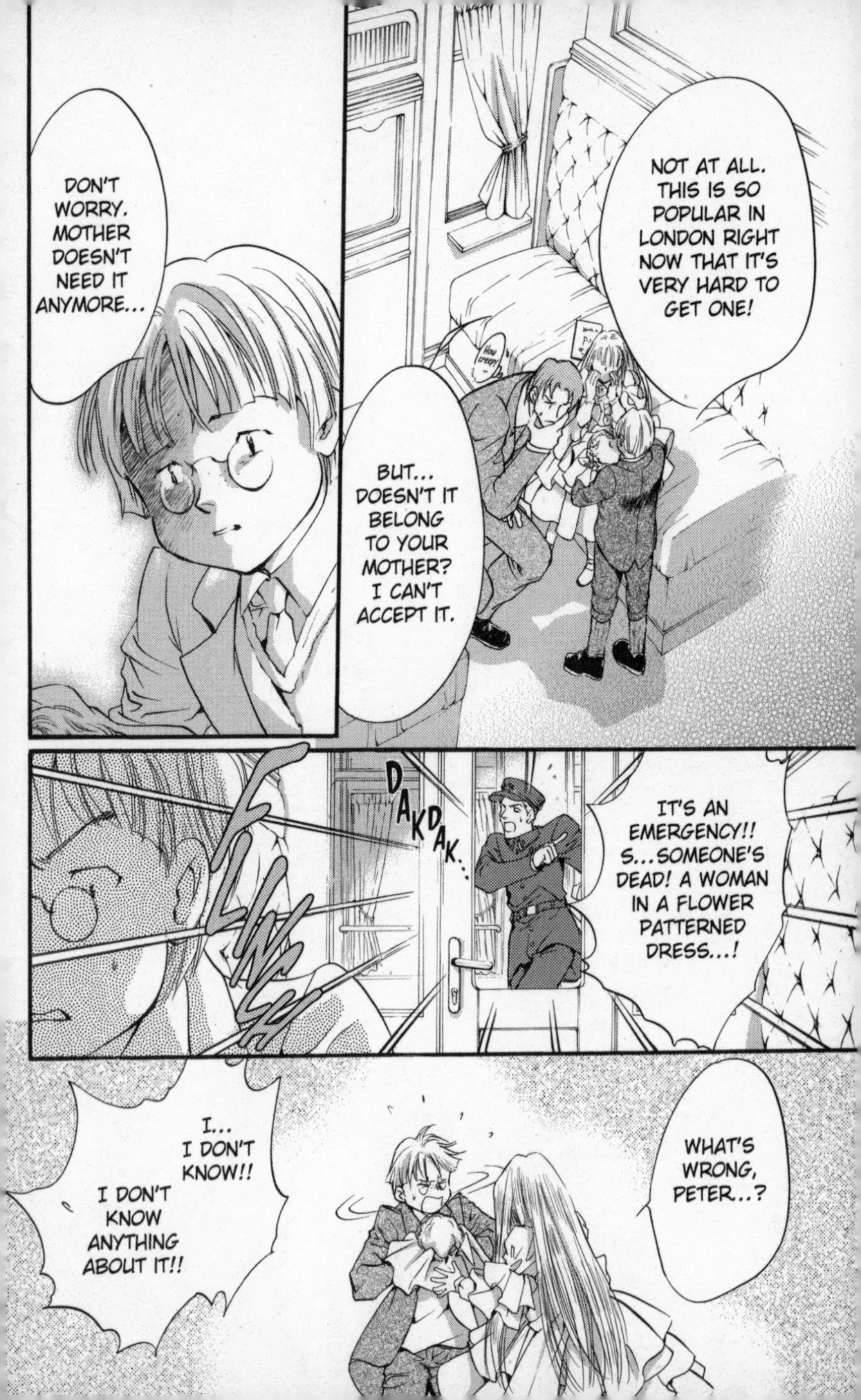
NOT AT ALL. THIS IS SO POPULAR IN LONDON RIGHT NOW THAT IT'S VERY HARD TO GET ONE!
BUT... DOESN'T IT BELONG TO YOUR MOTHER? I CAN'T ACCEPT IT.
DON'T WORRY. MOTHER DOESN'T NEED IT ANYMORE...
DAKDAK...
IT'S AN EMERGENCY!! S...SOMEONE'S DEAD! A WOMAN IN A FLOWER PATTERNED DRESS...!
WHAT'S WRONG, PETER...?
I... I DON'T KNOW!!
I DON'T KNOW ANYTHING ABOUT IT!!

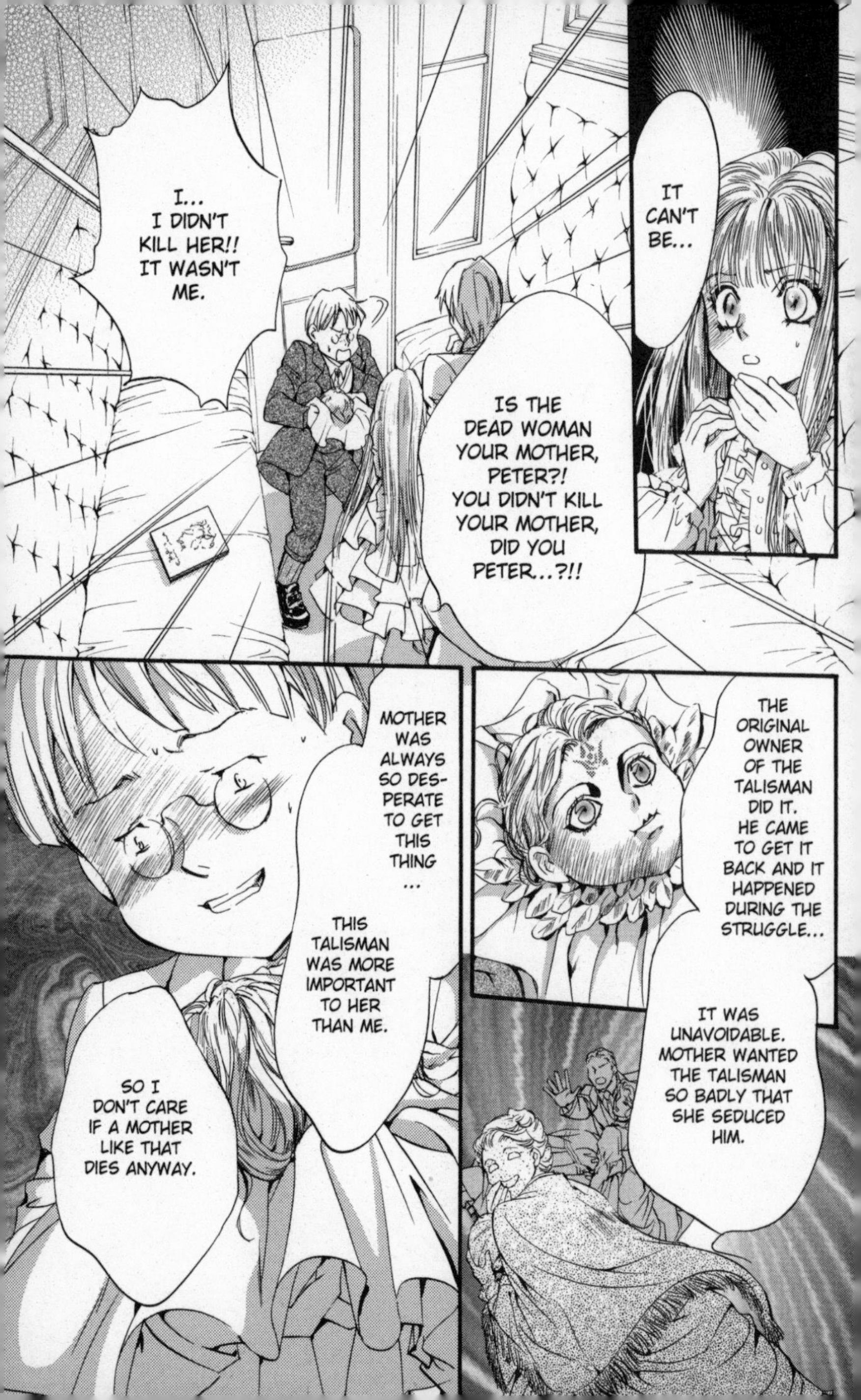
IT CAN'T BE...
IS THE DEAD WOMAN YOUR MOTHER, PETER?! YOU DIDN'T KILL YOUR MOTHER, DID YOU PETER...?!!
I... I DIDN'T KILL HER!! IT WASN'T ME.
THE ORIGINAL OWNER OF THE TALISMAN DID IT. HE CAME TO GET IT BACK AND IT HAPPENED DURING THE STRUGGLE...
IT WAS UNAVOIDABLE. MOTHER WANTED THE TALISMAN SO BADLY THAT SHE SEDUCED HIM.
MOTHER WAS ALWAYS SO DES-PERATE TO GET THIS THING ...
THIS TALISMAN WAS MORE IMPORTANT TO HER THAN ME.
SO I DON'T CARE IF A MOTHER LIKE THAT DIES ANYWAY.

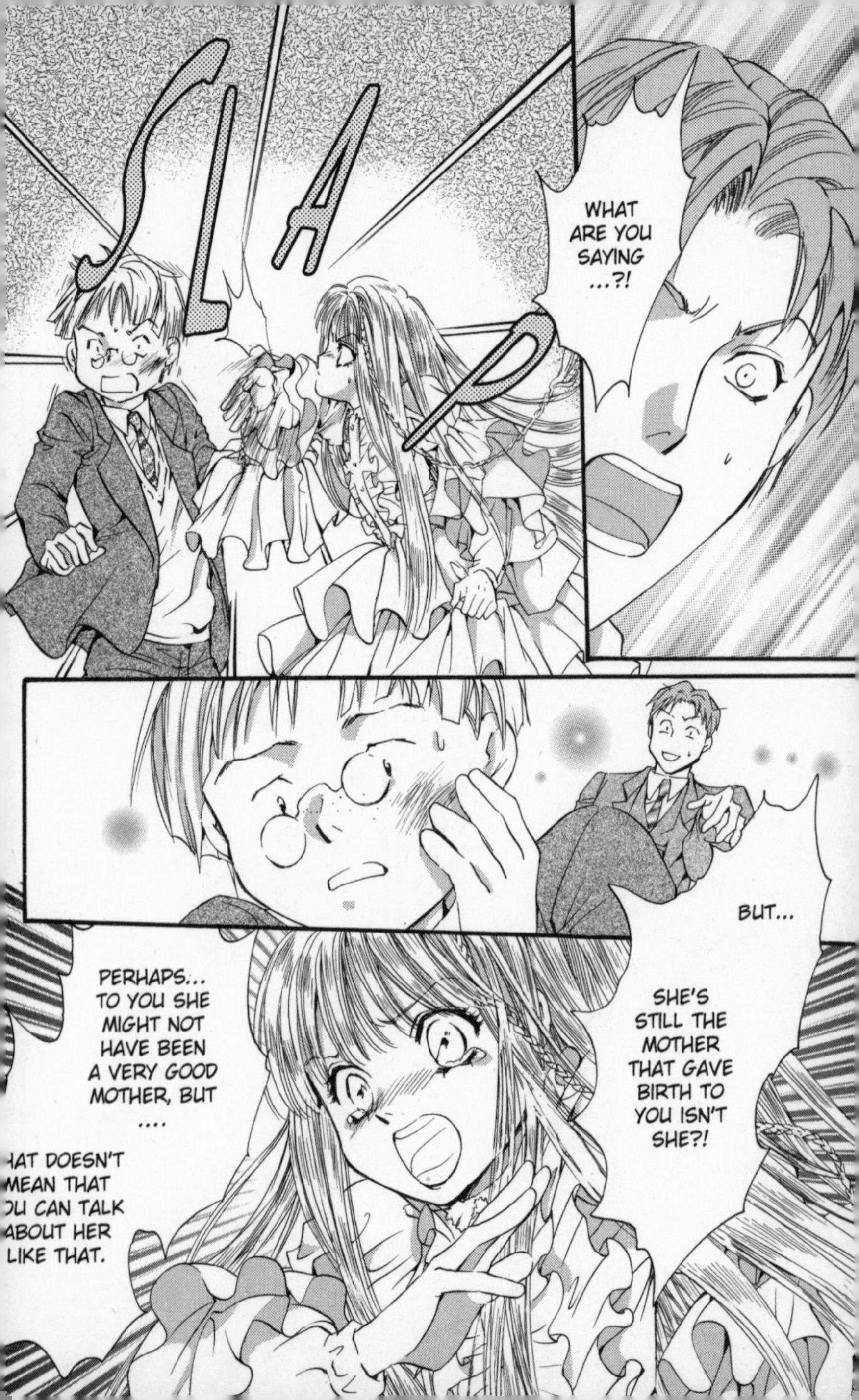
WHAT ARE YOU SAYING ...?!
SLAP
BUT...
SHE'S STILL THE MOTHER THAT GAVE BIRTH TO YOU ISN'T SHE?!
PERHAPS... TO YOU SHE MIGHT NOT HAVE BEEN A VERY GOOD MOTHER, BUT ....
HAT DOESN'T MEAN THAT OU CAN TALK ABOUT HER LIKE THAT.

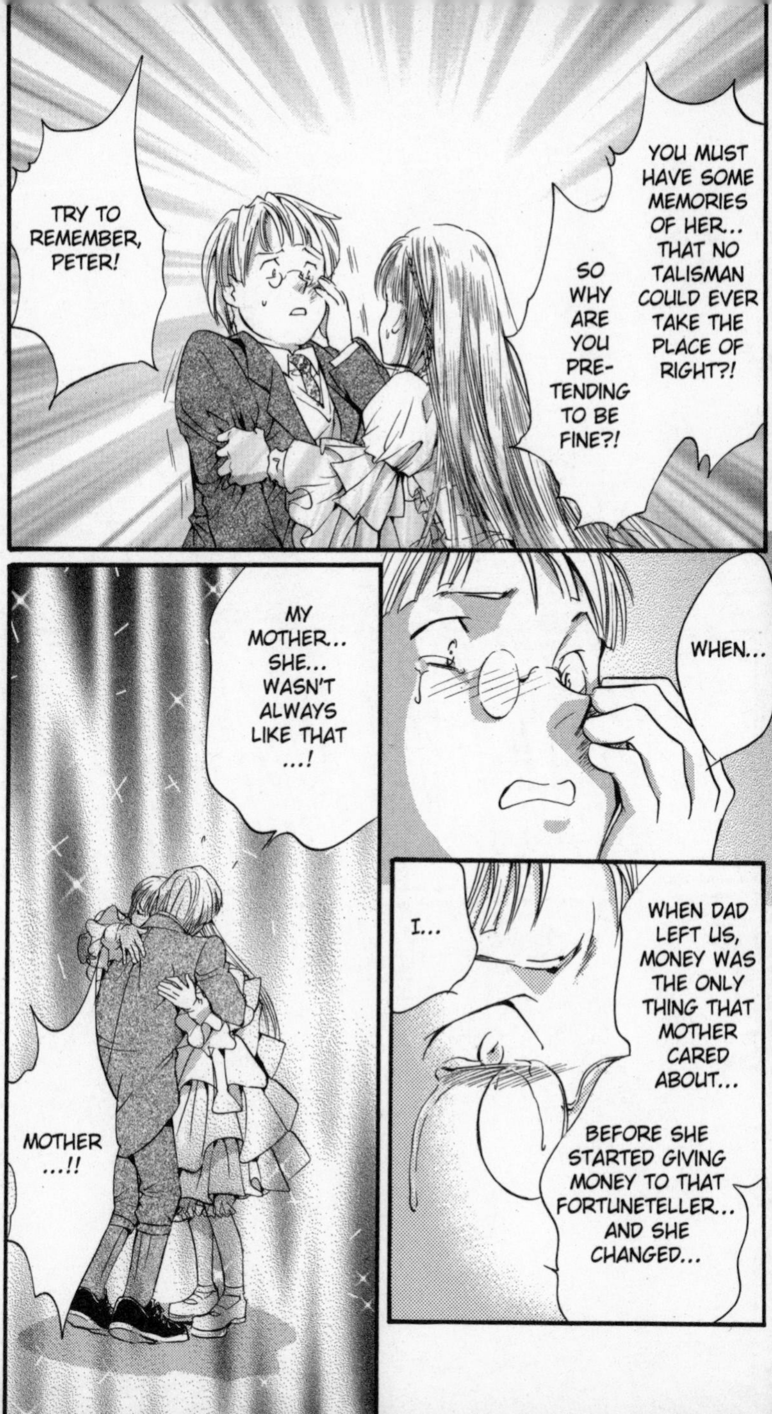
YOU MUST HAVE SOME MEMORIES OF HER... THAT NO TALISMAN COULD EVER TAKE THE PLACE OF RIGHT?!
SO WHY ARE YOU PRE-TENDING TO BE FINE?!
TRY TO REMEMBER, PETER!
WHEN...
WHEN DAD LEFT US, MONEY WAS THE ONLY THING THAT MOTHER CARED ABOUT...
I...
BEFORE SHE STARTED GIVING MONEY TO THAT FORTUNETELLER... AND SHE CHANGED...
MY MOTHER... SHE... WASN'T ALWAYS LIKE THAT ...!
MOTHER ...!!

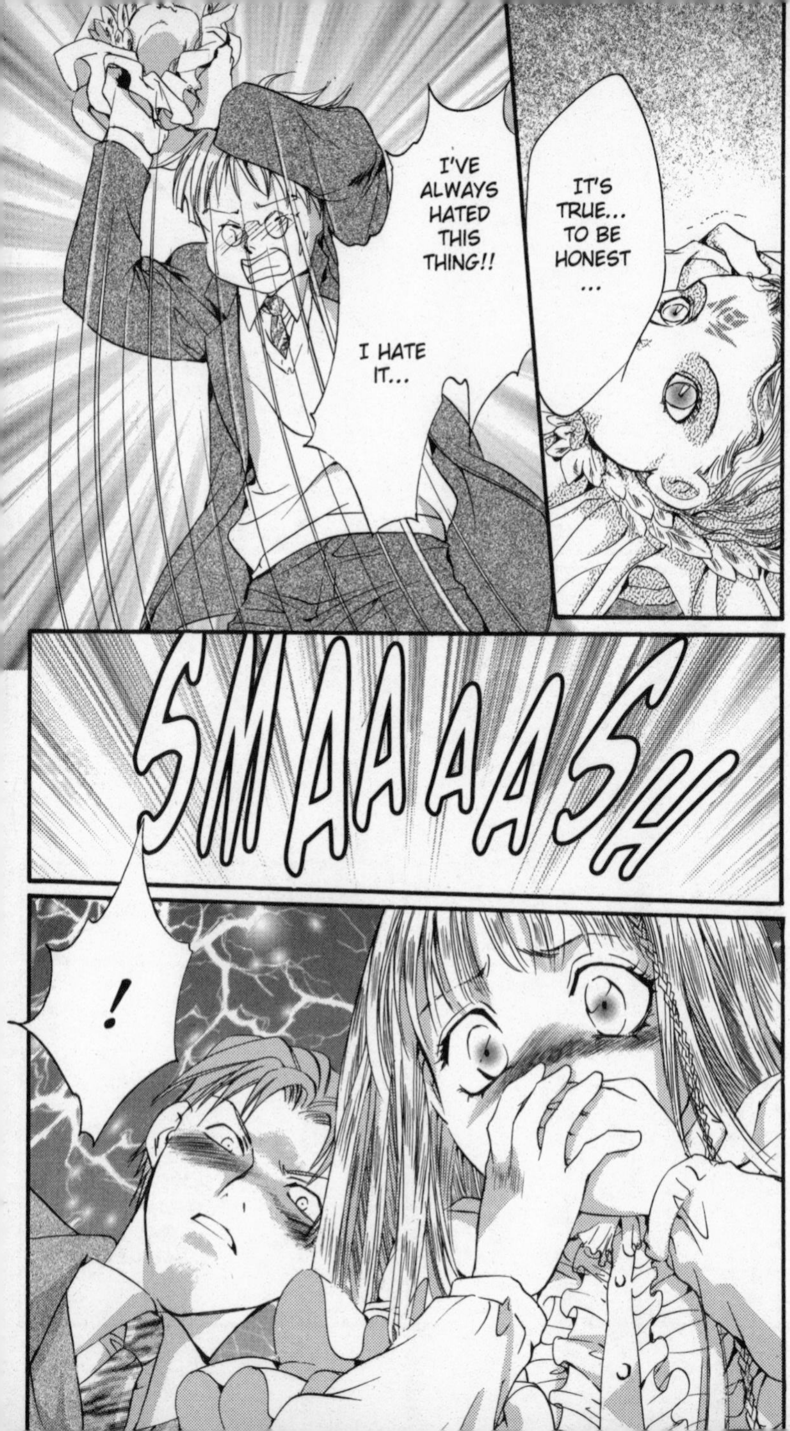
IT'S TRUE... TO BE HONEST ...
I'VE ALWAYS HATED THIS THING!!
I HATE IT...
SMAAAASH
!

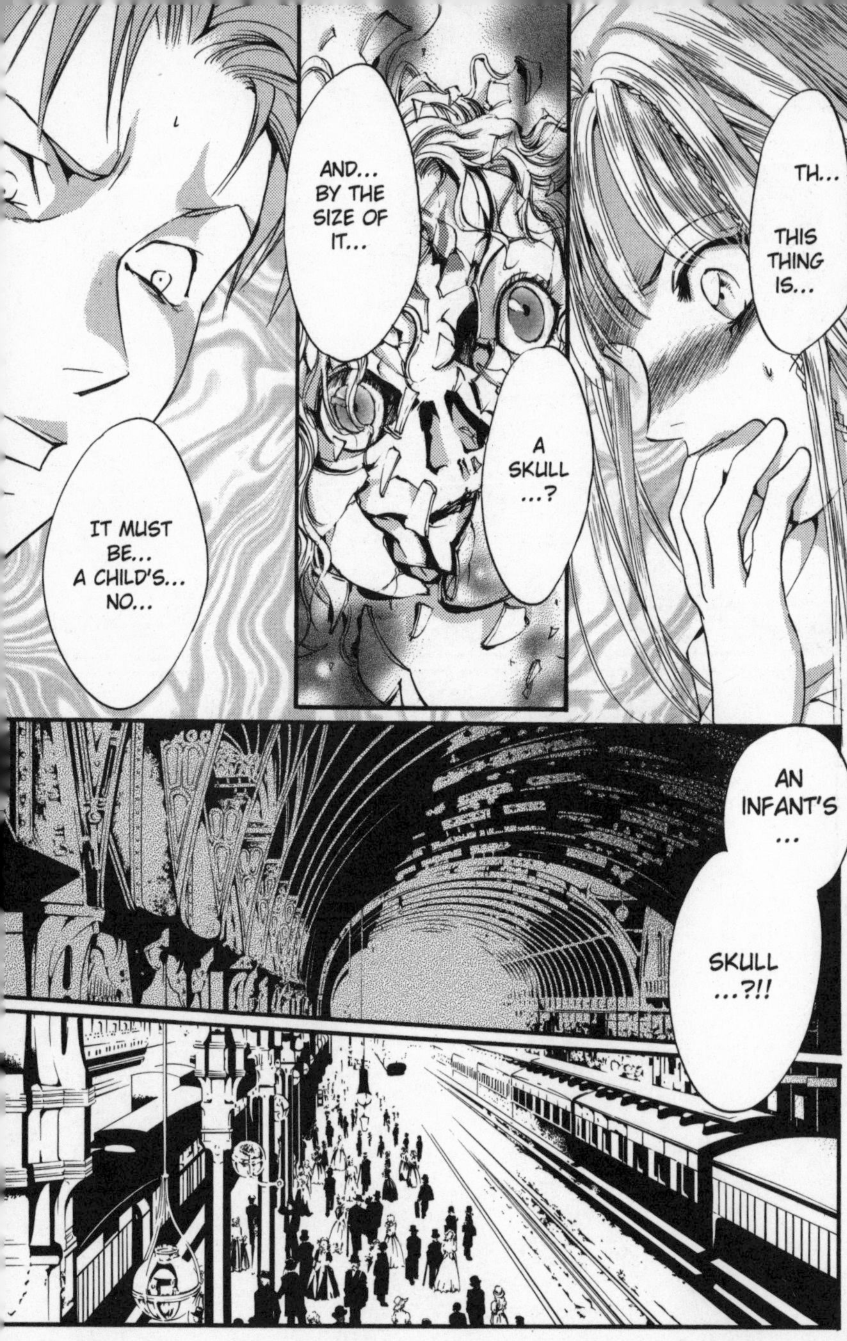
TH...
THIS THING IS...
A SKULL ...?
AND... BY THE SIZE OF IT...
IT MUST BE... A CHILD'S... NO...
AN INFANT'S ...
SKULL ...?!!

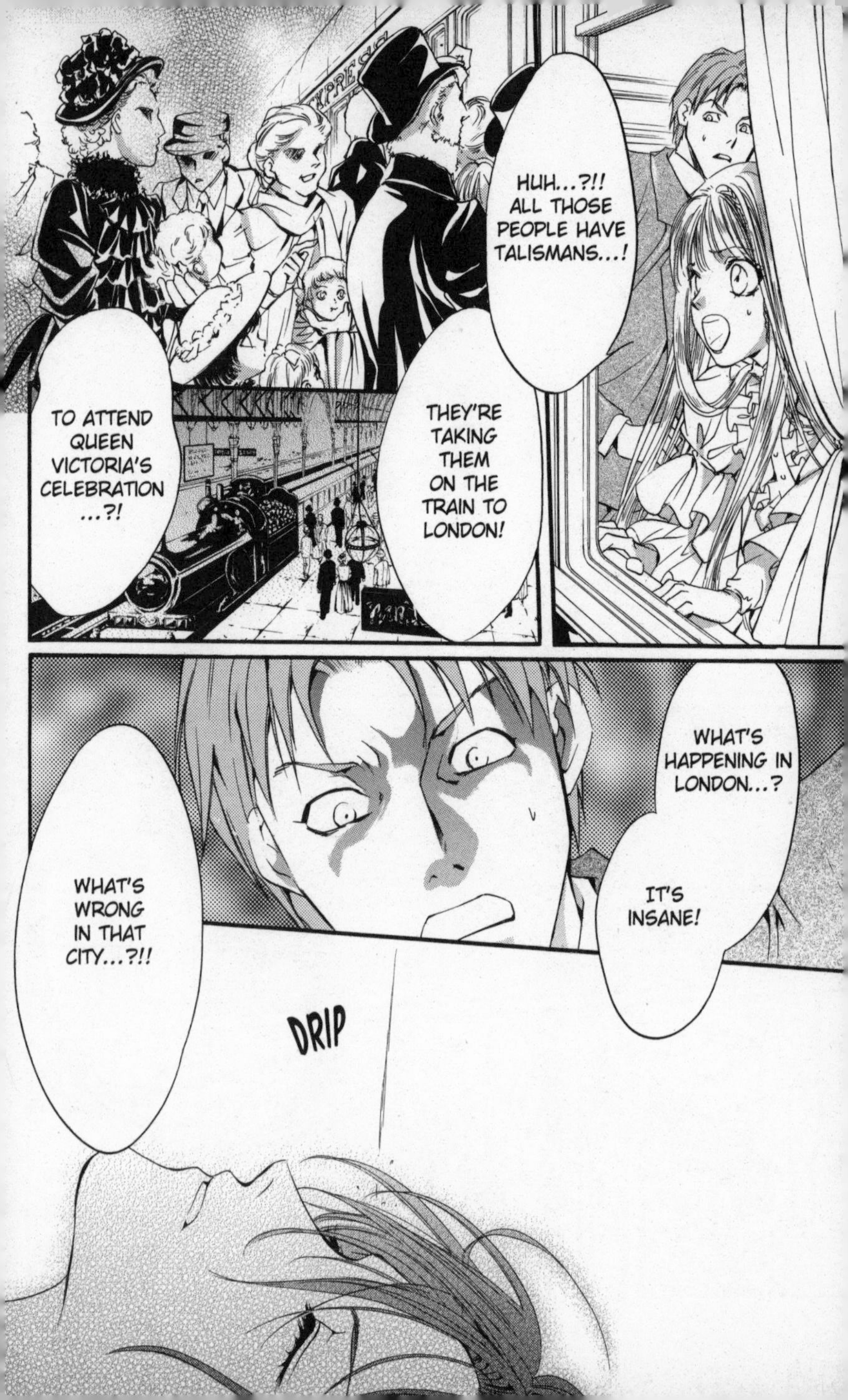
HUH...?!! ALL THOSE PEOPLE HAVE TALISMANS...!
THEY'RE TAKING THEM ON THE TRAIN TO LONDON!
TO ATTEND QUEEN VICTORIA'S CELEBRATION ...?!
WHAT'S HAPPENING IN LONDON...?
IT'S INSANE!
WHAT'S WRONG IN THAT CITY...?!!
DRIP

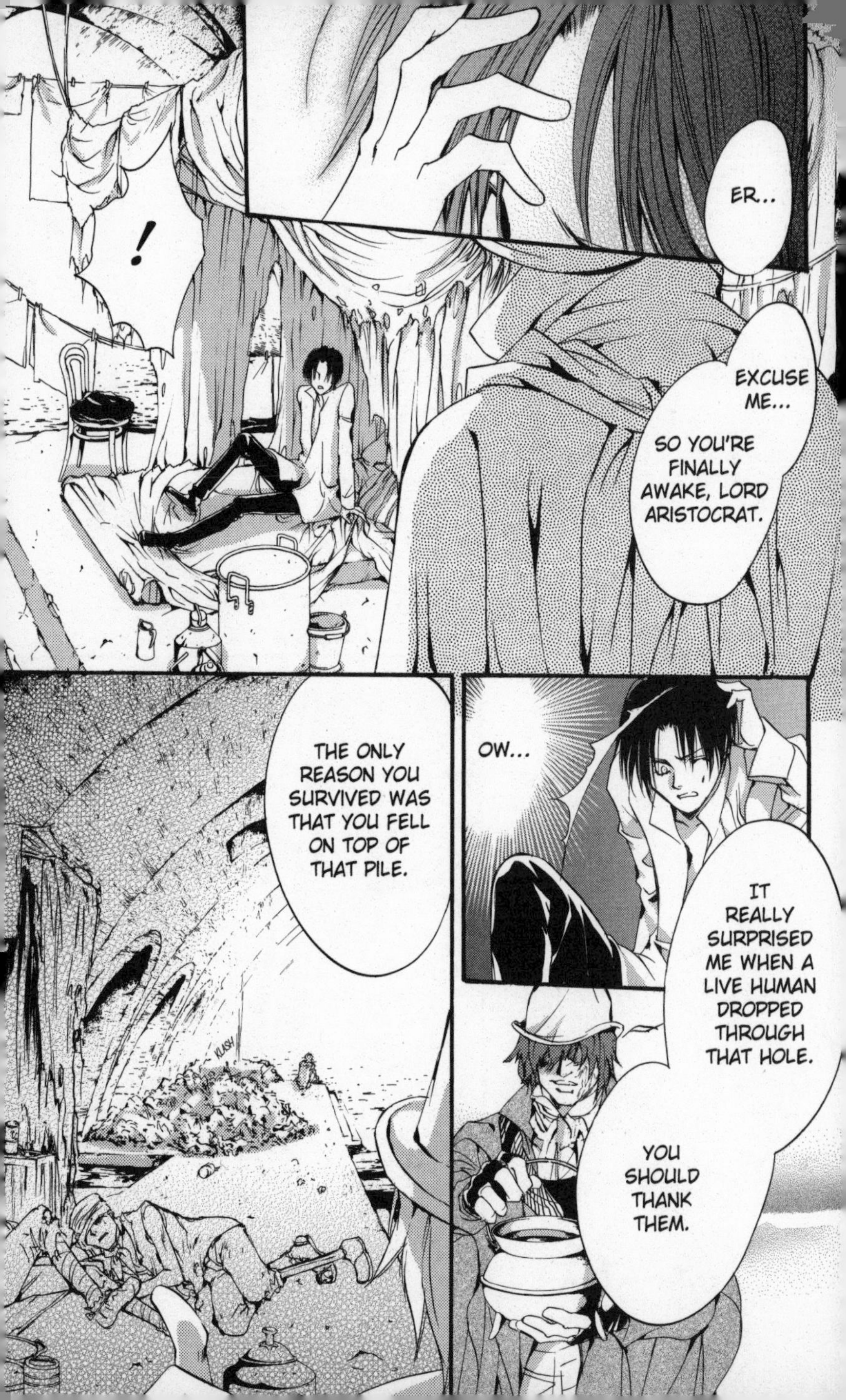
ER...
EXCUSE ME...
SO YOU'RE FINALLY AWAKE, LORD ARISTOCRAT.
!
OW...
IT REALLY SURPRISED ME WHEN A LIVE HUMAN DROPPED THROUGH THAT HOLE.
YOU SHOULD THANK THEM.
THE ONLY REASON YOU SURVIVED WAS THAT YOU FELL ON TOP OF THAT PILE.
KUSH

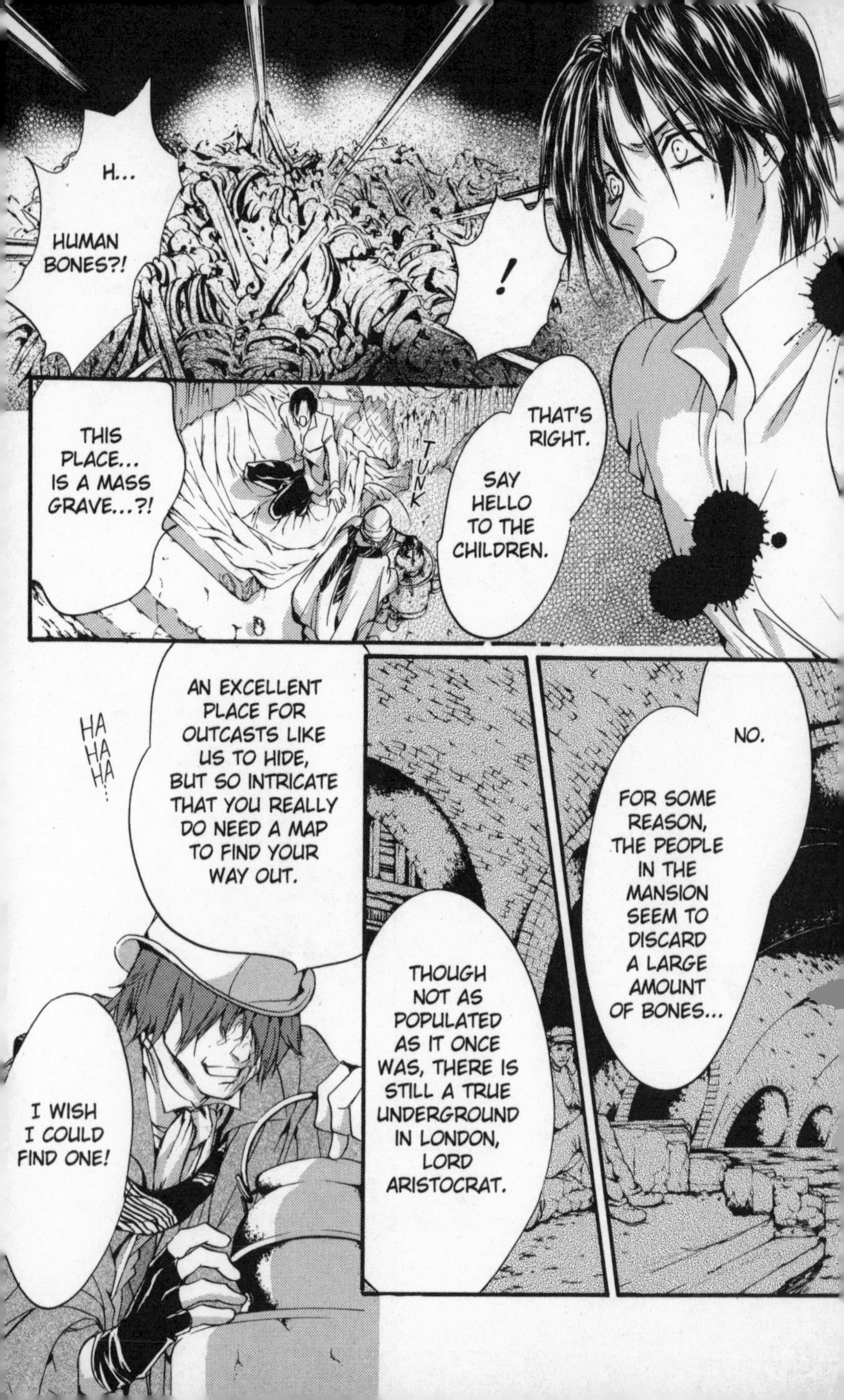
!
H...
HUMAN BONES?!
THIS PLACE... IS A MASS GRAVE...?!
TUNK
THAT'S RIGHT.
SAY HELLO TO THE CHILDREN.
NO.
FOR SOME REASON, THE PEOPLE IN THE MANSION SEEM TO DISCARD A LARGE AMOUNT OF BONES...
THOUGH NOT AS POPULATED AS IT ONCE WAS, THERE IS STILL A TRUE UNDERGROUND IN LONDON, LORD ARISTOCRAT.
AN EXCELLENT PLACE FOR OUTCASTS LIKE US TO HIDE, BUT SO INTRICATE THAT YOU REALLY DO NEED A MAP TO FIND YOUR WAY OUT.
HA HA HA...
I WISH I COULD FIND ONE!

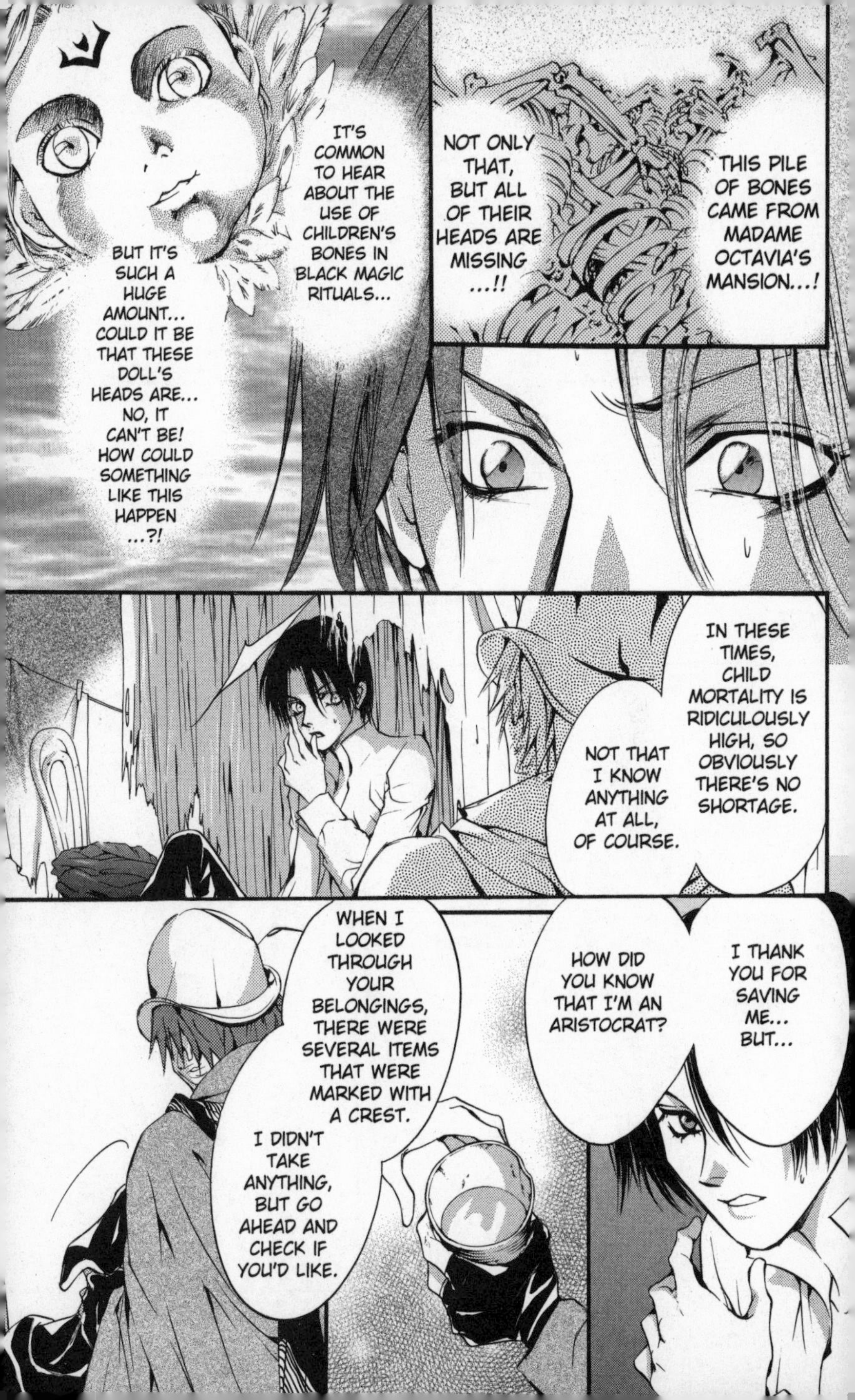

THIS PILE OF BONES CAME FROM MADAME OCTAVIA'S MANSION...!
NOT ONLY THAT, BUT ALL OF THEIR HEADS ARE MISSING...!!
IT'S COMMON TO HEAR ABOUT THE USE OF CHILDREN'S BONES IN BLACK MAGIC RITUALS...
BUT IT'S SUCH A HUGE AMOUNT... COULD IT BE THAT THESE DOLL'S HEADS ARE... NO, IT CAN'T BE! HOW COULD SOMETHING LIKE THIS HAPPEN...?!
IN THESE TIMES, CHILD MORTALITY IS RIDICULOUSLY HIGH, SO OBVIOUSLY THERE'S NO SHORTAGE.
NOT THAT I KNOW ANYTHING AT ALL, OF COURSE.
I THANK YOU FOR SAVING ME... BUT...
HOW DID YOU KNOW THAT I'M AN ARISTOCRAT?
WHEN I LOOKED THROUGH YOUR BELONGINGS, THERE WERE SEVERAL ITEMS THAT WERE MARKED WITH A CREST.
I DIDN'T TAKE ANYTHING, BUT GO AHEAD AND CHECK IF YOU'D LIKE.

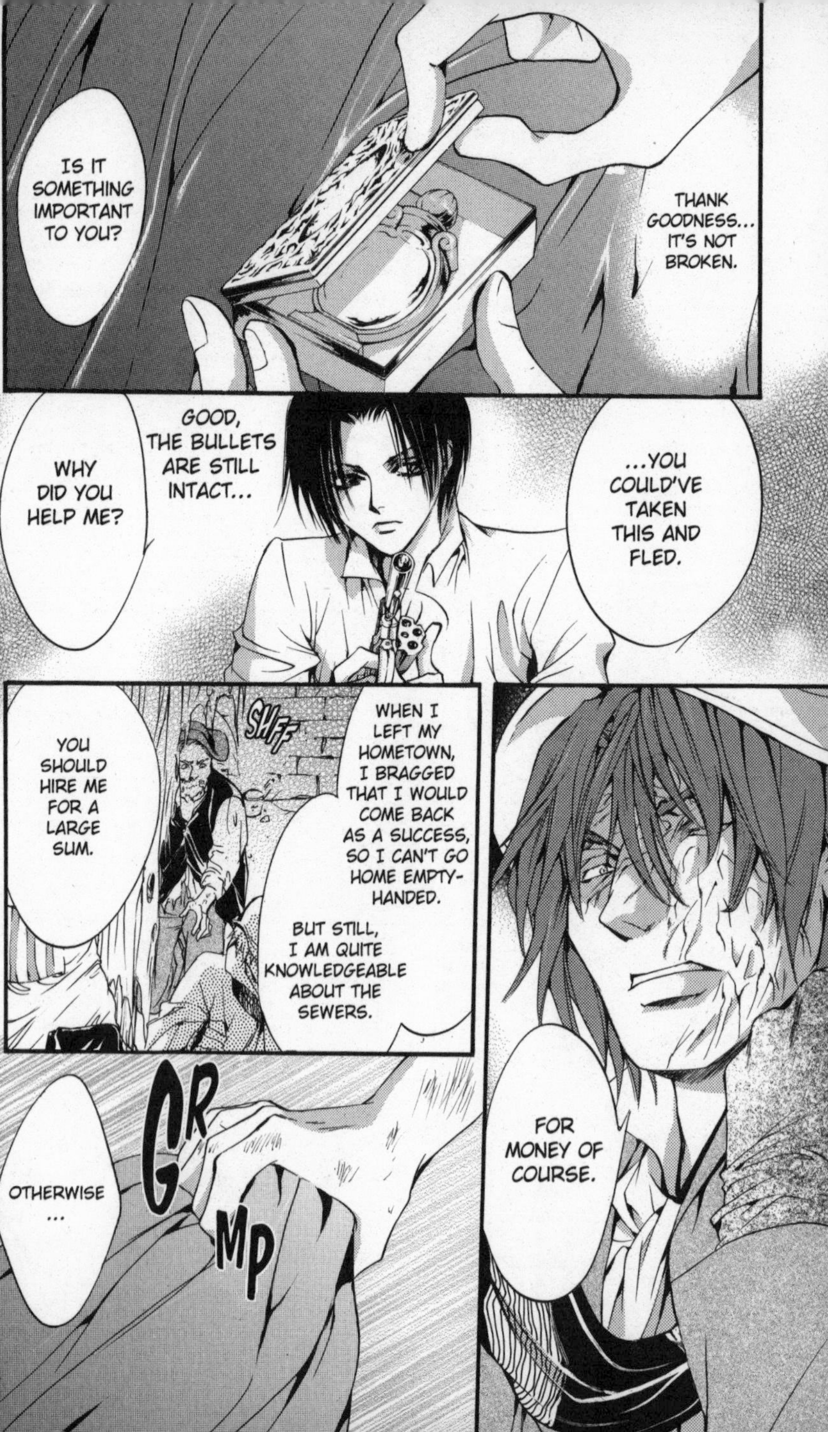
THANK GOODNESS... IT'S NOT BROKEN.
IS IT SOMETHING IMPORTANT TO YOU?
...YOU COULD'VE TAKEN THIS AND FLED.
GOOD, THE BULLETS ARE STILL INTACT...
WHY DID YOU HELP ME?
FOR MONEY OF COURSE.
SHFF
WHEN I LEFT MY HOMETOWN, I BRAGGED THAT I WOULD COME BACK AS A SUCCESS, SO I CAN'T GO HOME EMPTY-HANDED.
BUT STILL, I AM QUITE KNOWLEDGEABLE ABOUT THE SEWERS.
YOU SHOULD HIRE ME FOR A LARGE SUM.
GRMP
OTHERWISE...

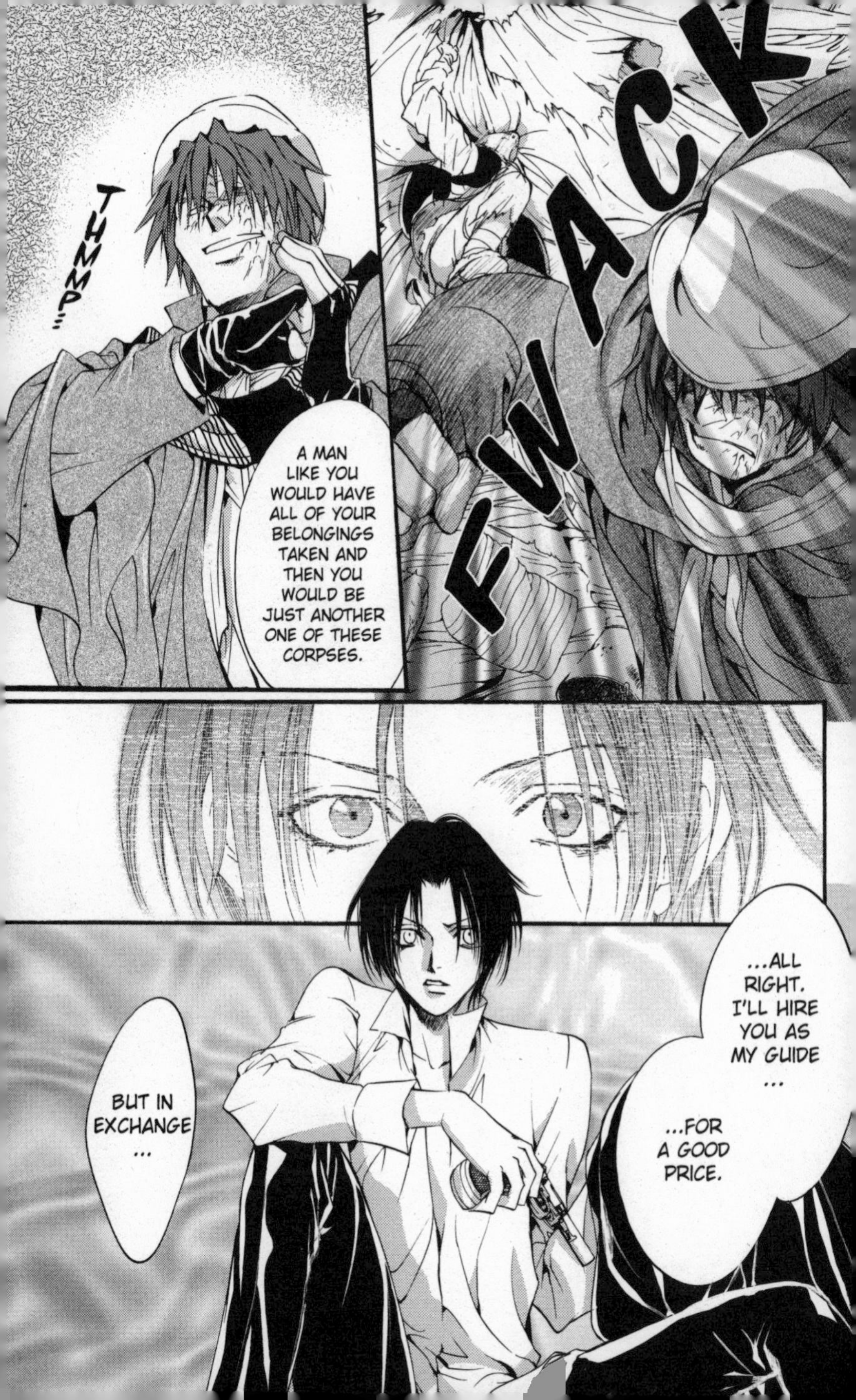
FWACK
THMMP...
A MAN LIKE YOU WOULD HAVE ALL OF YOUR BELONGINGS TAKEN AND THEN YOU WOULD BE JUST ANOTHER ONE OF THESE CORPSES.
...ALL RIGHT. I'LL HIRE YOU AS MY GUIDE ...
...FOR A GOOD PRICE.
BUT IN EXCHANGE ...

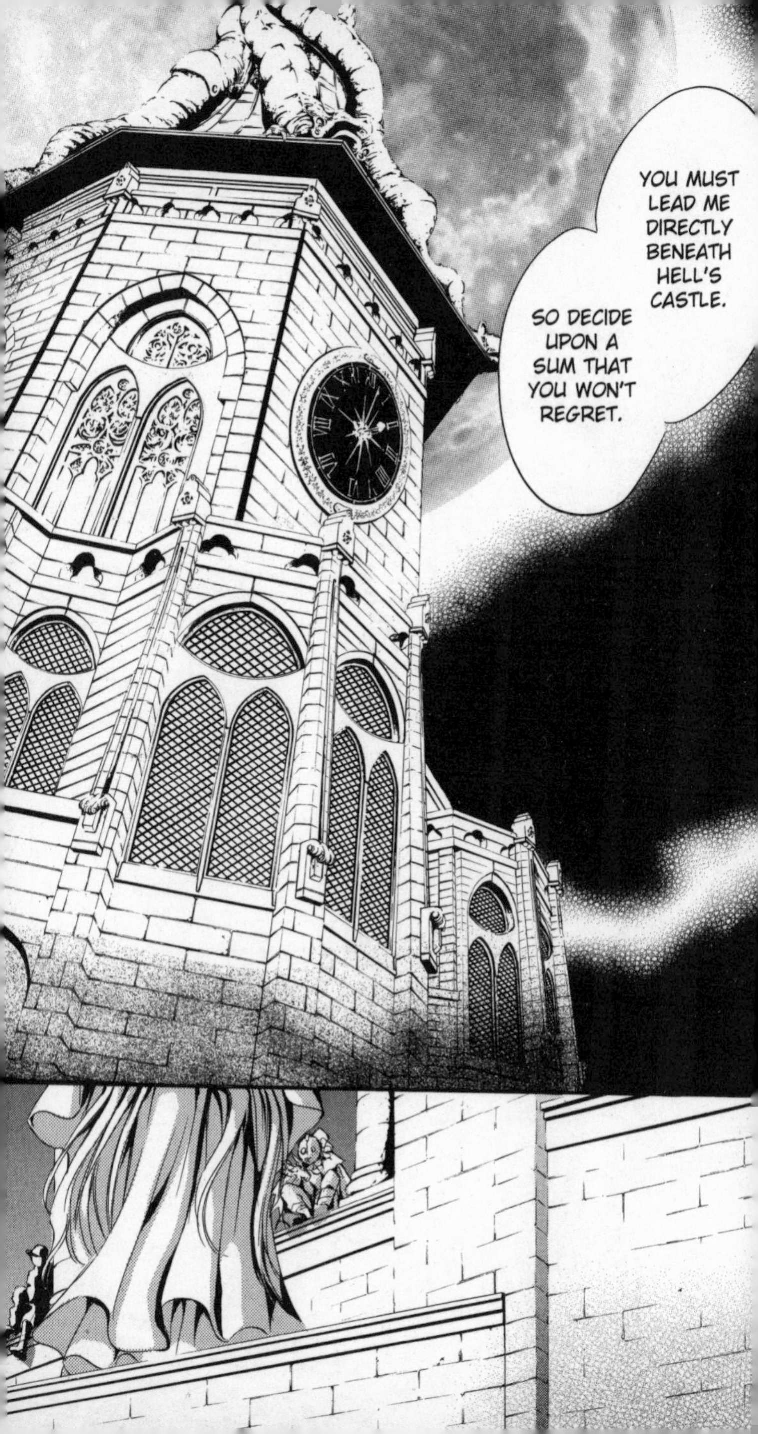
YOU MUST LEAD ME DIRECTLY BENEATH HELL'S CASTLE.
SO DECIDE UPON A SUM THAT YOU WON'T REGRET.

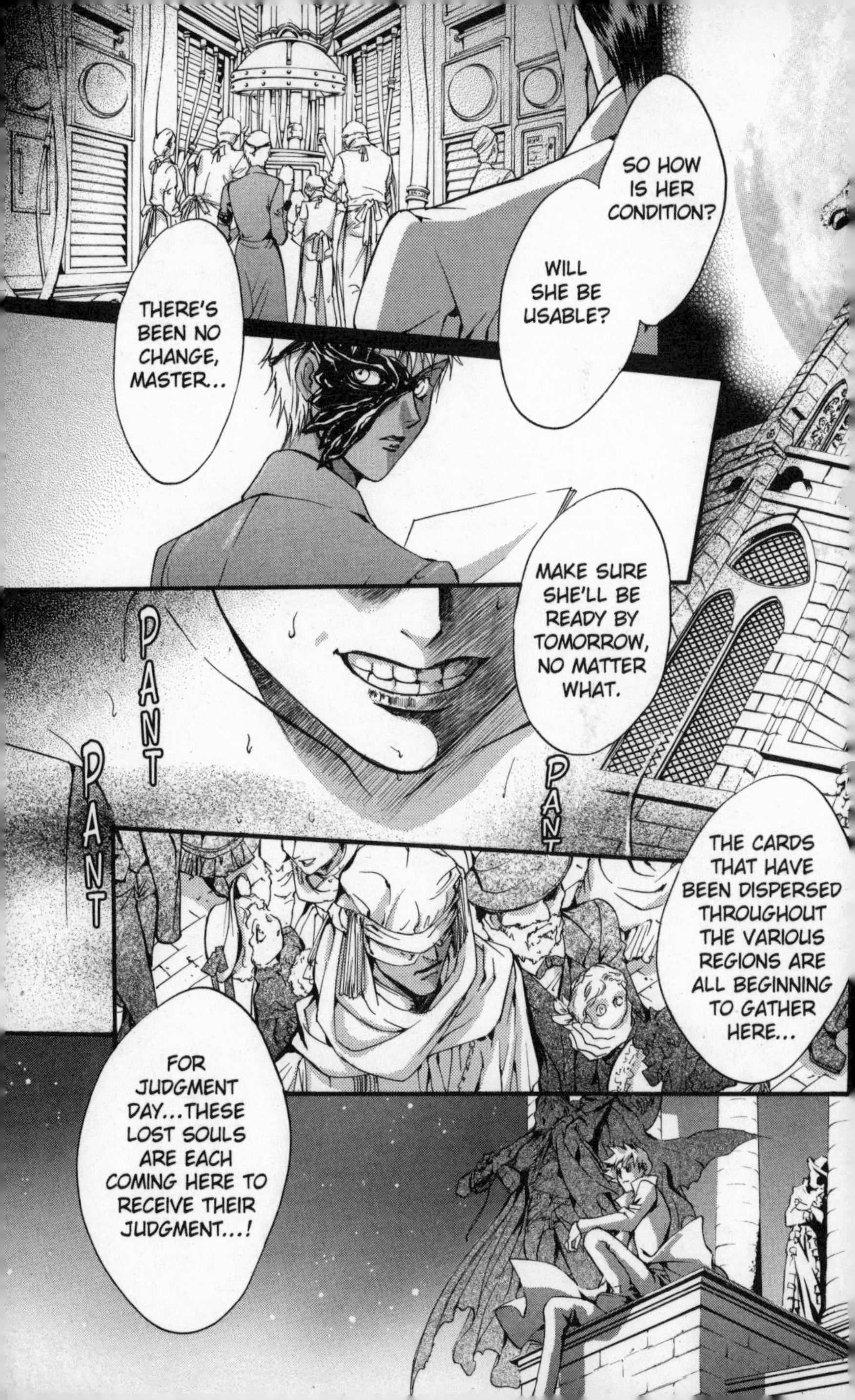
SO HOW IS HER CONDITION?
WILL SHE BE USABLE?
THERE'S BEEN NO CHANGE, MASTER...
MAKE SURE SHE'LL BE READY BY TOMORROW, NO MATTER WHAT.
PANT
PANT
PANT
THE CARDS THAT HAVE BEEN DISPERSED THROUGHOUT THE VARIOUS REGIONS ARE ALL BEGINNING TO GATHER HERE...
FOR JUDGMENT DAY...THESE LOST SOULS ARE EACH COMING HERE TO RECEIVE THEIR JUDGMENT...!

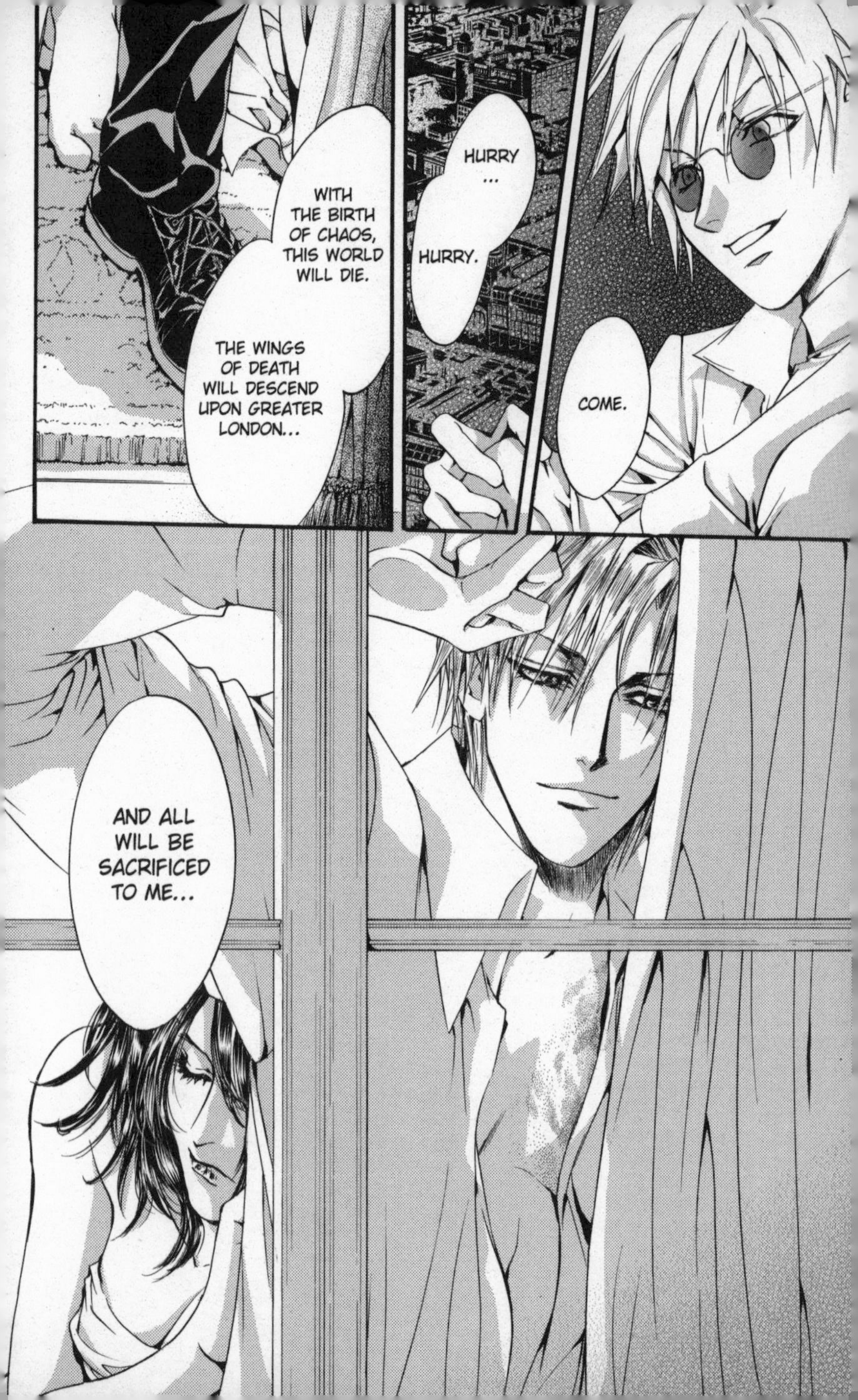
COME.
HURRY ...
HURRY.
WITH THE BIRTH OF CHAOS, THIS WORLD WILL DIE.
THE WINGS OF DEATH WILL DESCEND UPON GREATER LONDON...
AND ALL WILL BE SACRIFICED TO ME...

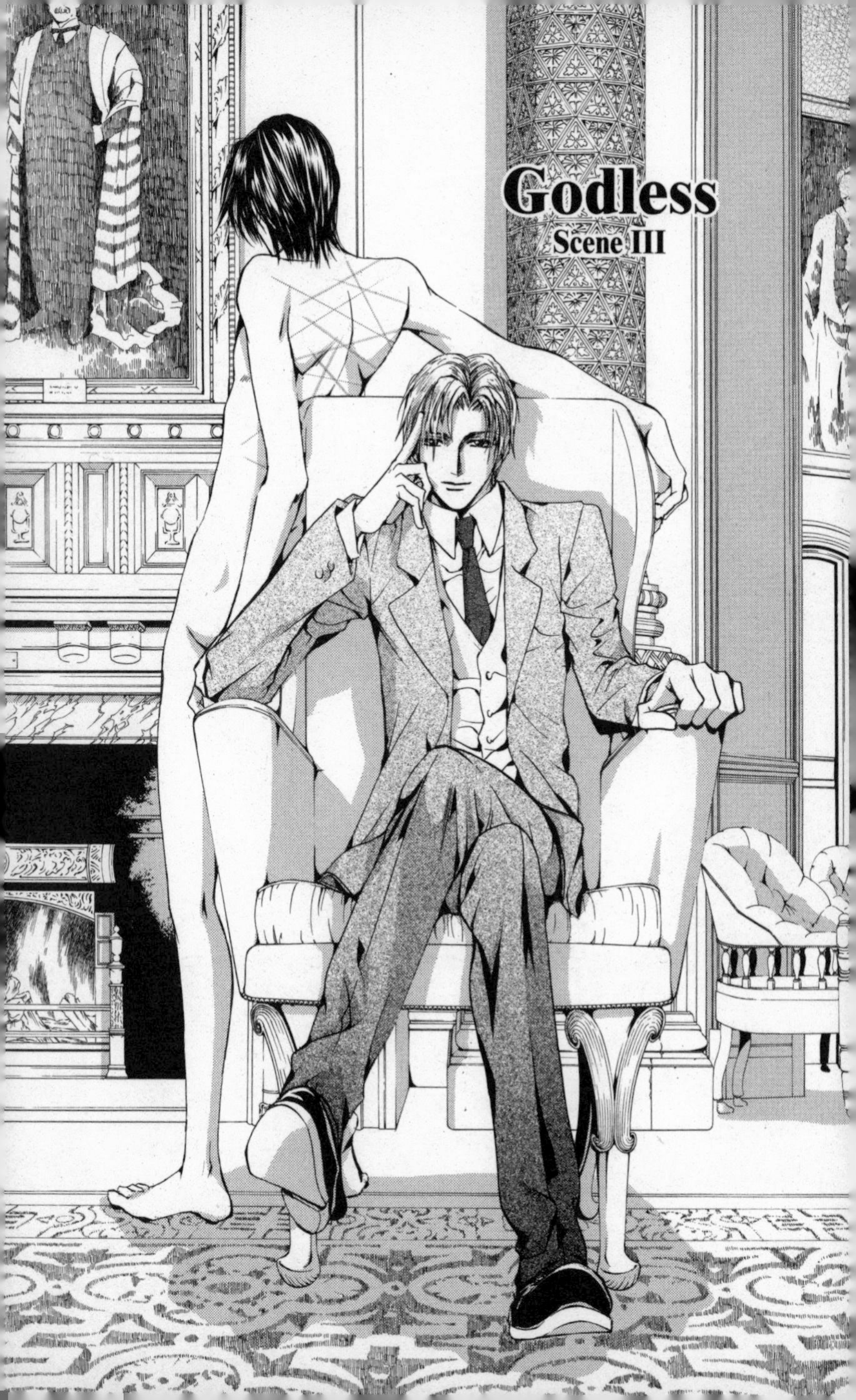
Godless
Scene III

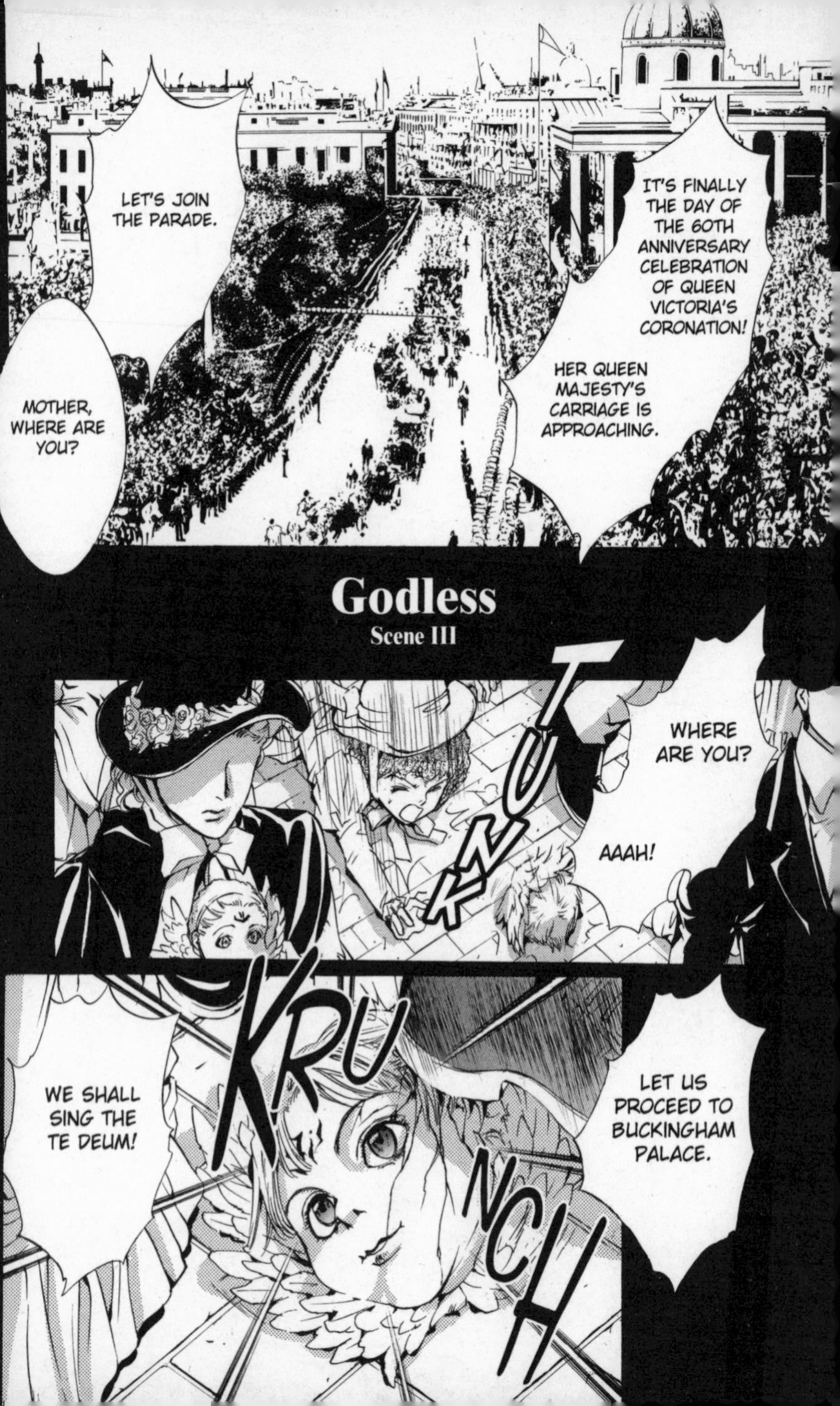
IT'S FINALLY THE DAY OF THE 60TH ANNIVERSARY CELEBRATION OF QUEEN VICTORIA'S CORONATION!
LET'S JOIN THE PARADE.
HER QUEEN MAJESTY'S CARRIAGE IS APPROACHING.
MOTHER, WHERE ARE YOU?
Godless
Scene III
WHERE ARE YOU?
AAAH!
TUNK
LET US PROCEED TO BUCKINGHAM PALACE.
WE SHALL SING THE TE DEUM!
KRUNCH

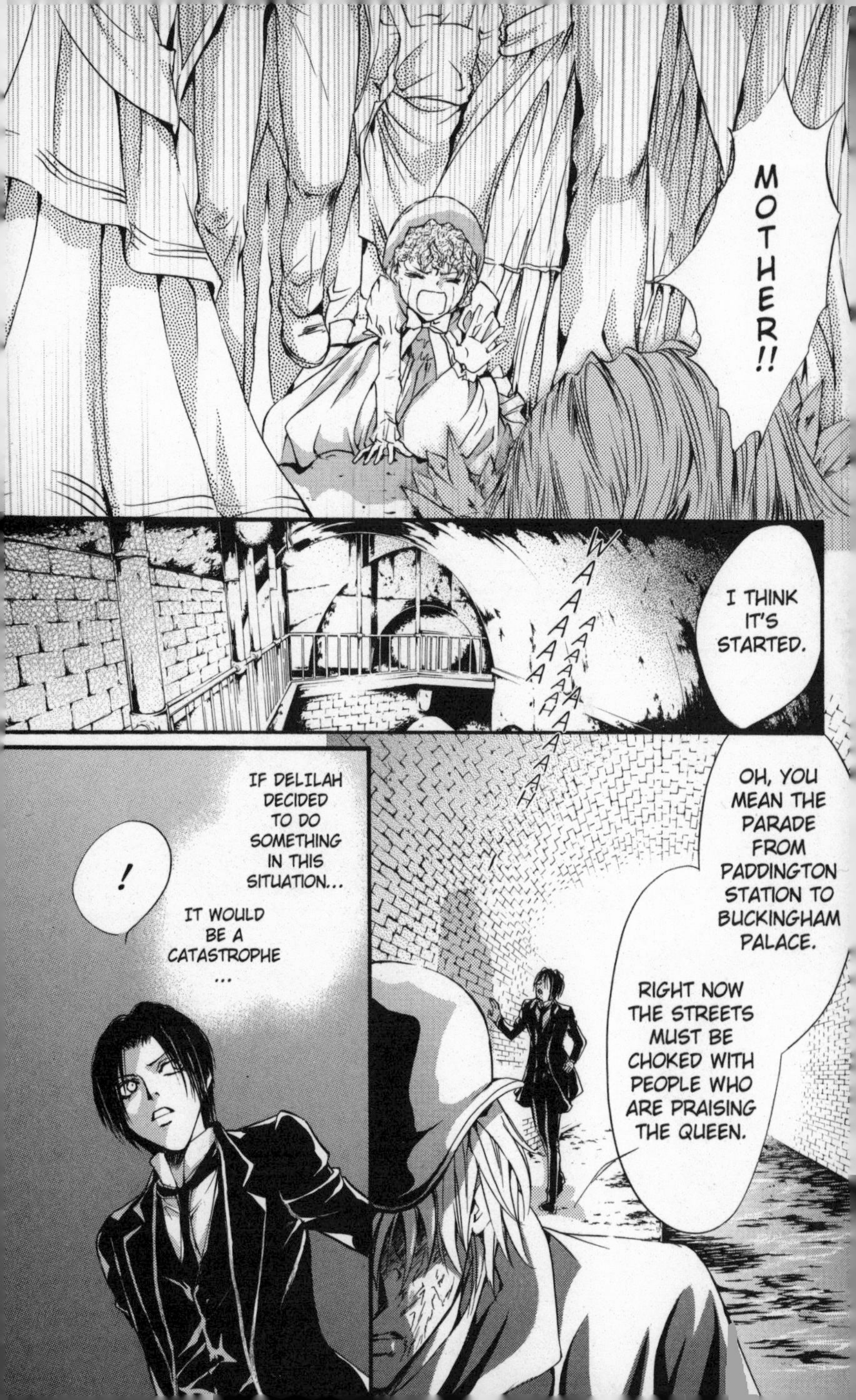
MOTHER!!
WAAAAAAAAAAAAAAAAAH
I THINK IT'S STARTED.
OH, YOU MEAN THE PARADE FROM PADDINGTON STATION TO BUCKINGHAM PALACE.
RIGHT NOW THE STREETS MUST BE CHOKED WITH PEOPLE WHO ARE PRAISING THE QUEEN.
IF DELILAH DECIDED TO DO SOMETHING IN THIS SITUATION...
IT WOULD BE A CATASTROPHE ...
!

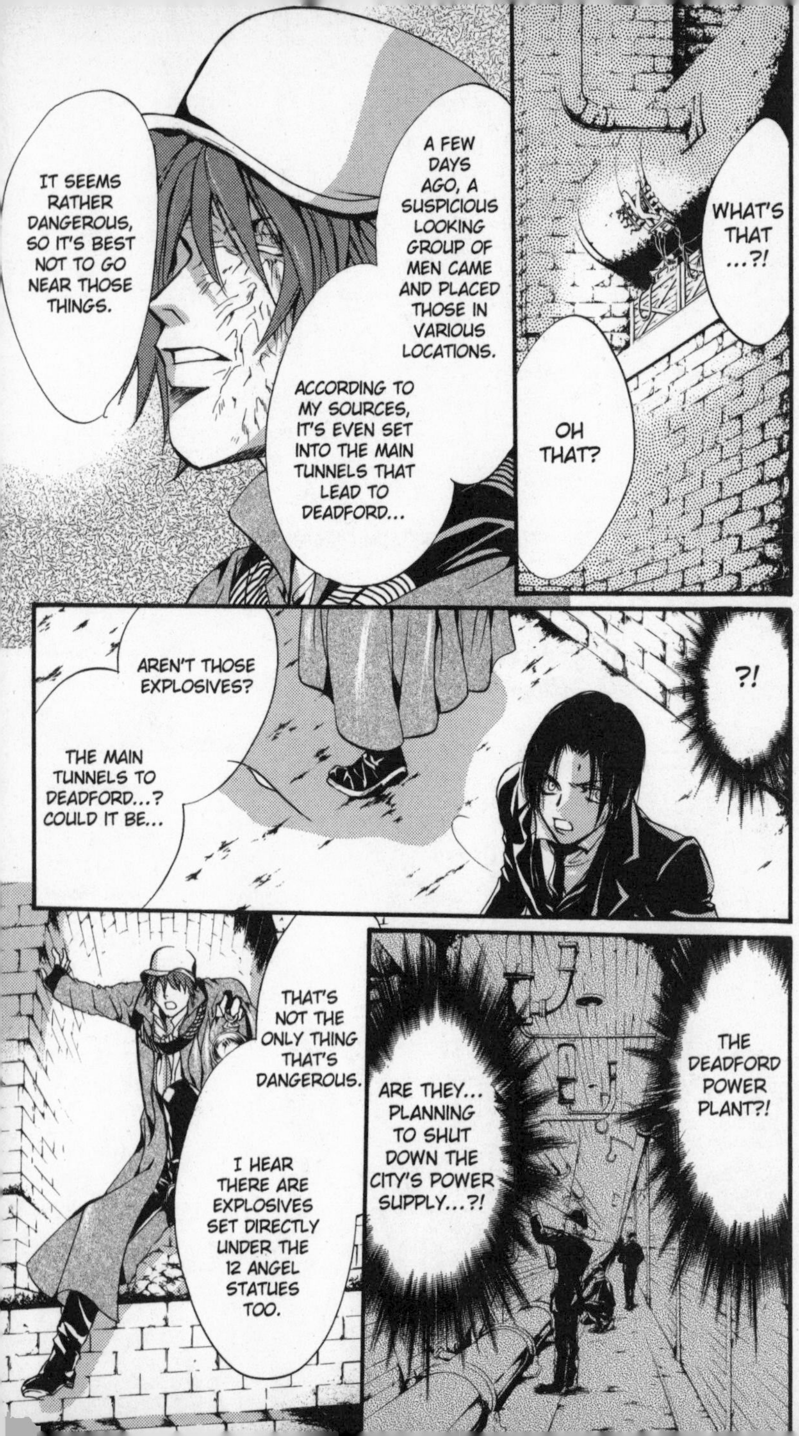
WHAT'S THAT ...?!
OH THAT?
A FEW DAYS AGO, A SUSPICIOUS LOOKING GROUP OF MEN CAME AND PLACED THOSE IN VARIOUS LOCATIONS.
ACCORDING TO MY SOURCES, IT'S EVEN SET INTO THE MAIN TUNNELS THAT LEAD TO DEADFORD...
IT SEEMS RATHER DANGEROUS, SO IT'S BEST NOT TO GO NEAR THOSE THINGS.
?!
AREN'T THOSE EXPLOSIVES?
THE MAIN TUNNELS TO DEADFORD...? COULD IT BE...
THE DEADFORD POWER PLANT?!
ARE THEY... PLANNING TO SHUT DOWN THE CITY'S POWER SUPPLY...?!
THAT'S NOT THE ONLY THING THAT'S DANGEROUS.
I HEAR THERE ARE EXPLOSIVES SET DIRECTLY UNDER THE 12 ANGEL STATUES TOO.

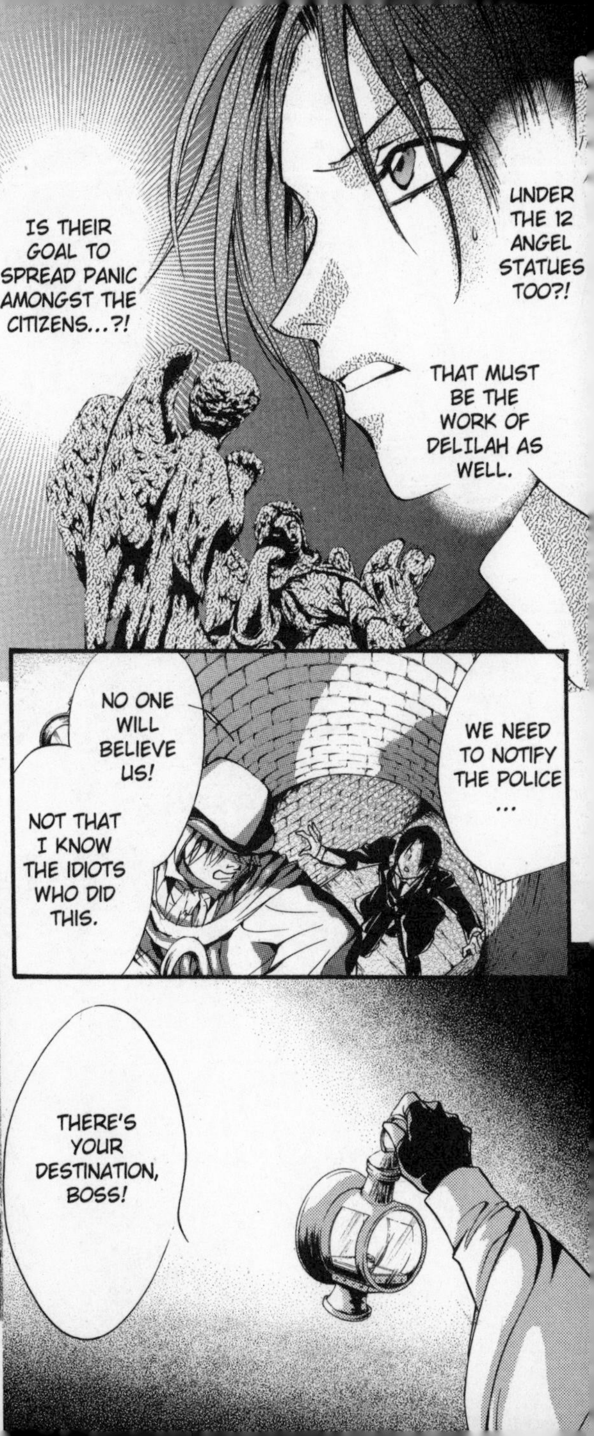
UNDER THE 12 ANGEL STATUES TOO?!
IS THEIR GOAL TO SPREAD PANIC AMONGST THE CITIZENS...?!
THAT MUST BE THE WORK OF DELILAH AS WELL.
WE NEED TO NOTIFY THE POLICE...
NO ONE WILL BELIEVE US!
NOT THAT I KNOW THE IDIOTS WHO DID THIS.
THERE'S YOUR DESTINATION, BOSS!

The 60th anniversary celebration of Queen Victoria's coronation... In reality it was on June, 21st and there was a parade of carriages from Paddington Station to Buckingham Palace. Of course an incident such as the one in the story never occurred and apparently order was maintained throughout the ceremony.

This is something that happened a while ago but since this is the last volume I think I'll mention it. Plus it was mentioned recently in a fan letter. Um... The reason Riff's name was written in kanji in the previous series is because in the overseas version of the manga, such as the Taiwanese version, Riff's name was in kanji. Of course Cain and Mary's names were all in kanji too. [EDITOR'S NOTE: THIS OF COURSE, REFERS TO THE JAPANESE EDITION OF *GODCHILD* 8 AND DOES NOT APPLY TO THE VIZ MEDIA AMERICAN EDITION, BUT THE AUTHOR'S NOTE HAS BEEN TRANSLATED DIRECTLY TO RETAIN HER ORIGINAL INTENT.]

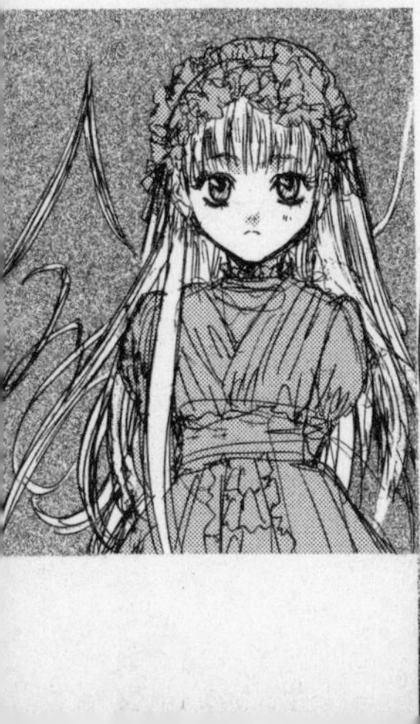

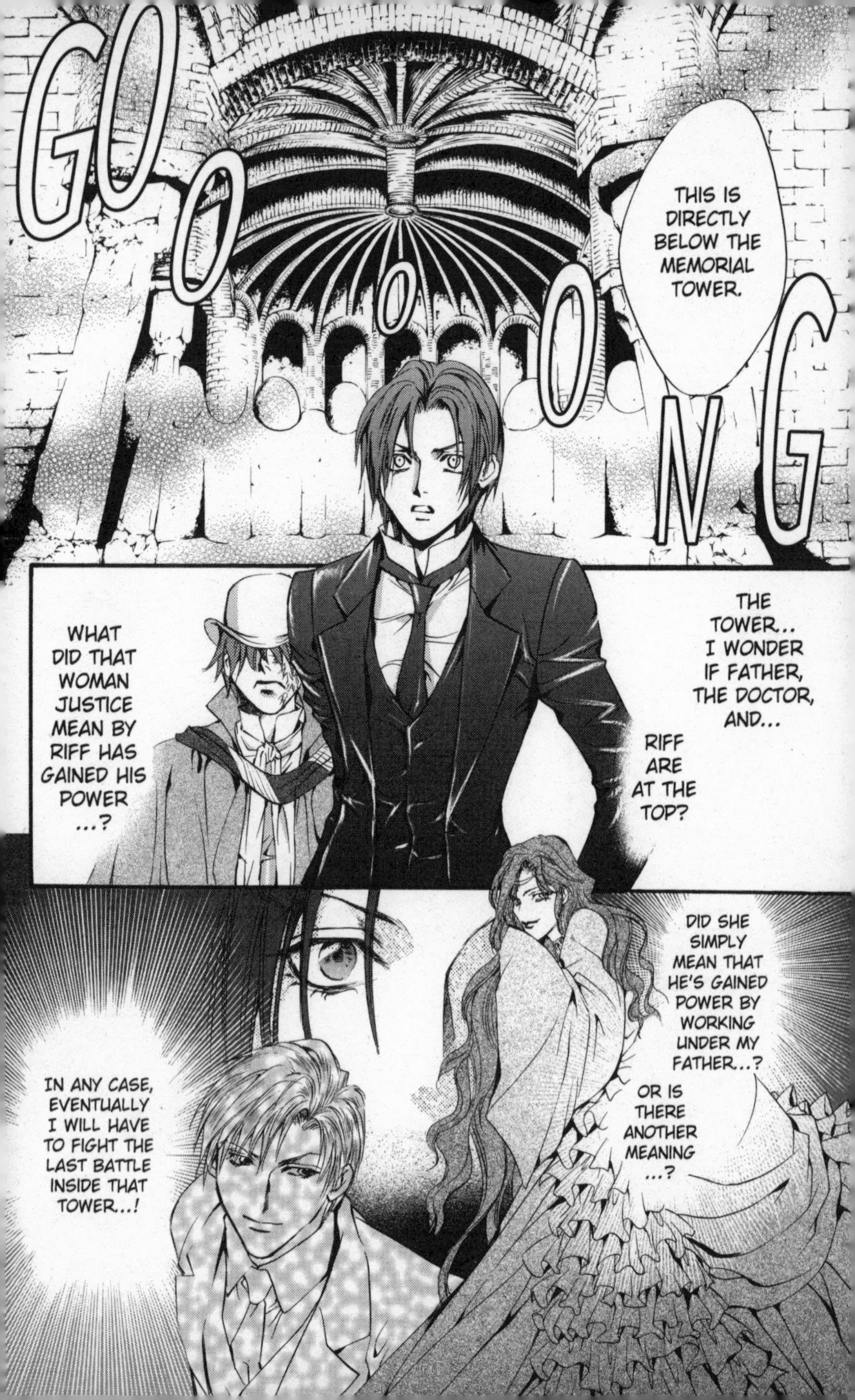
THIS IS DIRECTLY BELOW THE MEMORIAL TOWER.
GOOOOONG
THE TOWER... I WONDER IF FATHER, THE DOCTOR, AND...
RIFF ARE AT THE TOP?
WHAT DID THAT WOMAN JUSTICE MEAN BY RIFF HAS GAINED HIS POWER ...?
DID SHE SIMPLY MEAN THAT HE'S GAINED POWER BY WORKING UNDER MY FATHER...?
OR IS THERE ANOTHER MEANING ...?
IN ANY CASE, EVENTUALLY I WILL HAVE TO FIGHT THE LAST BATTLE INSIDE THAT TOWER...!

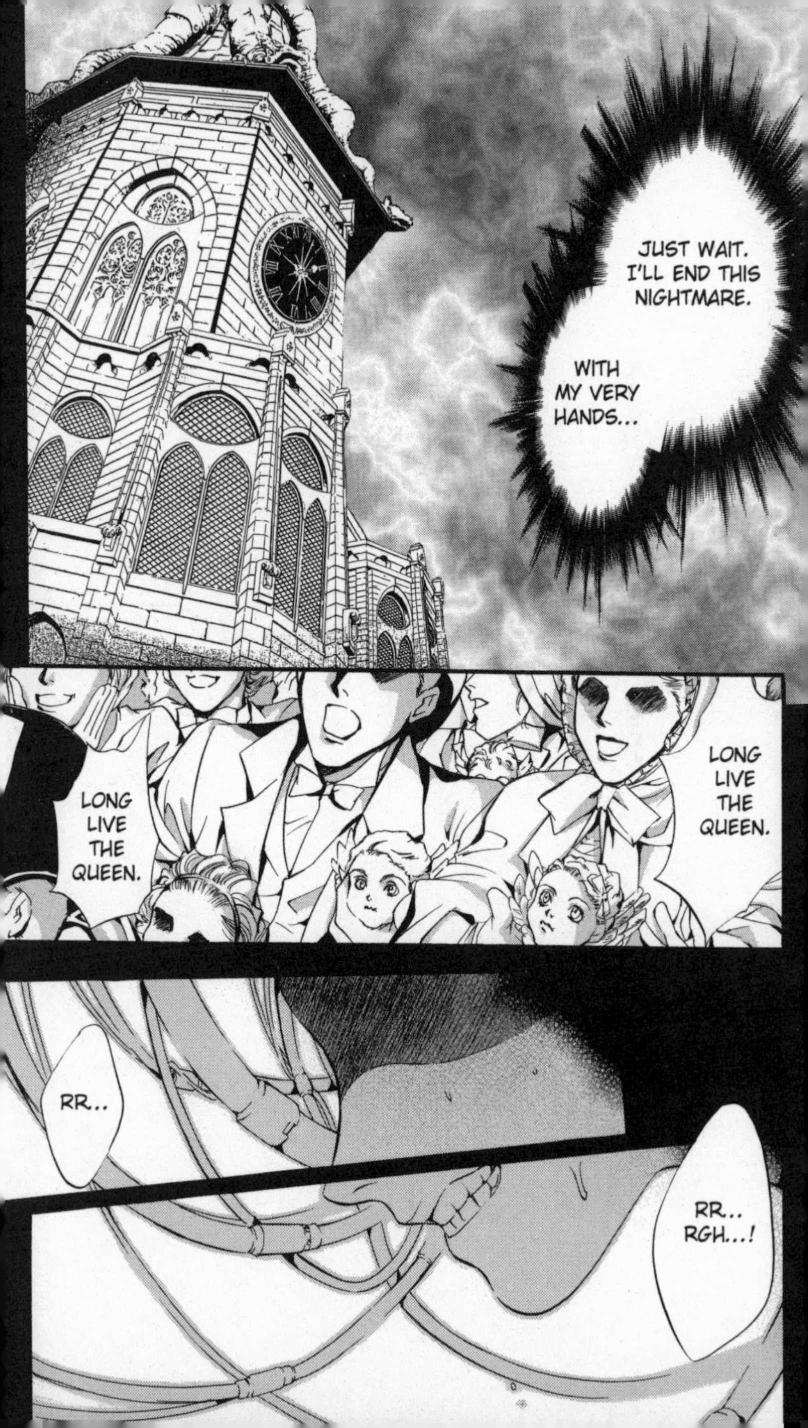
JUST WAIT. I'LL END THIS NIGHTMARE.
WITH MY VERY HANDS...
LONG LIVE THE QUEEN.
LONG LIVE THE QUEEN.
RR...
RR... RGH...!

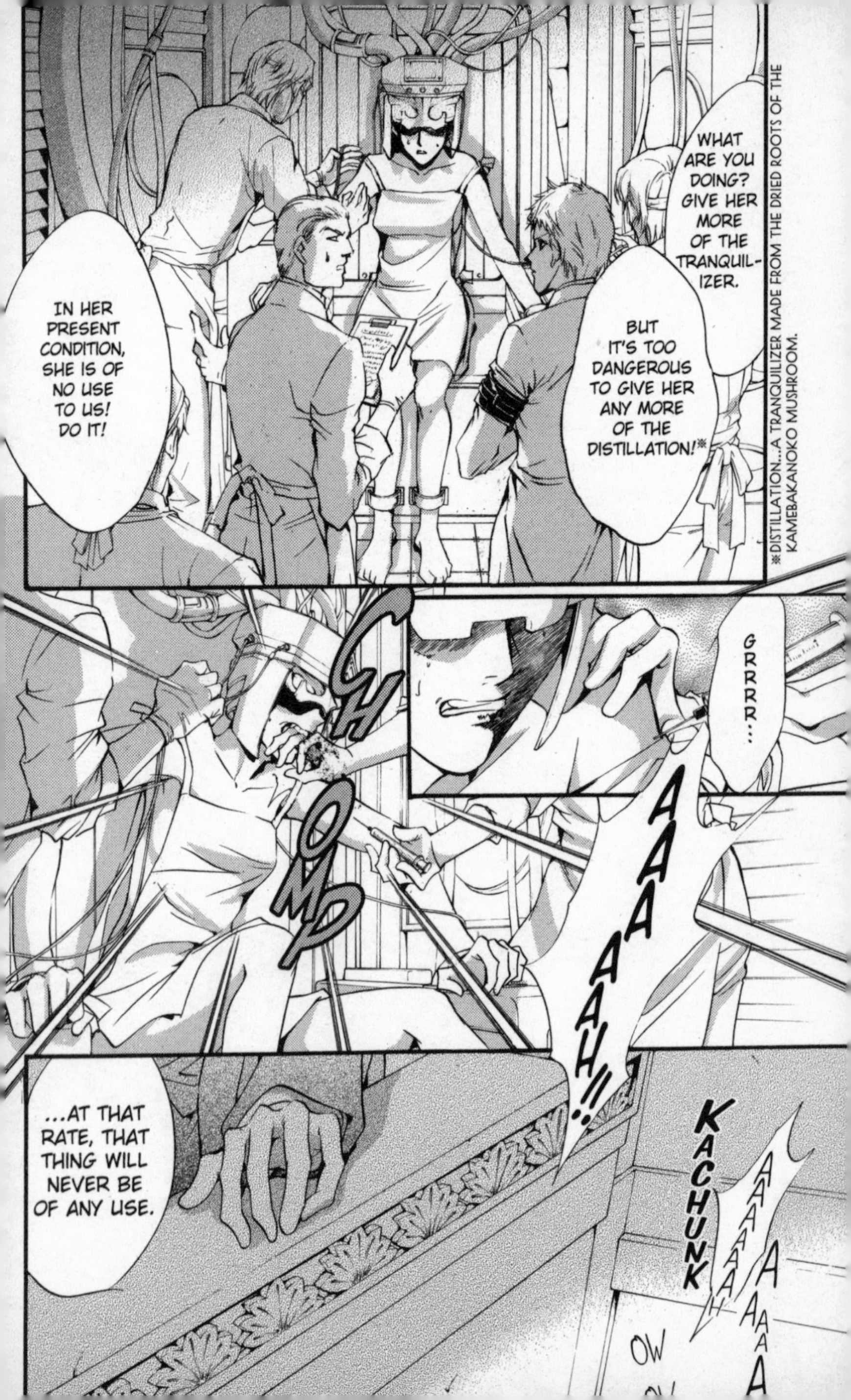
WHAT ARE YOU DOING? GIVE HER MORE OF THE TRANQUIL-IZER.
BUT IT'S TOO DANGEROUS TO GIVE HER ANY MORE OF THE DISTILLATION!※
IN HER PRESENT CONDITION, SHE IS OF NO USE TO US! DO IT!
GRRRR...
CHOMP
AAAAAAH!!
KACHUNK
AAAAAAAAAH
OW
...AT THAT RATE, THAT THING WILL NEVER BE OF ANY USE.

※DISTILLATION...A TRANQUILIZER MADE FROM THE DRIED ROOTS OF THE KAMEBAKANOKO MUSHROOM.

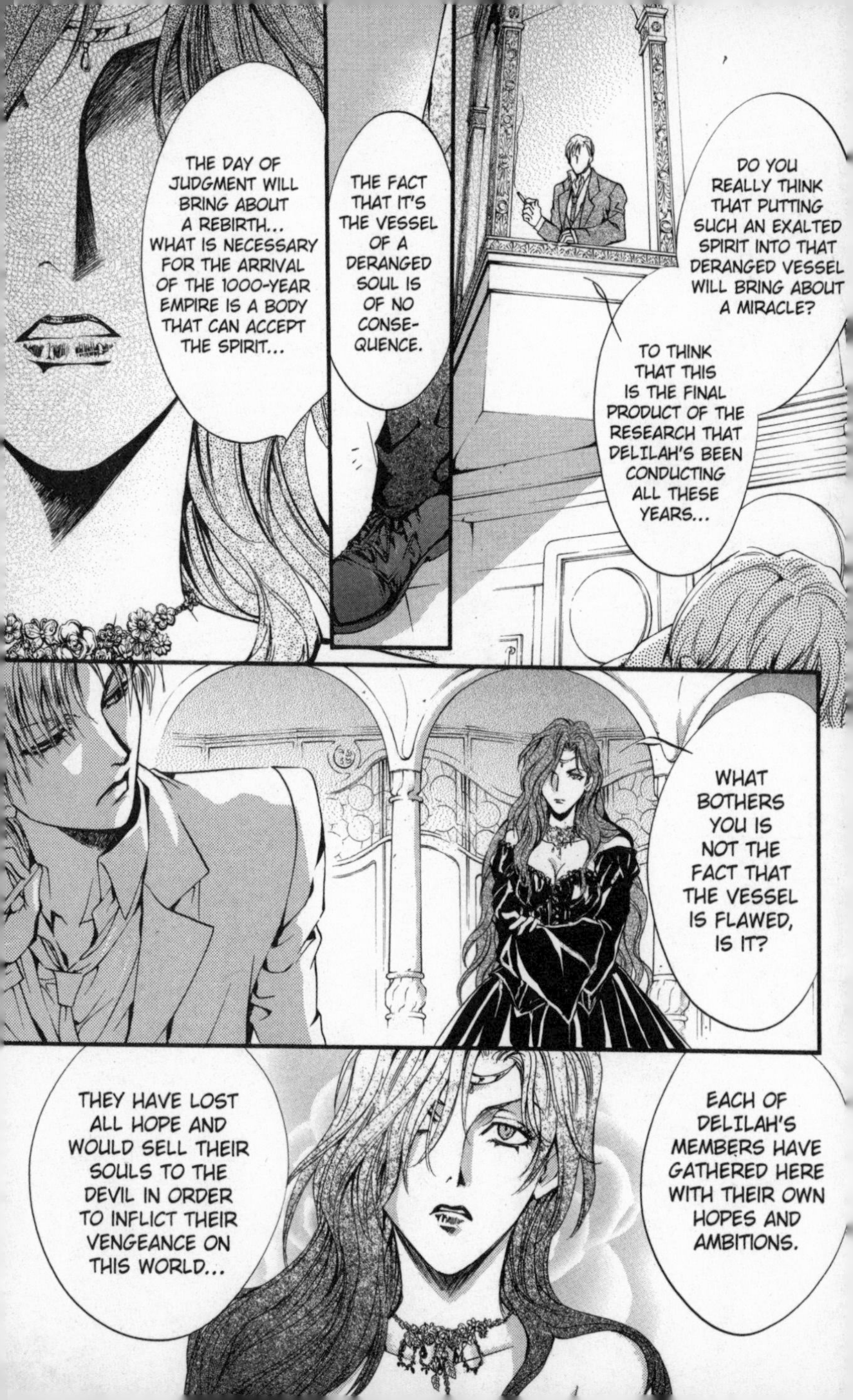
DO YOU REALLY THINK THAT PUTTING SUCH AN EXALTED SPIRIT INTO THAT DERANGED VESSEL WILL BRING ABOUT A MIRACLE?
TO THINK THAT THIS IS THE FINAL PRODUCT OF THE RESEARCH THAT DELILAH'S BEEN CONDUCTING ALL THESE YEARS...
THE FACT THAT IT'S THE VESSEL OF A DERANGED SOUL IS OF NO CONSE-QUENCE.
THE DAY OF JUDGMENT WILL BRING ABOUT A REBIRTH... WHAT IS NECESSARY FOR THE ARRIVAL OF THE 1000-YEAR EMPIRE IS A BODY THAT CAN ACCEPT THE SPIRIT...
WHAT BOTHERS YOU IS NOT THE FACT THAT THE VESSEL IS FLAWED, IS IT?
EACH OF DELILAH'S MEMBERS HAVE GATHERED HERE WITH THEIR OWN HOPES AND AMBITIONS.
THEY HAVE LOST ALL HOPE AND WOULD SELL THEIR SOULS TO THE DEVIL IN ORDER TO INFLICT THEIR VENGEANCE ON THIS WORLD...

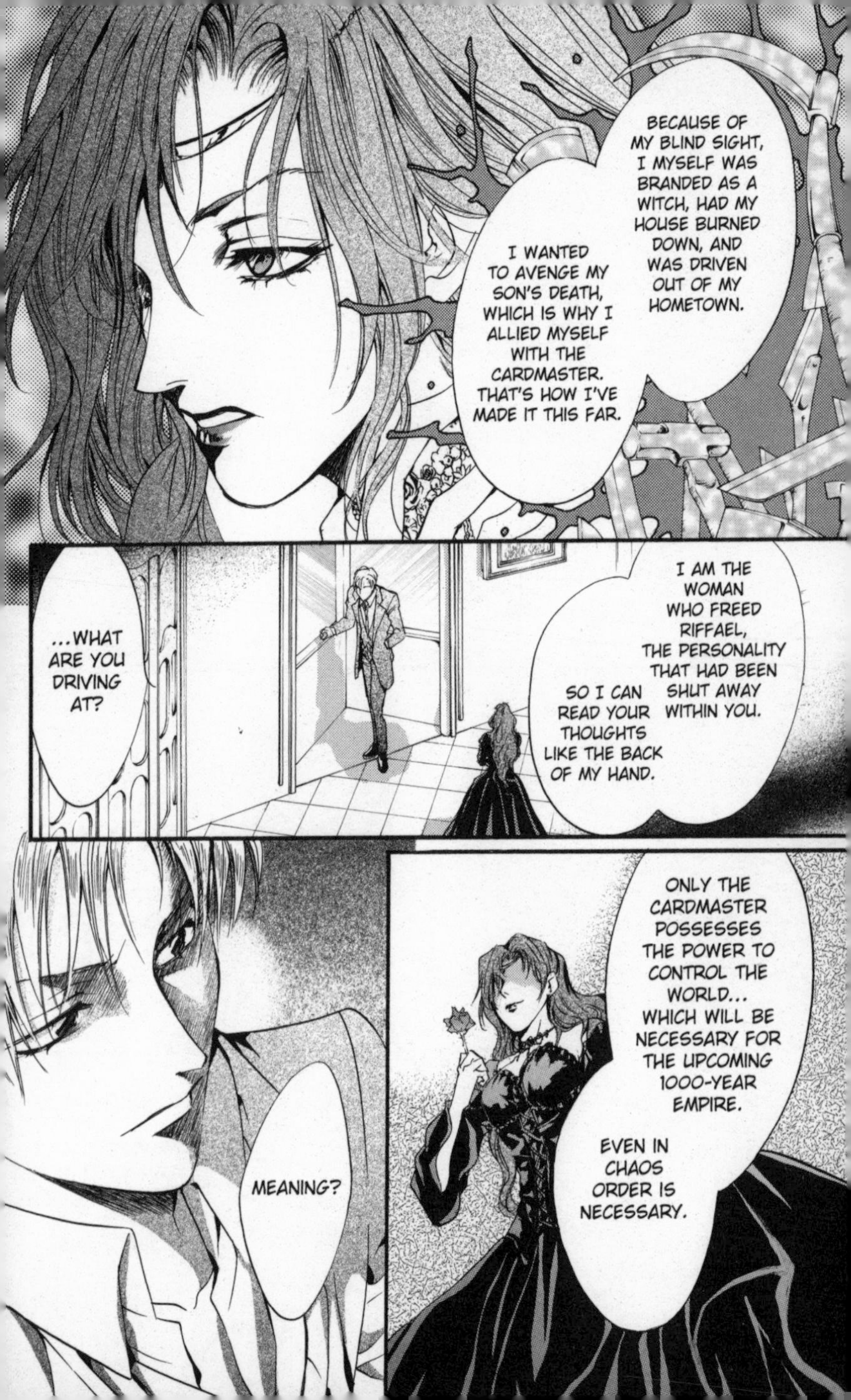
BECAUSE OF MY BLIND SIGHT, I MYSELF WAS BRANDED AS A WITCH, HAD MY HOUSE BURNED DOWN, AND WAS DRIVEN OUT OF MY HOMETOWN.
I WANTED TO AVENGE MY SON'S DEATH, WHICH IS WHY I ALLIED MYSELF WITH THE CARDMASTER. THAT'S HOW I'VE MADE IT THIS FAR.
I AM THE WOMAN WHO FREED RIFFAEL, THE PERSONALITY THAT HAD BEEN SHUT AWAY WITHIN YOU.
SO I CAN READ YOUR THOUGHTS LIKE THE BACK OF MY HAND.
...WHAT ARE YOU DRIVING AT?
ONLY THE CARDMASTER POSSESSES THE POWER TO CONTROL THE WORLD... WHICH WILL BE NECESSARY FOR THE UPCOMING 1000-YEAR EMPIRE.
EVEN IN CHAOS ORDER IS NECESSARY.
MEANING?

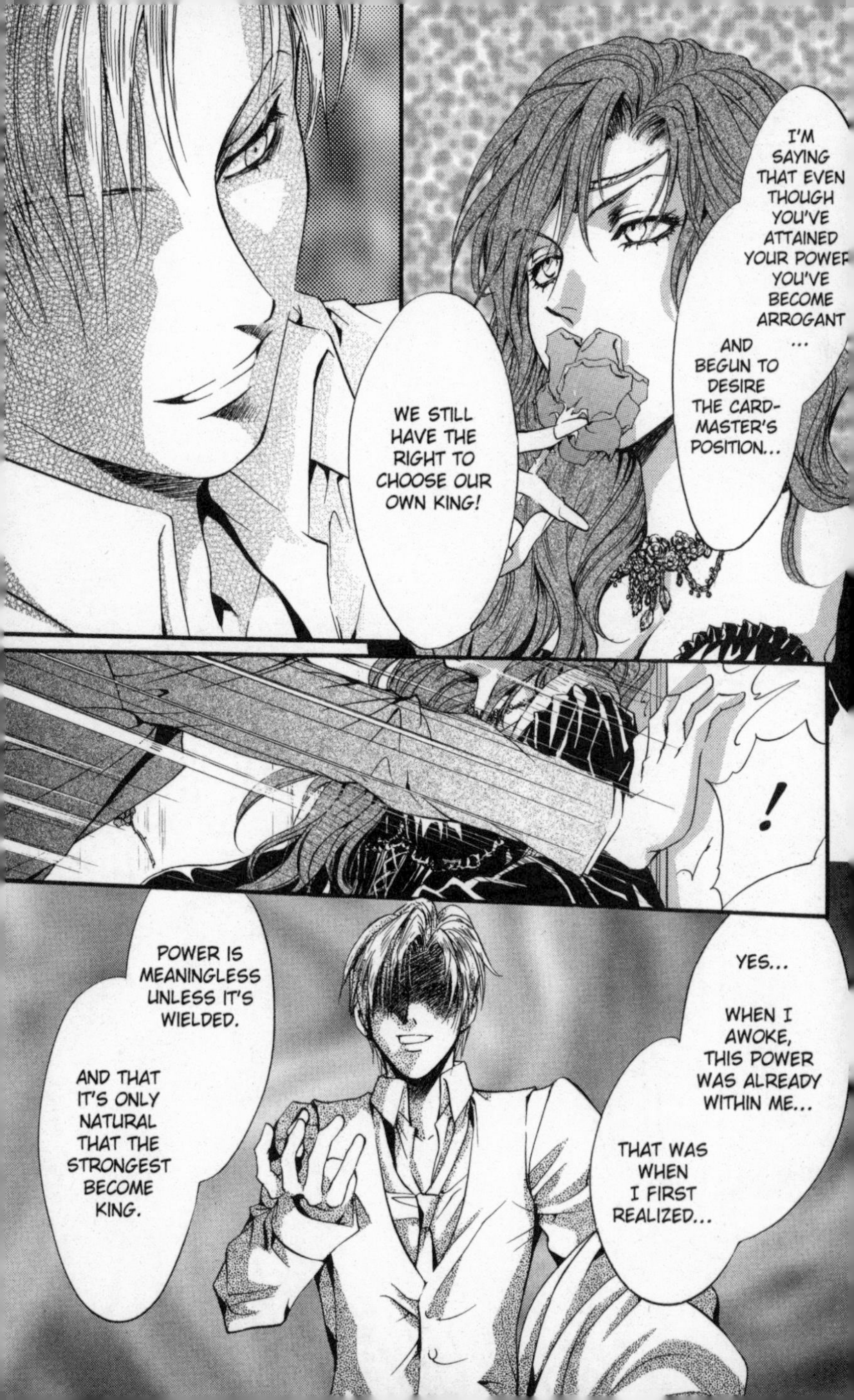
I'M SAYING THAT EVEN THOUGH YOU'VE ATTAINED YOUR POWER YOU'VE BECOME ARROGANT ...
AND BEGUN TO DESIRE THE CARD-MASTER'S POSITION...
WE STILL HAVE THE RIGHT TO CHOOSE OUR OWN KING!
!
YES...
WHEN I AWOKE, THIS POWER WAS ALREADY WITHIN ME...
THAT WAS WHEN I FIRST REALIZED...
POWER IS MEANINGLESS UNLESS IT'S WIELDED.
AND THAT IT'S ONLY NATURAL THAT THE STRONGEST BECOME KING.

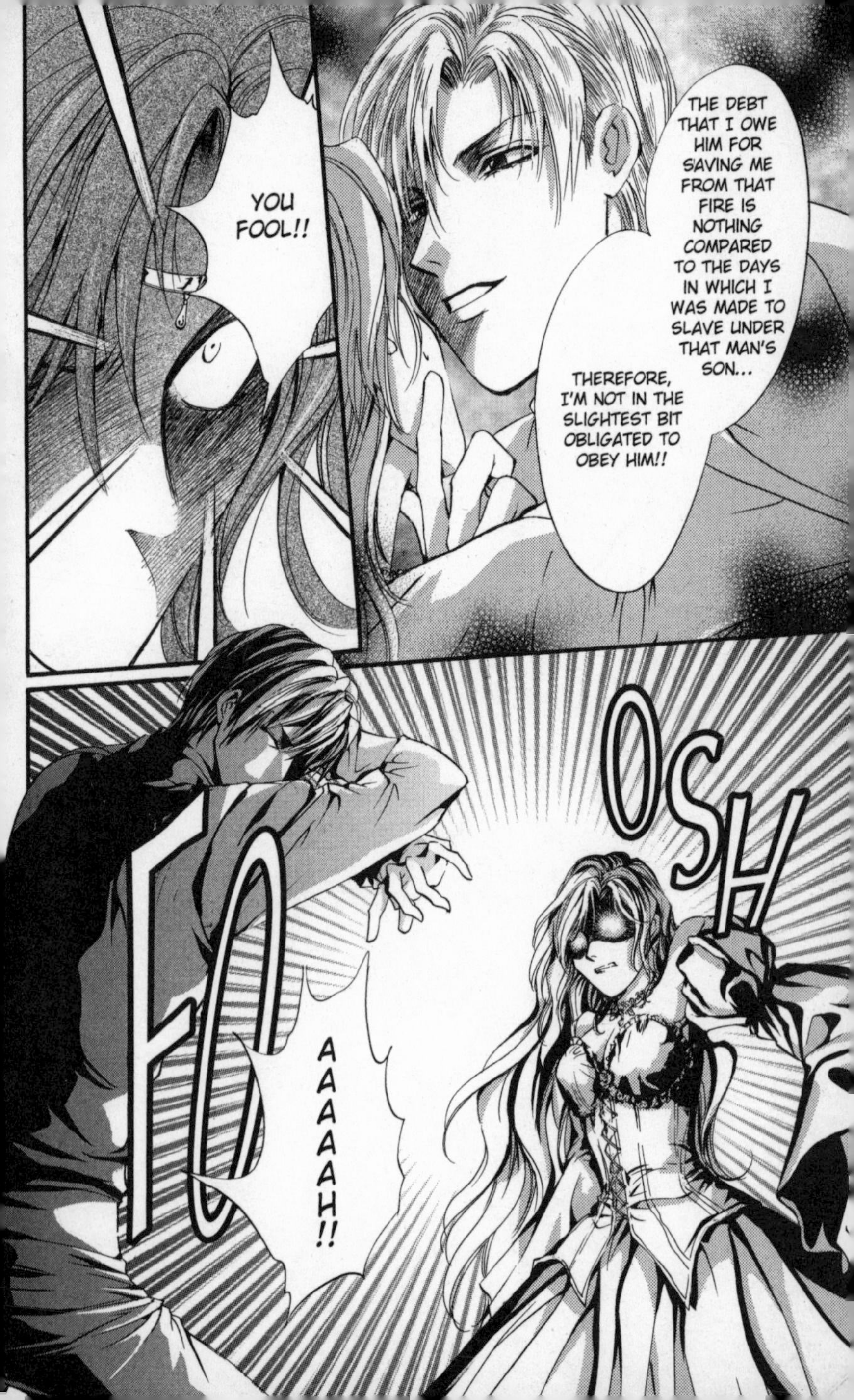
THE DEBT THAT I OWE HIM FOR SAVING ME FROM THAT FIRE IS NOTHING COMPARED TO THE DAYS IN WHICH I WAS MADE TO SLAVE UNDER THAT MAN'S SON...
THEREFORE, I'M NOT IN THE SLIGHTEST BIT OBLIGATED TO OBEY HIM!!
YOU FOOL!!
FOOSH
AAAAAAH!!

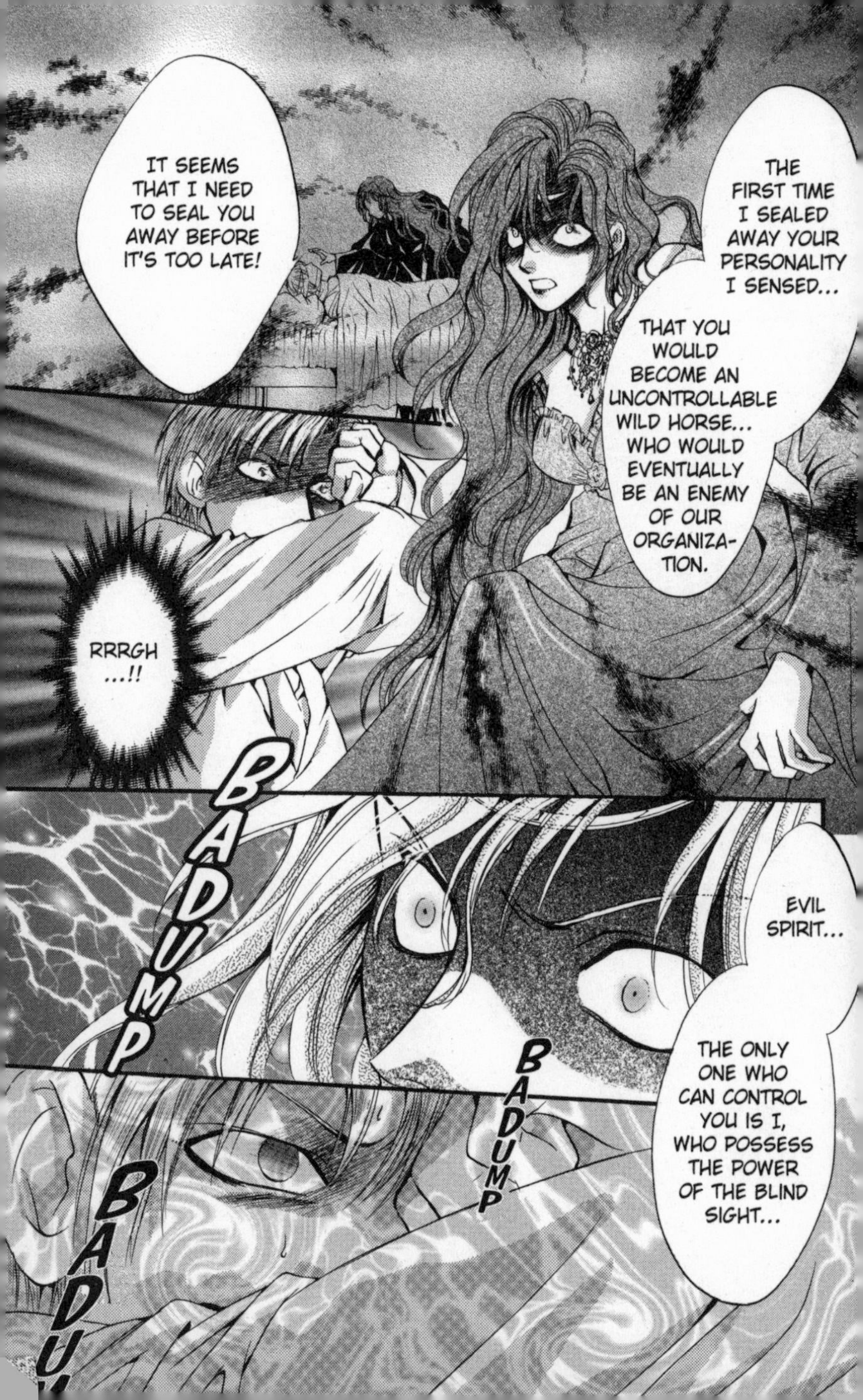
THE FIRST TIME I SEALED AWAY YOUR PERSONALITY I SENSED...
THAT YOU WOULD BECOME AN UNCONTROLLABLE WILD HORSE... WHO WOULD EVENTUALLY BE AN ENEMY OF OUR ORGANIZATION.
IT SEEMS THAT I NEED TO SEAL YOU AWAY BEFORE IT'S TOO LATE!
RRRGH ...!!
BADUMP
EVIL SPIRIT...
THE ONLY ONE WHO CAN CONTROL YOU IS I, WHO POSSESS THE POWER OF THE BLIND SIGHT...
BADUMP
BADU

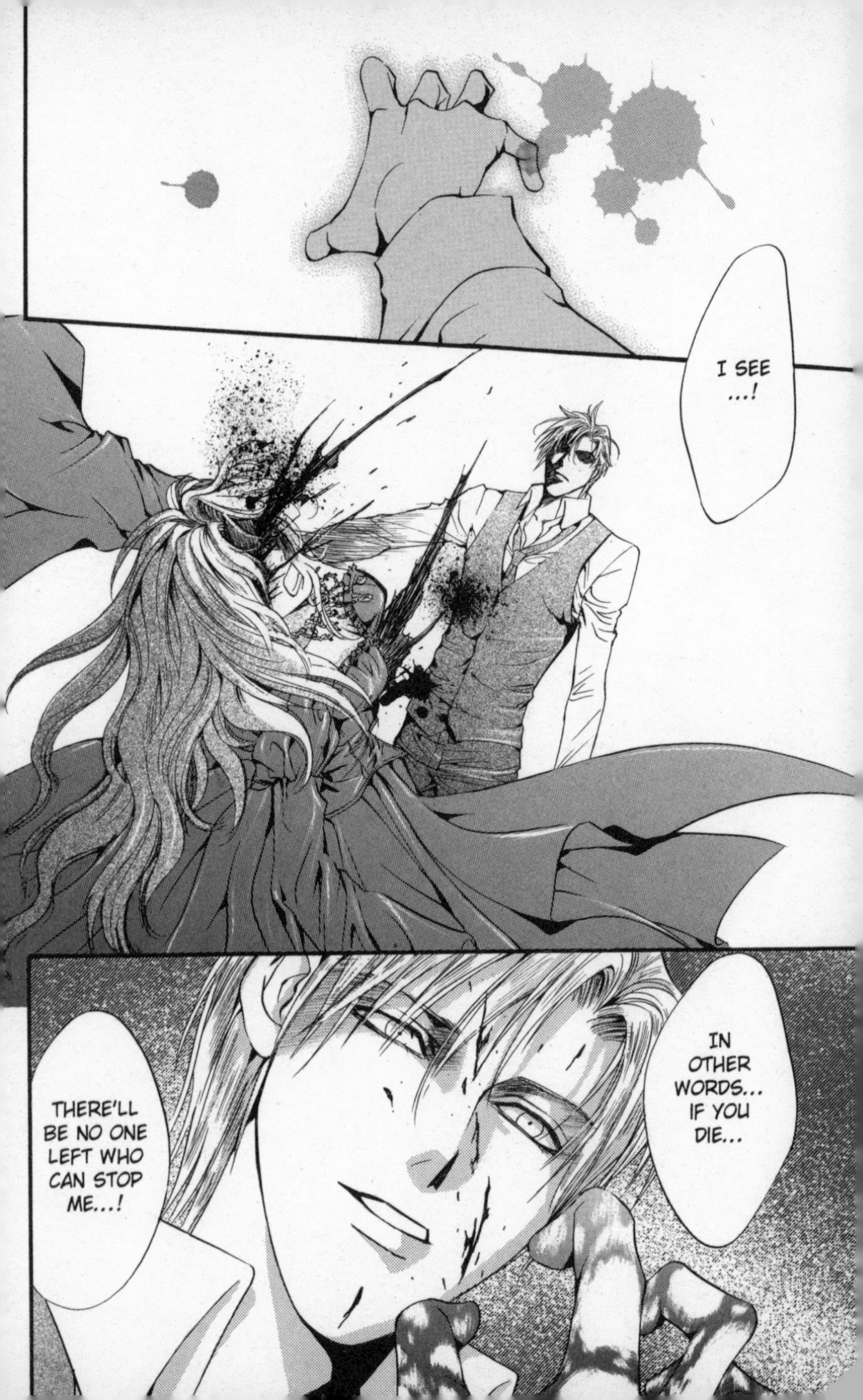
I SEE ...!
IN OTHER WORDS... IF YOU DIE...
THERE'LL BE NO ONE LEFT WHO CAN STOP ME...!

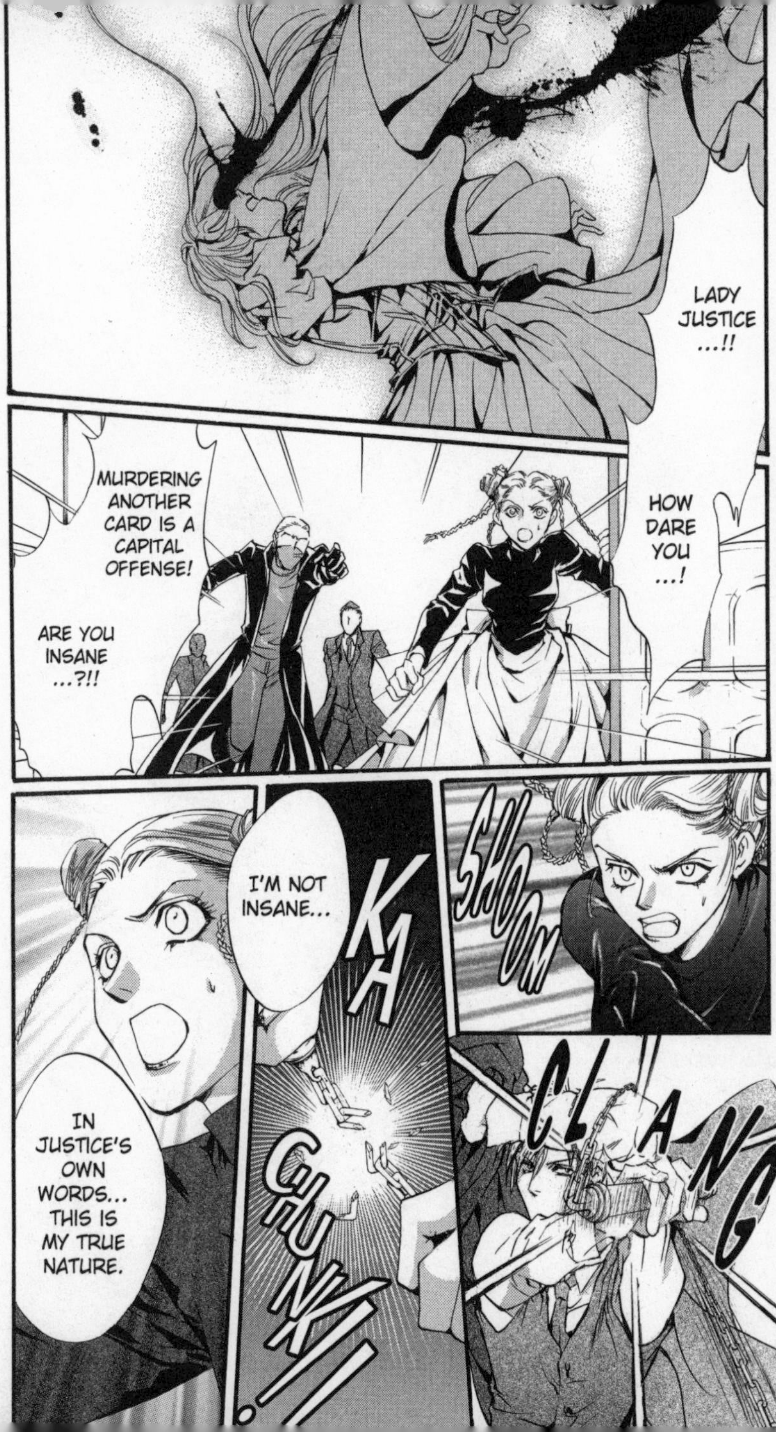
LADY JUSTICE ...!!
HOW DARE YOU ...!
MURDERING ANOTHER CARD IS A CAPITAL OFFENSE!
ARE YOU INSANE ...?!!
SHOOM
CLANG
I'M NOT INSANE...
KA
CHUNK!!
IN JUSTICE'S OWN WORDS... THIS IS MY TRUE NATURE.

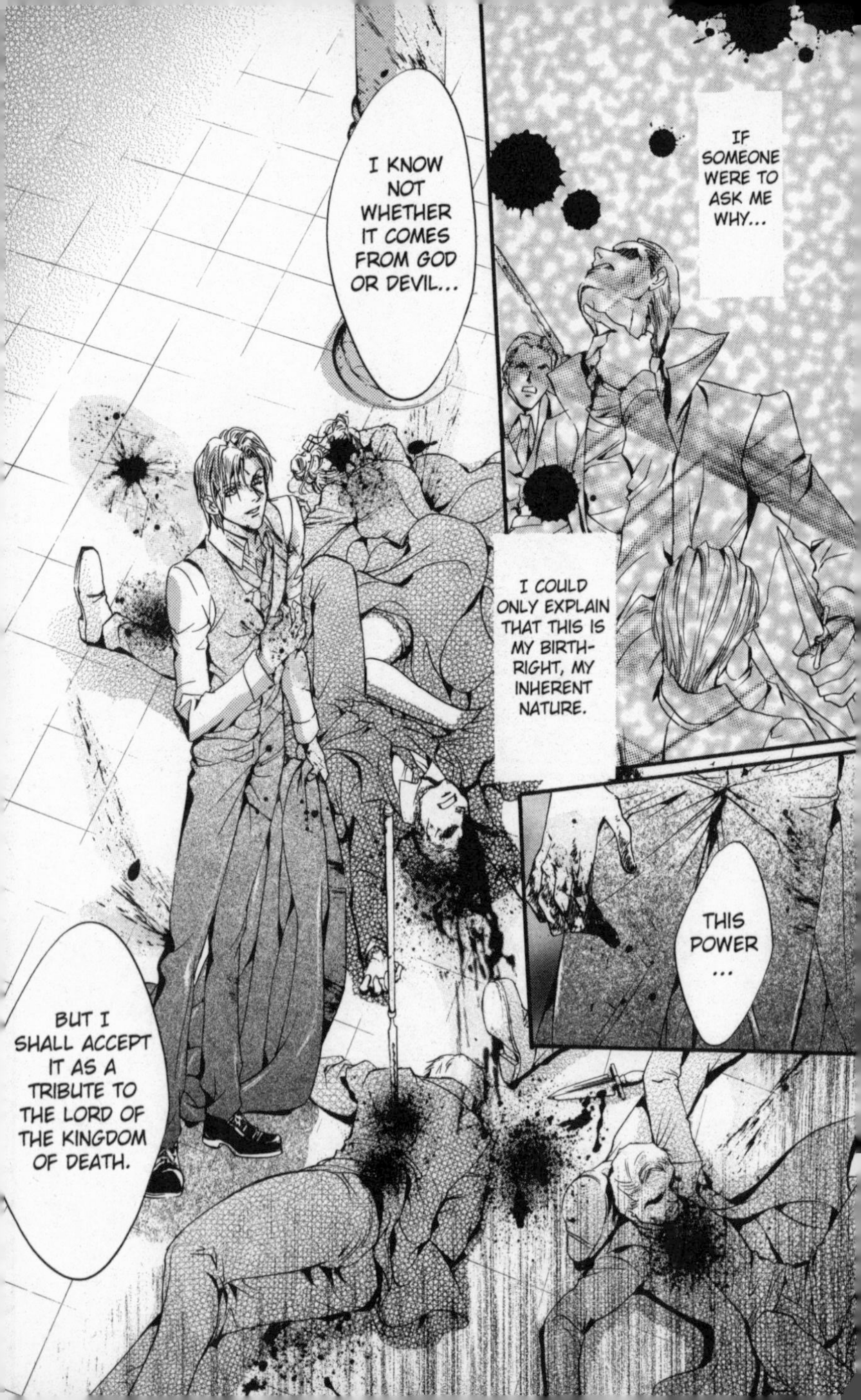
IF SOMEONE WERE TO ASK ME WHY...
I COULD ONLY EXPLAIN THAT THIS IS MY BIRTH-RIGHT, MY INHERENT NATURE.
THIS POWER ...
I KNOW NOT WHETHER IT COMES FROM GOD OR DEVIL...
BUT I SHALL ACCEPT IT AS A TRIBUTE TO THE LORD OF THE KINGDOM OF DEATH.

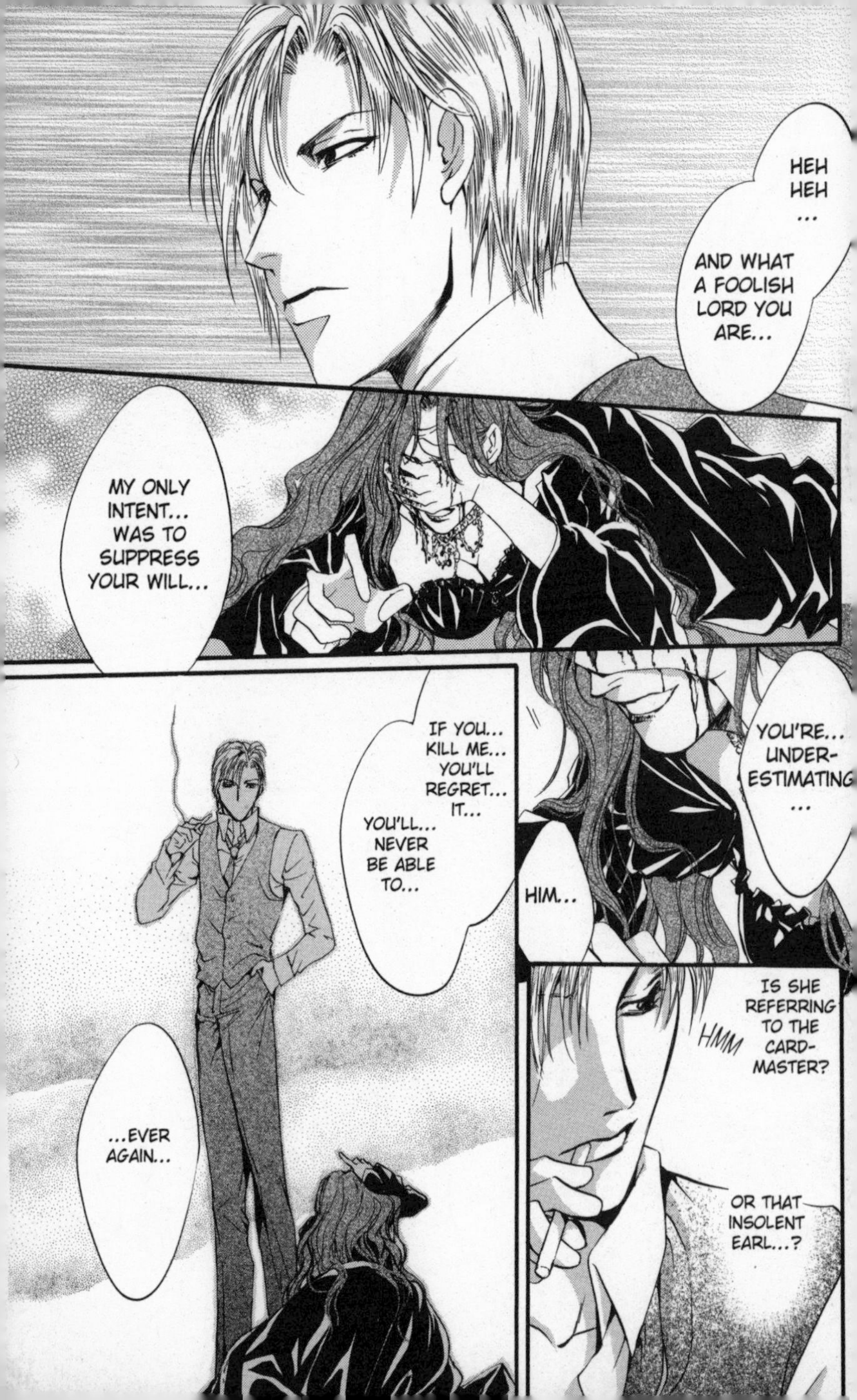
HEH HEH ...
AND WHAT A FOOLISH LORD YOU ARE...
MY ONLY INTENT... WAS TO SUPPRESS YOUR WILL...
YOU'RE... UNDER-ESTIMATING ...
HIM...
HMM
IS SHE REFERRING TO THE CARD-MASTER?
OR THAT INSOLENT EARL...?
IF YOU... KILL ME... YOU'LL REGRET... IT...
YOU'LL... NEVER BE ABLE TO...
...EVER AGAIN...

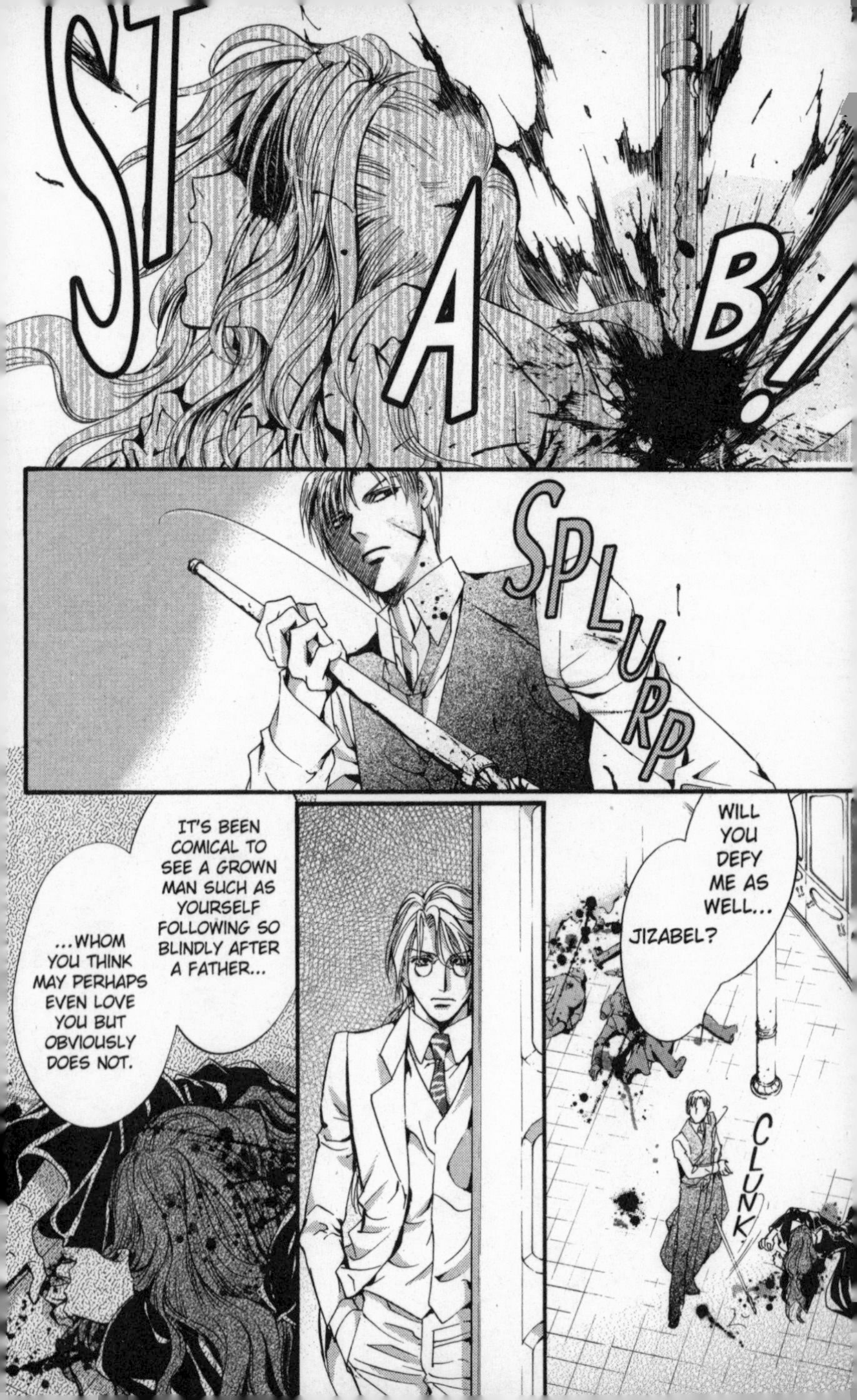
STAB!!
SPLURP
WILL YOU DEFY ME AS WELL...
JIZABEL?
CLUNK
IT'S BEEN COMICAL TO SEE A GROWN MAN SUCH AS YOURSELF FOLLOWING SO BLINDLY AFTER A FATHER...
...WHOM YOU THINK MAY PERHAPS EVEN LOVE YOU BUT OBVIOUSLY DOES NOT.

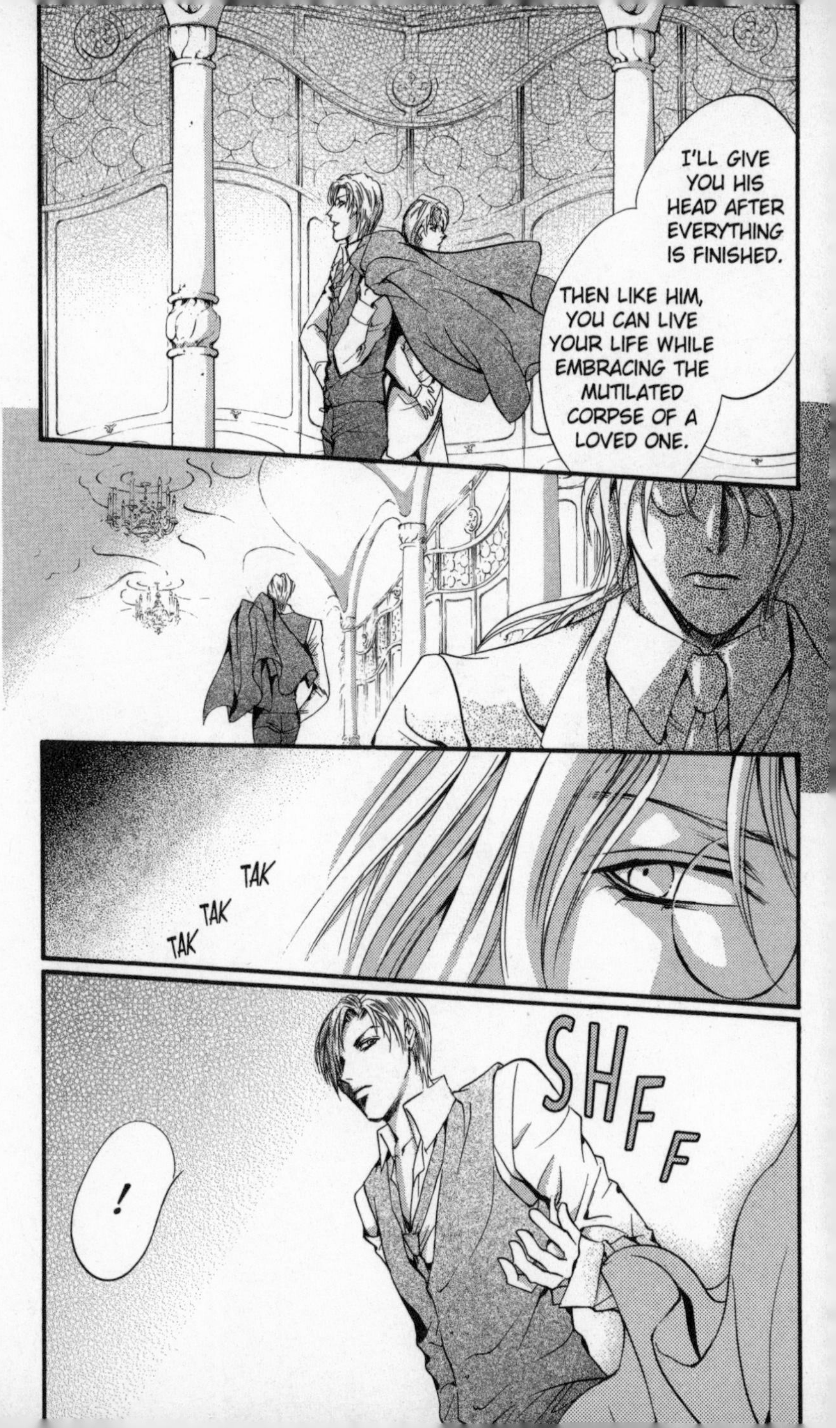
I'LL GIVE YOU HIS HEAD AFTER EVERYTHING IS FINISHED.
THEN LIKE HIM, YOU CAN LIVE YOUR LIFE WHILE EMBRACING THE MUTILATED CORPSE OF A LOVED ONE.
TAK
TAK
TAK
SHFFF
!

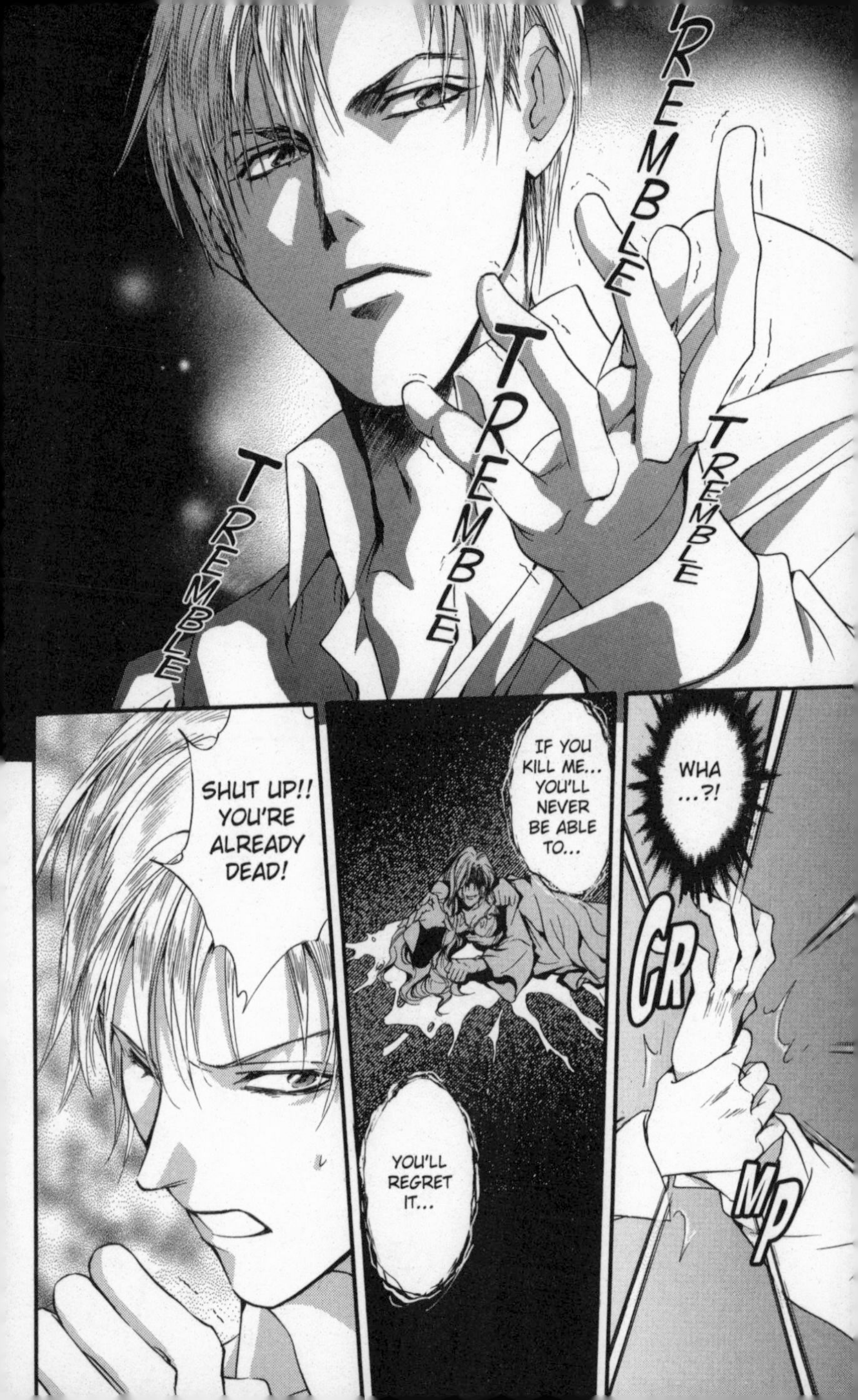
REMBLE
TREMBLE
TREMBLE
TREMBLE
WHA ...?!
CR
MP
IF YOU KILL ME... YOU'LL NEVER BE ABLE TO...
YOU'LL REGRET IT...
SHUT UP!! YOU'RE ALREADY DEAD!

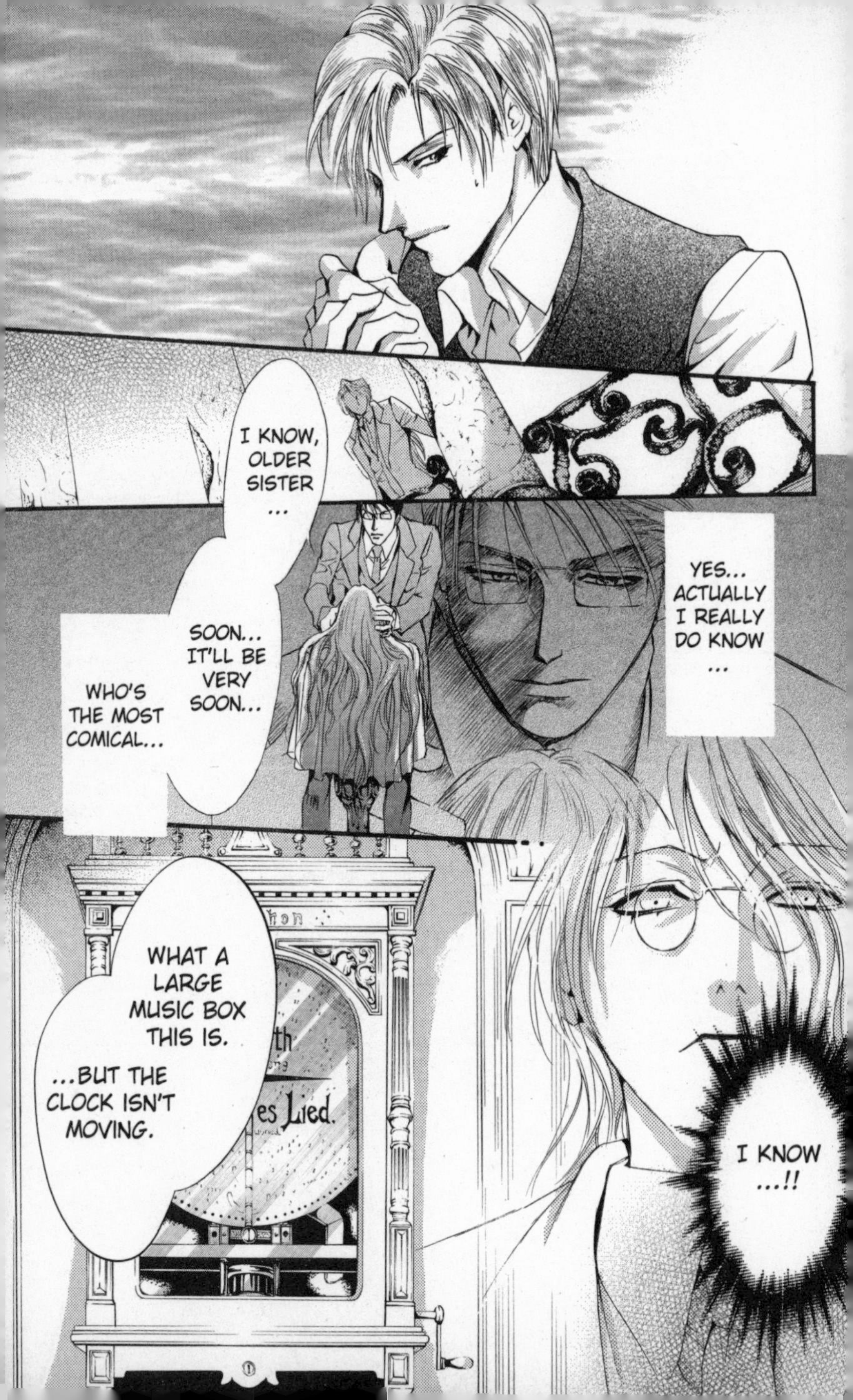
I KNOW, OLDER SISTER...
YES... ACTUALLY I REALLY DO KNOW...
SOON... IT'LL BE VERY SOON...
WHO'S THE MOST COMICAL...
I KNOW...!!
WHAT A LARGE MUSIC BOX THIS IS.
...BUT THE CLOCK ISN'T MOVING.

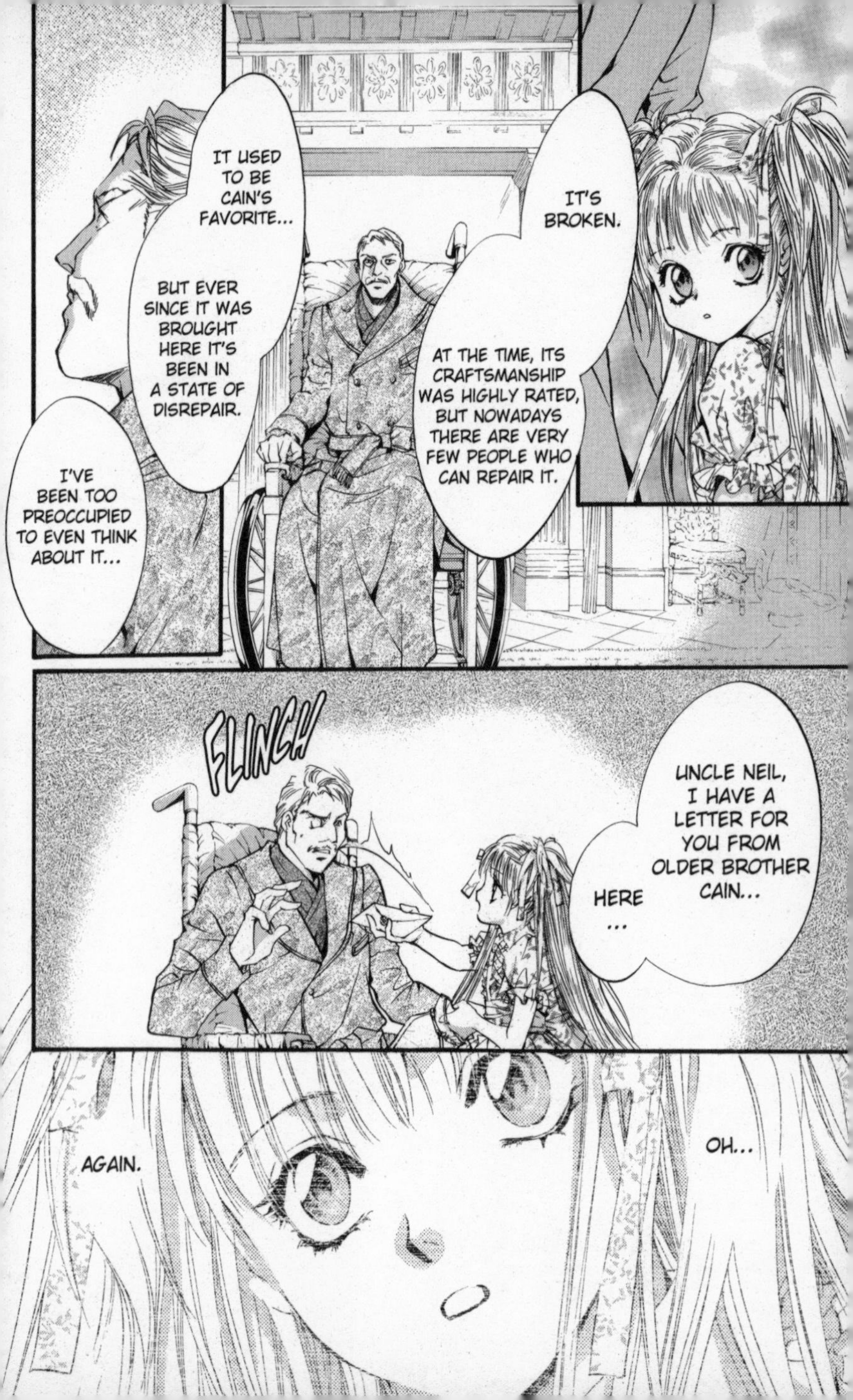

IT'S BROKEN.
IT USED TO BE CAIN'S FAVORITE...
BUT EVER SINCE IT WAS BROUGHT HERE IT'S BEEN IN A STATE OF DISREPAIR.
AT THE TIME, ITS CRAFTSMANSHIP WAS HIGHLY RATED, BUT NOWADAYS THERE ARE VERY FEW PEOPLE WHO CAN REPAIR IT.
I'VE BEEN TOO PREOCCUPIED TO EVEN THINK ABOUT IT...
UNCLE NEIL, I HAVE A LETTER FOR YOU FROM OLDER BROTHER CAIN...
HERE...
FLINCH!
OH...
AGAIN.

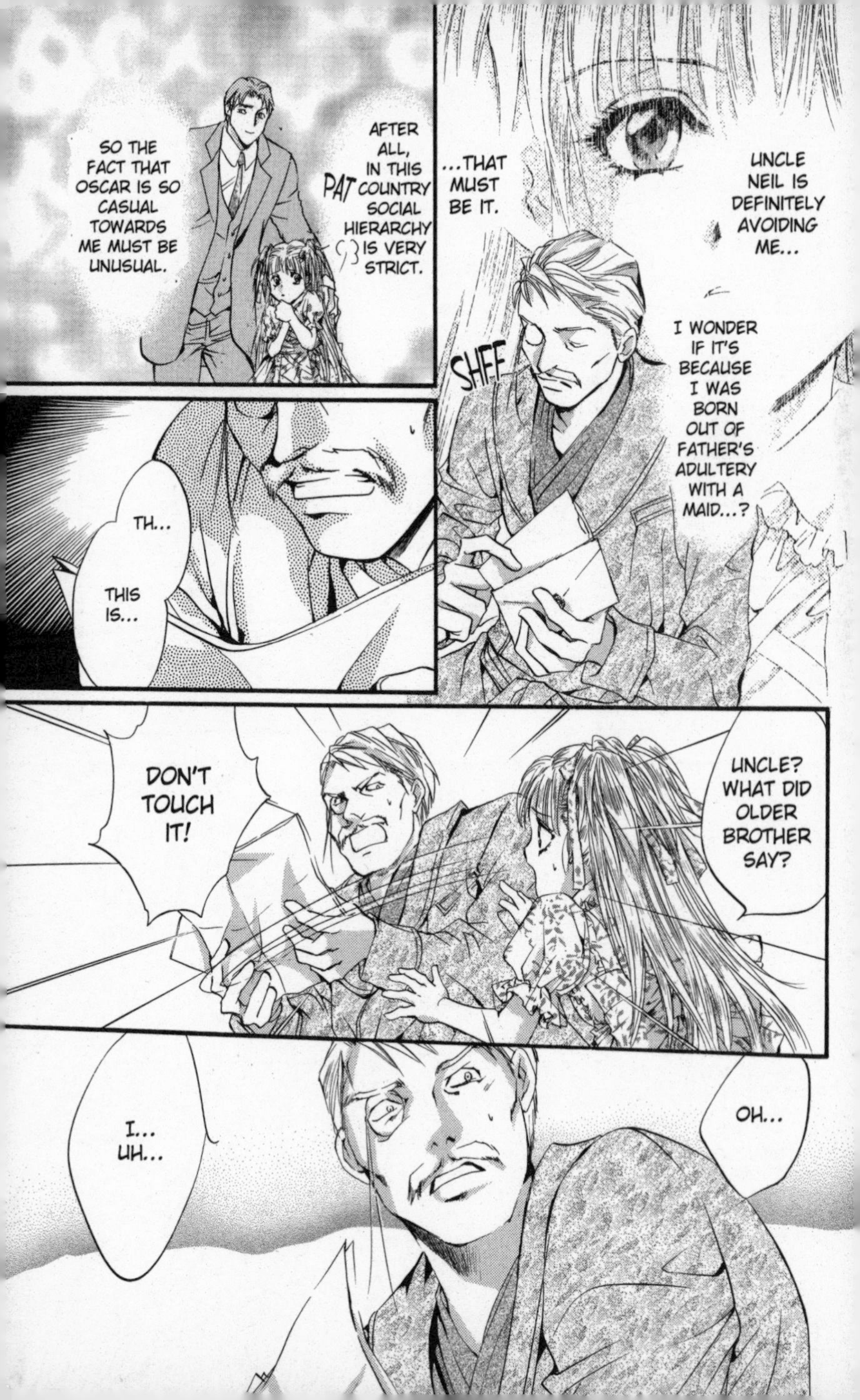
UNCLE NEIL IS DEFINITELY AVOIDING ME...
...THAT MUST BE IT.
I WONDER IF IT'S BECAUSE I WAS BORN OUT OF FATHER'S ADULTERY WITH A MAID...?
SHFF
AFTER ALL, IN THIS COUNTRY SOCIAL HIERARCHY IS VERY STRICT.
PAT
SO THE FACT THAT OSCAR IS SO CASUAL TOWARDS ME MUST BE UNUSUAL.
TH...
THIS IS...
UNCLE? WHAT DID OLDER BROTHER SAY?
DON'T TOUCH IT!
OH...
I... UH...

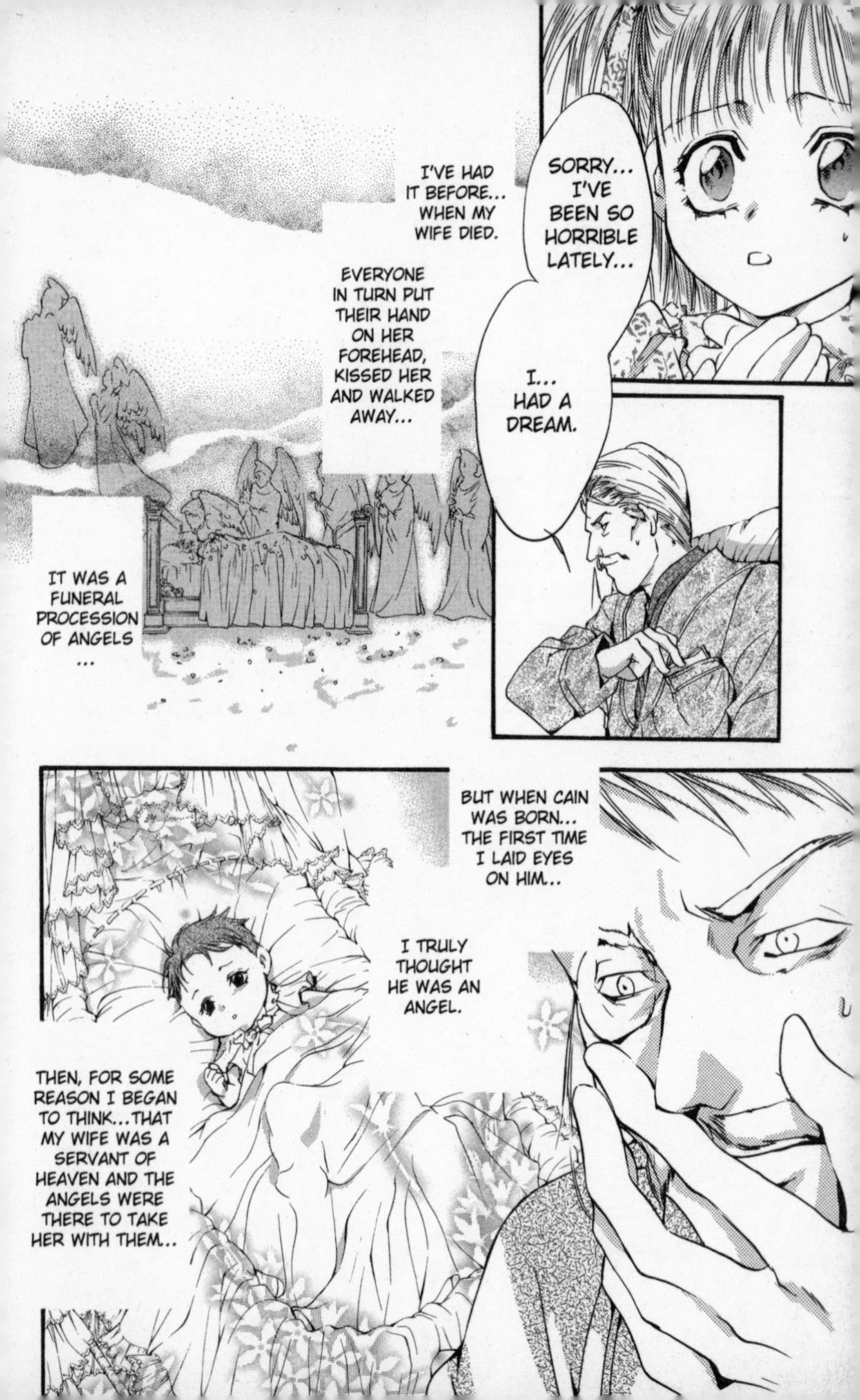
SORRY... I'VE BEEN SO HORRIBLE LATELY...
I... HAD A DREAM.
I'VE HAD IT BEFORE... WHEN MY WIFE DIED.
EVERYONE IN TURN PUT THEIR HAND ON HER FOREHEAD, KISSED HER AND WALKED AWAY...
IT WAS A FUNERAL PROCESSION OF ANGELS...
BUT WHEN CAIN WAS BORN... THE FIRST TIME I LAID EYES ON HIM...
I TRULY THOUGHT HE WAS AN ANGEL.
THEN, FOR SOME REASON I BEGAN TO THINK...THAT MY WIFE WAS A SERVANT OF HEAVEN AND THE ANGELS WERE THERE TO TAKE HER WITH THEM...

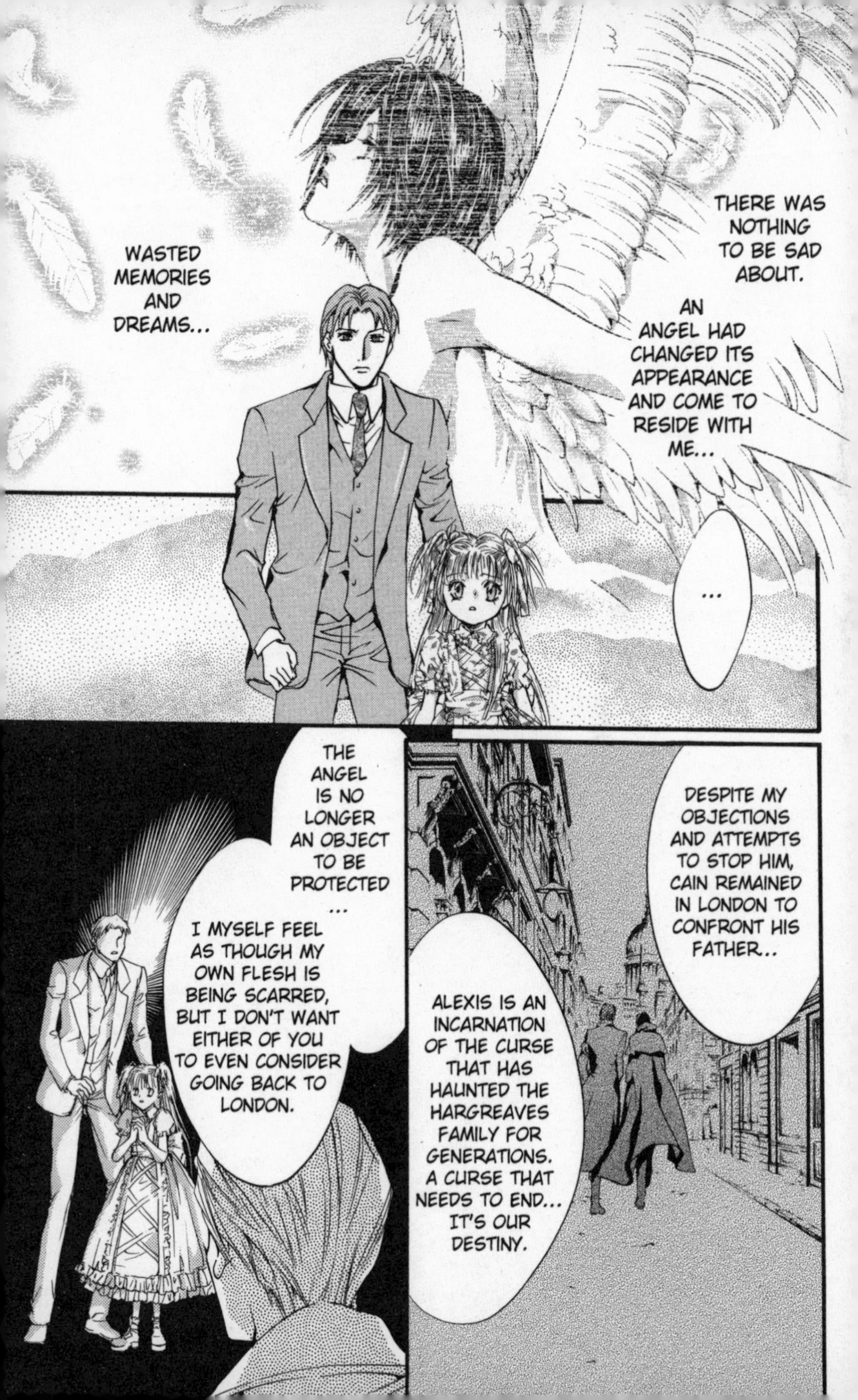
THERE WAS NOTHING TO BE SAD ABOUT.
AN ANGEL HAD CHANGED ITS APPEARANCE AND COME TO RESIDE WITH ME...
WASTED MEMORIES AND DREAMS...
...
DESPITE MY OBJECTIONS AND ATTEMPTS TO STOP HIM, CAIN REMAINED IN LONDON TO CONFRONT HIS FATHER...
ALEXIS IS AN INCARNATION OF THE CURSE THAT HAS HAUNTED THE HARGREAVES FAMILY FOR GENERATIONS. A CURSE THAT NEEDS TO END... IT'S OUR DESTINY.
THE ANGEL IS NO LONGER AN OBJECT TO BE PROTECTED...
I MYSELF FEEL AS THOUGH MY OWN FLESH IS BEING SCARRED, BUT I DON'T WANT EITHER OF YOU TO EVEN CONSIDER GOING BACK TO LONDON.

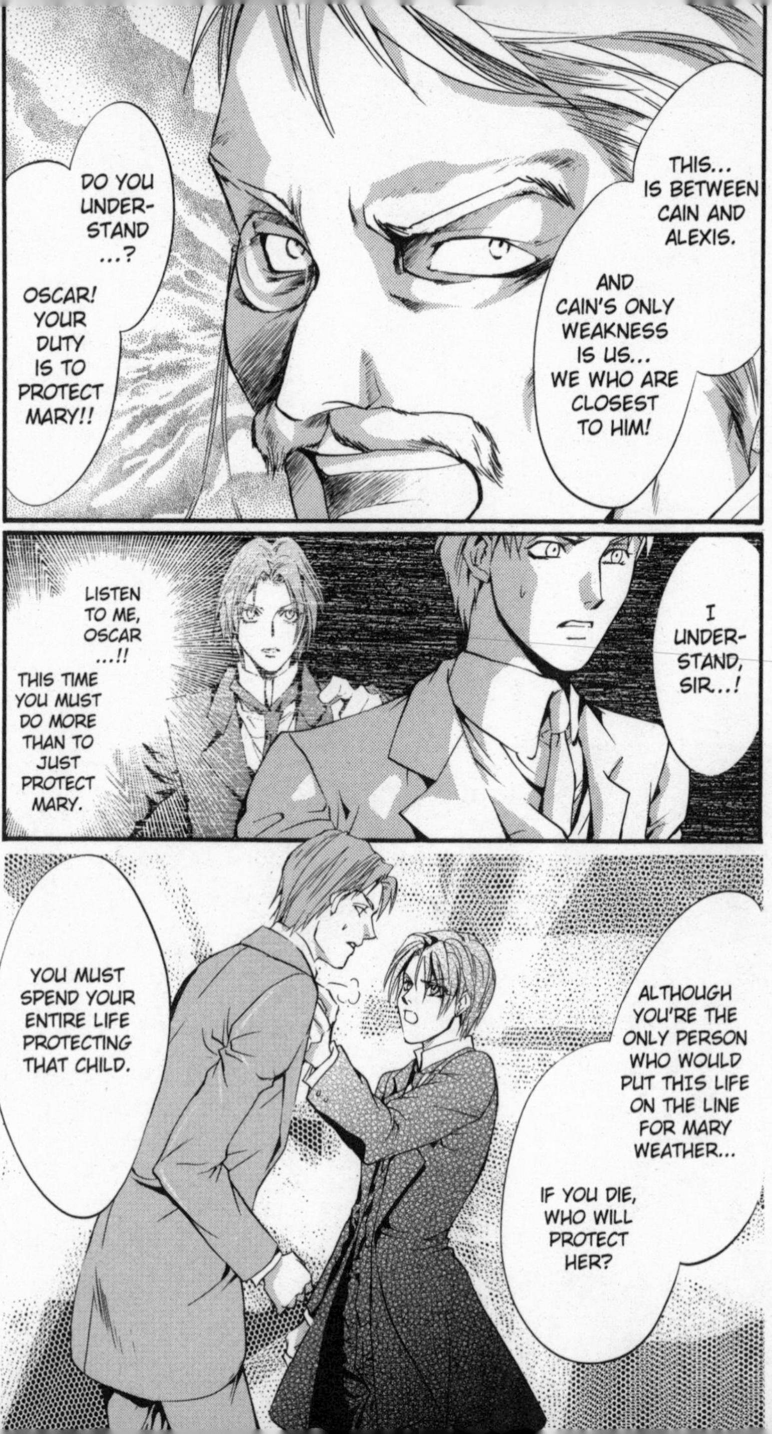
THIS... IS BETWEEN CAIN AND ALEXIS.
AND CAIN'S ONLY WEAKNESS IS US... WE WHO ARE CLOSEST TO HIM!
DO YOU UNDERSTAND ...?
OSCAR! YOUR DUTY IS TO PROTECT MARY!!
I UNDERSTAND, SIR...!
LISTEN TO ME, OSCAR ...!!
THIS TIME YOU MUST DO MORE THAN TO JUST PROTECT MARY.
ALTHOUGH YOU'RE THE ONLY PERSON WHO WOULD PUT THIS LIFE ON THE LINE FOR MARY WEATHER...
IF YOU DIE, WHO WILL PROTECT HER?
YOU MUST SPEND YOUR ENTIRE LIFE PROTECTING THAT CHILD.

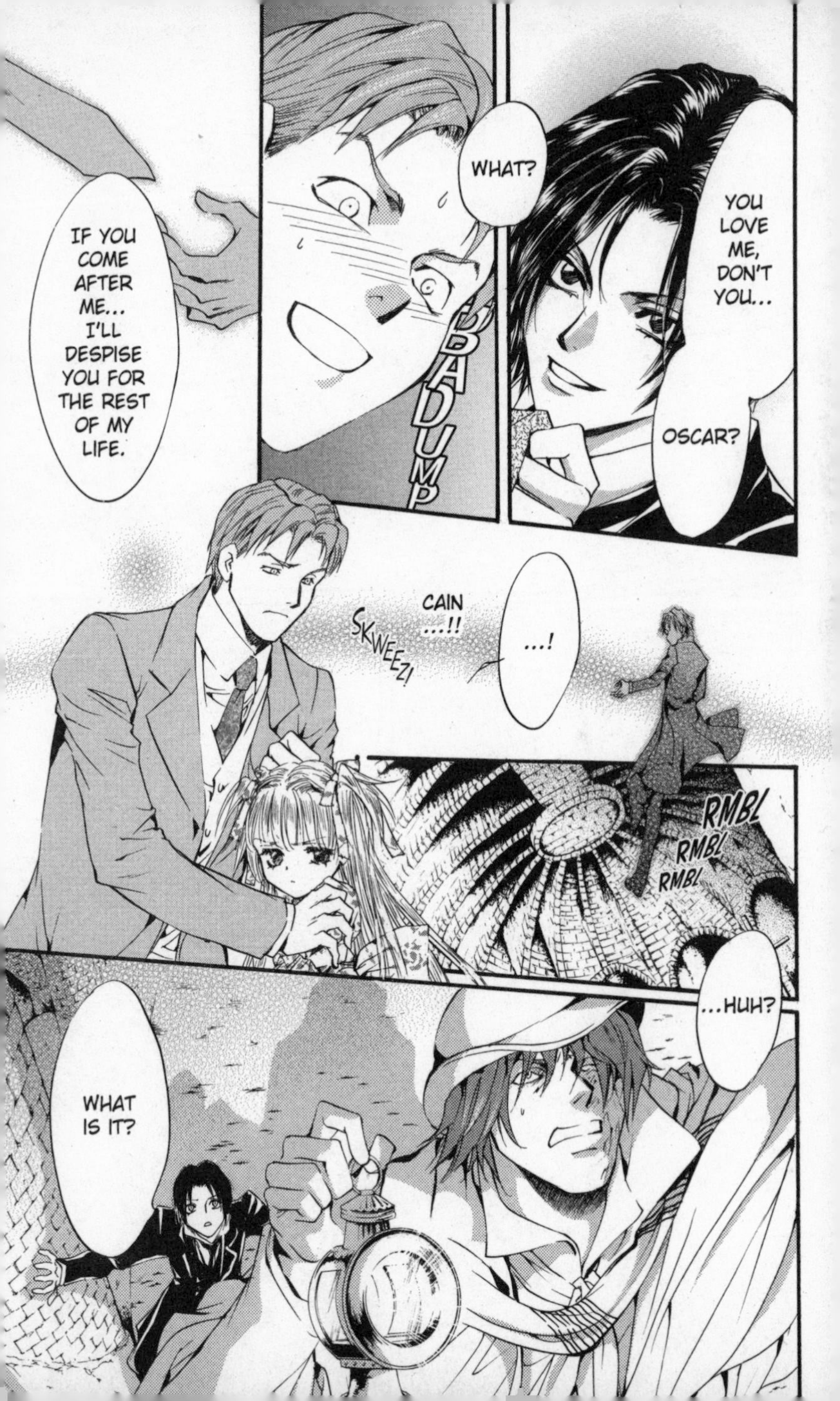
YOU LOVE ME, DON'T YOU...
OSCAR?
WHAT?
BADUMP
IF YOU COME AFTER ME... I'LL DESPISE YOU FOR THE REST OF MY LIFE.
...!
CAIN ...!!
SKWEEZ!
RMBL RMBL RMBL
...HUH?
WHAT IS IT?

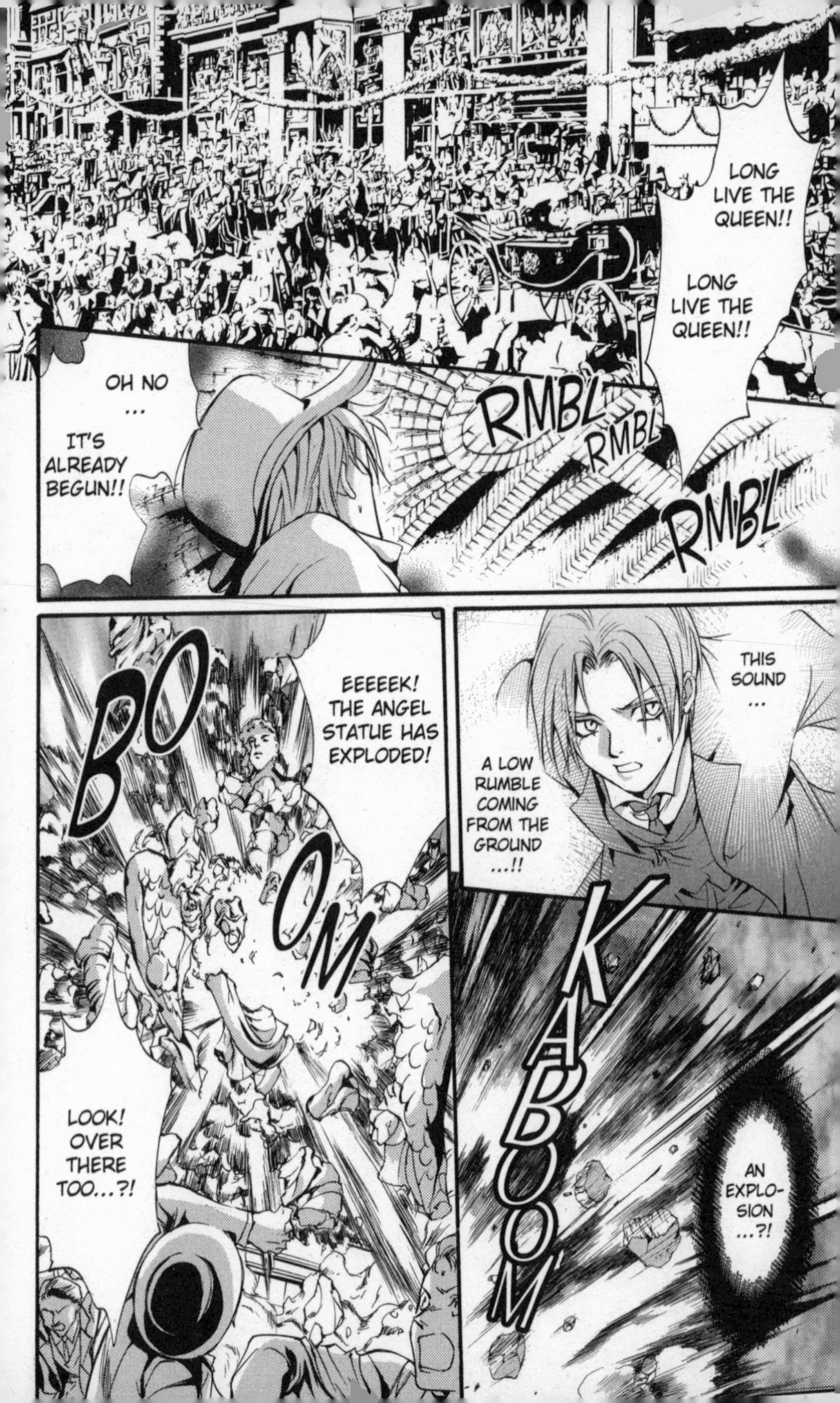
LONG LIVE THE QUEEN!!
LONG LIVE THE QUEEN!!
RMBL
RMBL
RMBL
OH NO ... IT'S ALREADY BEGUN!!
THIS SOUND ...
A LOW RUMBLE COMING FROM THE GROUND ...!!
KABOOM
AN EXPLOSION ...?!
EEEEEK! THE ANGEL STATUE HAS EXPLODED!
BOOM
LOOK! OVER THERE TOO...?!

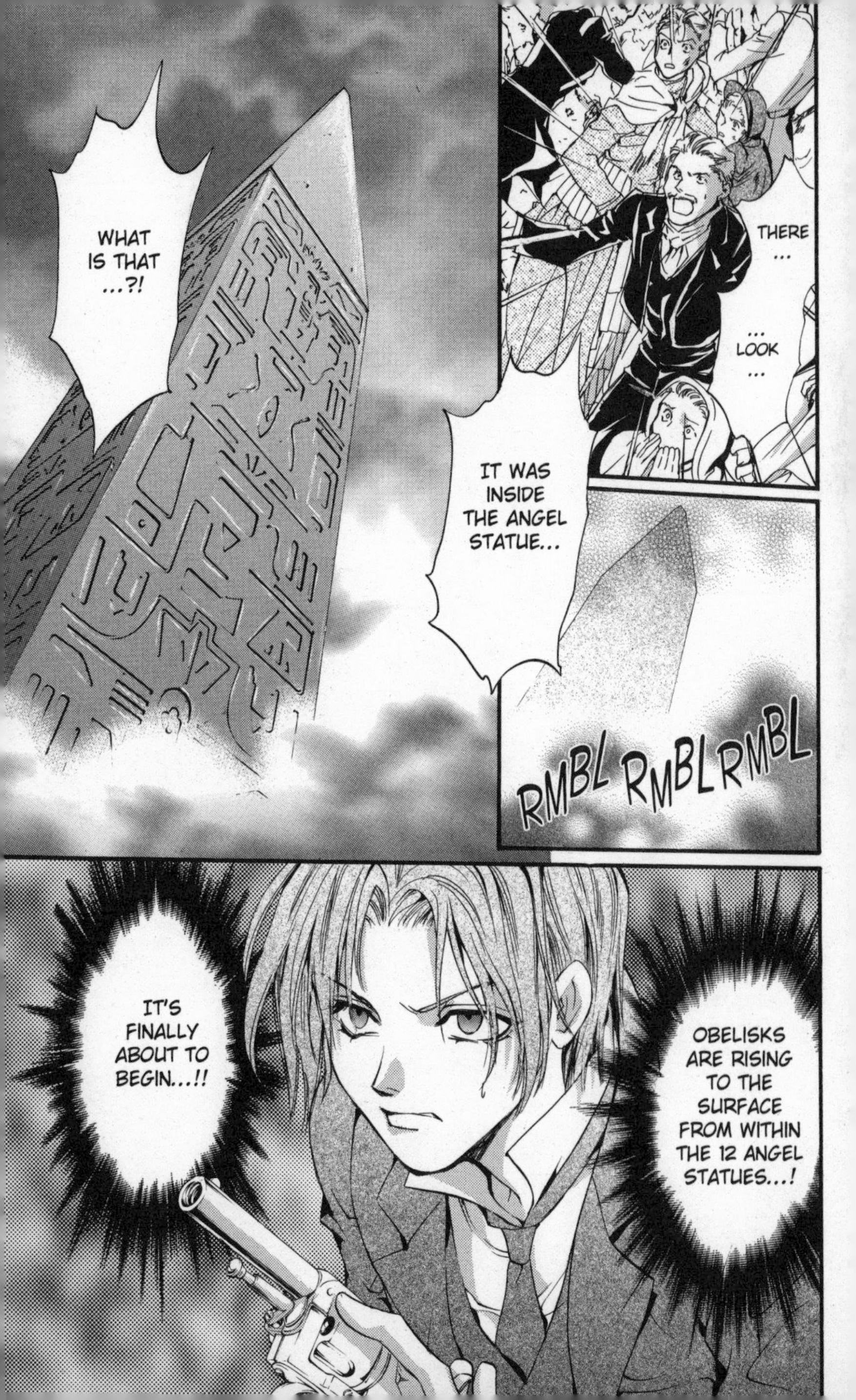
THERE ...
... LOOK ...
IT WAS INSIDE THE ANGEL STATUE...
RMBL RMBL RMBL
WHAT IS THAT ...?!
OBELISKS ARE RISING TO THE SURFACE FROM WITHIN THE 12 ANGEL STATUES...!
IT'S FINALLY ABOUT TO BEGIN...!!

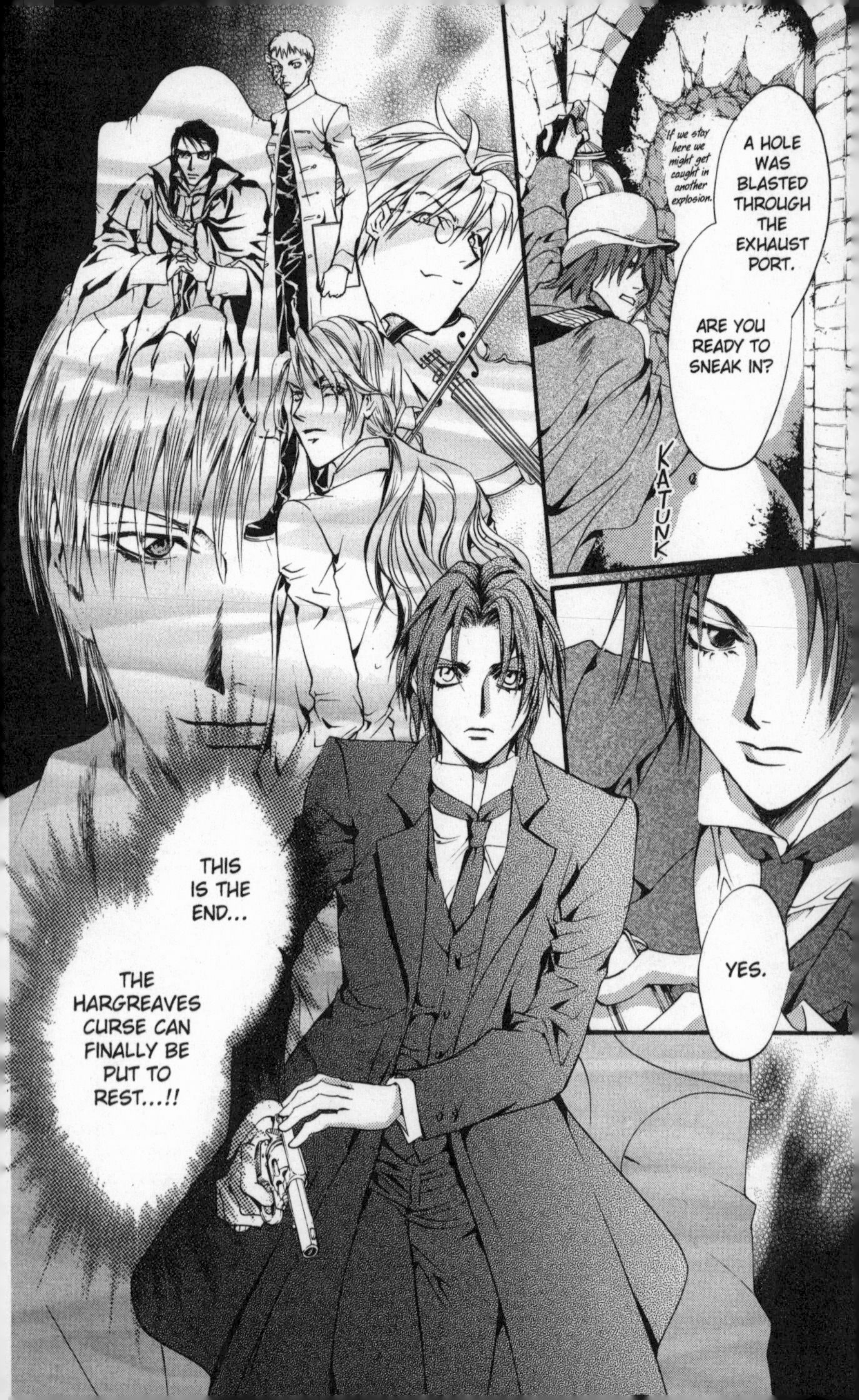
A HOLE WAS BLASTED THROUGH THE EXHAUST PORT.
If we stay here we might get caught in another explosion.
ARE YOU READY TO SNEAK IN?
KATUNK
YES.
THIS IS THE END...
THE HARGREAVES CURSE CAN FINALLY BE PUT TO REST...!!

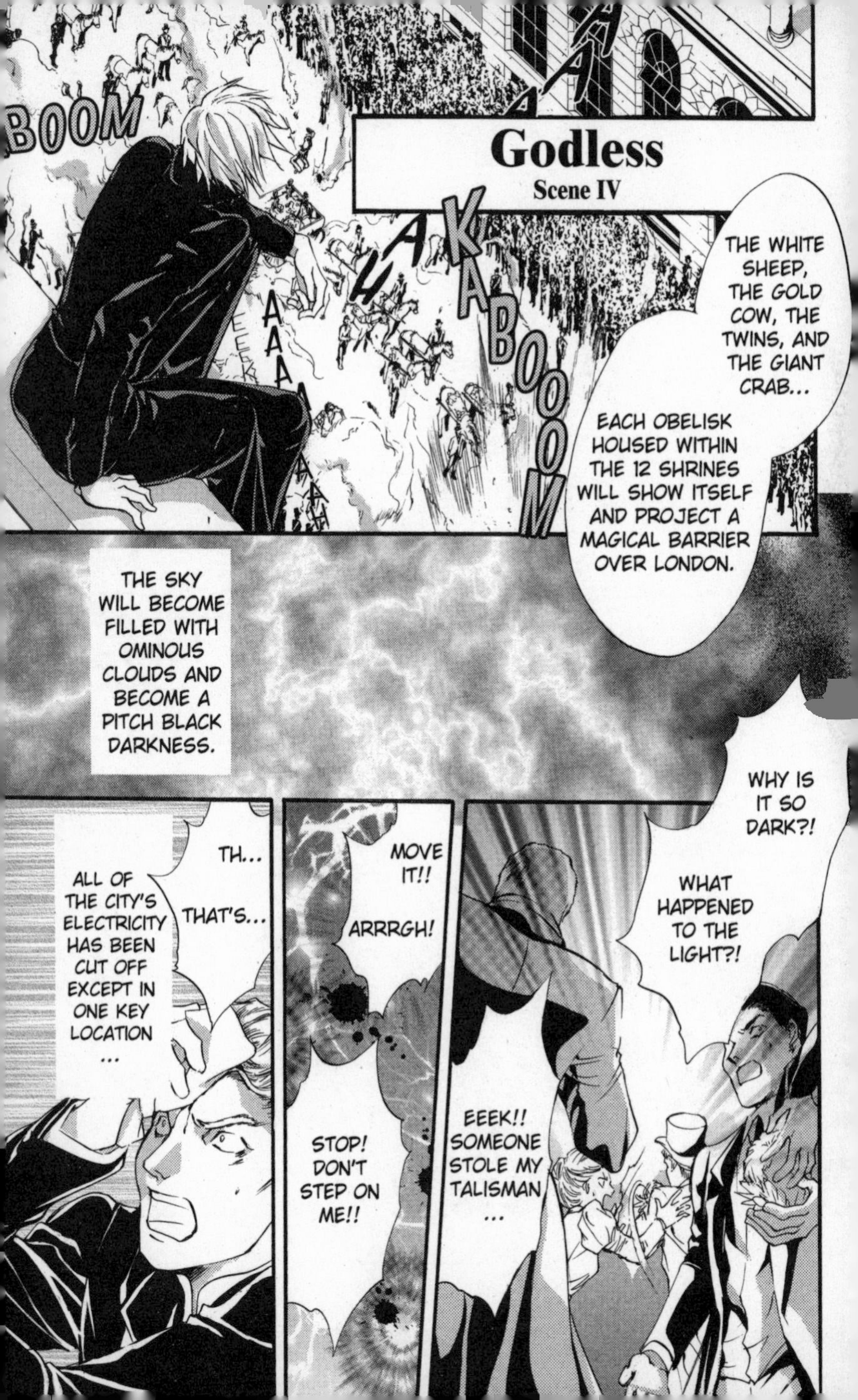
Godless
Scene IV
BOOM
KABOOOM
THE WHITE SHEEP, THE GOLD COW, THE TWINS, AND THE GIANT CRAB...
EACH OBELISK HOUSED WITHIN THE 12 SHRINES WILL SHOW ITSELF AND PROJECT A MAGICAL BARRIER OVER LONDON.
THE SKY WILL BECOME FILLED WITH OMINOUS CLOUDS AND BECOME A PITCH BLACK DARKNESS.
WHY IS IT SO DARK?!
WHAT HAPPENED TO THE LIGHT?!
EEEK!! SOMEONE STOLE MY TALISMAN...
MOVE IT!!
ARRRGH!
STOP! DON'T STEP ON ME!!
TH...
THAT'S...
ALL OF THE CITY'S ELECTRICITY HAS BEEN CUT OFF EXCEPT IN ONE KEY LOCATION...

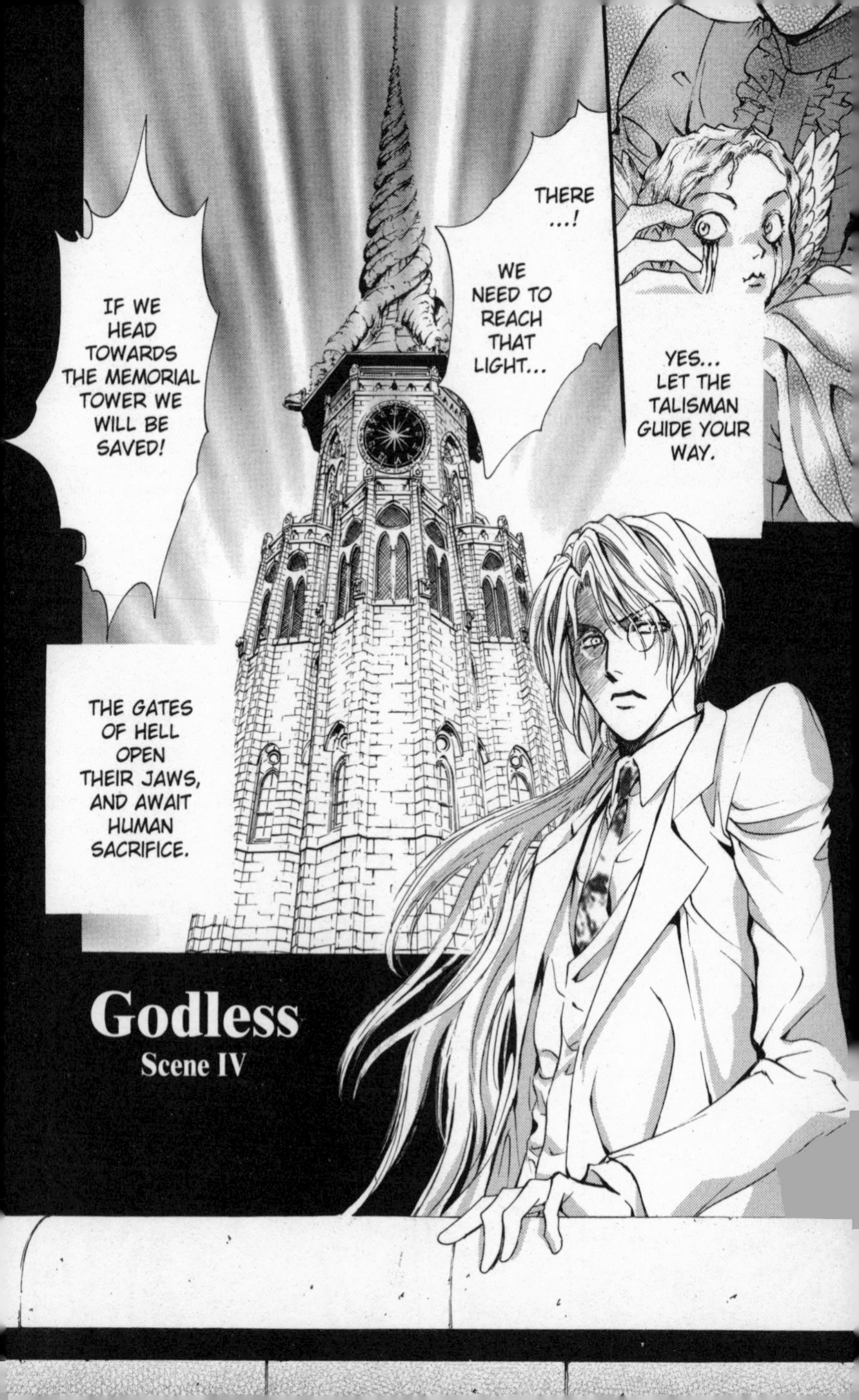
YES... LET THE TALISMAN GUIDE YOUR WAY.
THERE ...!
WE NEED TO REACH THAT LIGHT...
IF WE HEAD TOWARDS THE MEMORIAL TOWER WE WILL BE SAVED!
THE GATES OF HELL OPEN THEIR JAWS, AND AWAIT HUMAN SACRIFICE.
Godless
Scene IV

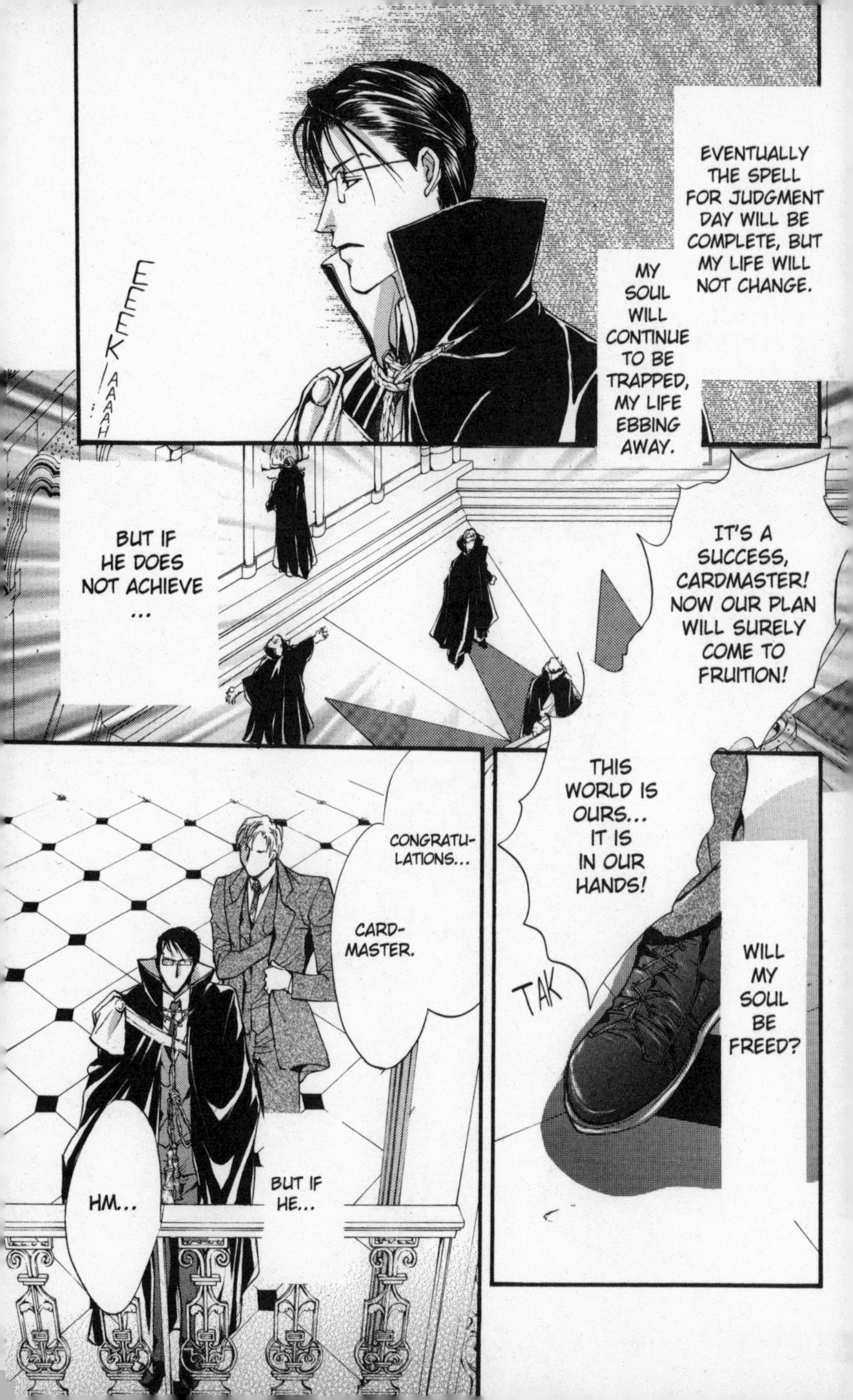
EVENTUALLY THE SPELL FOR JUDGMENT DAY WILL BE COMPLETE, BUT MY LIFE WILL NOT CHANGE.
MY SOUL WILL CONTINUE TO BE TRAPPED, MY LIFE EBBING AWAY.
EEEEK! AAAAH!
IT'S A SUCCESS, CARDMASTER! NOW OUR PLAN WILL SURELY COME TO FRUITION!
BUT IF HE DOES NOT ACHIEVE ...
THIS WORLD IS OURS... IT IS IN OUR HANDS!
TAK
WILL MY SOUL BE FREED?
CONGRATULATIONS...
CARDMASTER.
BUT IF HE...
HM...

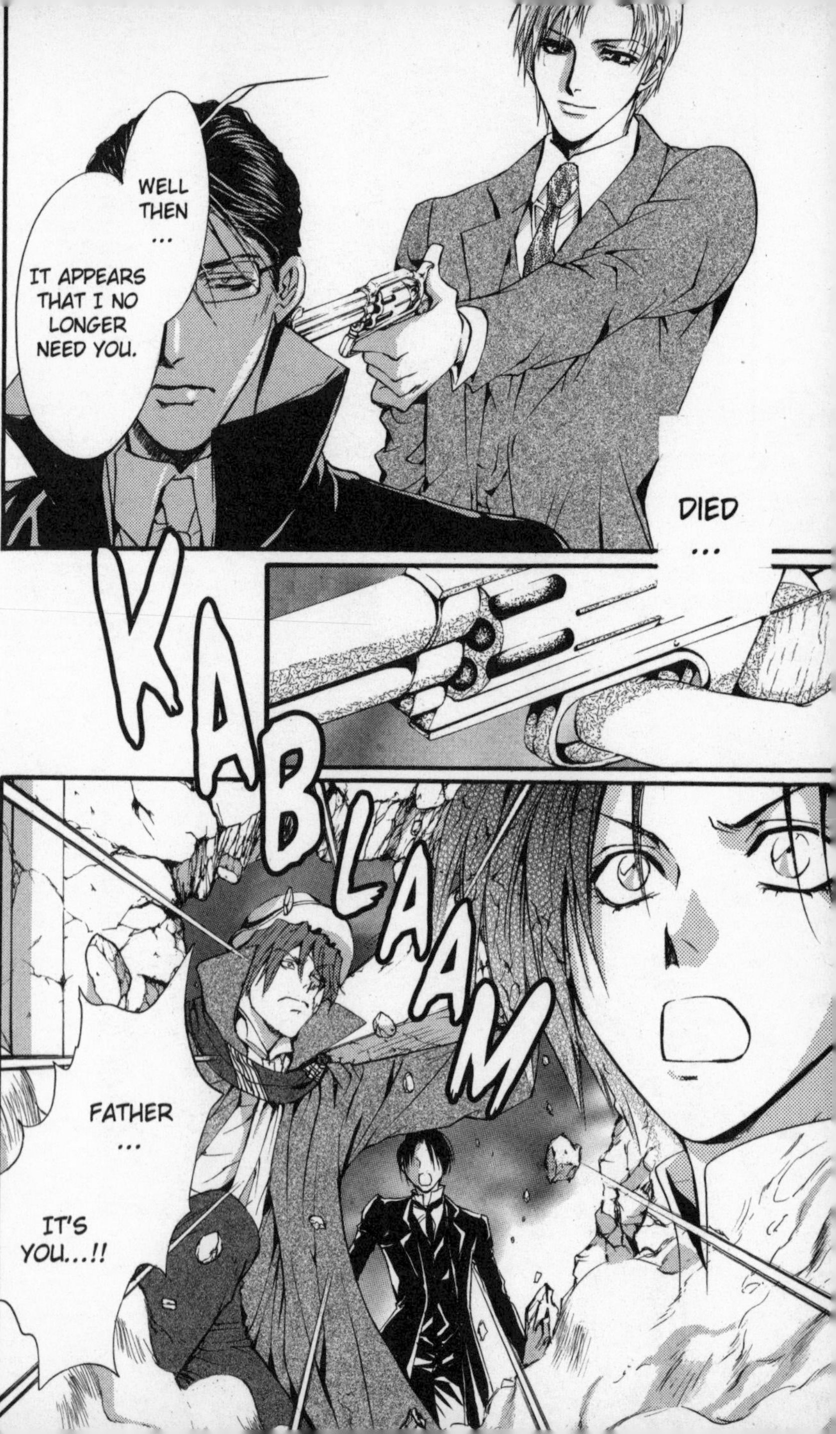
WELL THEN ... IT APPEARS THAT I NO LONGER NEED YOU.
DIED ...
KABLAAM
FATHER ... IT'S YOU...!!

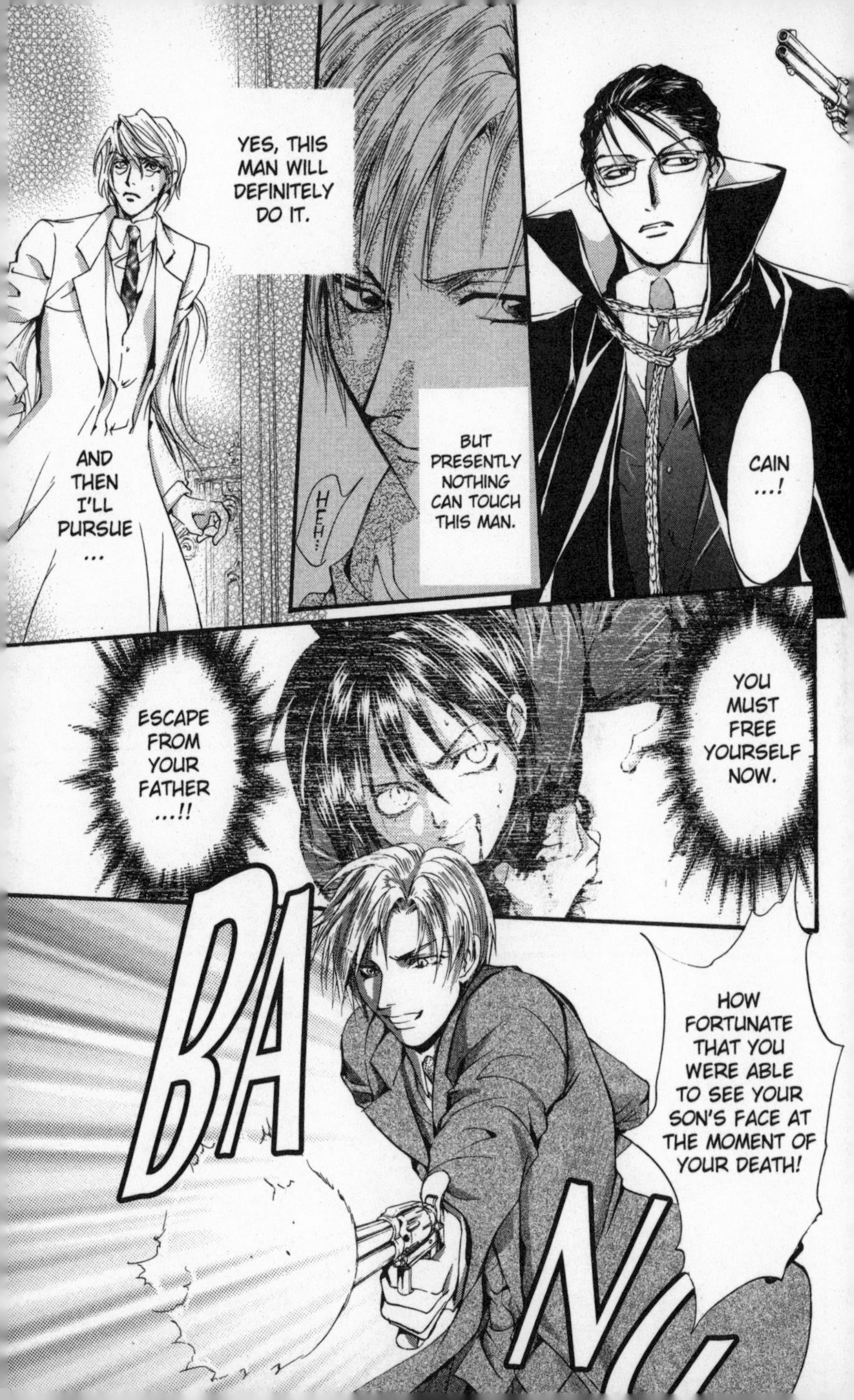
CAIN ...!
YES, THIS MAN WILL DEFINITELY DO IT.
BUT PRESENTLY NOTHING CAN TOUCH THIS MAN.
HEH!
AND THEN I'LL PURSUE ...
YOU MUST FREE YOURSELF NOW.
ESCAPE FROM YOUR FATHER ...!!
HOW FORTUNATE THAT YOU WERE ABLE TO SEE YOUR SON'S FACE AT THE MOMENT OF YOUR DEATH!
BA
N

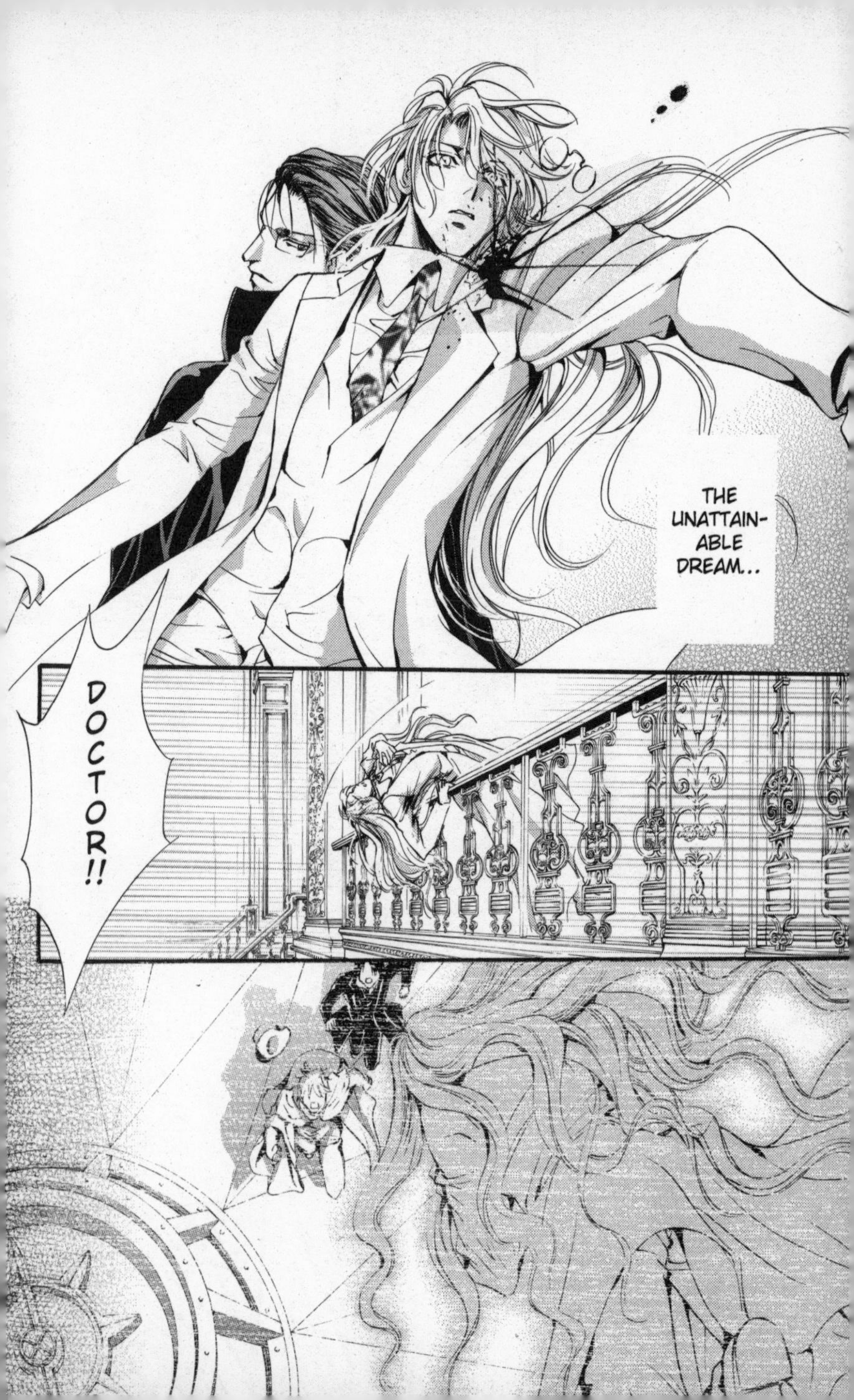
THE UNATTAIN-ABLE DREAM...
DOCTOR!!

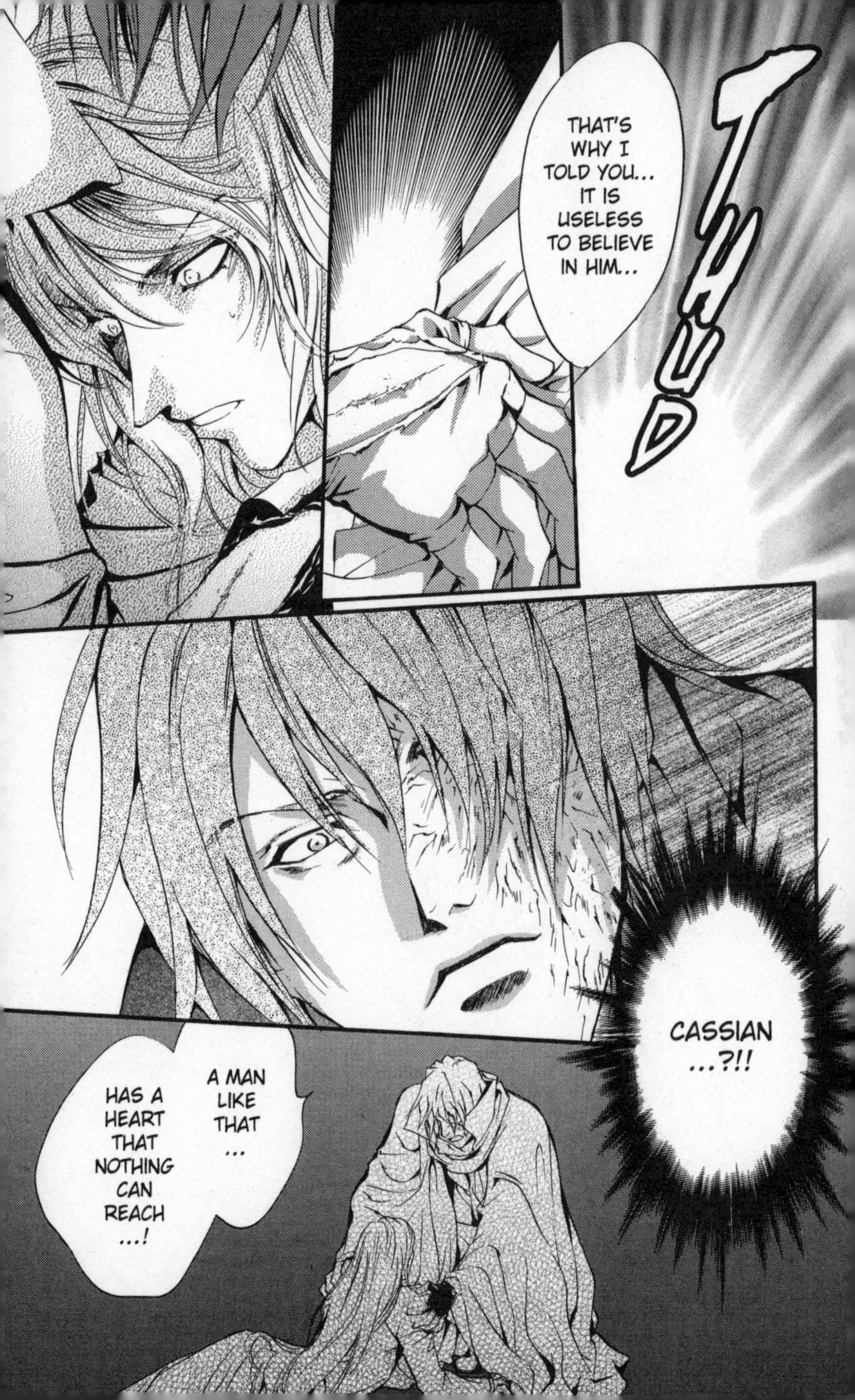
THAT'S WHY I TOLD YOU... IT IS USELESS TO BELIEVE IN HIM...
THUD
CASSIAN ...?!!
A MAN LIKE THAT ...
HAS A HEART THAT NOTHING CAN REACH ...!

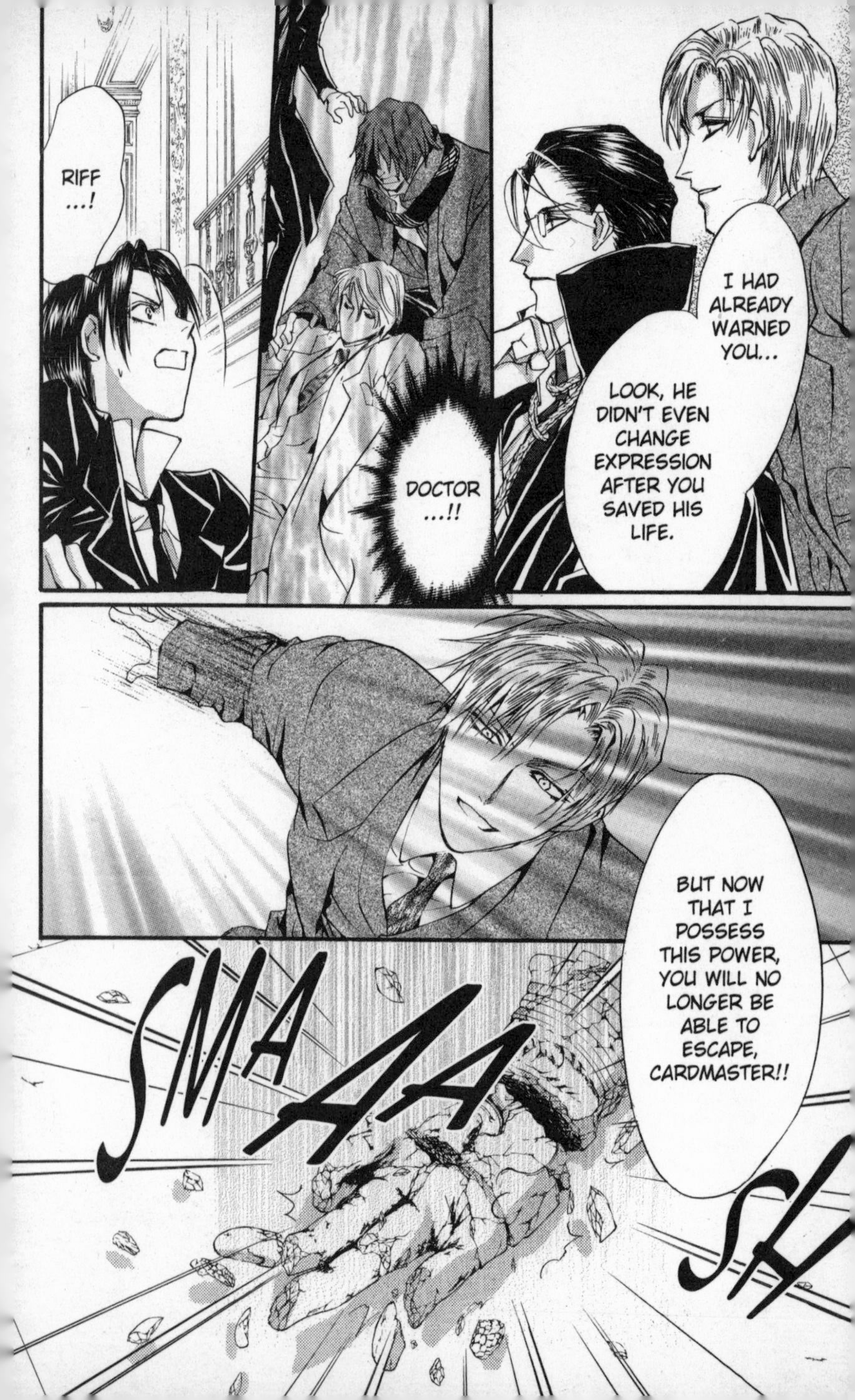
I HAD ALREADY WARNED YOU...
LOOK, HE DIDN'T EVEN CHANGE EXPRESSION AFTER YOU SAVED HIS LIFE.
DOCTOR ...!!
RIFF ...!
BUT NOW THAT I POSSESS THIS POWER, YOU WILL NO LONGER BE ABLE TO ESCAPE, CARDMASTER!!
SMAAA
SH

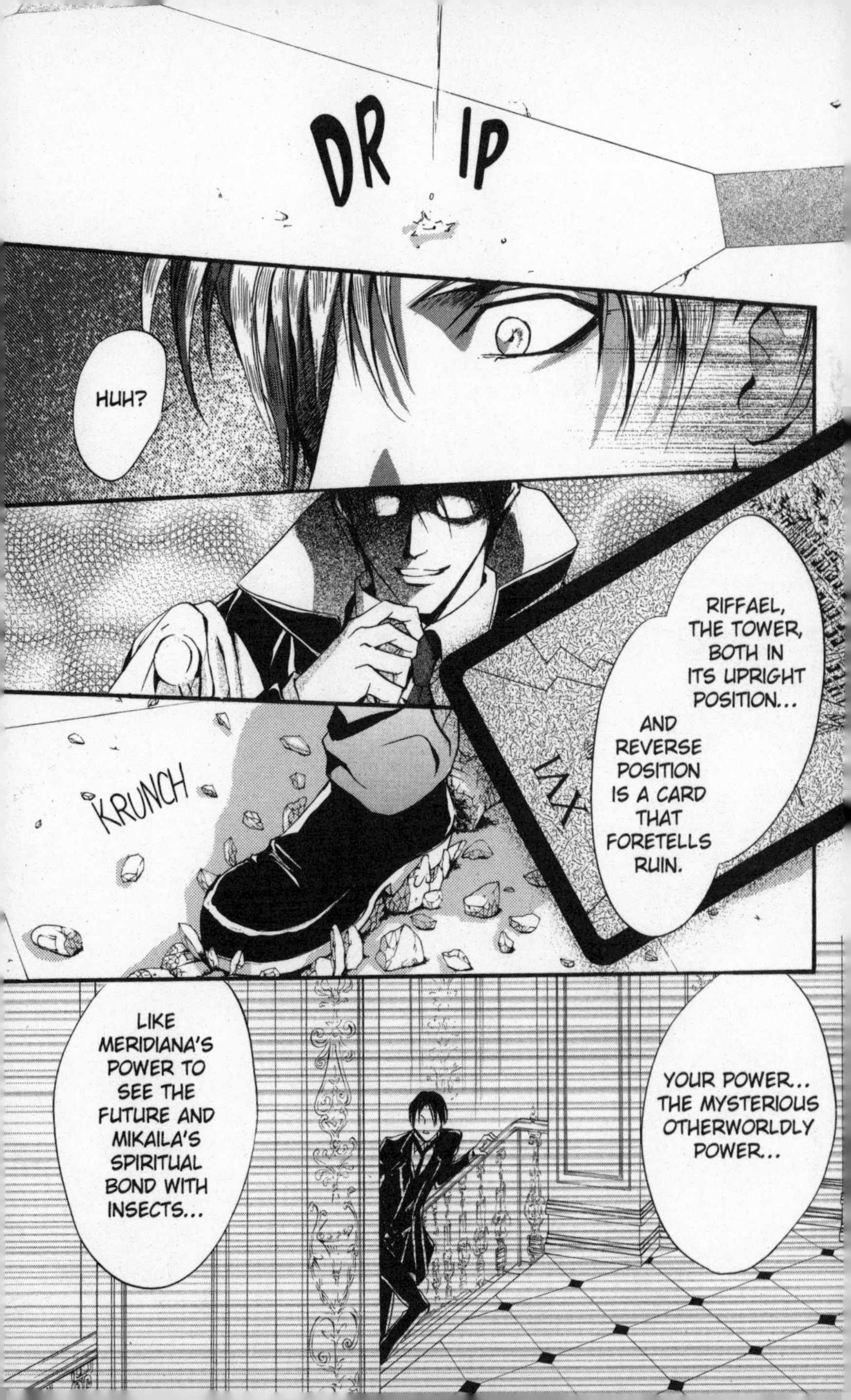
DR IP
HUH?
RIFFAEL, THE TOWER, BOTH IN ITS UPRIGHT POSITION...
AND REVERSE POSITION IS A CARD THAT FORETELLS RUIN.
KRUNCH
YOUR POWER... THE MYSTERIOUS OTHERWORLDLY POWER...
LIKE MERIDIANA'S POWER TO SEE THE FUTURE AND MIKAILA'S SPIRITUAL BOND WITH INSECTS...

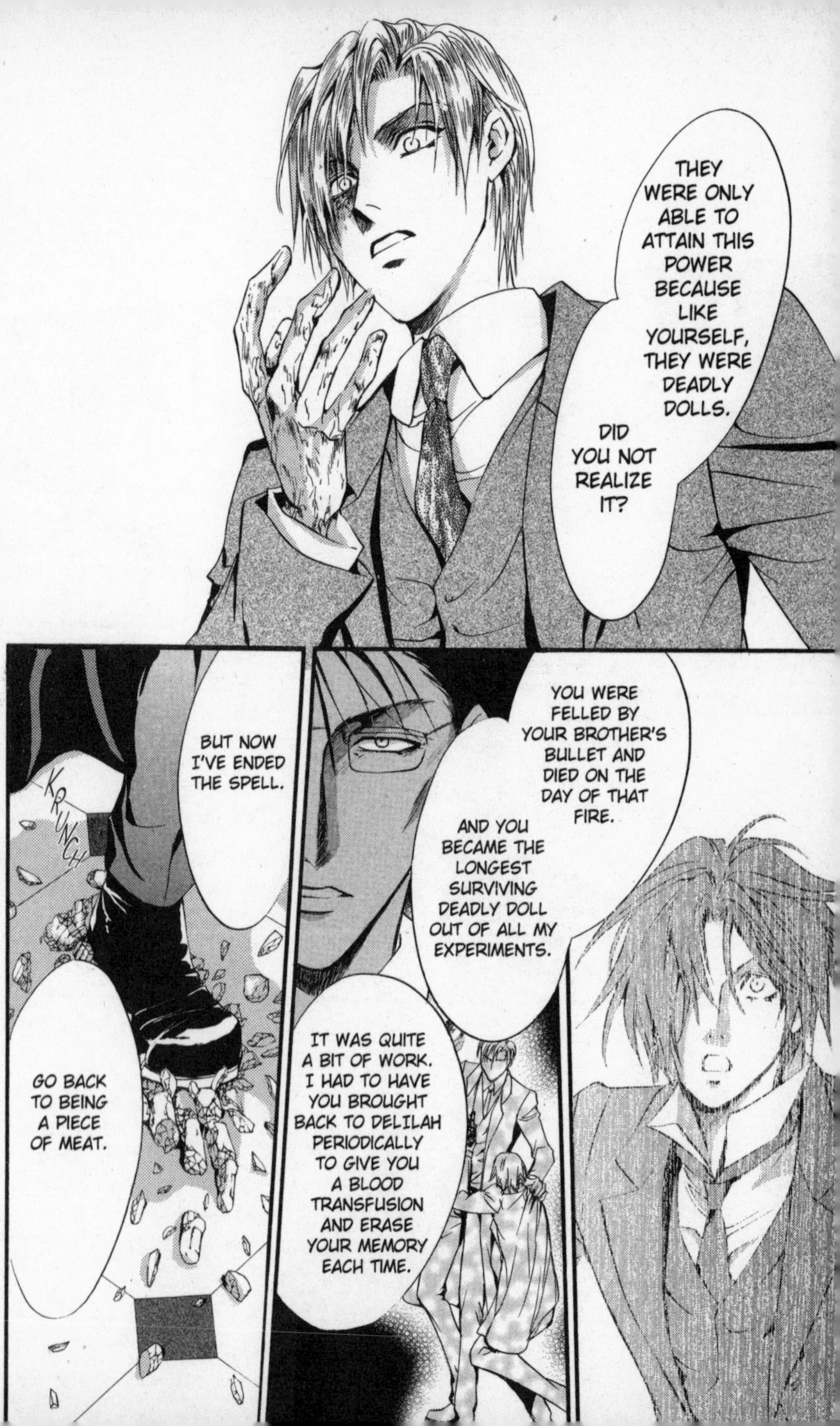
THEY WERE ONLY ABLE TO ATTAIN THIS POWER BECAUSE LIKE YOURSELF, THEY WERE DEADLY DOLLS.
DID YOU NOT REALIZE IT?
YOU WERE FELLED BY YOUR BROTHER'S BULLET AND DIED ON THE DAY OF THAT FIRE.
AND YOU BECAME THE LONGEST SURVIVING DEADLY DOLL OUT OF ALL MY EXPERIMENTS.
IT WAS QUITE A BIT OF WORK. I HAD TO HAVE YOU BROUGHT BACK TO DELILAH PERIODICALLY TO GIVE YOU A BLOOD TRANSFUSION AND ERASE YOUR MEMORY EACH TIME.
BUT NOW I'VE ENDED THE SPELL.
KRUNCH
GO BACK TO BEING A PIECE OF MEAT.

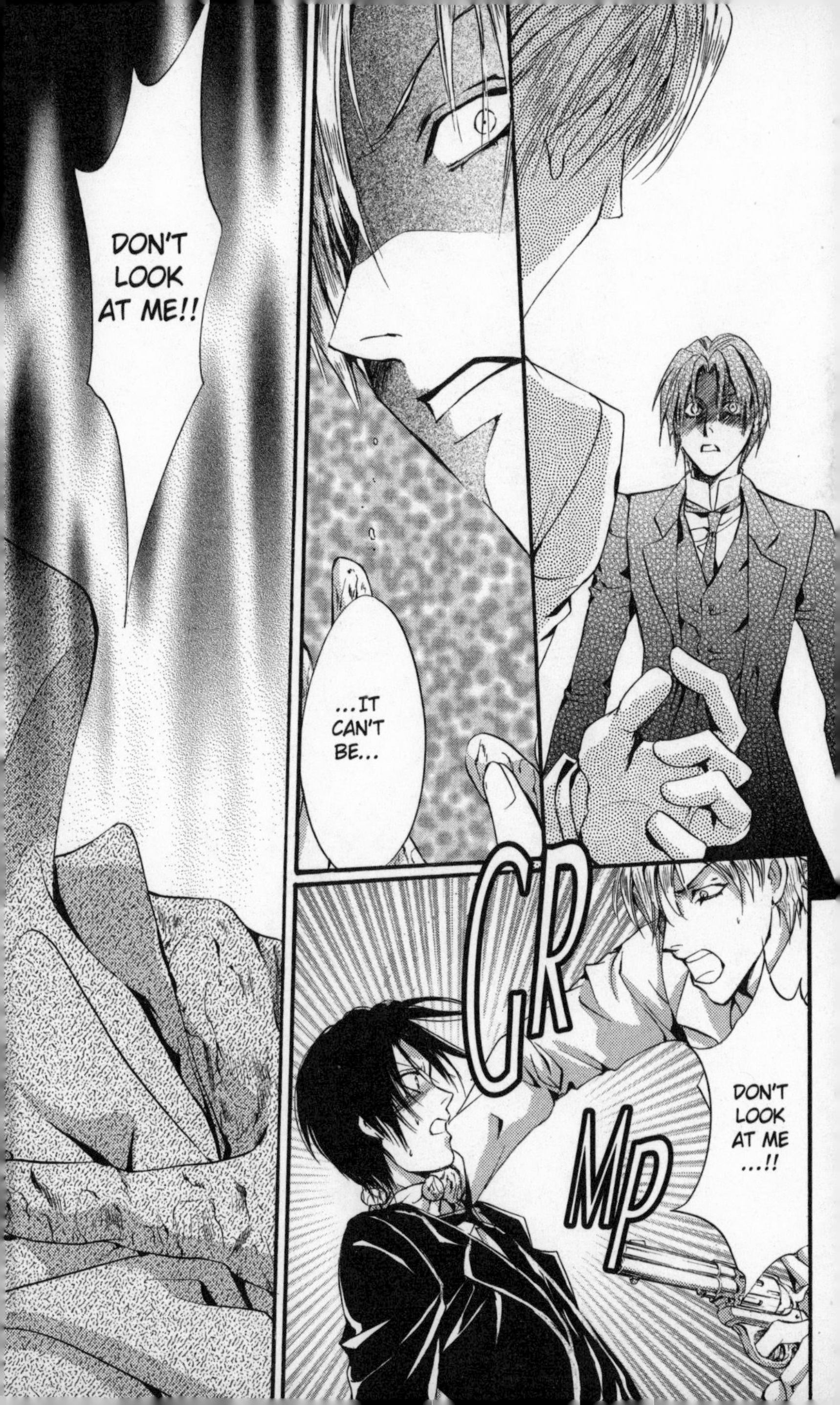
...IT CAN'T BE...
GRMP
DON'T LOOK AT ME ...!!
DON'T LOOK AT ME!!

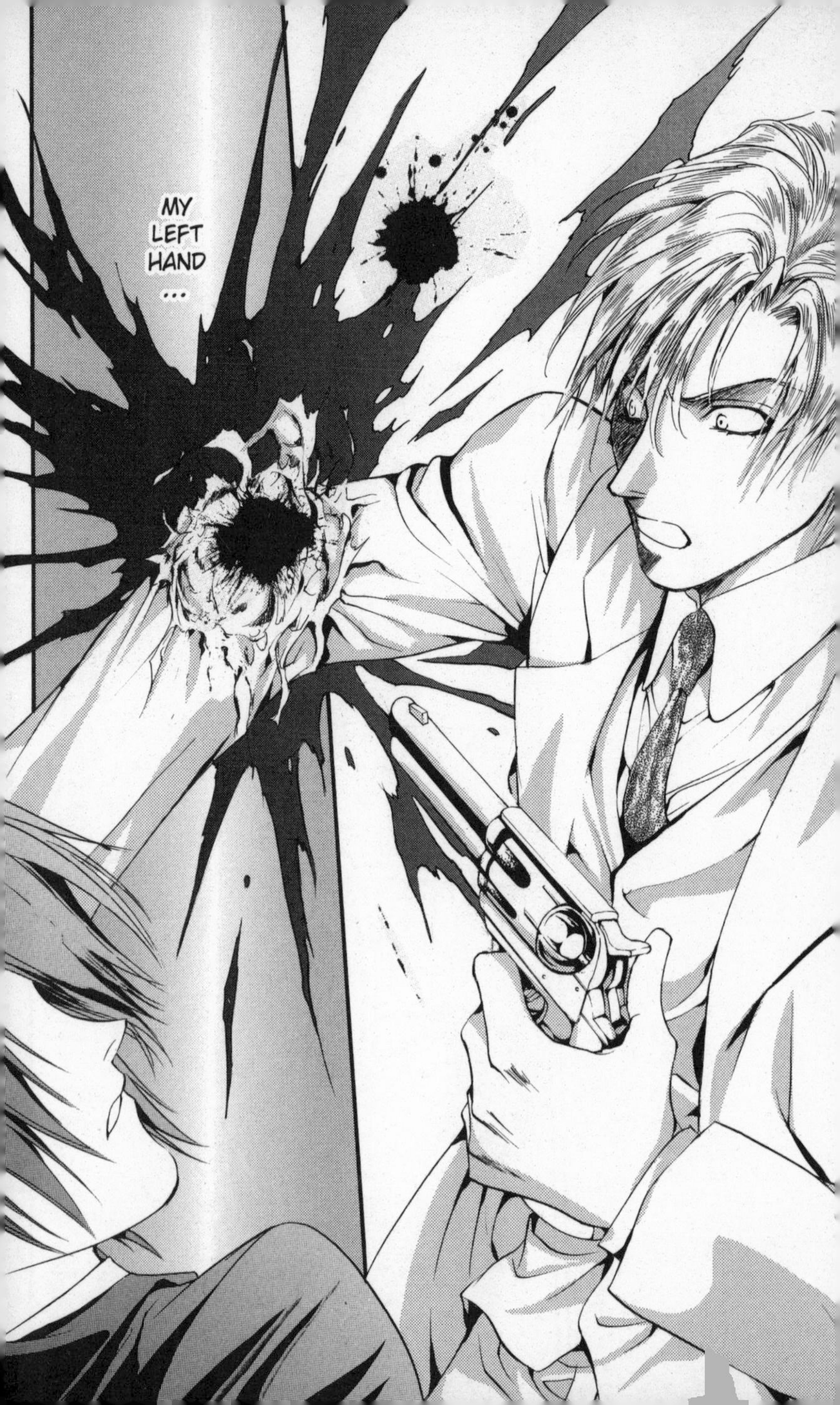
MY LEFT HAND ...

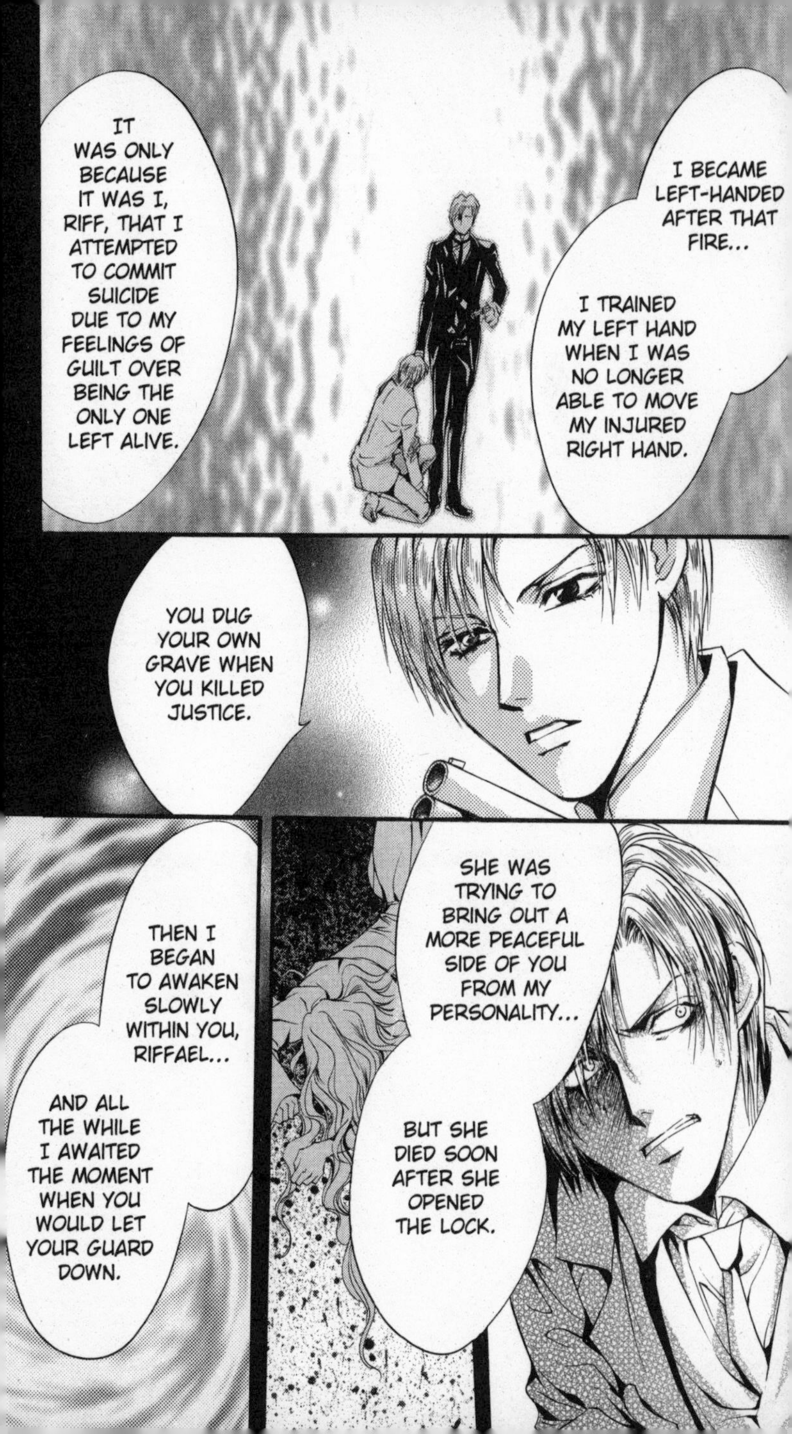
I BECAME LEFT-HANDED AFTER THAT FIRE...
I TRAINED MY LEFT HAND WHEN I WAS NO LONGER ABLE TO MOVE MY INJURED RIGHT HAND.
IT WAS ONLY BECAUSE IT WAS I, RIFF, THAT I ATTEMPTED TO COMMIT SUICIDE DUE TO MY FEELINGS OF GUILT OVER BEING THE ONLY ONE LEFT ALIVE.
YOU DUG YOUR OWN GRAVE WHEN YOU KILLED JUSTICE.
SHE WAS TRYING TO BRING OUT A MORE PEACEFUL SIDE OF YOU FROM MY PERSONALITY...
BUT SHE DIED SOON AFTER SHE OPENED THE LOCK.
THEN I BEGAN TO AWAKEN SLOWLY WITHIN YOU, RIFFAEL...
AND ALL THE WHILE I AWAITED THE MOMENT WHEN YOU WOULD LET YOUR GUARD DOWN.

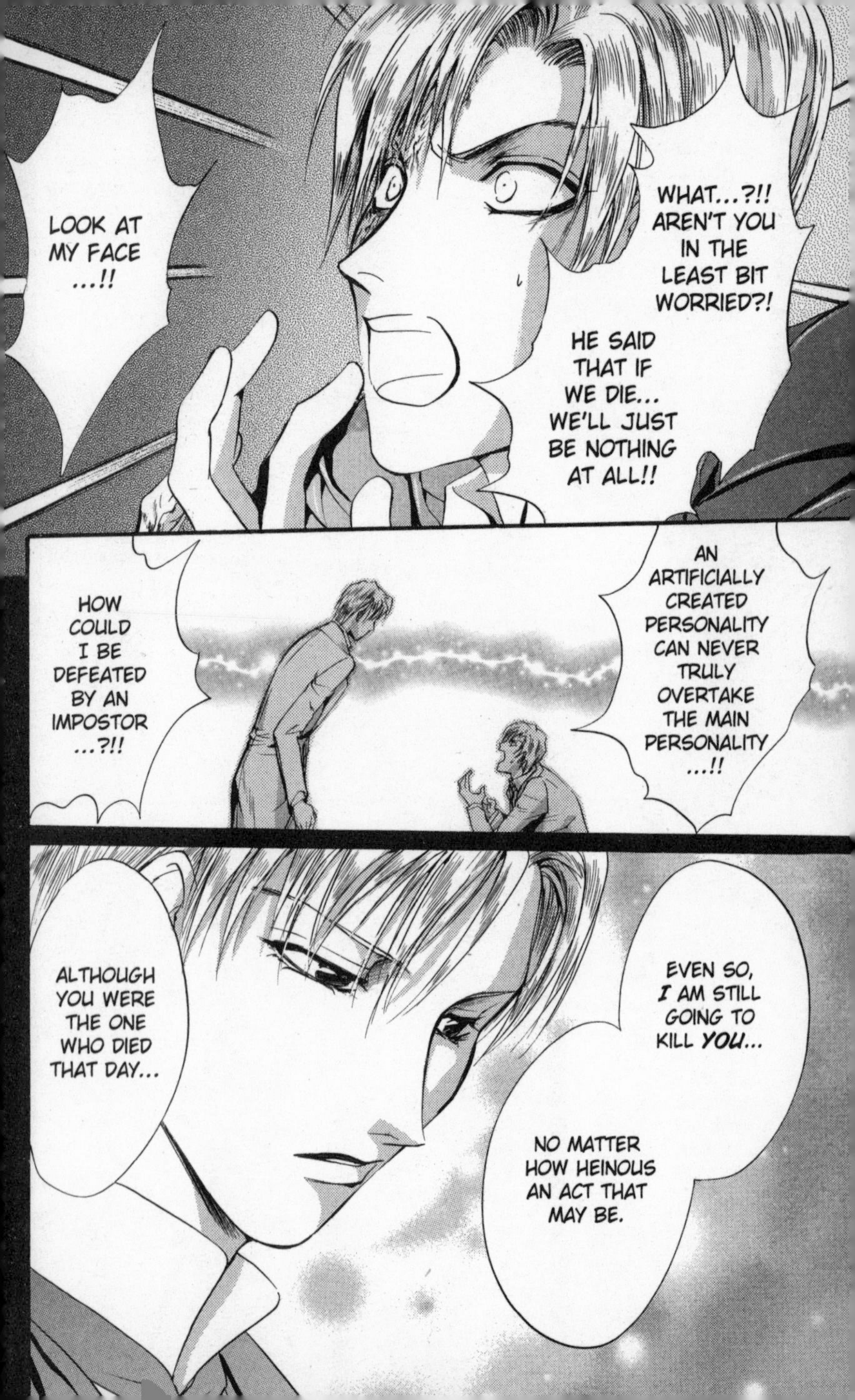
WHAT...?!! AREN'T YOU IN THE LEAST BIT WORRIED?!
HE SAID THAT IF WE DIE... WE'LL JUST BE NOTHING AT ALL!!
LOOK AT MY FACE ...!!
AN ARTIFICIALLY CREATED PERSONALITY CAN NEVER TRULY OVERTAKE THE MAIN PERSONALITY ...!!
HOW COULD I BE DEFEATED BY AN IMPOSTOR ...?!!
EVEN SO, *I* AM STILL GOING TO KILL ***YOU***...
NO MATTER HOW HEINOUS AN ACT THAT MAY BE.
ALTHOUGH YOU WERE THE ONE WHO DIED THAT DAY...

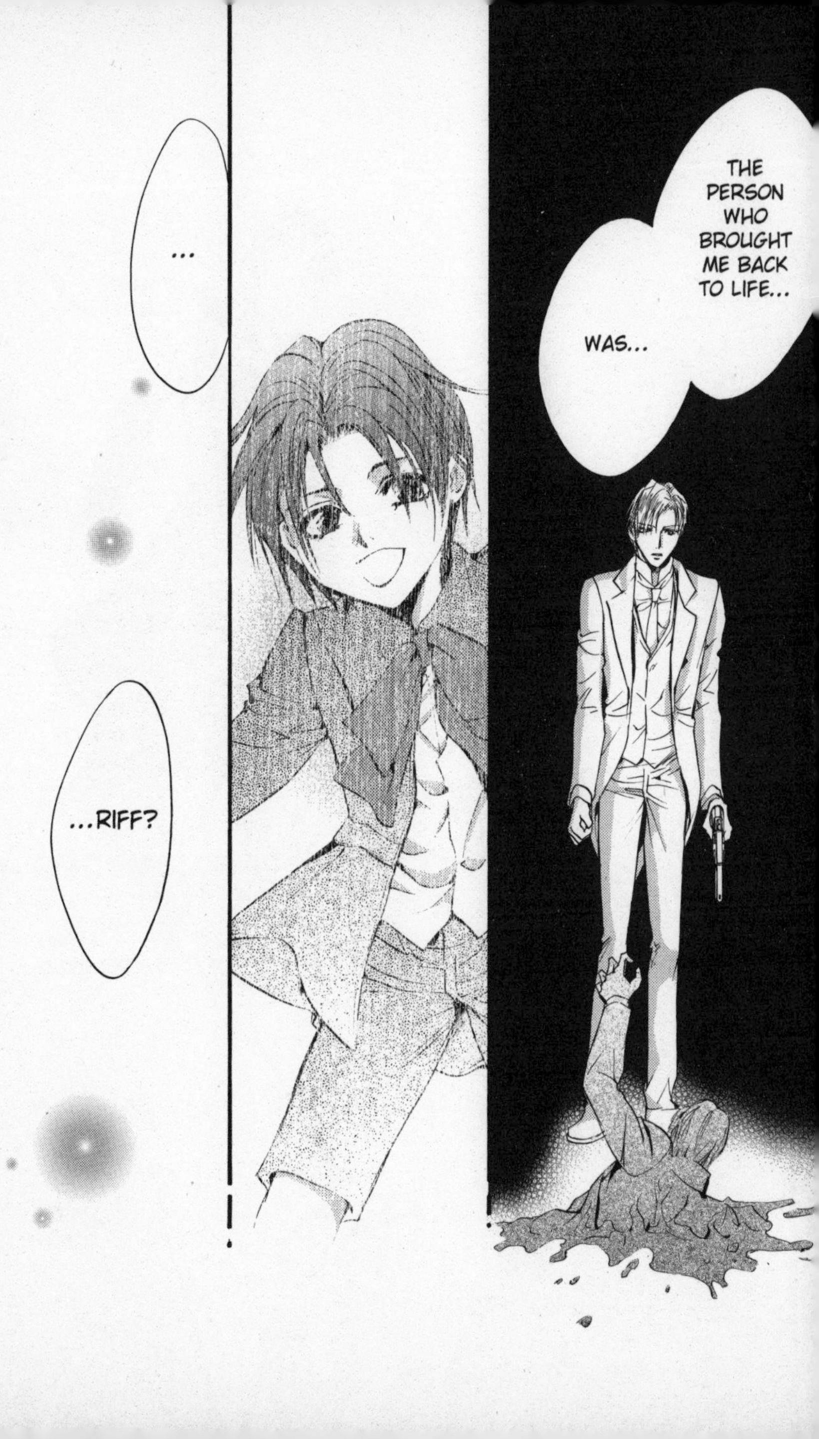
THE PERSON WHO BROUGHT ME BACK TO LIFE...
WAS...
...
...RIFF?

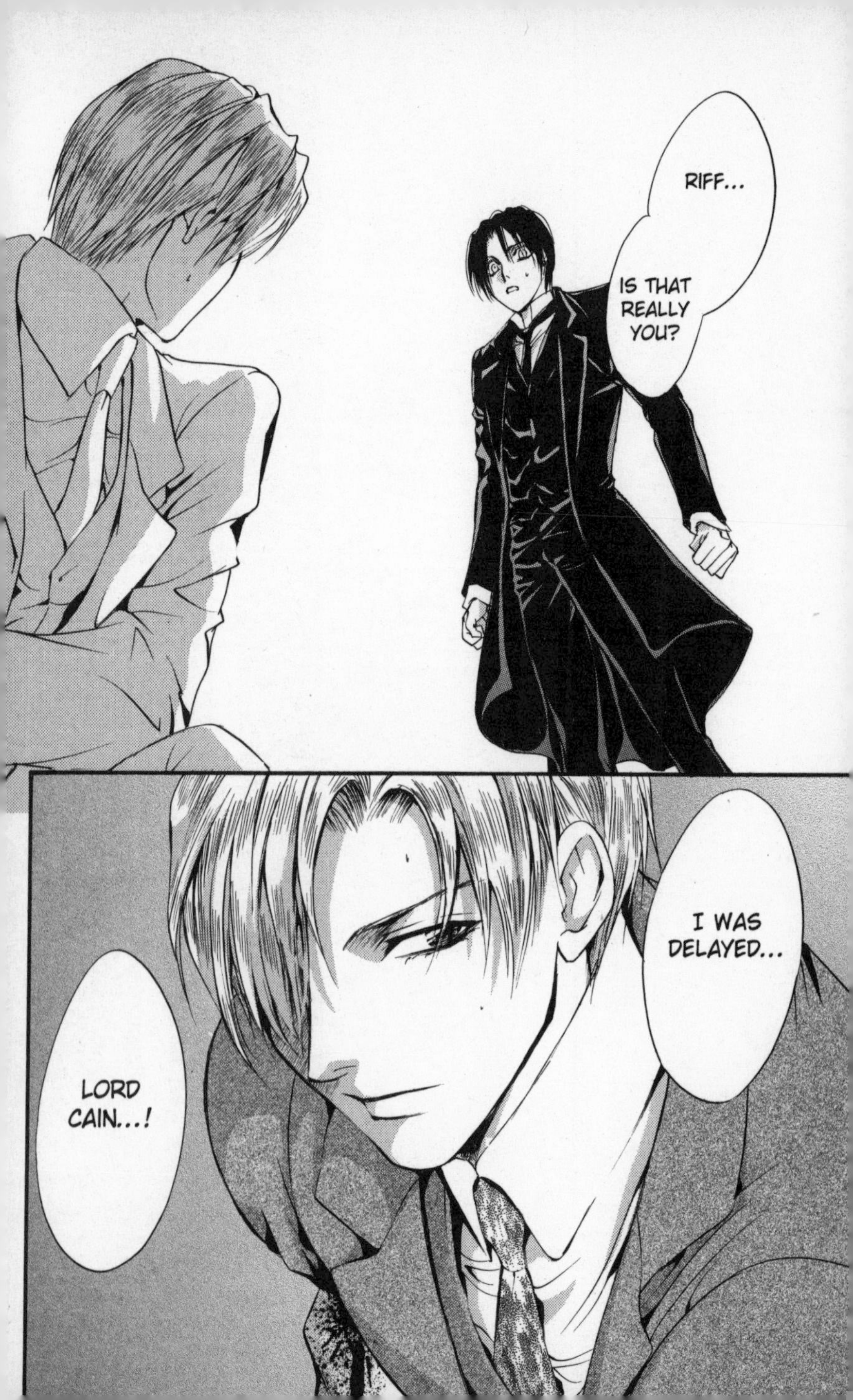
RIFF...
IS THAT REALLY YOU?
I WAS DELAYED...
LORD CAIN...!

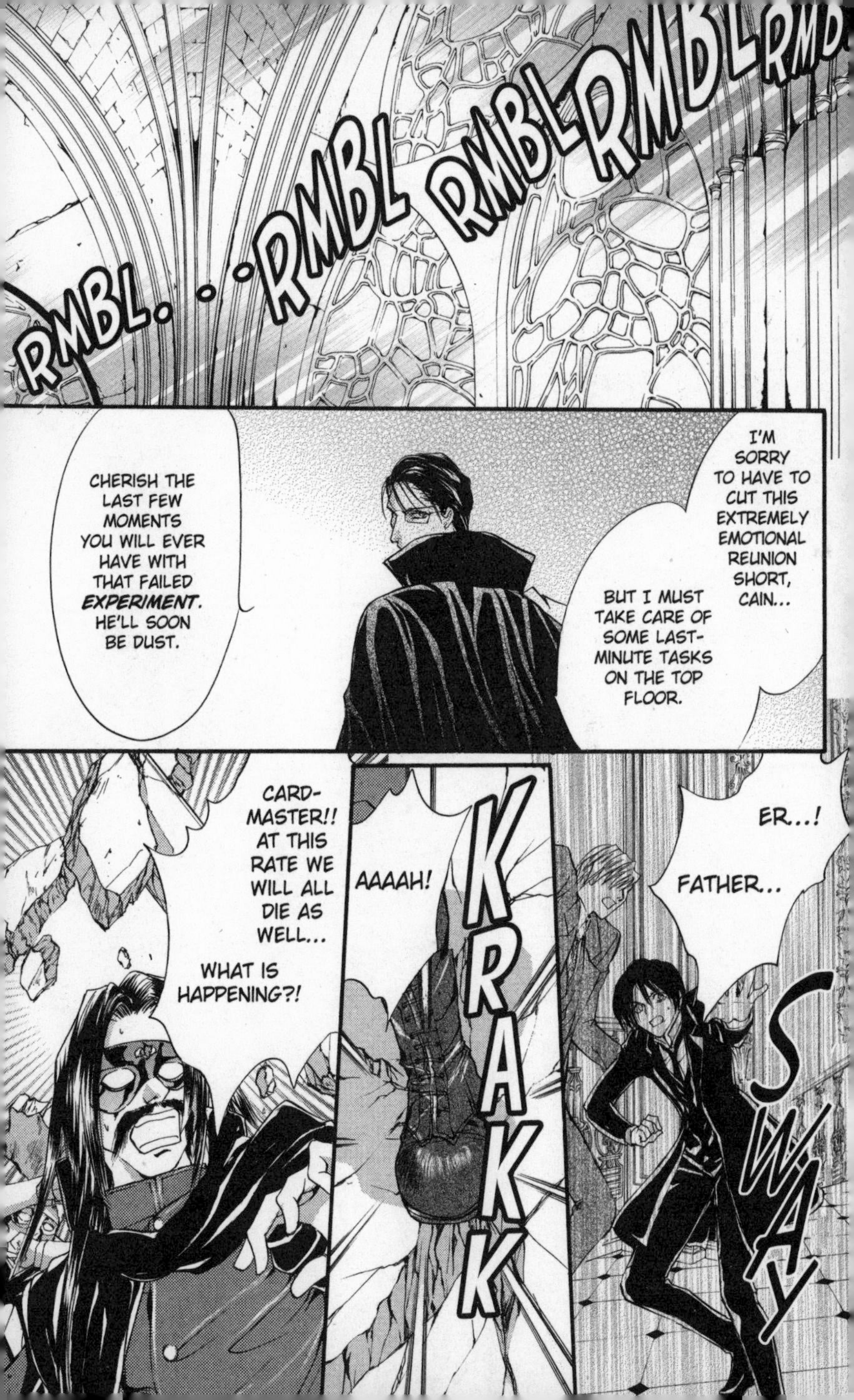
RMBL. . .RMBL RMBL RMBLRMBLRMBL
I'M SORRY TO HAVE TO CUT THIS EXTREMELY EMOTIONAL REUNION SHORT, CAIN...
BUT I MUST TAKE CARE OF SOME LAST-MINUTE TASKS ON THE TOP FLOOR.
CHERISH THE LAST FEW MOMENTS YOU WILL EVER HAVE WITH THAT FAILED *EXPERIMENT*. HE'LL SOON BE DUST.
ER...!
FATHER...
SWAY
KRAKK
AAAAH!
CARD-MASTER!! AT THIS RATE WE WILL ALL DIE AS WELL...
WHAT IS HAPPENING?!

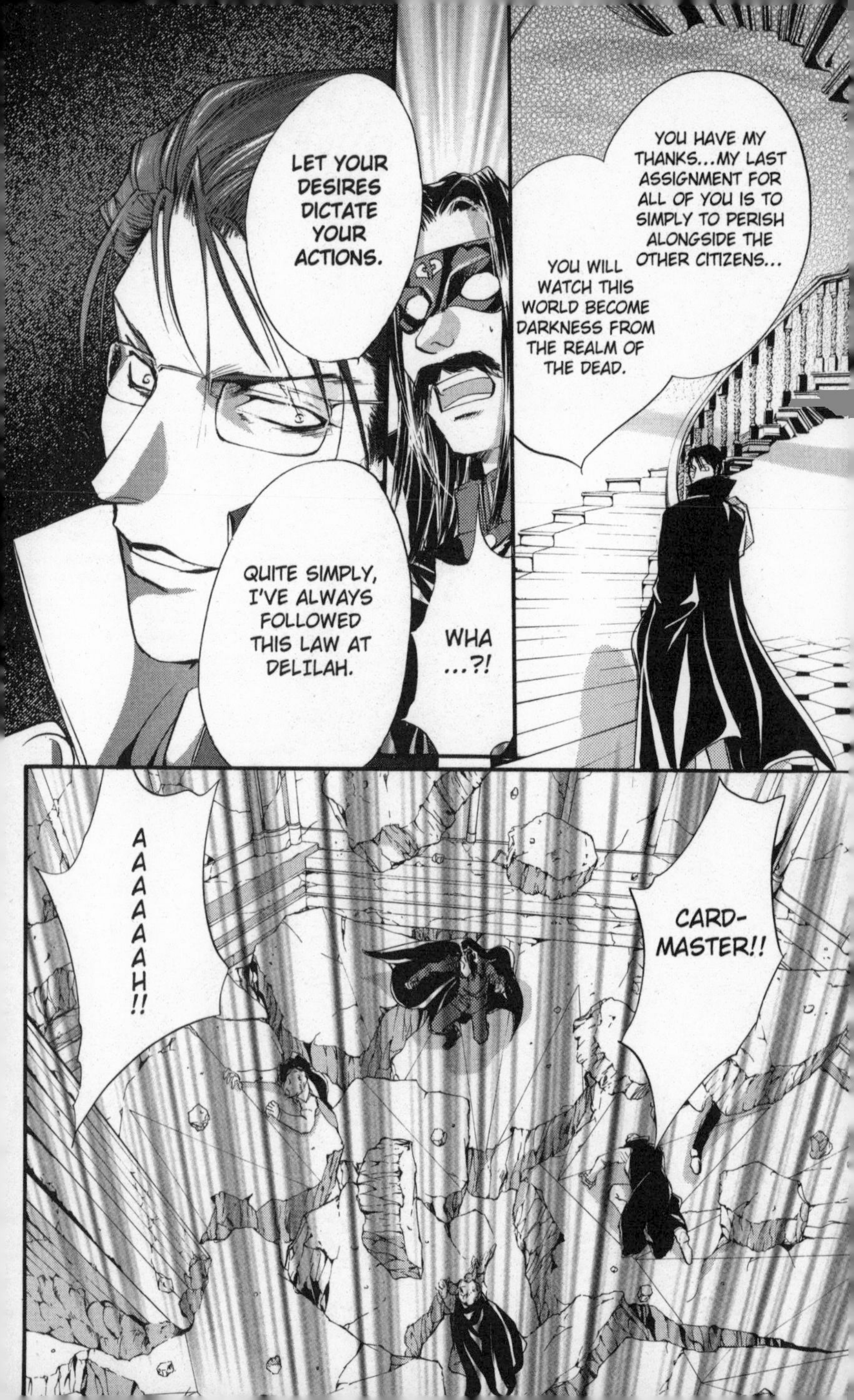
YOU HAVE MY THANKS...MY LAST ASSIGNMENT FOR ALL OF YOU IS TO SIMPLY TO PERISH ALONGSIDE THE OTHER CITIZENS...
YOU WILL WATCH THIS WORLD BECOME DARKNESS FROM THE REALM OF THE DEAD.
LET YOUR DESIRES DICTATE YOUR ACTIONS.
WHA ...?!
QUITE SIMPLY, I'VE ALWAYS FOLLOWED THIS LAW AT DELILAH.
CARD-MASTER!!
AAAAAAAAH!!

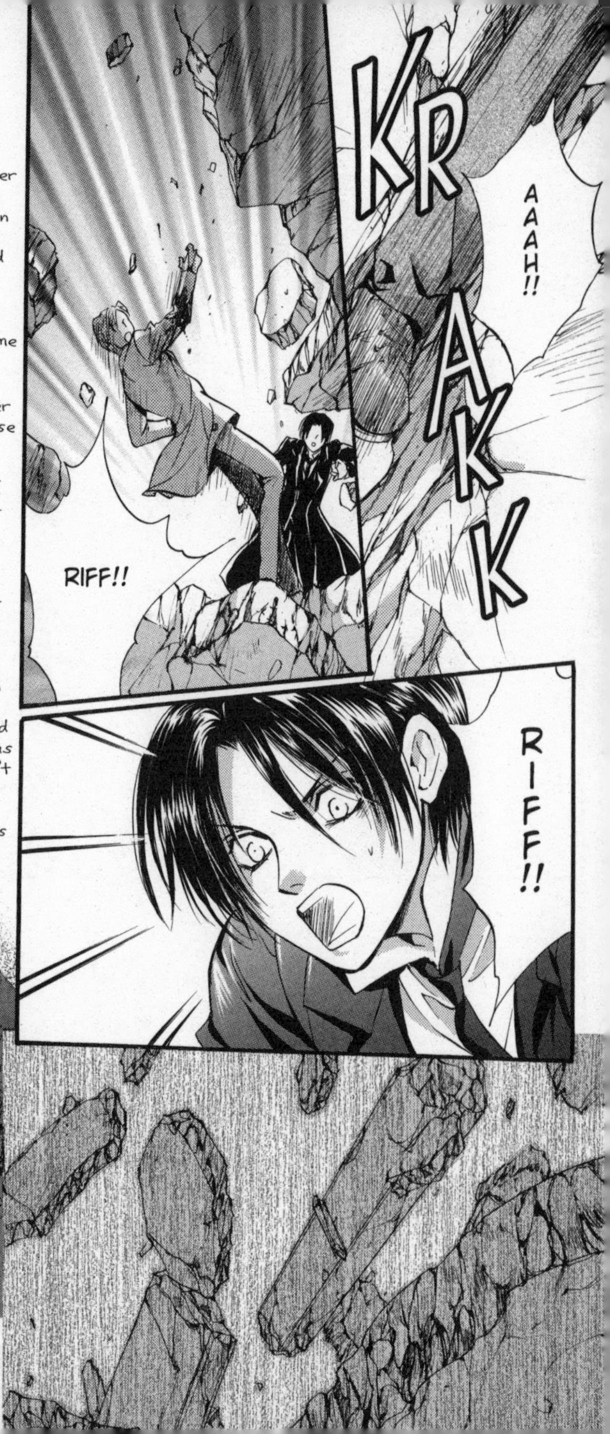
KRAAKK
AAAH!!
RIFF!!
RIFF!!

Justice is a character that I've liked since she first appeared in the previous series. Apparently she used to have a family, so maybe it was after they died that her true personality came out?

I enjoyed drawing her subordinates because there hadn't been very many female characters lately. I wanted a little sexiness in the visuals.

Also, I thought that there would be more readers who would say that they preferred Cassian when he had the appearance of a 12-year-old boy, but maybe I was wrong and they didn't really care for that body so much. Or maybe those letters will be coming in the future?

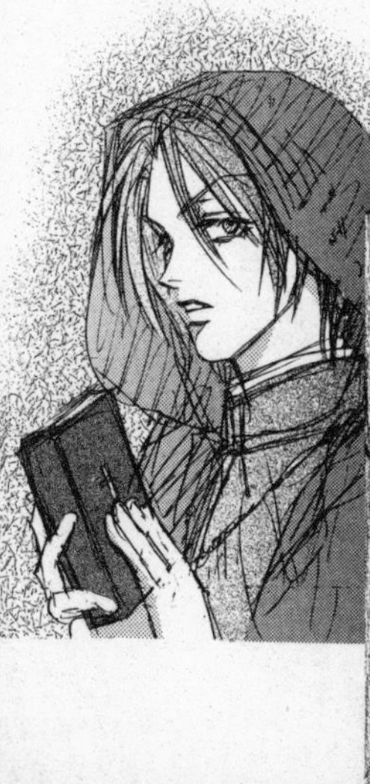

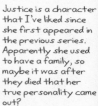

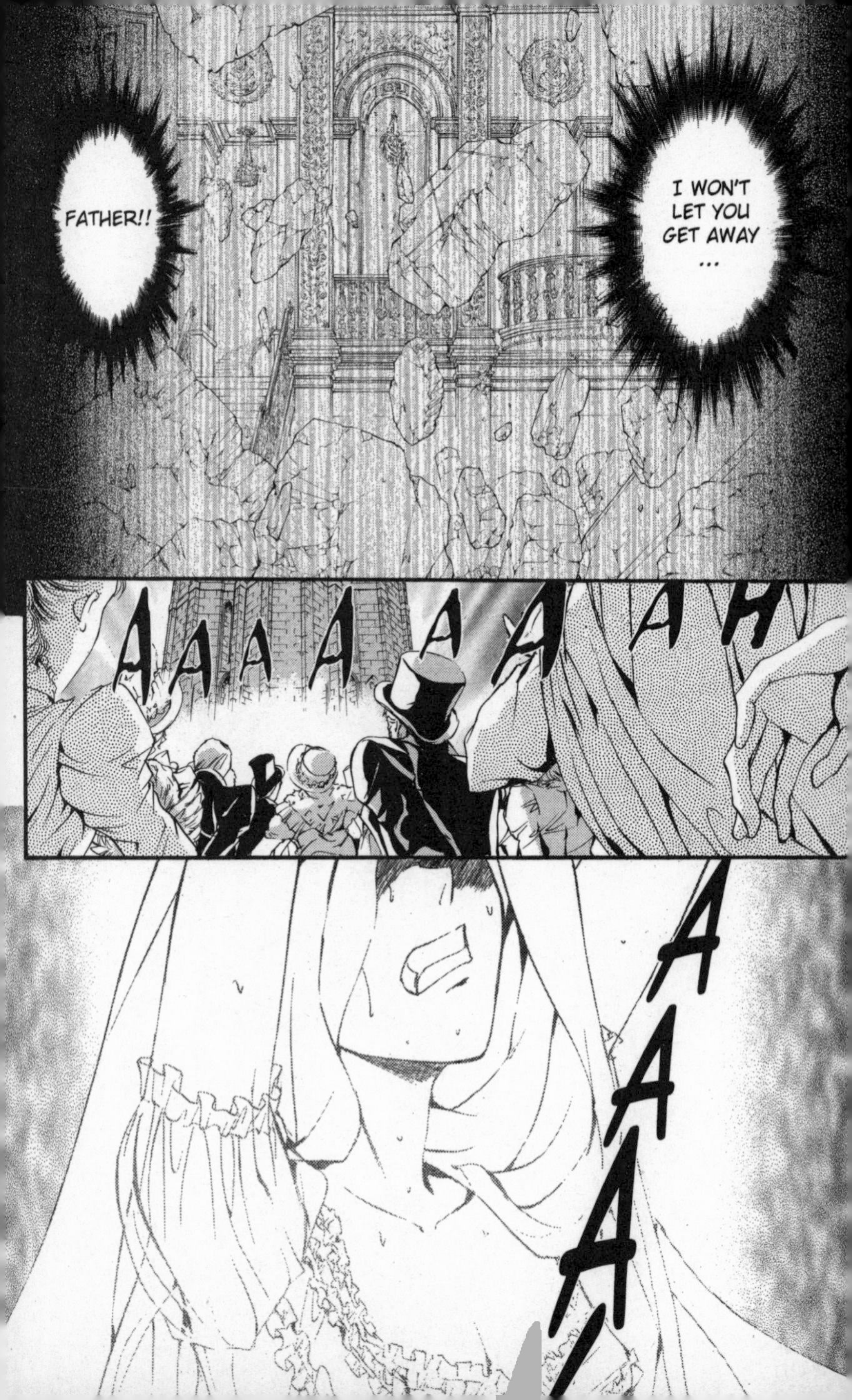
I WON'T LET YOU GET AWAY ...
FATHER!!
AAAAAAAH
AAAA!

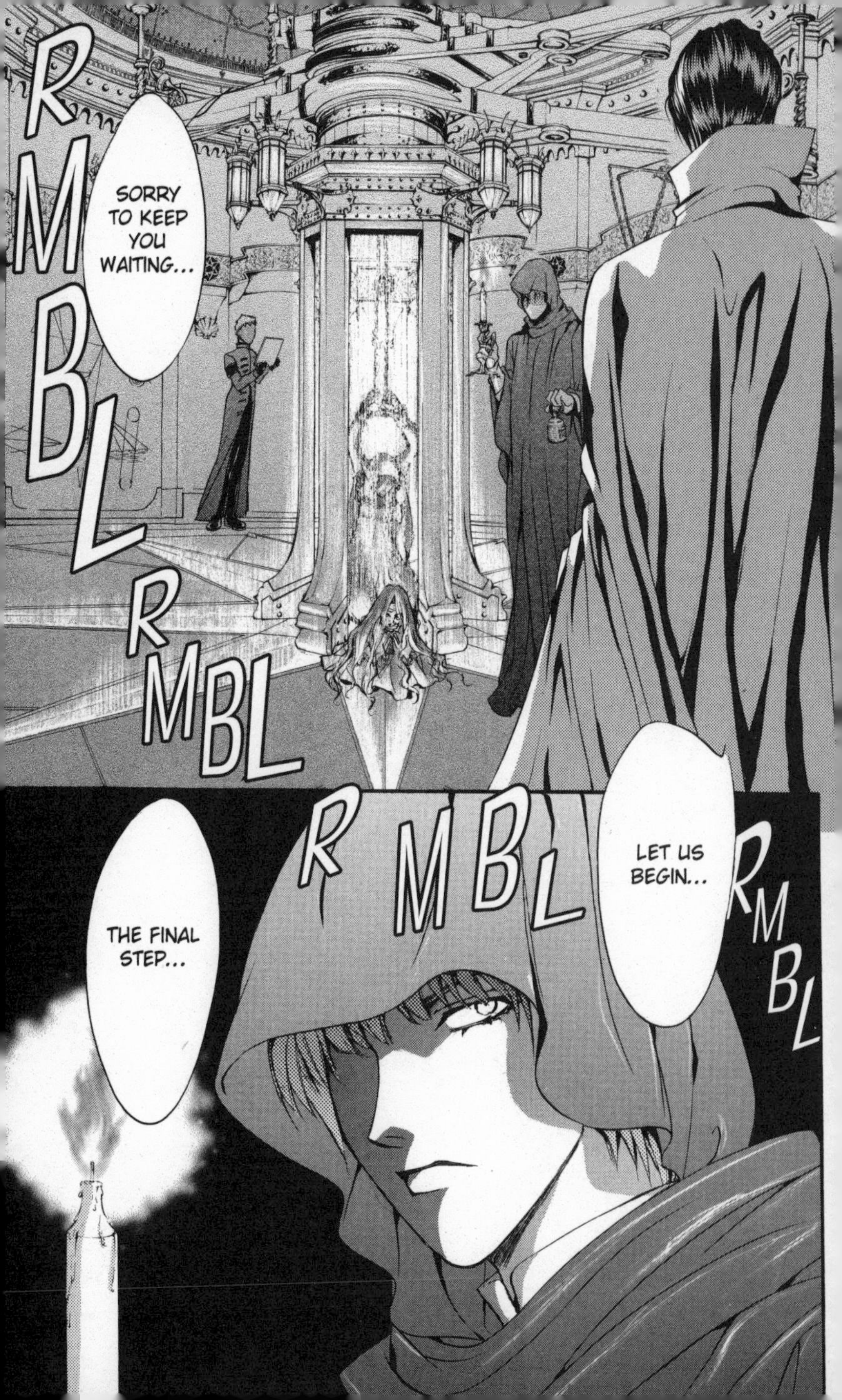
RMBL
SORRY TO KEEP YOU WAITING...
RMBL
RMBL
LET US BEGIN...
RMBL
THE FINAL STEP...

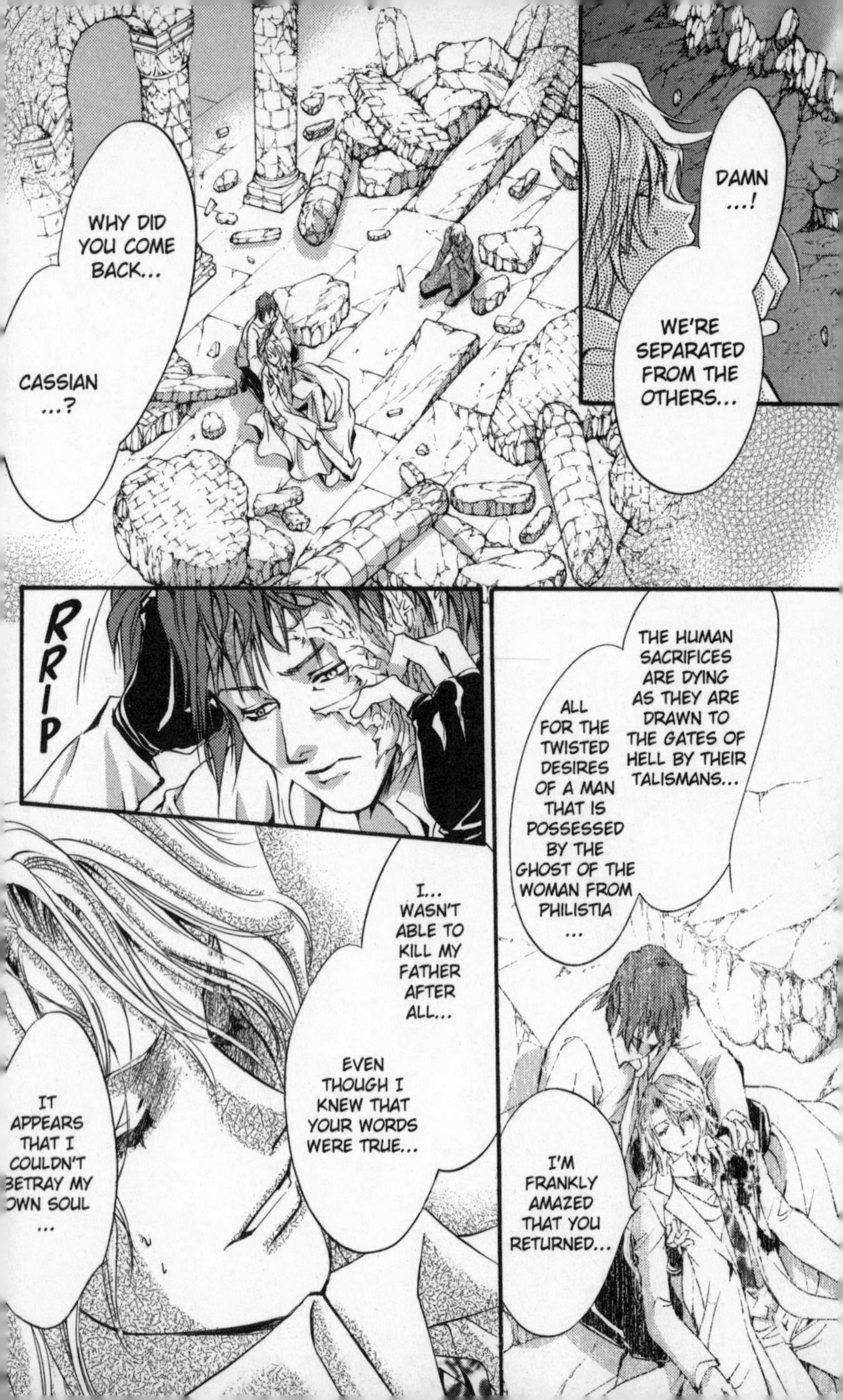
DAMN ...!
WE'RE SEPARATED FROM THE OTHERS...
WHY DID YOU COME BACK...
CASSIAN ...?
THE HUMAN SACRIFICES ARE DYING AS THEY ARE DRAWN TO THE GATES OF HELL BY THEIR TALISMANS...
ALL FOR THE TWISTED DESIRES OF A MAN THAT IS POSSESSED BY THE GHOST OF THE WOMAN FROM PHILISTIA ...
I'M FRANKLY AMAZED THAT YOU RETURNED...
RRIP
I... WASN'T ABLE TO KILL MY FATHER AFTER ALL...
EVEN THOUGH I KNEW THAT YOUR WORDS WERE TRUE...
IT APPEARS THAT I COULDN'T BETRAY MY OWN SOUL ...

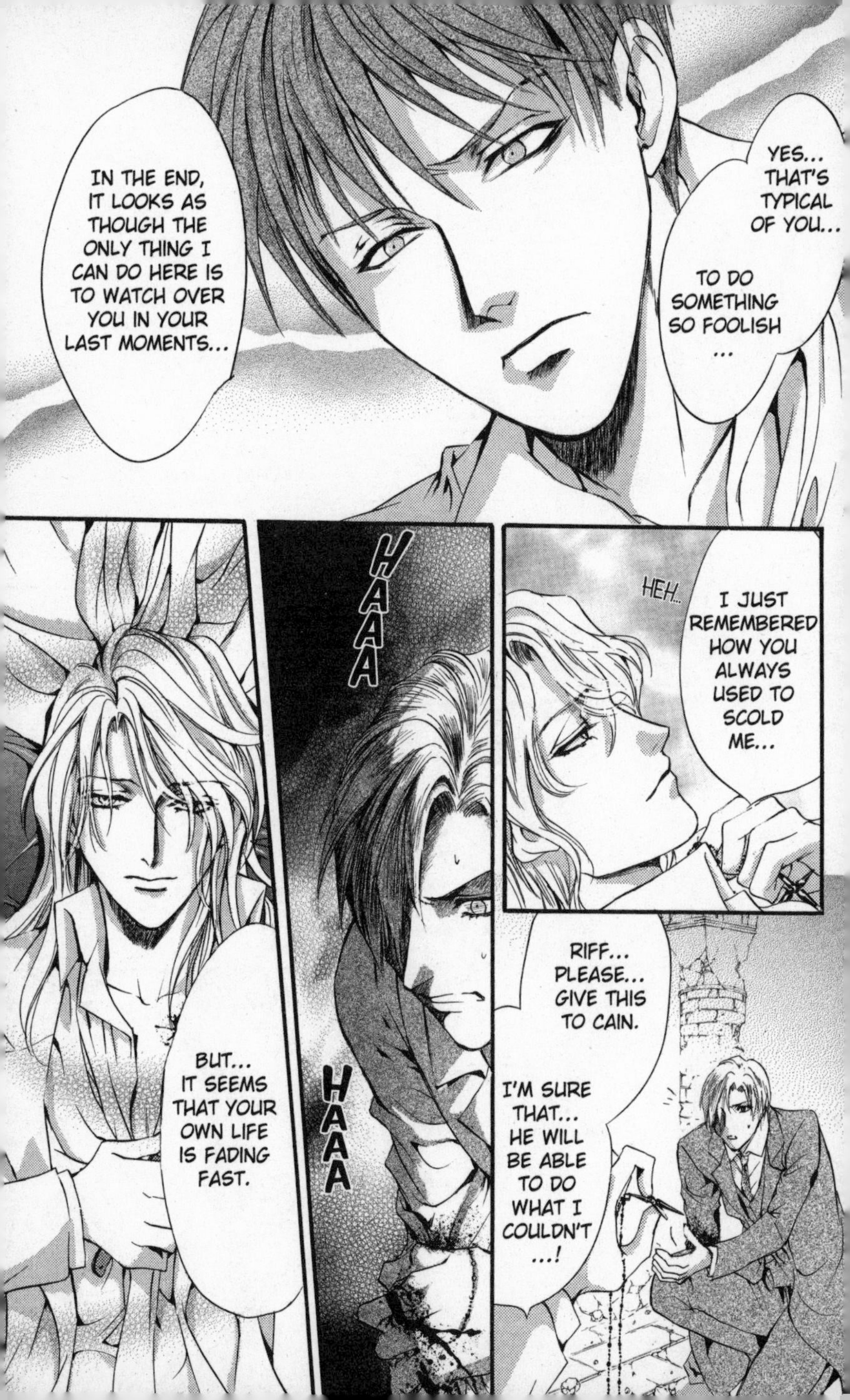
YES... THAT'S TYPICAL OF YOU...
TO DO SOMETHING SO FOOLISH ...
IN THE END, IT LOOKS AS THOUGH THE ONLY THING I CAN DO HERE IS TO WATCH OVER YOU IN YOUR LAST MOMENTS...
I JUST REMEMBERED HOW YOU ALWAYS USED TO SCOLD ME...
HEH..
RIFF... PLEASE... GIVE THIS TO CAIN.
I'M SURE THAT... HE WILL BE ABLE TO DO WHAT I COULDN'T ...!
HAAAA
HAAA
BUT... IT SEEMS THAT YOUR OWN LIFE IS FADING FAST.

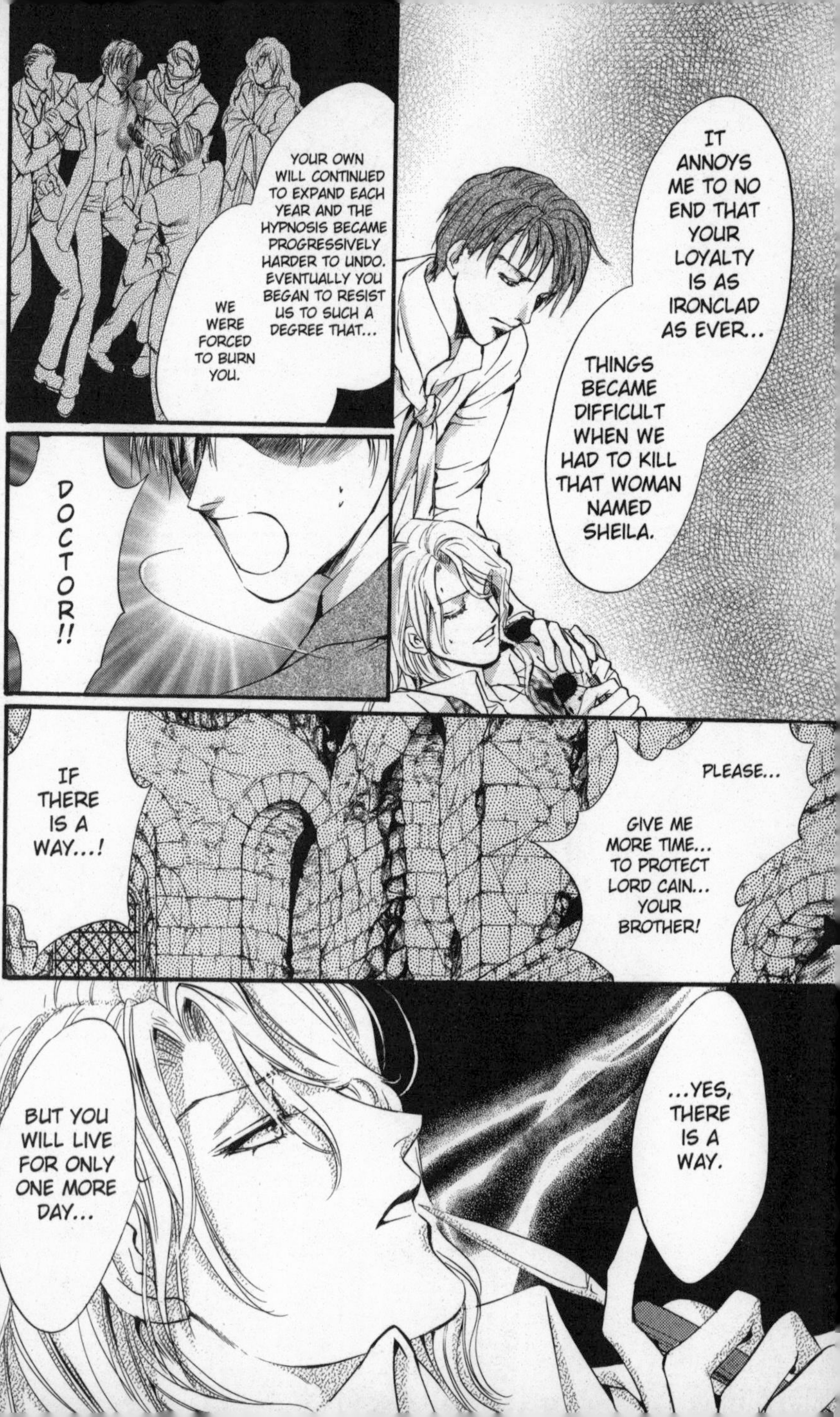
IT ANNOYS ME TO NO END THAT YOUR LOYALTY IS AS IRONCLAD AS EVER...
THINGS BECAME DIFFICULT WHEN WE HAD TO KILL THAT WOMAN NAMED SHEILA.
YOUR OWN WILL CONTINUED TO EXPAND EACH YEAR AND THE HYPNOSIS BECAME PROGRESSIVELY HARDER TO UNDO. EVENTUALLY YOU BEGAN TO RESIST US TO SUCH A DEGREE THAT...
WE WERE FORCED TO BURN YOU.
DOCTOR!!
PLEASE...
GIVE ME MORE TIME... TO PROTECT LORD CAIN... YOUR BROTHER!
IF THERE IS A WAY...!
...YES, THERE IS A WAY.
BUT YOU WILL LIVE FOR ONLY ONE MORE DAY...

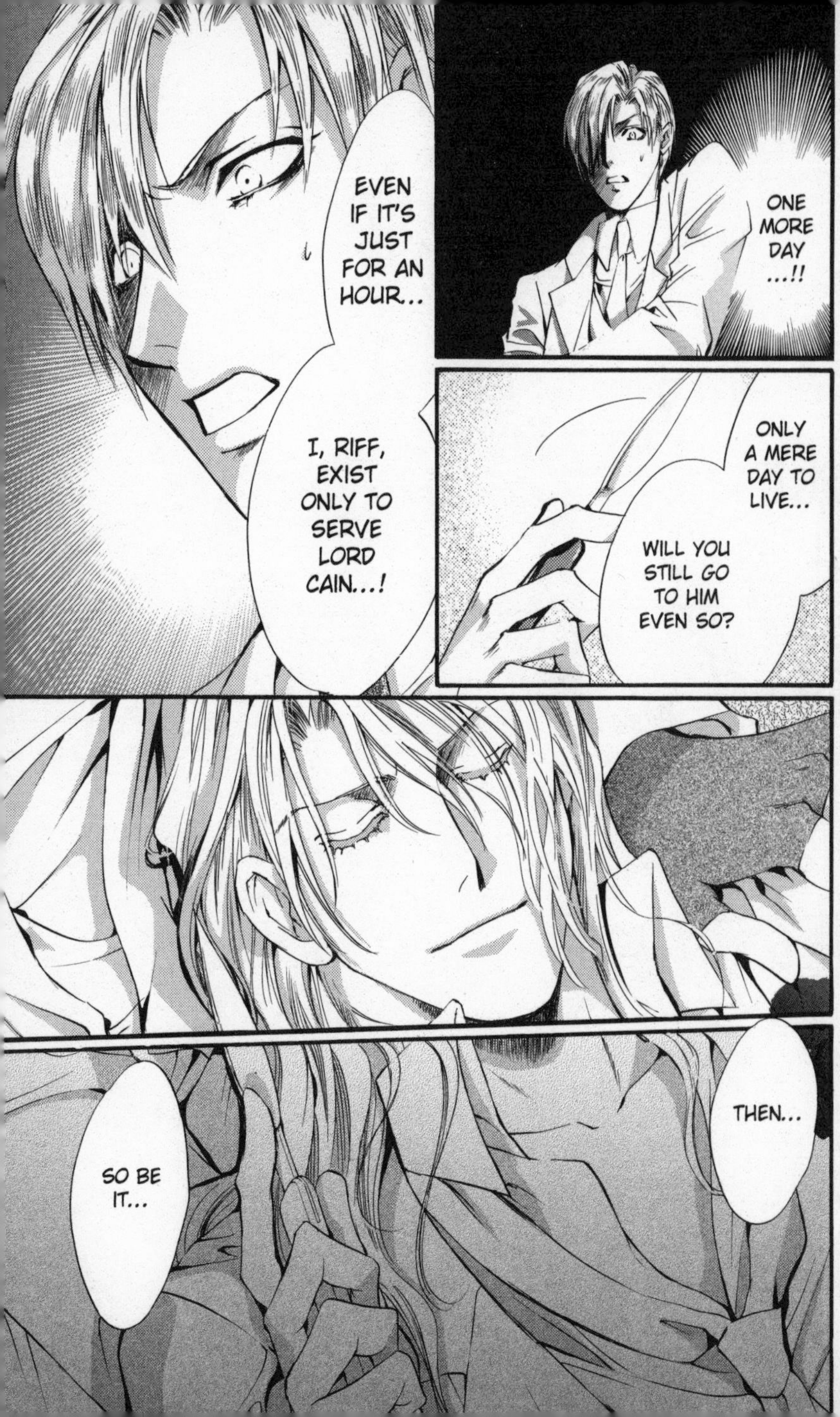
ONE MORE DAY ...!!
ONLY A MERE DAY TO LIVE...
WILL YOU STILL GO TO HIM EVEN SO?
EVEN IF IT'S JUST FOR AN HOUR...
I, RIFF, EXIST ONLY TO SERVE LORD CAIN...!
THEN...
SO BE IT...

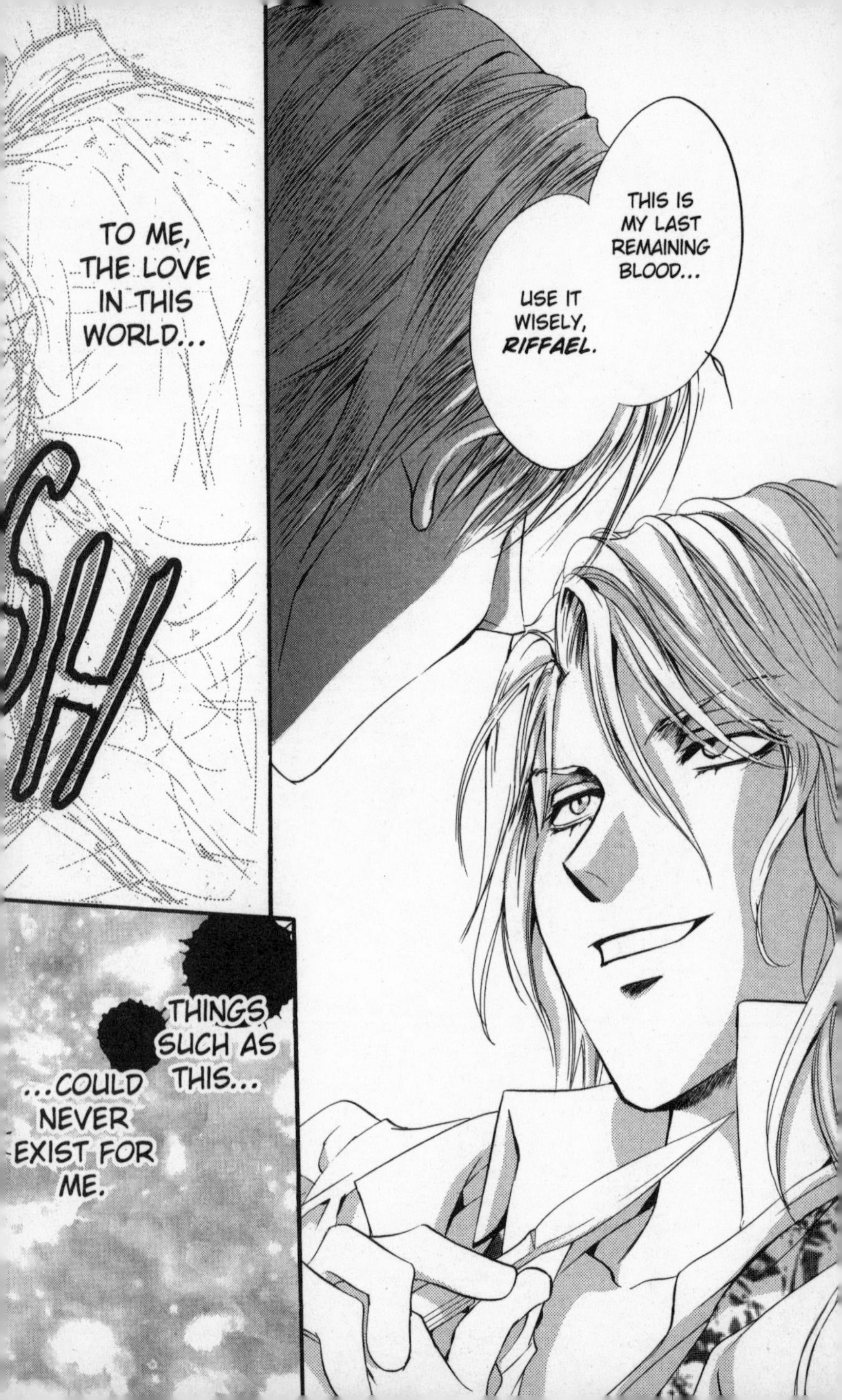
THIS IS MY LAST REMAINING BLOOD...
USE IT WISELY, *RIFFAEL*.
TO ME, THE LOVE IN THIS WORLD...
SH
THINGS SUCH AS THIS...
...COULD NEVER EXIST FOR ME.

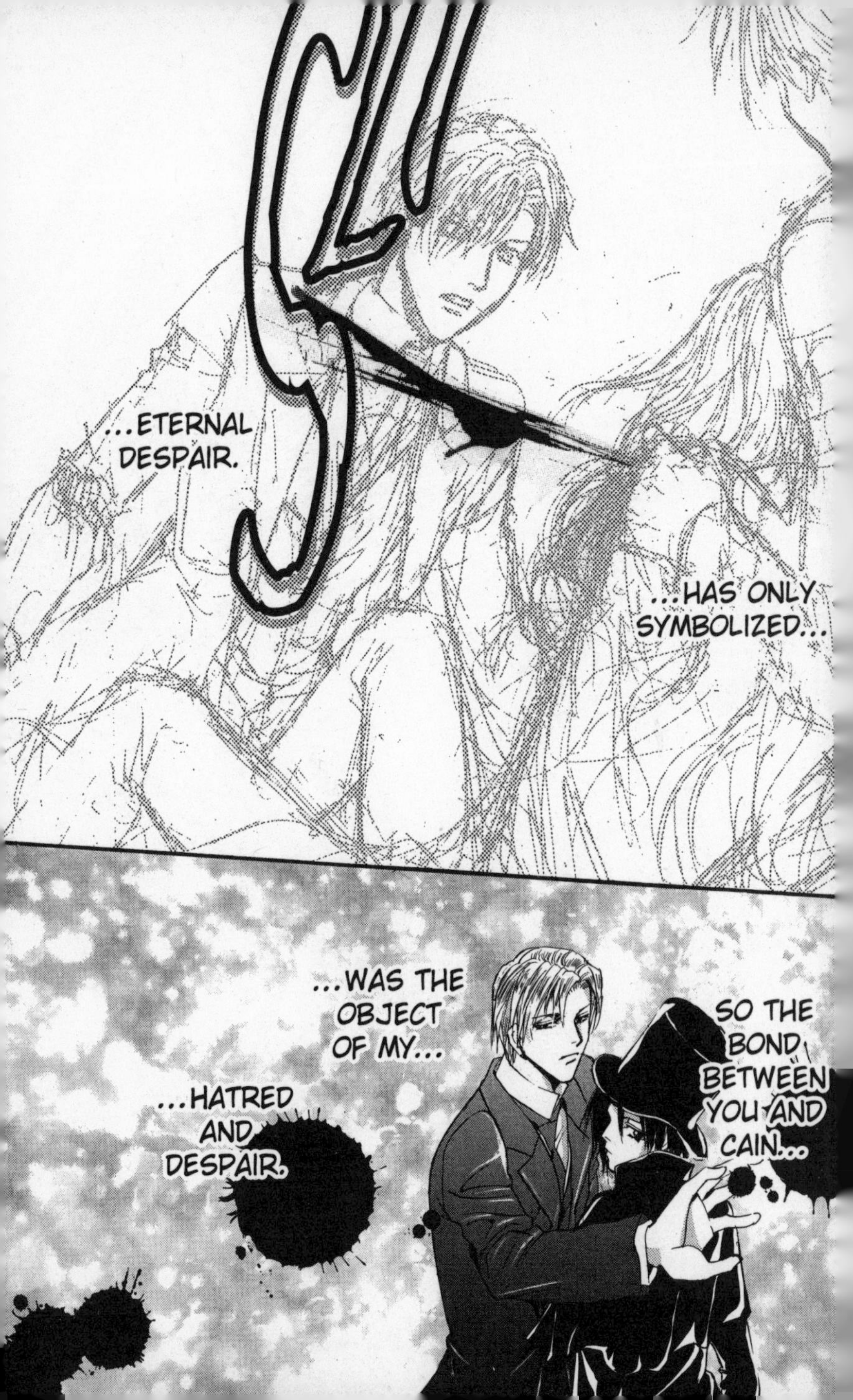
...HAS ONLY SYMBOLIZED...
...ETERNAL DESPAIR.
SO THE BOND BETWEEN YOU AND CAIN...
...WAS THE OBJECT OF MY...
...HATRED AND DESPAIR.

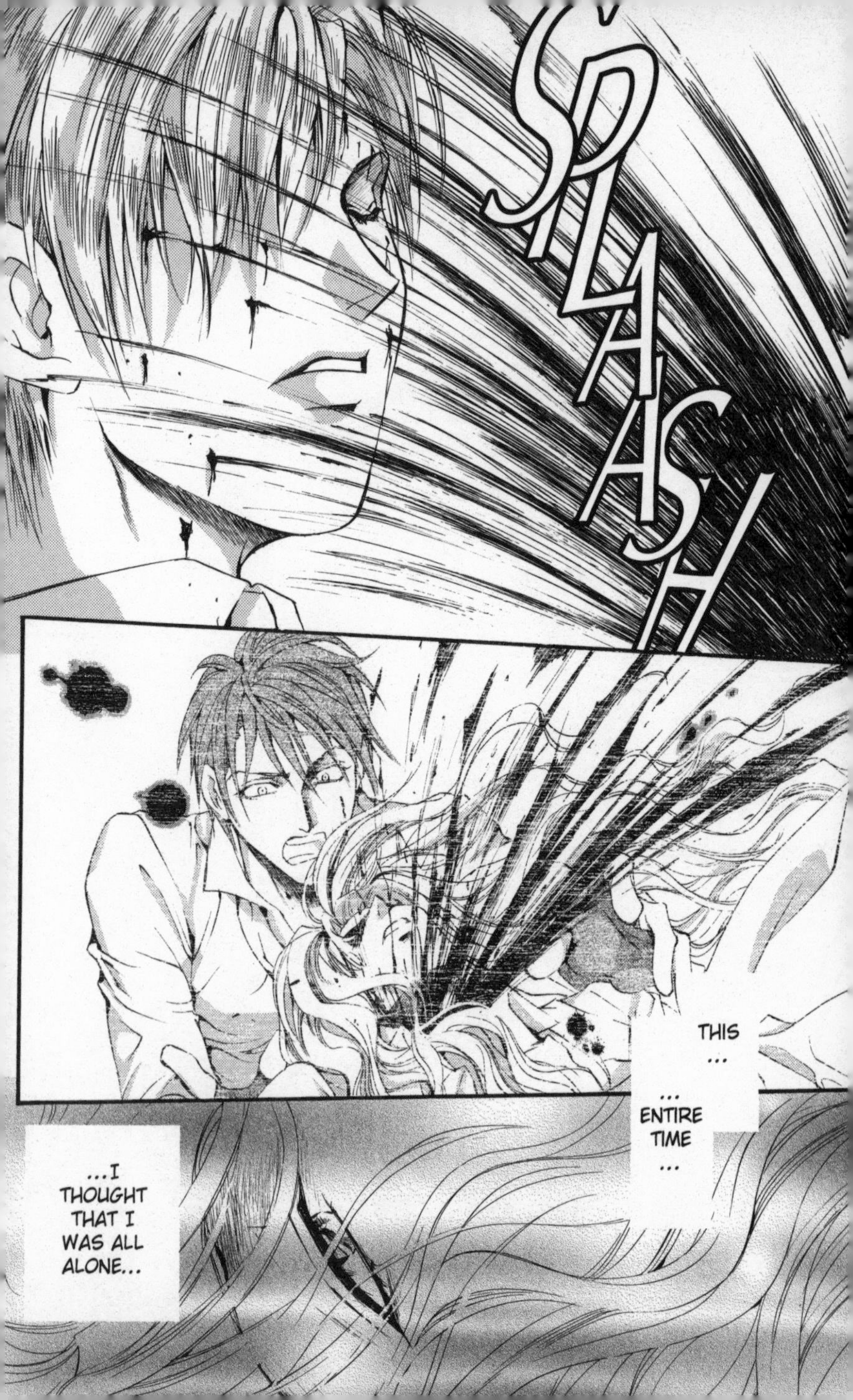
SPLASH
THIS ...
... ENTIRE TIME ...
...I THOUGHT THAT I WAS ALL ALONE...

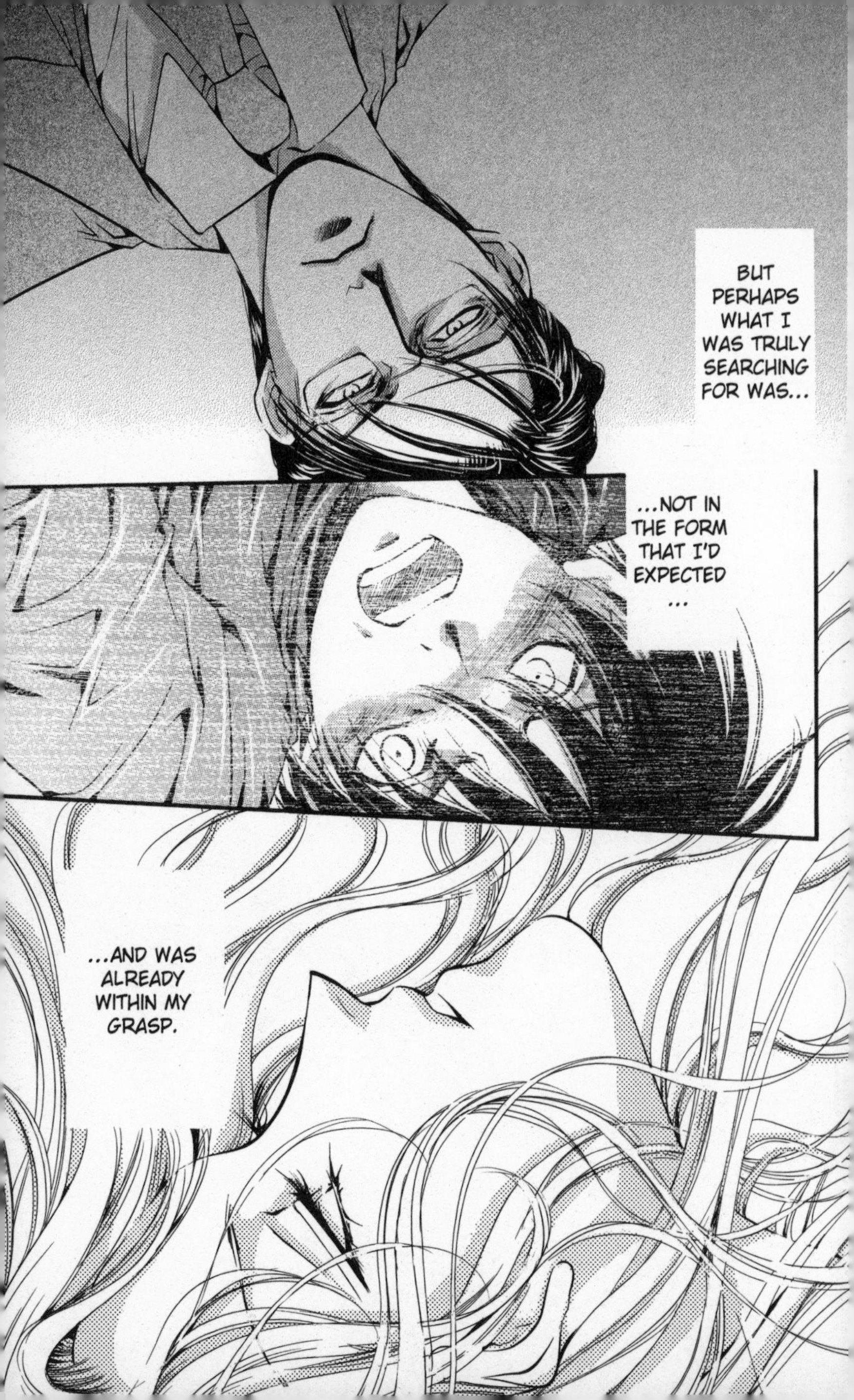
BUT PERHAPS WHAT I WAS TRULY SEARCHING FOR WAS...
...NOT IN THE FORM THAT I'D EXPECTED...
...AND WAS ALREADY WITHIN MY GRASP.

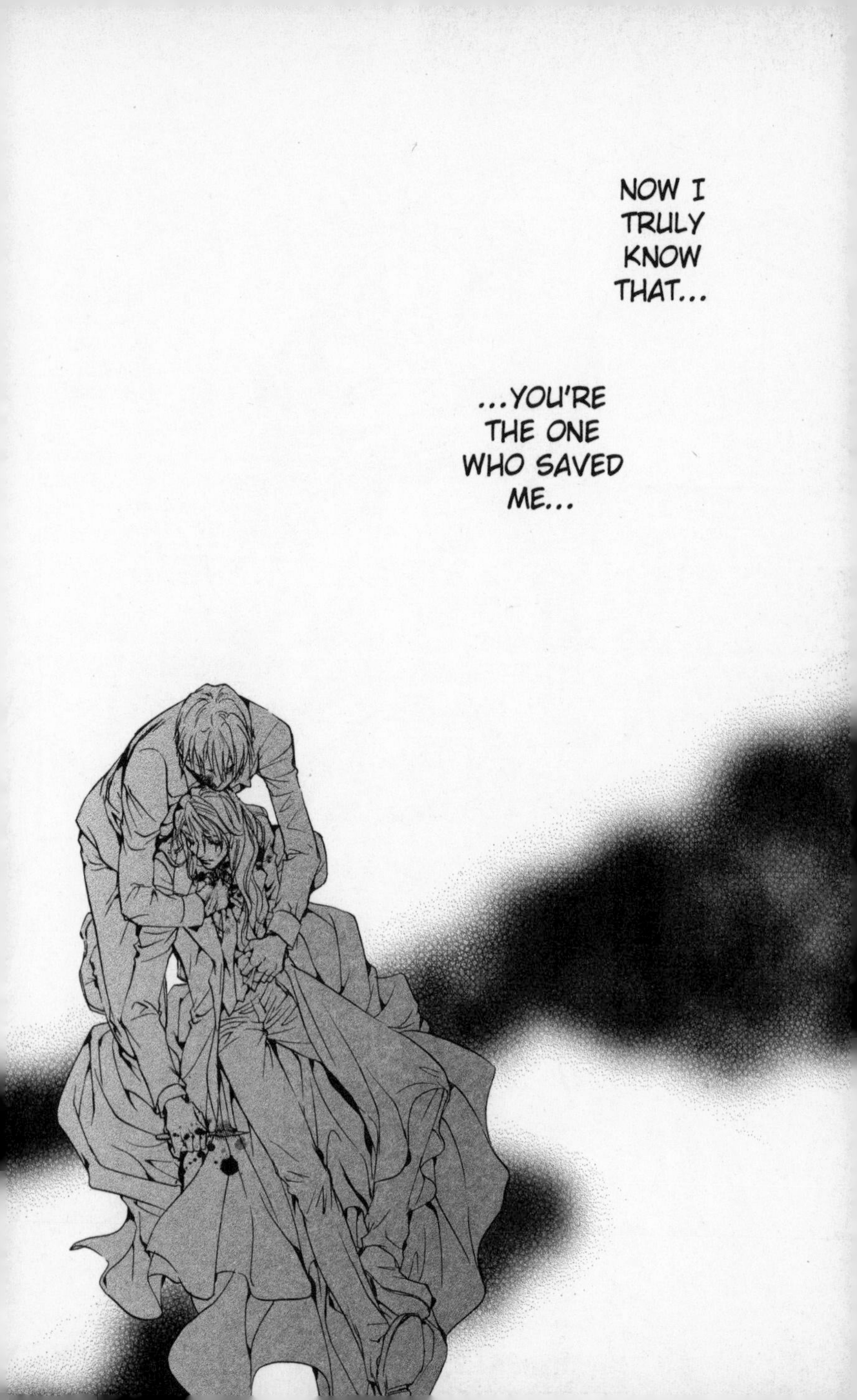
NOW I TRULY KNOW THAT...
...YOU'RE THE ONE WHO SAVED ME...

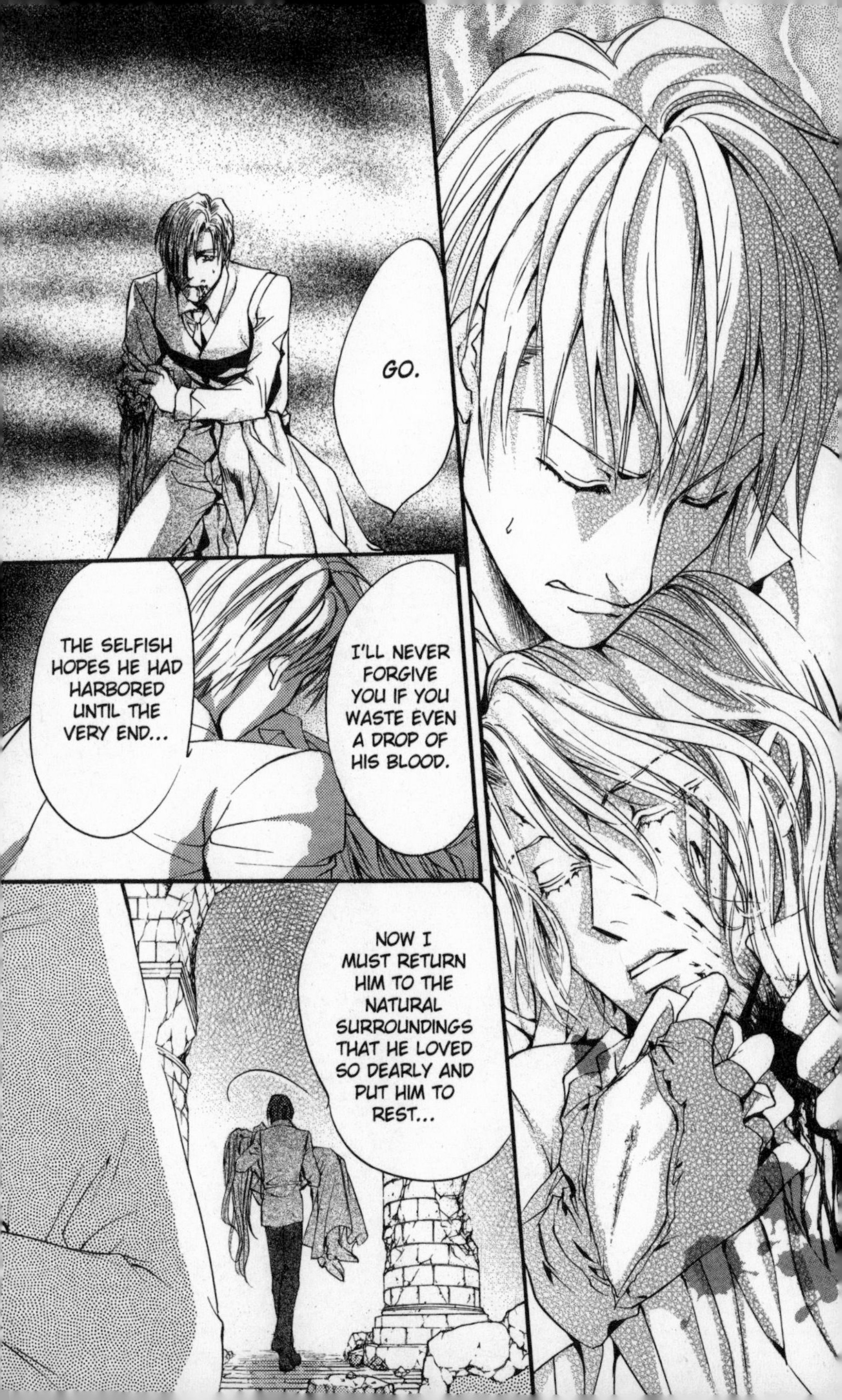
GO.
I'LL NEVER FORGIVE YOU IF YOU WASTE EVEN A DROP OF HIS BLOOD.
THE SELFISH HOPES HE HAD HARBORED UNTIL THE VERY END...
NOW I MUST RETURN HIM TO THE NATURAL SURROUNDINGS THAT HE LOVED SO DEARLY AND PUT HIM TO REST...

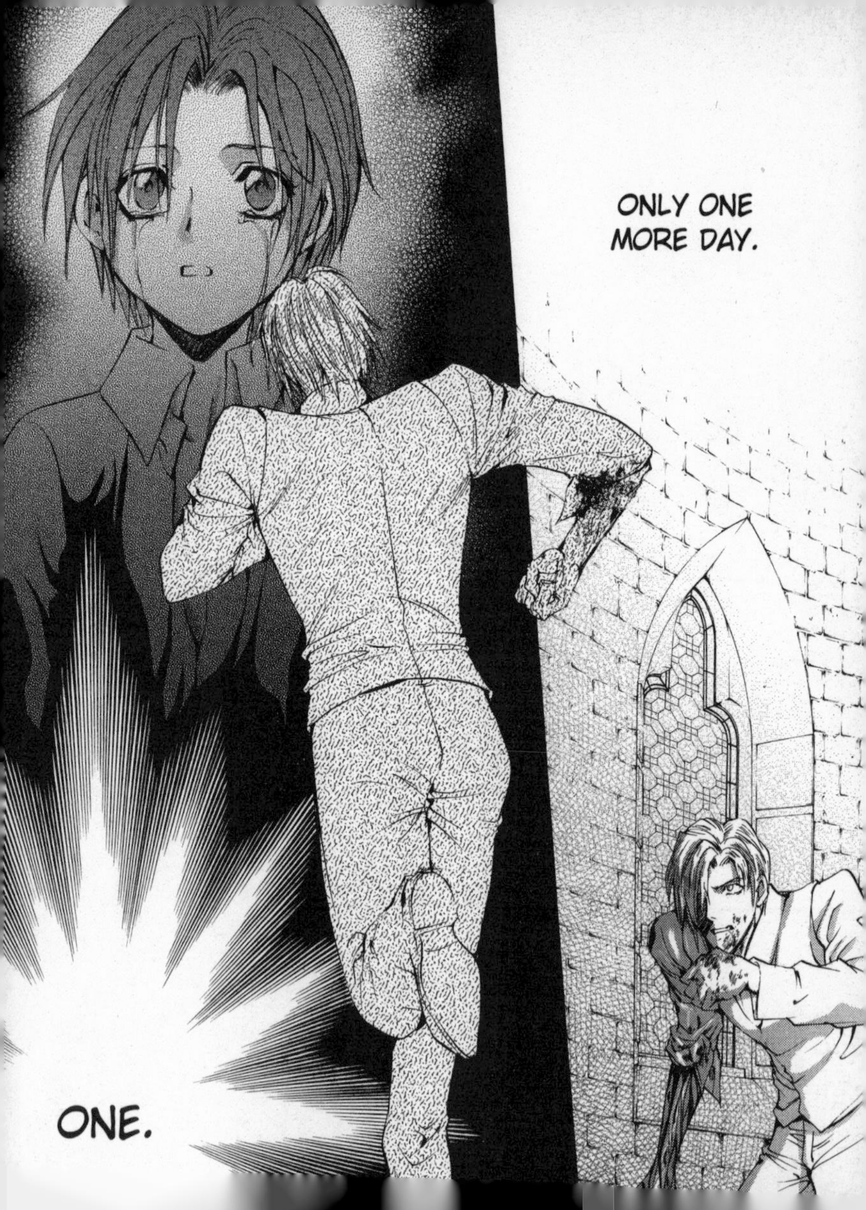
ONLY ONE MORE DAY.
ONE.

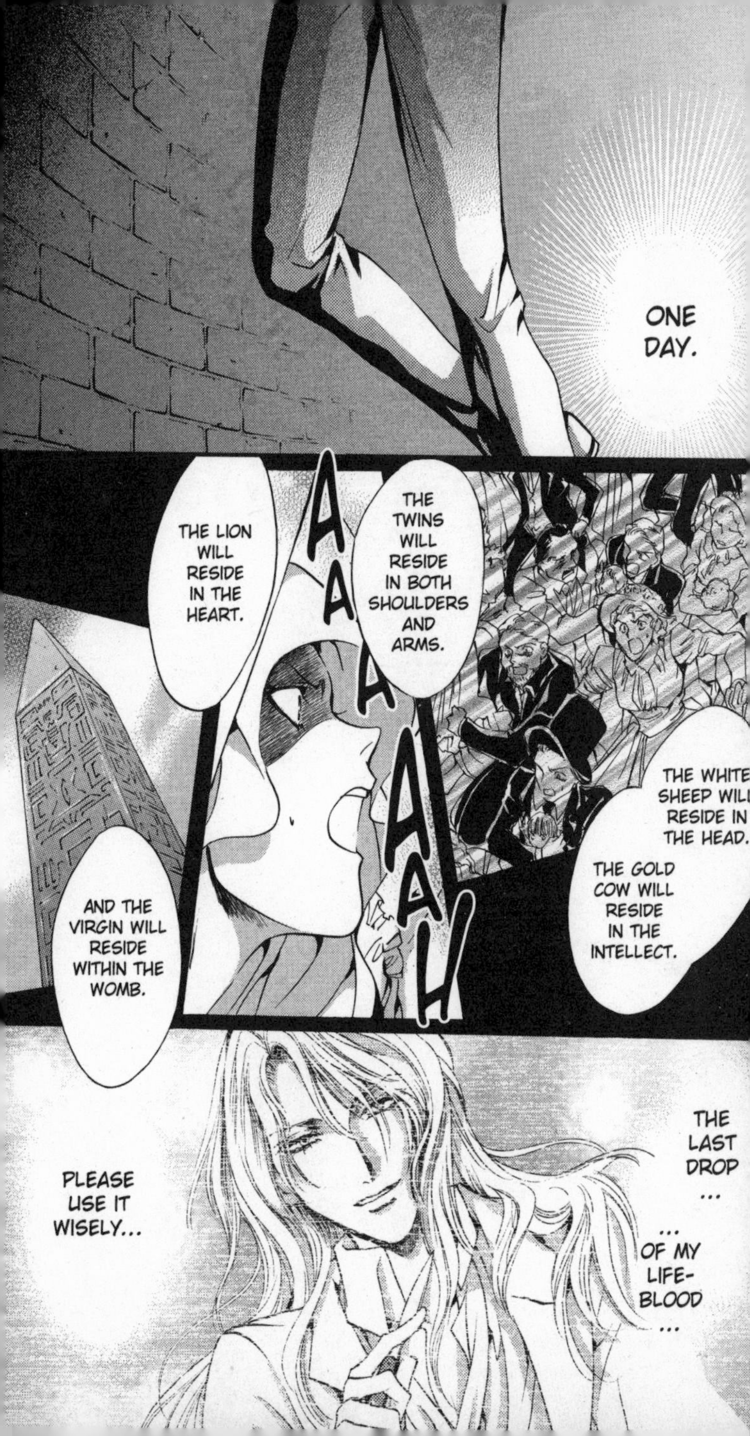
ONE DAY.
THE WHITE SHEEP WILL RESIDE IN THE HEAD.
THE GOLD COW WILL RESIDE IN THE INTELLECT.
THE TWINS WILL RESIDE IN BOTH SHOULDERS AND ARMS.
AAAAAH
THE LION WILL RESIDE IN THE HEART.
AND THE VIRGIN WILL RESIDE WITHIN THE WOMB.
THE LAST DROP ...
... OF MY LIFE-BLOOD ...
PLEASE USE IT WISELY...

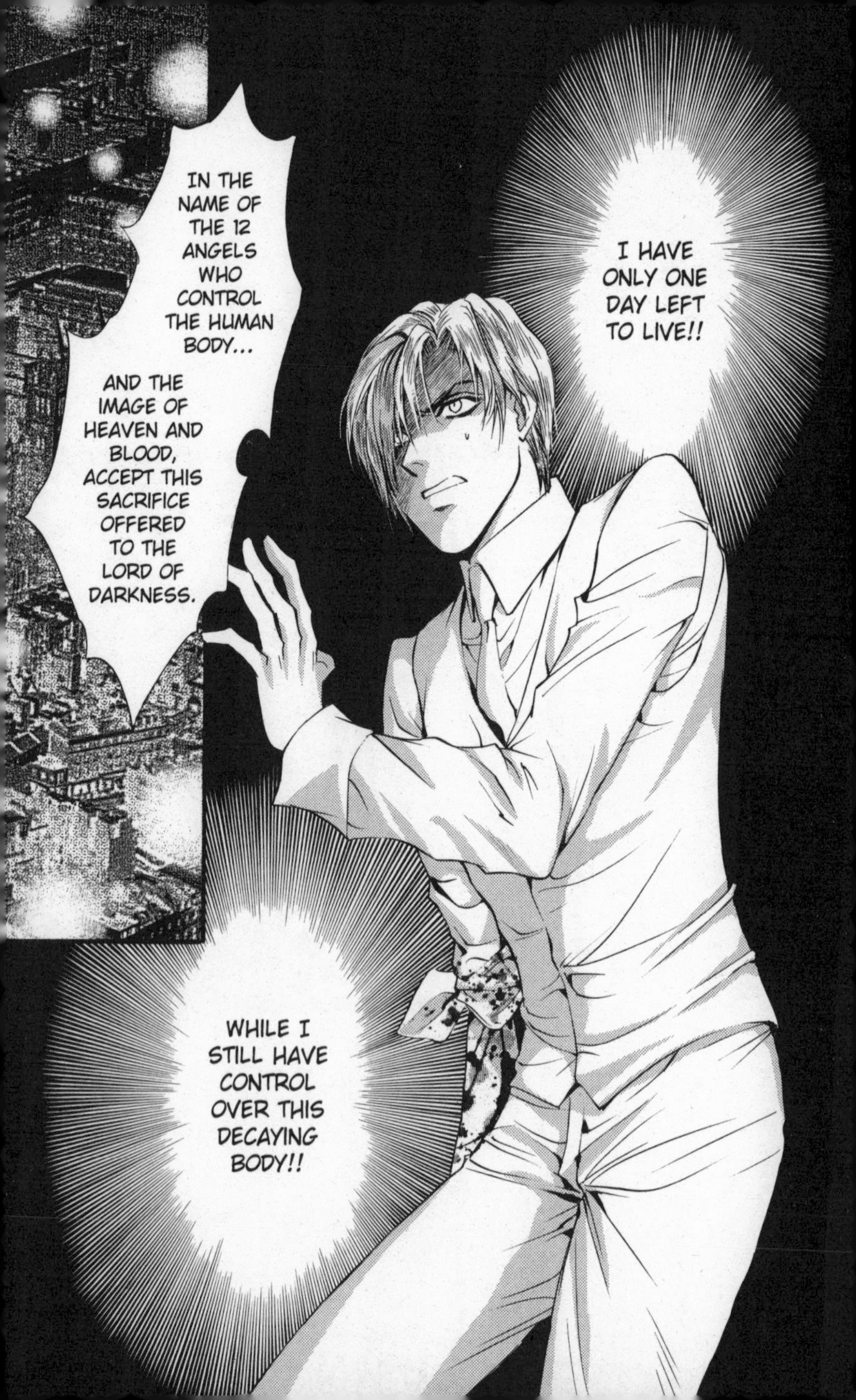
I HAVE ONLY ONE DAY LEFT TO LIVE!!
IN THE NAME OF THE 12 ANGELS WHO CONTROL THE HUMAN BODY... AND THE IMAGE OF HEAVEN AND BLOOD, ACCEPT THIS SACRIFICE OFFERED TO THE LORD OF DARKNESS.
WHILE I STILL HAVE CONTROL OVER THIS DECAYING BODY!!

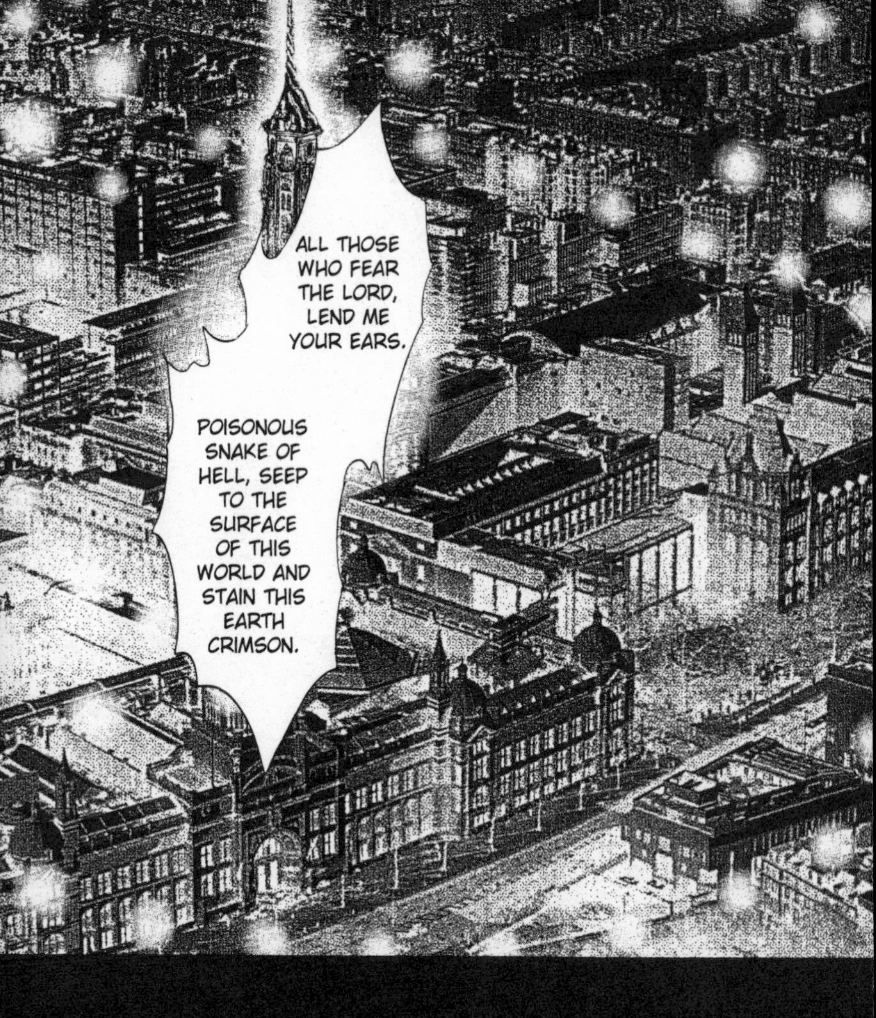
ALL THOSE WHO FEAR THE LORD, LEND ME YOUR EARS.
POISONOUS SNAKE OF HELL, SEEP TO THE SURFACE OF THIS WORLD AND STAIN THIS EARTH CRIMSON.

Godless

Scene V

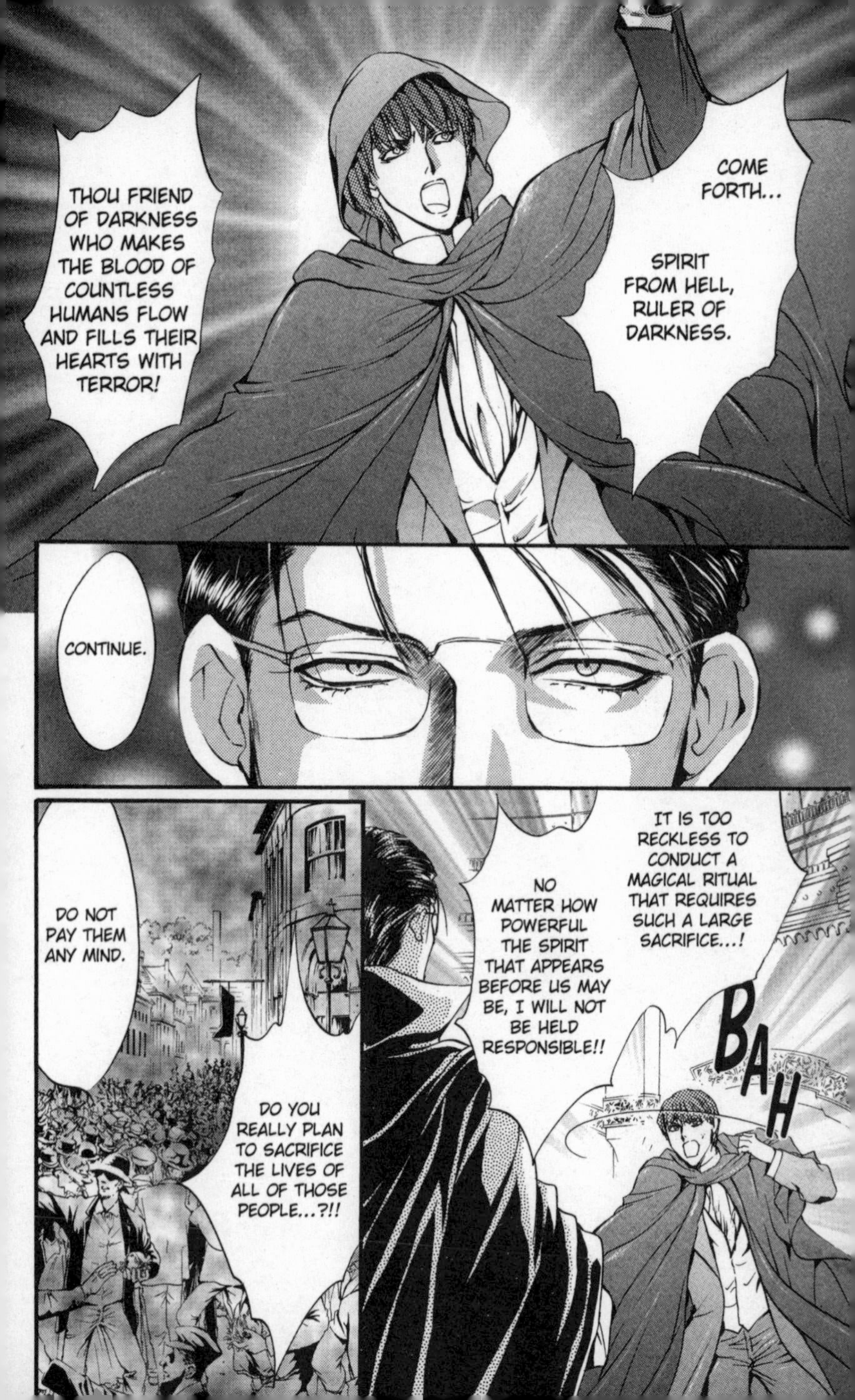
COME FORTH...
SPIRIT FROM HELL, RULER OF DARKNESS.
THOU FRIEND OF DARKNESS WHO MAKES THE BLOOD OF COUNTLESS HUMANS FLOW AND FILLS THEIR HEARTS WITH TERROR!
CONTINUE.
IT IS TOO RECKLESS TO CONDUCT A MAGICAL RITUAL THAT REQUIRES SUCH A LARGE SACRIFICE...!
NO MATTER HOW POWERFUL THE SPIRIT THAT APPEARS BEFORE US MAY BE, I WILL NOT BE HELD RESPONSIBLE!!
BAH
DO YOU REALLY PLAN TO SACRIFICE THE LIVES OF ALL OF THOSE PEOPLE...?!!
DO NOT PAY THEM ANY MIND.

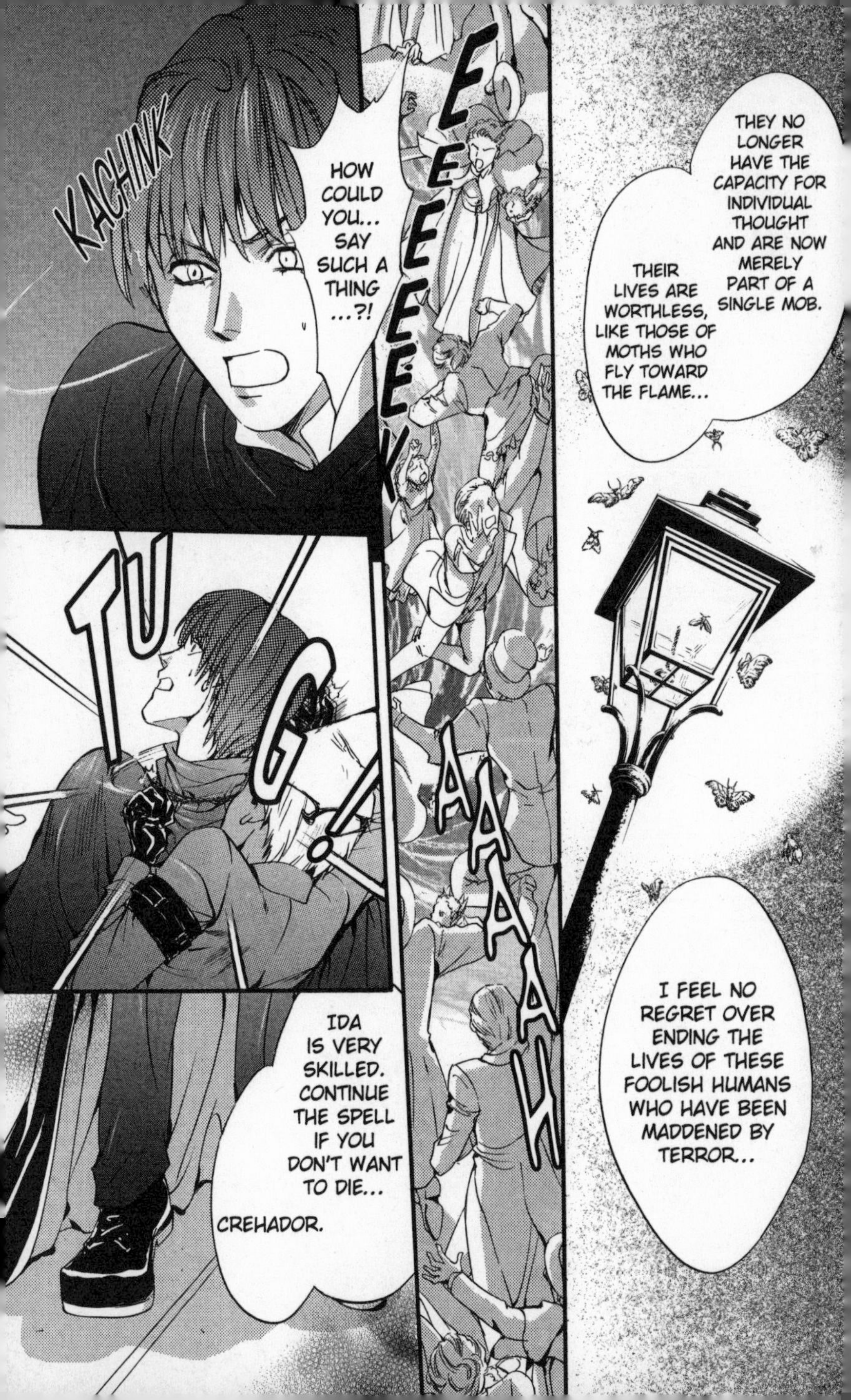
THEY NO LONGER HAVE THE CAPACITY FOR INDIVIDUAL THOUGHT AND ARE NOW MERELY PART OF A SINGLE MOB.
THEIR LIVES ARE WORTHLESS, LIKE THOSE OF MOTHS WHO FLY TOWARD THE FLAME...
I FEEL NO REGRET OVER ENDING THE LIVES OF THESE FOOLISH HUMANS WHO HAVE BEEN MADDENED BY TERROR...
KACHINK
HOW COULD YOU... SAY SUCH A THING ...?!
EEEEEEEK
TUG!
AAAAAH
IDA IS VERY SKILLED. CONTINUE THE SPELL IF YOU DON'T WANT TO DIE...
CREHADOR.

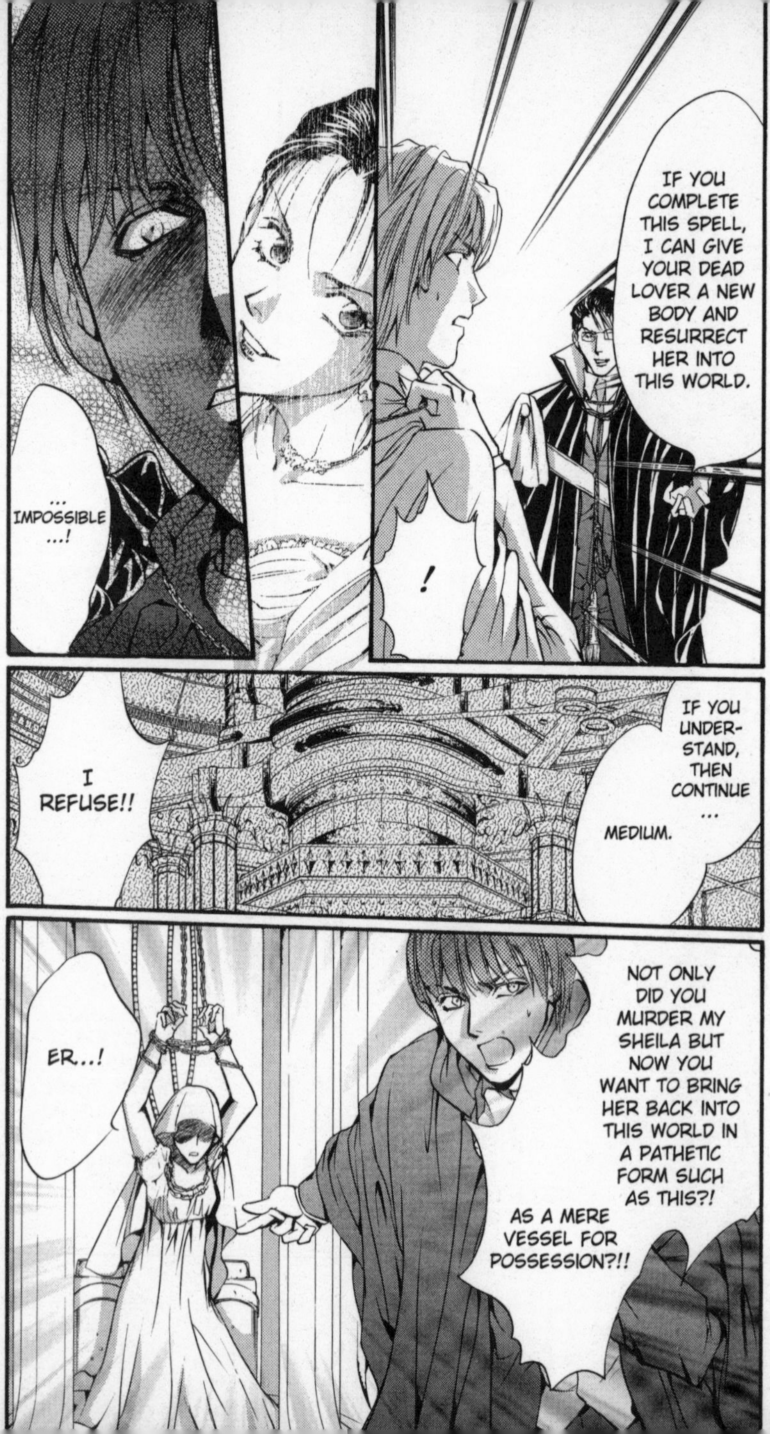
IF YOU COMPLETE THIS SPELL, I CAN GIVE YOUR DEAD LOVER A NEW BODY AND RESURRECT HER INTO THIS WORLD.
!
...IMPOSSIBLE...!
IF YOU UNDER-STAND, THEN CONTINUE ... MEDIUM.
I REFUSE!!
NOT ONLY DID YOU MURDER MY SHEILA BUT NOW YOU WANT TO BRING HER BACK INTO THIS WORLD IN A PATHETIC FORM SUCH AS THIS?!
AS A MERE VESSEL FOR POSSESSION?!!
ER...!

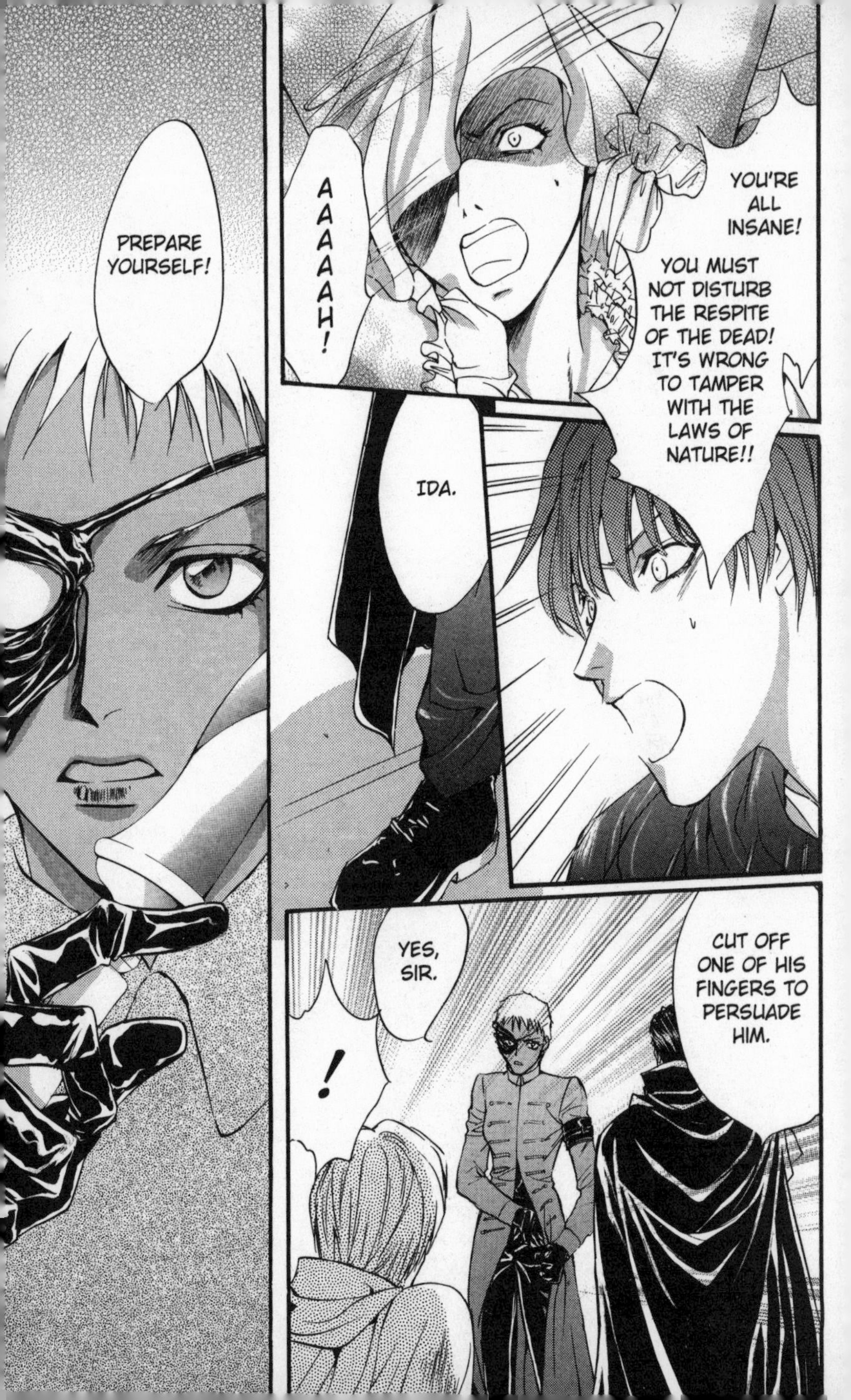
YOU'RE ALL INSANE!
YOU MUST NOT DISTURB THE RESPITE OF THE DEAD! IT'S WRONG TO TAMPER WITH THE LAWS OF NATURE!!
AAAAAH!
IDA.
CUT OFF ONE OF HIS FINGERS TO PERSUADE HIM.
YES, SIR.
!
PREPARE YOURSELF!

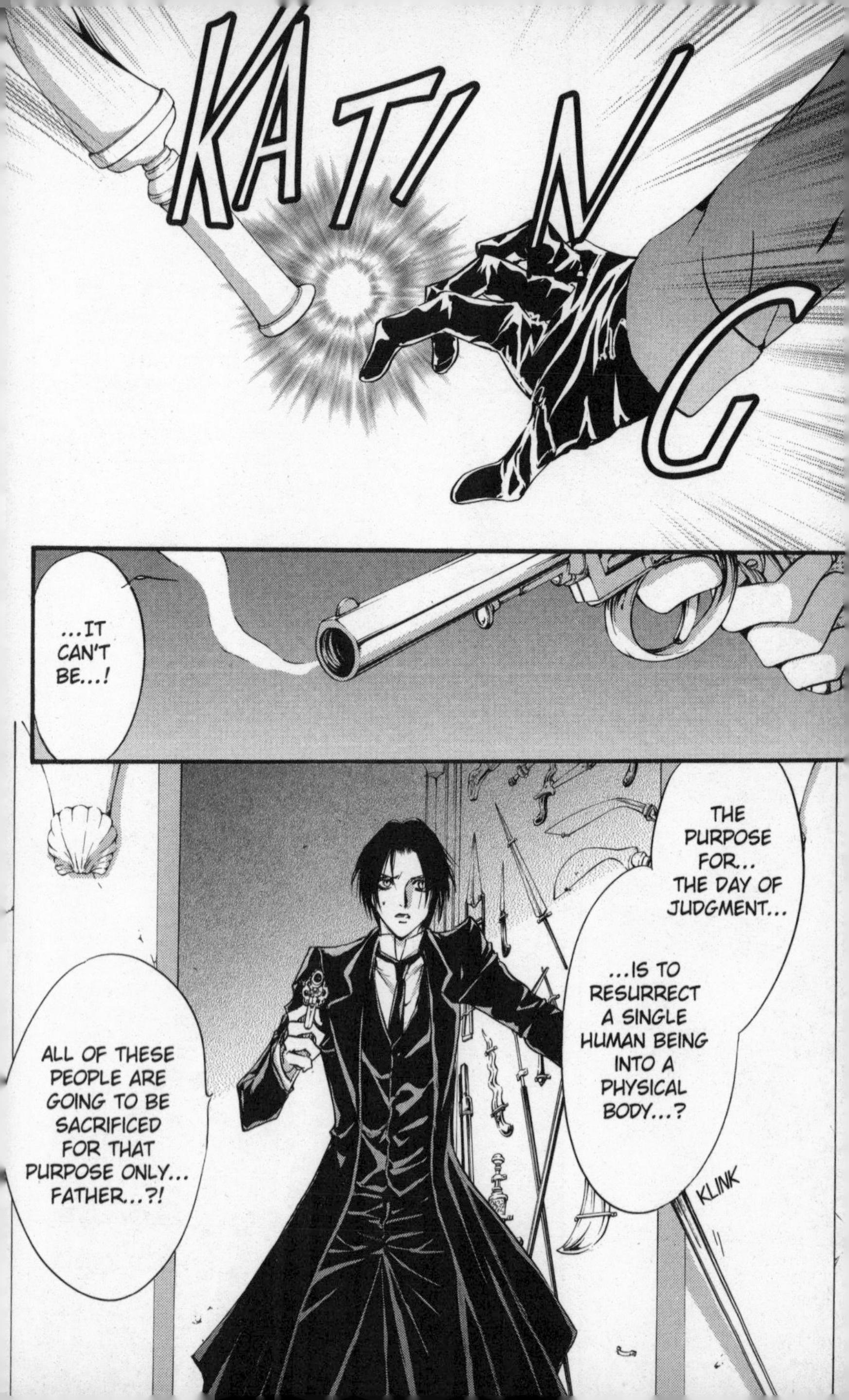
KATINC
...IT CAN'T BE...!
THE PURPOSE FOR... THE DAY OF JUDGMENT...
...IS TO RESURRECT A SINGLE HUMAN BEING INTO A PHYSICAL BODY...?
KLINK
ALL OF THESE PEOPLE ARE GOING TO BE SACRIFICED FOR THAT PURPOSE ONLY... FATHER...?!

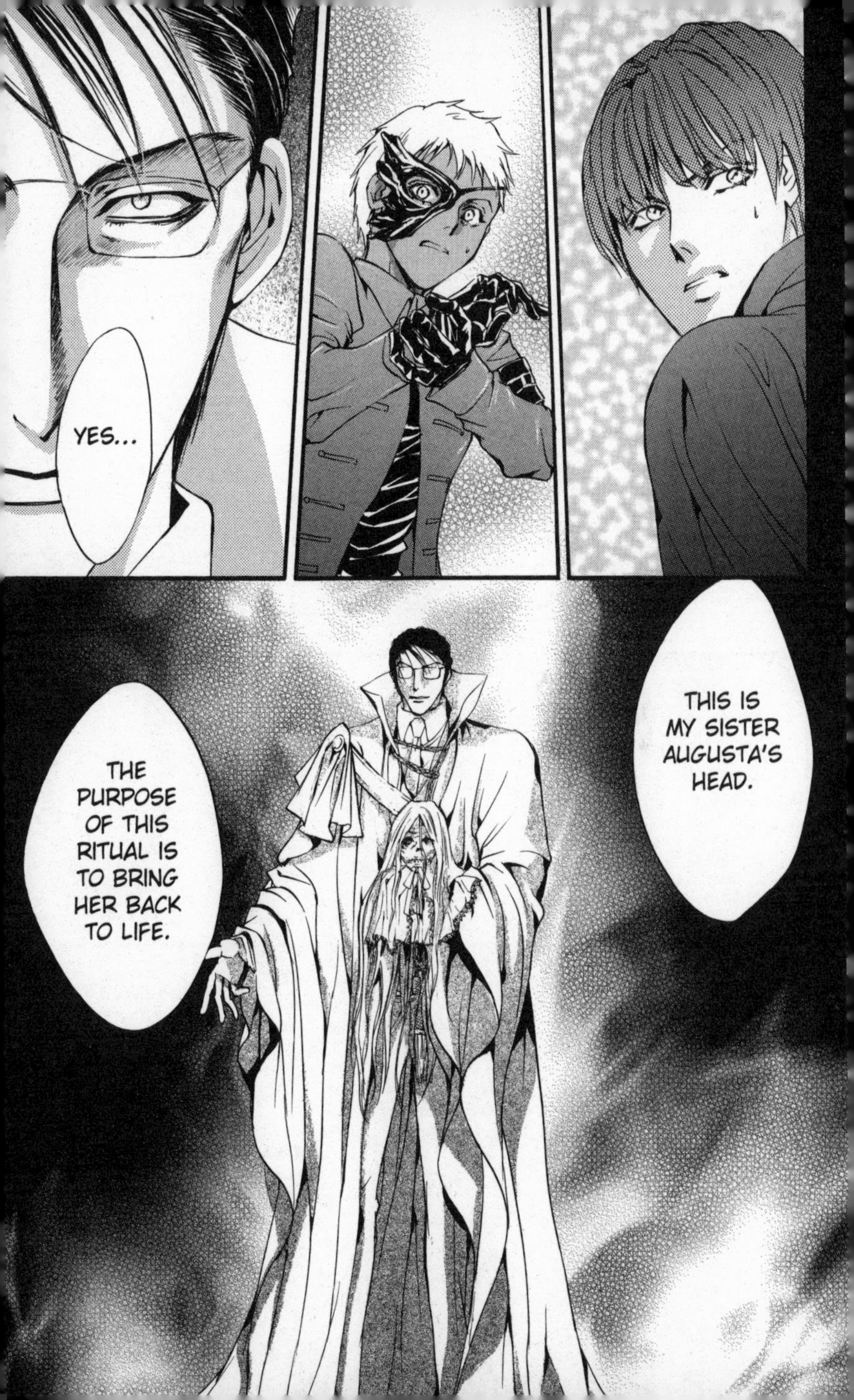
YES...
THIS IS MY SISTER AUGUSTA'S HEAD.
THE PURPOSE OF THIS RITUAL IS TO BRING HER BACK TO LIFE.

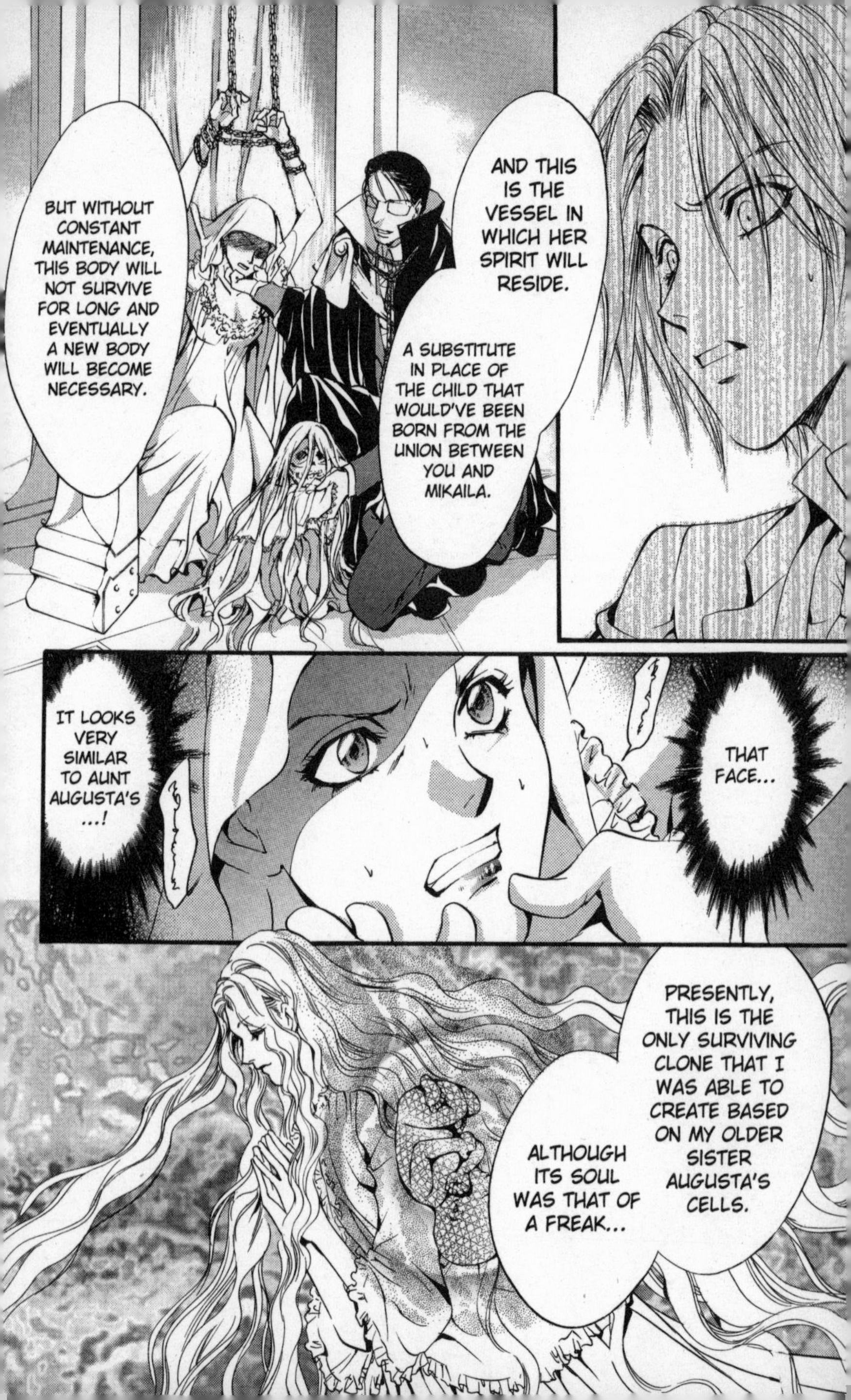
AND THIS IS THE VESSEL IN WHICH HER SPIRIT WILL RESIDE.
A SUBSTITUTE IN PLACE OF THE CHILD THAT WOULD'VE BEEN BORN FROM THE UNION BETWEEN YOU AND MIKAILA.
BUT WITHOUT CONSTANT MAINTENANCE, THIS BODY WILL NOT SURVIVE FOR LONG AND EVENTUALLY A NEW BODY WILL BECOME NECESSARY.
THAT FACE...
IT LOOKS VERY SIMILAR TO AUNT AUGUSTA'S ...!
PRESENTLY, THIS IS THE ONLY SURVIVING CLONE THAT I WAS ABLE TO CREATE BASED ON MY OLDER SISTER AUGUSTA'S CELLS.
ALTHOUGH ITS SOUL WAS THAT OF A FREAK...

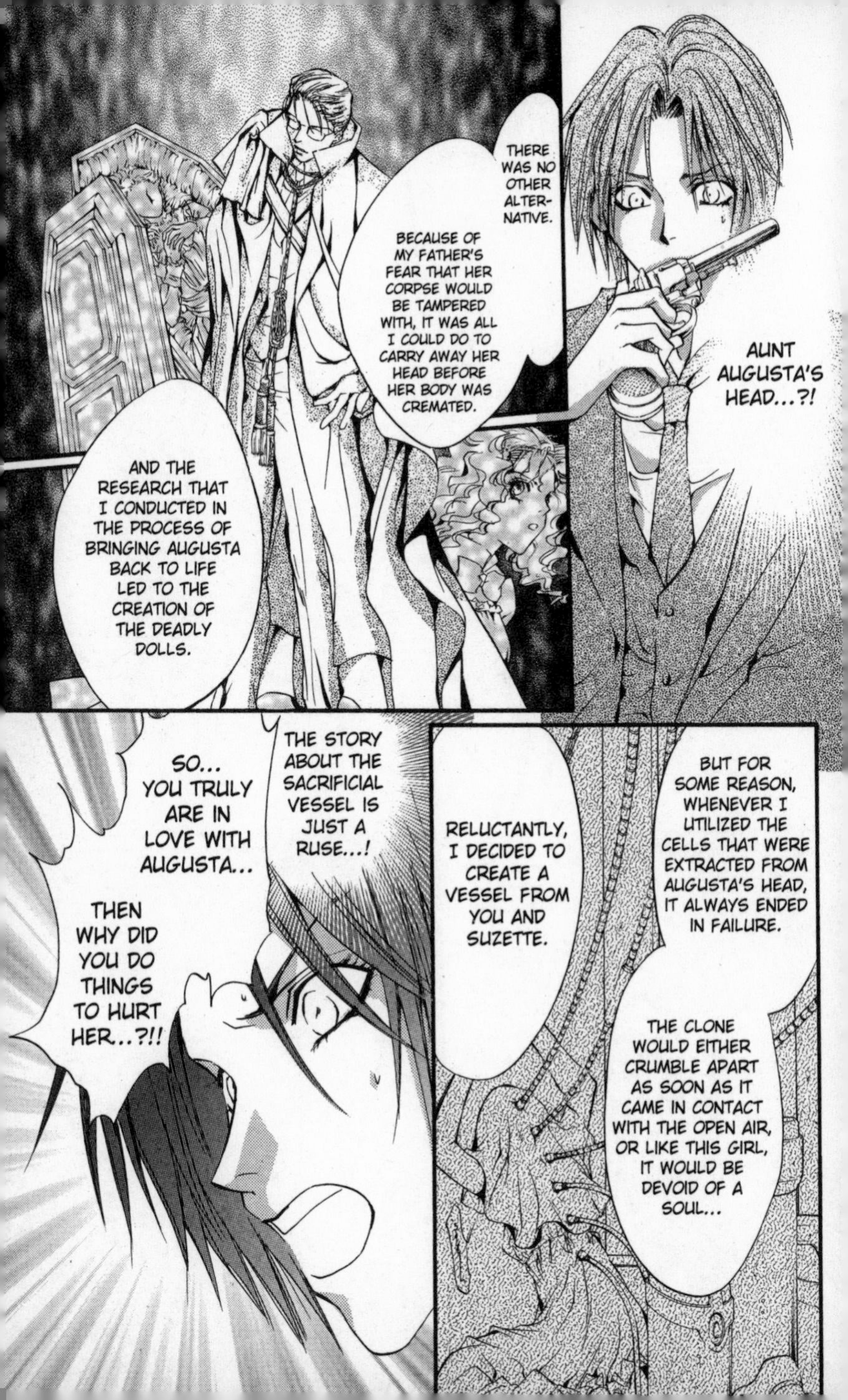
AUNT AUGUSTA'S HEAD...?!
THERE WAS NO OTHER ALTER-NATIVE.
BECAUSE OF MY FATHER'S FEAR THAT HER CORPSE WOULD BE TAMPERED WITH, IT WAS ALL I COULD DO TO CARRY AWAY HER HEAD BEFORE HER BODY WAS CREMATED.
AND THE RESEARCH THAT I CONDUCTED IN THE PROCESS OF BRINGING AUGUSTA BACK TO LIFE LED TO THE CREATION OF THE DEADLY DOLLS.
BUT FOR SOME REASON, WHENEVER I UTILIZED THE CELLS THAT WERE EXTRACTED FROM AUGUSTA'S HEAD, IT ALWAYS ENDED IN FAILURE.
THE CLONE WOULD EITHER CRUMBLE APART AS SOON AS IT CAME IN CONTACT WITH THE OPEN AIR, OR LIKE THIS GIRL, IT WOULD BE DEVOID OF A SOUL...
RELUCTANTLY, I DECIDED TO CREATE A VESSEL FROM YOU AND SUZETTE.
THE STORY ABOUT THE SACRIFICIAL VESSEL IS JUST A RUSE...!
SO... YOU TRULY ARE IN LOVE WITH AUGUSTA...
THEN WHY DID YOU DO THINGS TO HURT HER...?!!

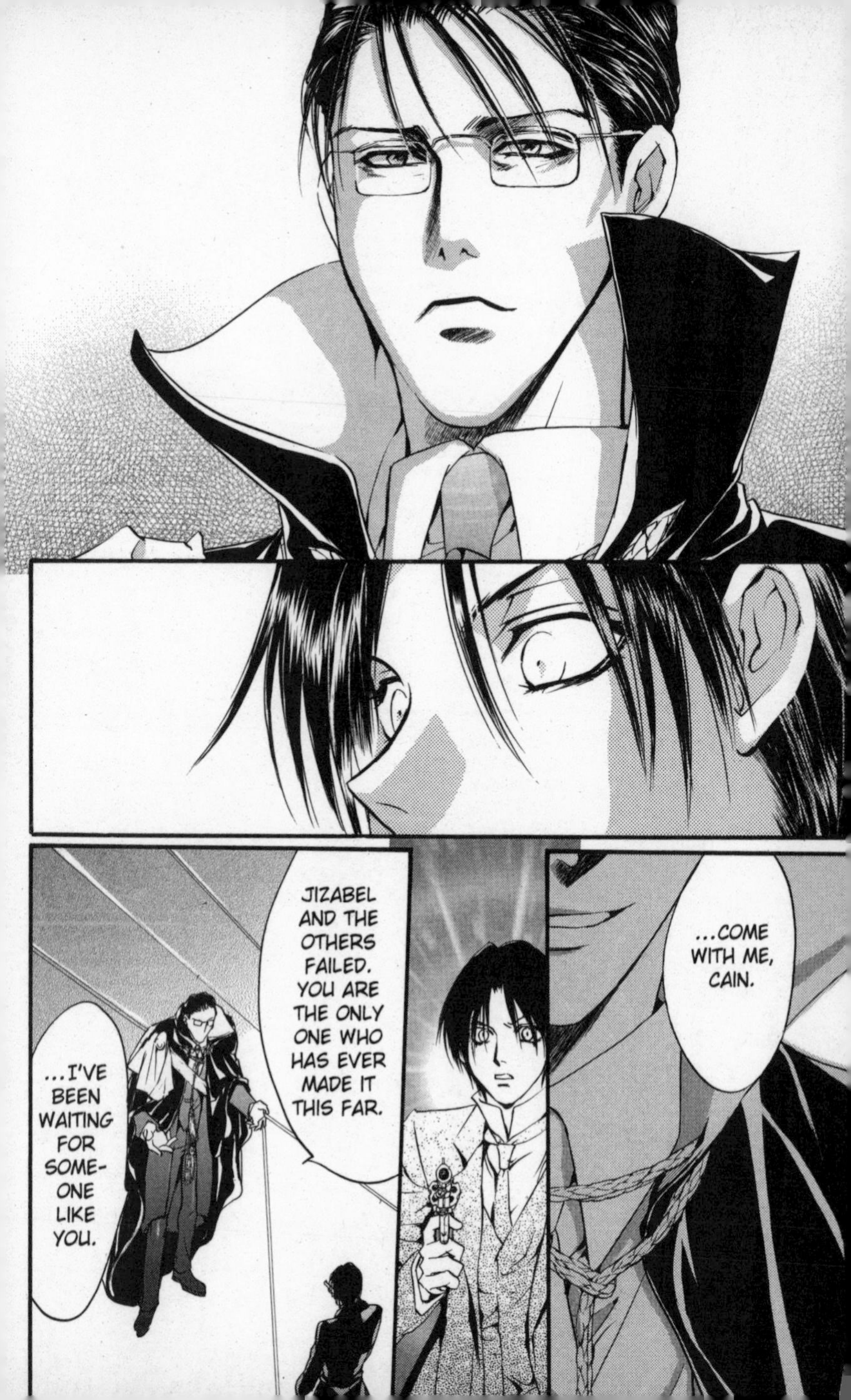
...COME WITH ME, CAIN.
JIZABEL AND THE OTHERS FAILED. YOU ARE THE ONLY ONE WHO HAS EVER MADE IT THIS FAR.
...I'VE BEEN WAITING FOR SOME-ONE LIKE YOU.

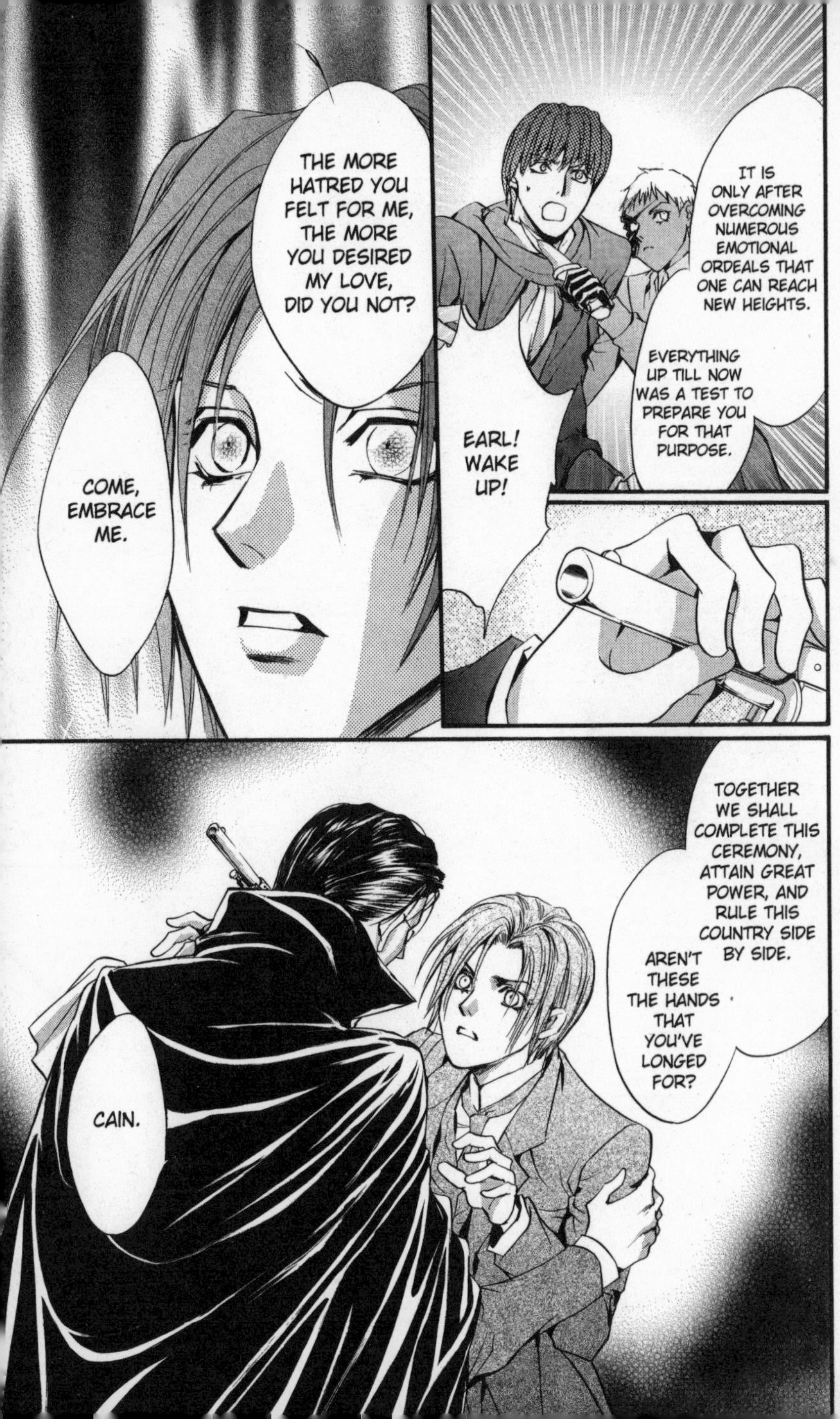
IT IS ONLY AFTER OVERCOMING NUMEROUS EMOTIONAL ORDEALS THAT ONE CAN REACH NEW HEIGHTS.
EVERYTHING UP TILL NOW WAS A TEST TO PREPARE YOU FOR THAT PURPOSE.
EARL! WAKE UP!
THE MORE HATRED YOU FELT FOR ME, THE MORE YOU DESIRED MY LOVE, DID YOU NOT?
COME, EMBRACE ME.
TOGETHER WE SHALL COMPLETE THIS CEREMONY, ATTAIN GREAT POWER, AND RULE THIS COUNTRY SIDE BY SIDE.
AREN'T THESE THE HANDS THAT YOU'VE LONGED FOR?
CAIN.

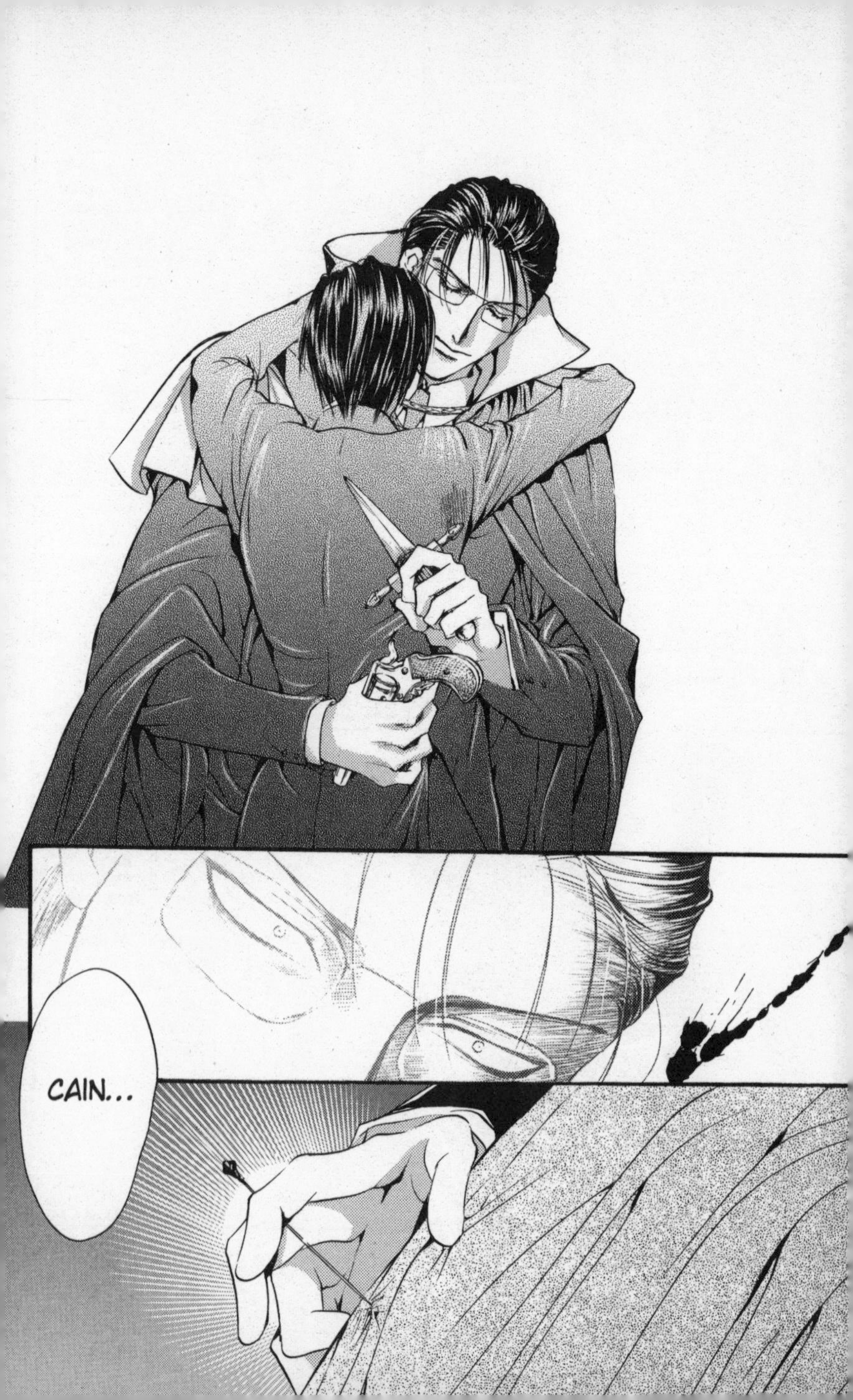
CAIN...

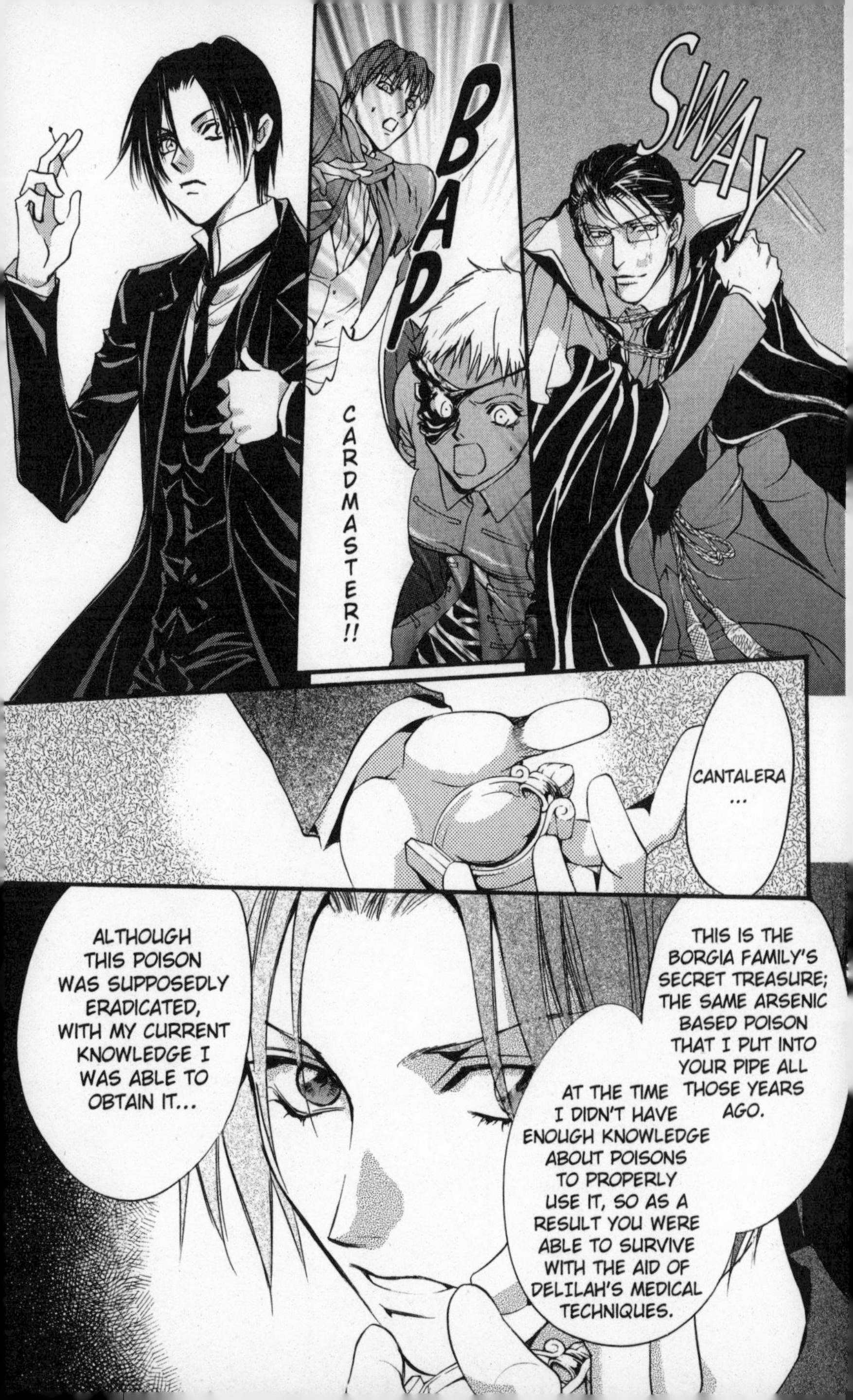
SWAY
BAP
CARDMASTER!!
CANTALERA ...
THIS IS THE BORGIA FAMILY'S SECRET TREASURE; THE SAME ARSENIC BASED POISON THAT I PUT INTO YOUR PIPE ALL THOSE YEARS AGO.
AT THE TIME I DIDN'T HAVE ENOUGH KNOWLEDGE ABOUT POISONS TO PROPERLY USE IT, SO AS A RESULT YOU WERE ABLE TO SURVIVE WITH THE AID OF DELILAH'S MEDICAL TECHNIQUES.
ALTHOUGH THIS POISON WAS SUPPOSEDLY ERADICATED, WITH MY CURRENT KNOWLEDGE I WAS ABLE TO OBTAIN IT...

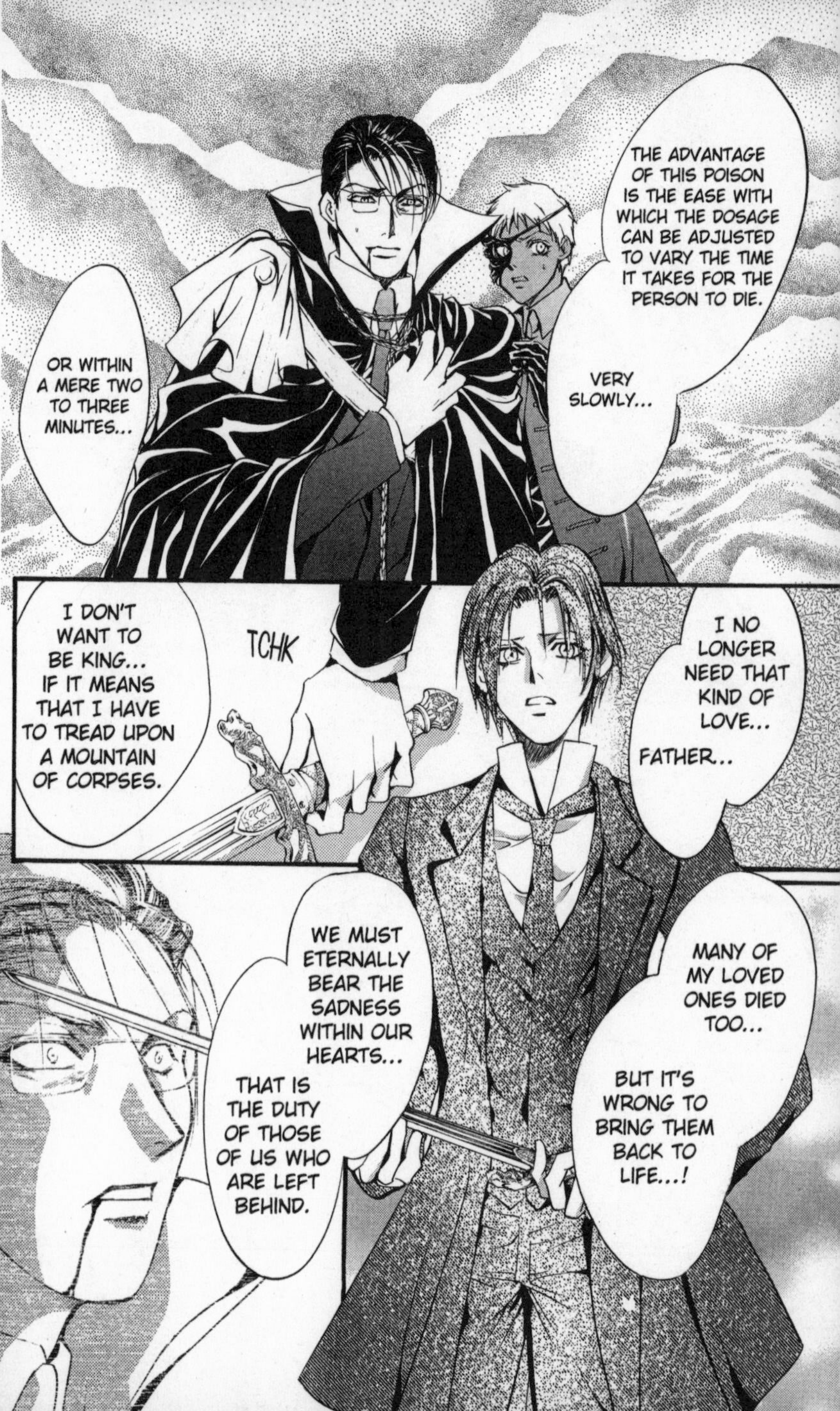
THE ADVANTAGE OF THIS POISON IS THE EASE WITH WHICH THE DOSAGE CAN BE ADJUSTED TO VARY THE TIME IT TAKES FOR THE PERSON TO DIE.
VERY SLOWLY...
OR WITHIN A MERE TWO TO THREE MINUTES...
I NO LONGER NEED THAT KIND OF LOVE...
FATHER...
TCHK
I DON'T WANT TO BE KING... IF IT MEANS THAT I HAVE TO TREAD UPON A MOUNTAIN OF CORPSES.
MANY OF MY LOVED ONES DIED TOO...
BUT IT'S WRONG TO BRING THEM BACK TO LIFE...!
WE MUST ETERNALLY BEAR THE SADNESS WITHIN OUR HEARTS...
THAT IS THE DUTY OF THOSE OF US WHO ARE LEFT BEHIND.

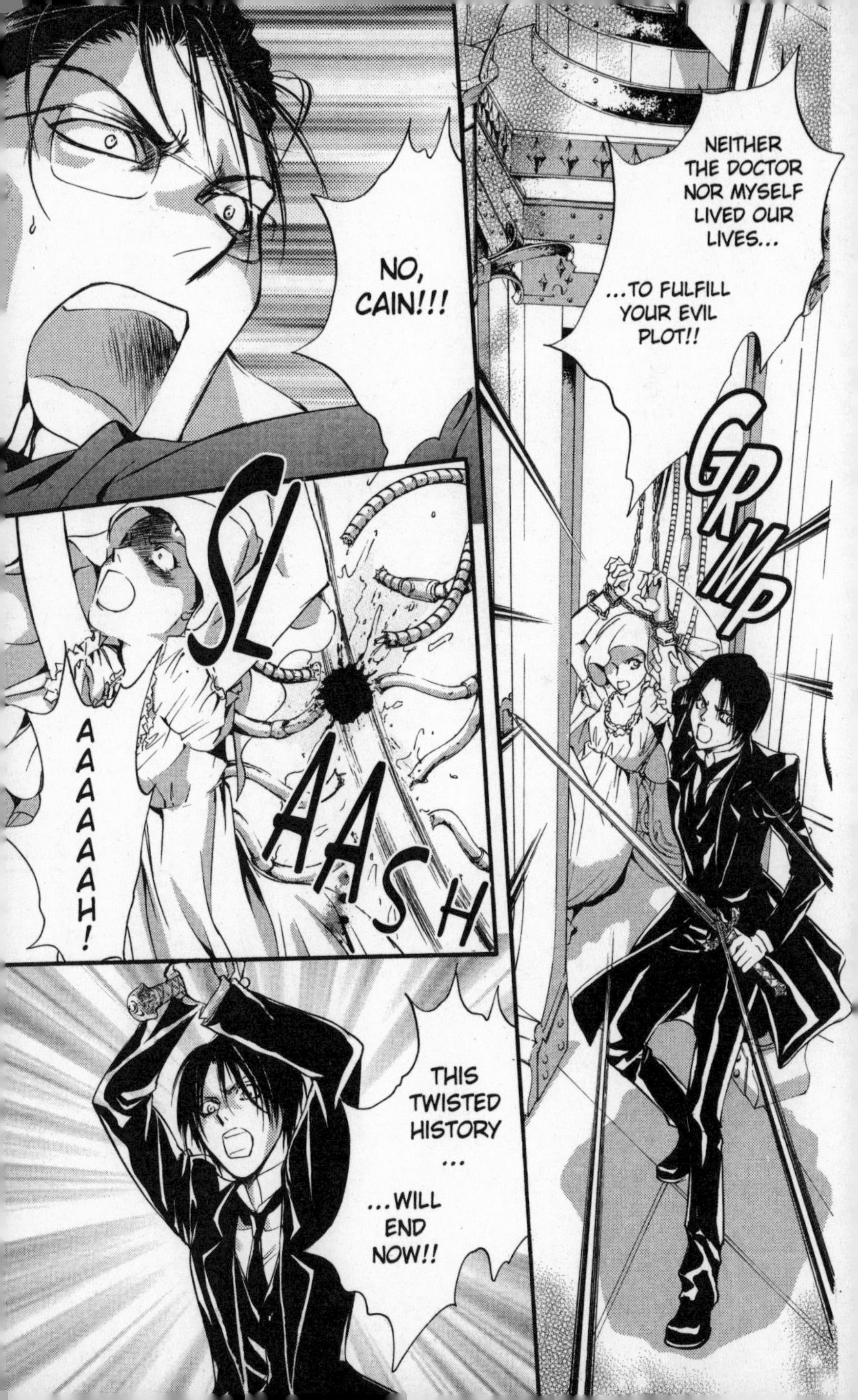
NEITHER THE DOCTOR NOR MYSELF LIVED OUR LIVES...
...TO FULFILL YOUR EVIL PLOT!!
GRMP
NO, CAIN!!!
SLAASH
AAAAAAAH!
THIS TWISTED HISTORY...
...WILL END NOW!!

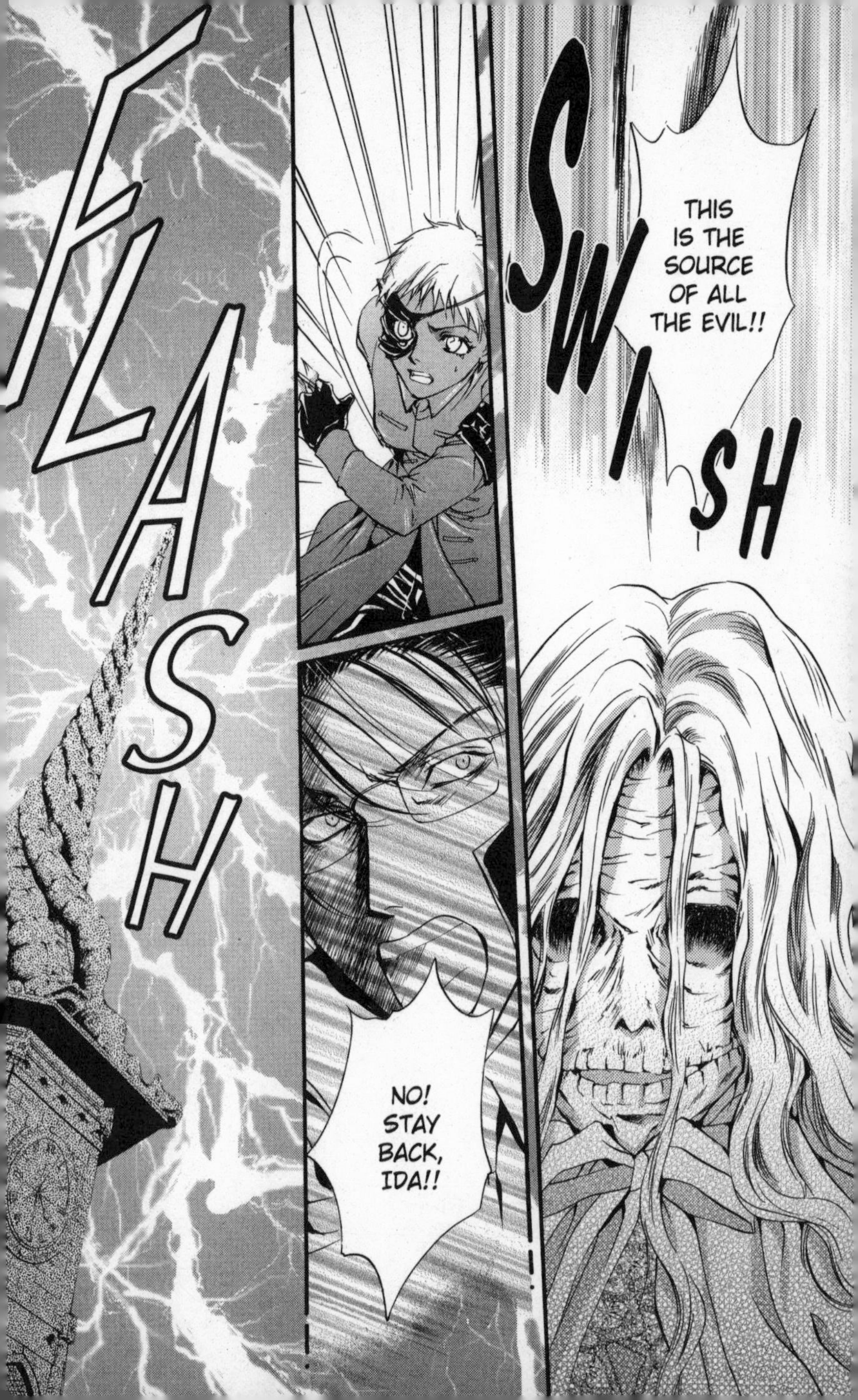
SWISH
THIS IS THE SOURCE OF ALL THE EVIL!!
NO! STAY BACK, IDA!!
FLASH

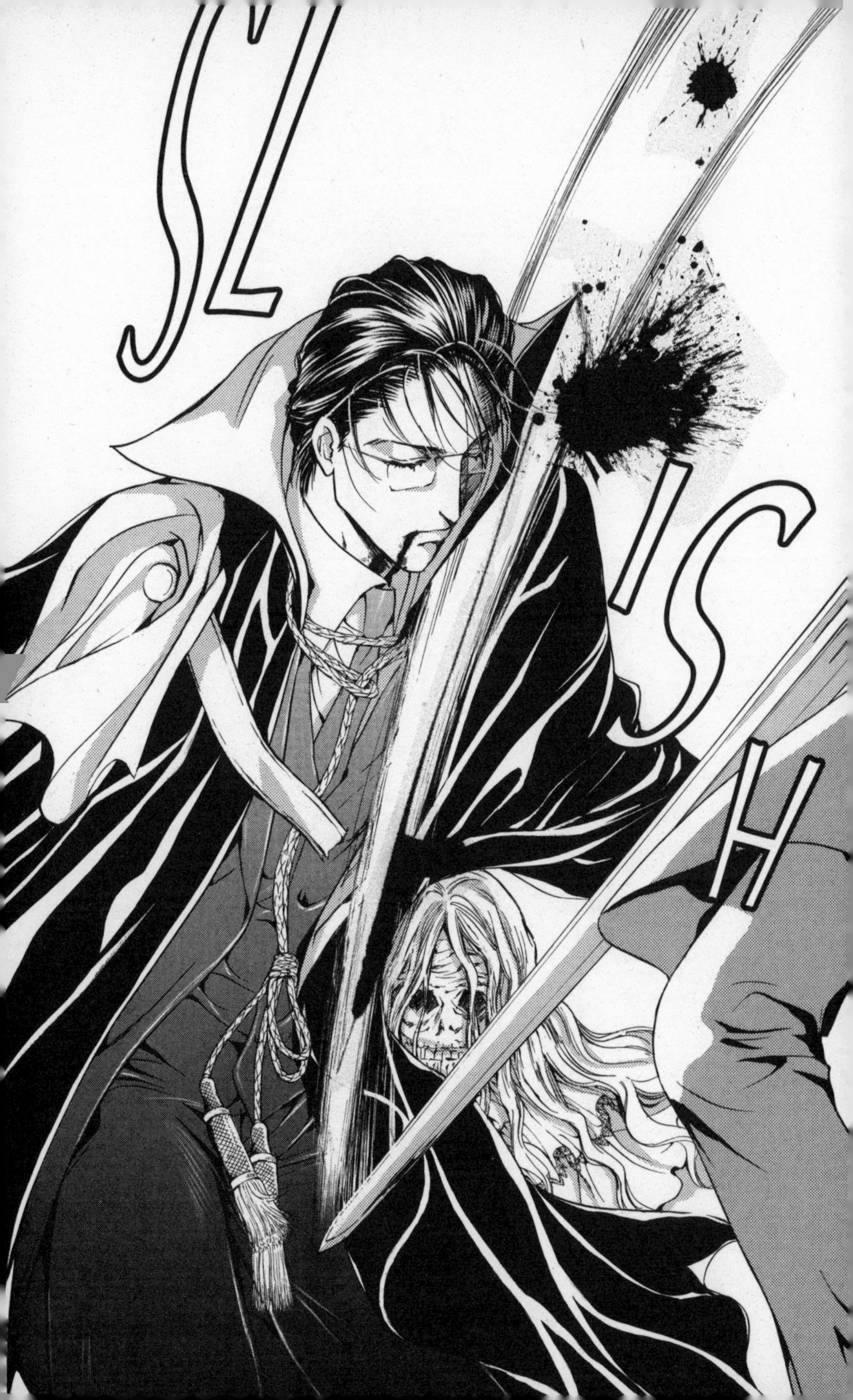
SLISH

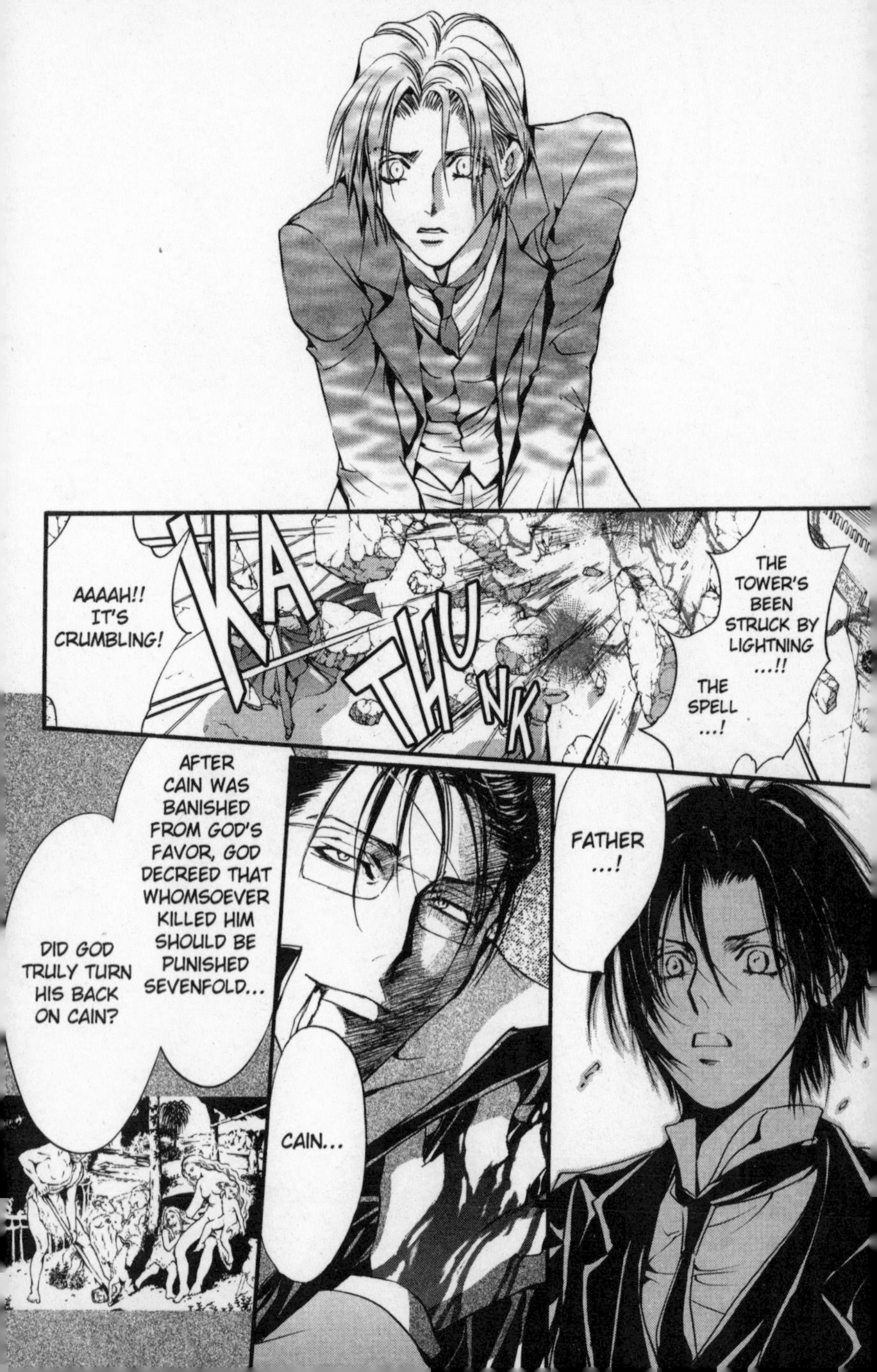
THE TOWER'S BEEN STRUCK BY LIGHTNING ...!!
THE SPELL ...!
KA THUNK
AAAAH!! IT'S CRUMBLING!
FATHER ...!
AFTER CAIN WAS BANISHED FROM GOD'S FAVOR, GOD DECREED THAT WHOMSOEVER KILLED HIM SHOULD BE PUNISHED SEVENFOLD...
DID GOD TRULY TURN HIS BACK ON CAIN?
CAIN...

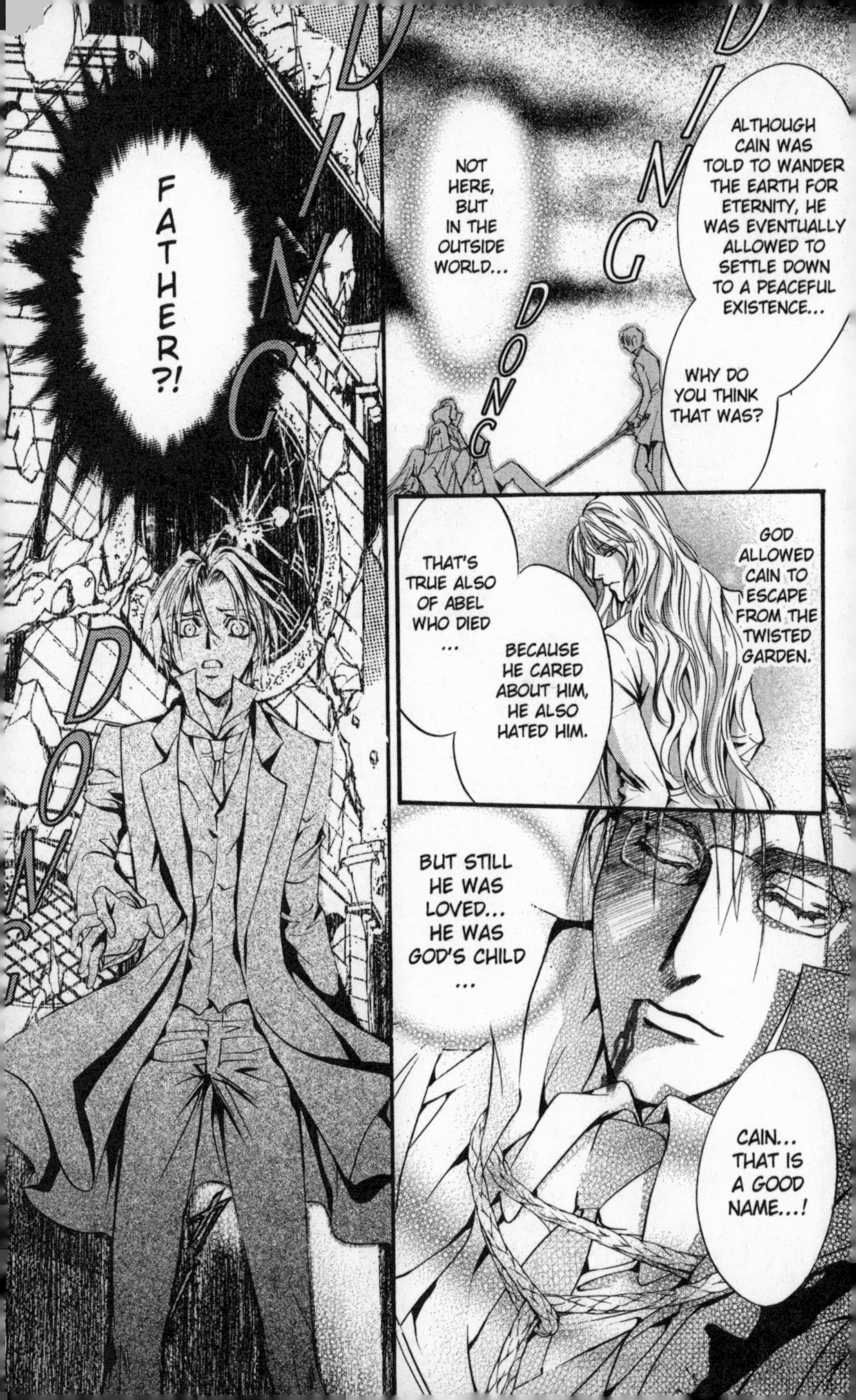
DING
ALTHOUGH CAIN WAS TOLD TO WANDER THE EARTH FOR ETERNITY, HE WAS EVENTUALLY ALLOWED TO SETTLE DOWN TO A PEACEFUL EXISTENCE...
NOT HERE, BUT IN THE OUTSIDE WORLD...
WHY DO YOU THINK THAT WAS?
DONG
GOD ALLOWED CAIN TO ESCAPE FROM THE TWISTED GARDEN.
THAT'S TRUE ALSO OF ABEL WHO DIED...
BECAUSE HE CARED ABOUT HIM, HE ALSO HATED HIM.
BUT STILL HE WAS LOVED... HE WAS GOD'S CHILD...
CAIN... THAT IS A GOOD NAME...!
DING
FATHER?!
DONG

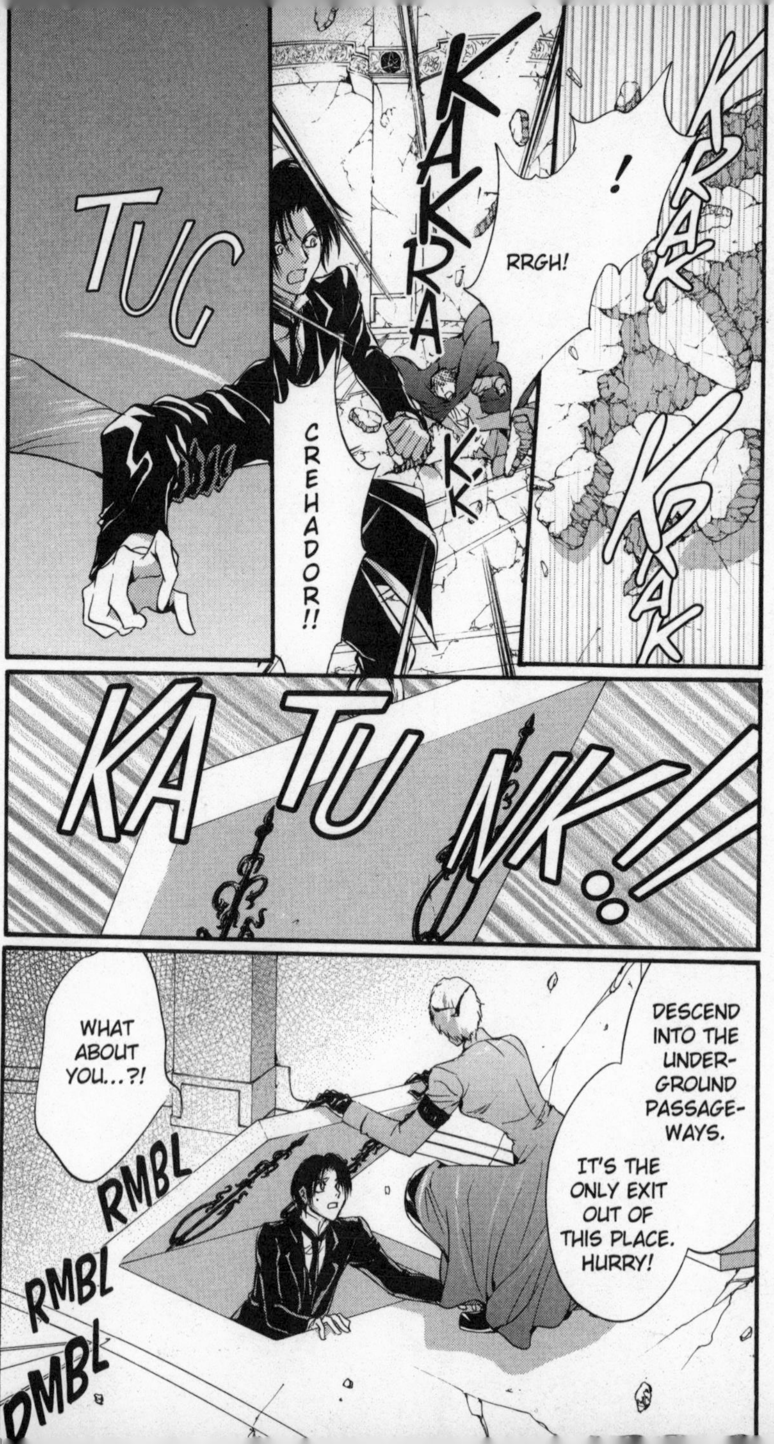
KRAK
!
KRAK
KAKRA
RRGH!
K.K
CREHADOR!!
TUC
KATUNK!!
DESCEND INTO THE UNDERGROUND PASSAGEWAYS.
IT'S THE ONLY EXIT OUT OF THIS PLACE. HURRY!
WHAT ABOUT YOU...?!
RMBL
RMBL
DMBL

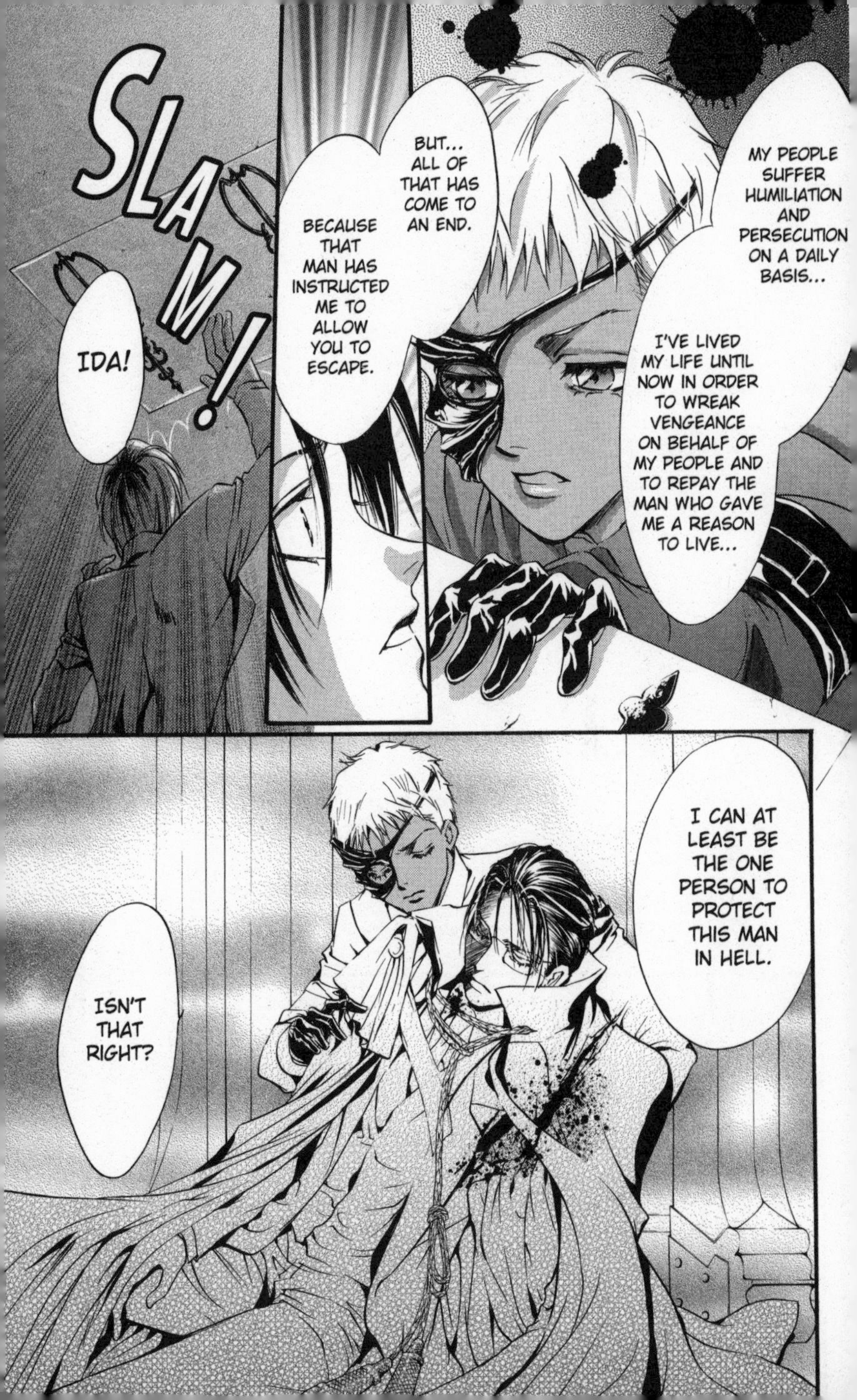
MY PEOPLE SUFFER HUMILIATION AND PERSECUTION ON A DAILY BASIS...
I'VE LIVED MY LIFE UNTIL NOW IN ORDER TO WREAK VENGEANCE ON BEHALF OF MY PEOPLE AND TO REPAY THE MAN WHO GAVE ME A REASON TO LIVE...
BUT... ALL OF THAT HAS COME TO AN END.
BECAUSE THAT MAN HAS INSTRUCTED ME TO ALLOW YOU TO ESCAPE.
SLAM!
IDA!
I CAN AT LEAST BE THE ONE PERSON TO PROTECT THIS MAN IN HELL.
ISN'T THAT RIGHT?

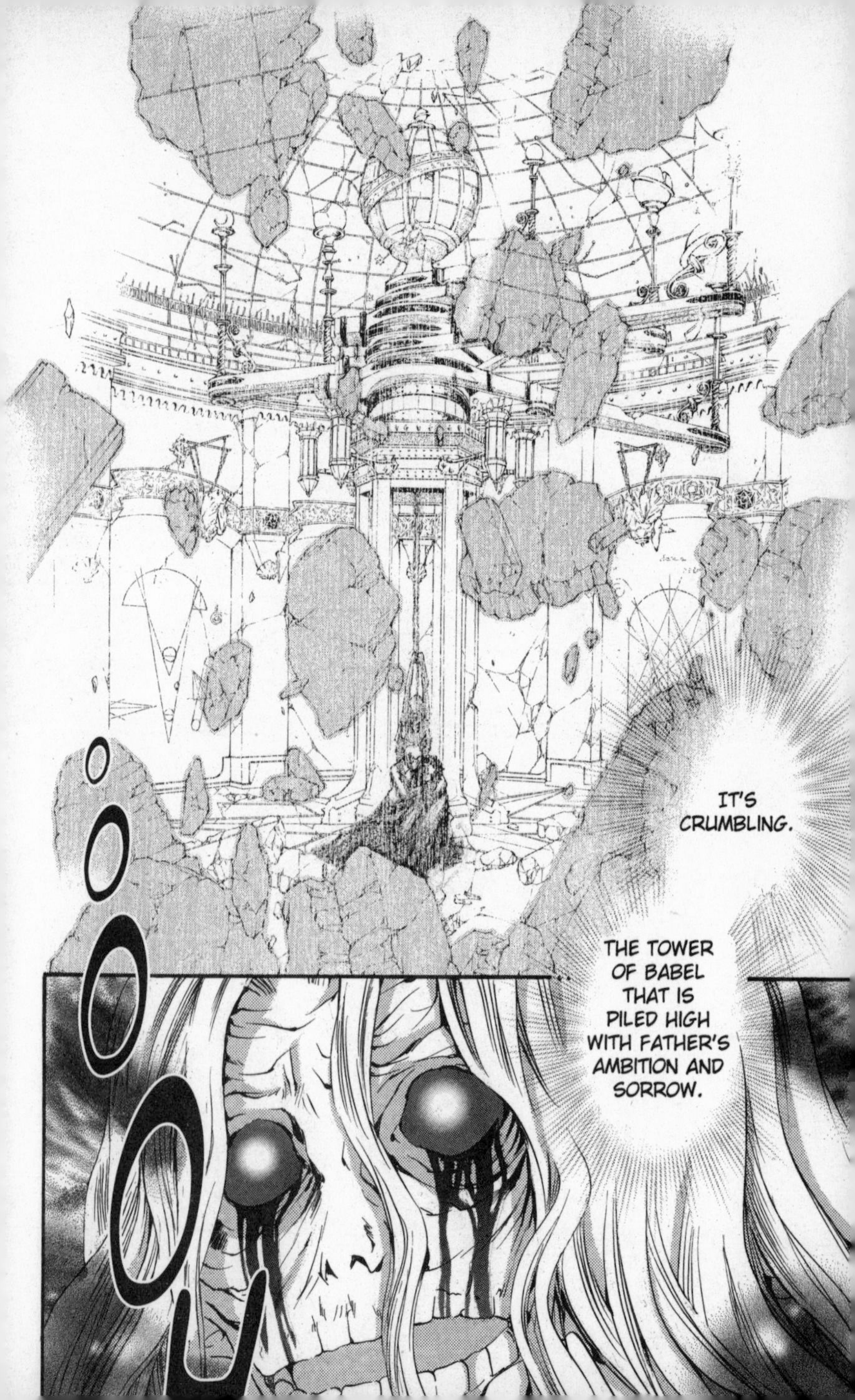
IT'S CRUMBLING.
THE TOWER OF BABEL THAT IS PILED HIGH WITH FATHER'S AMBITION AND SORROW.
OOOOO

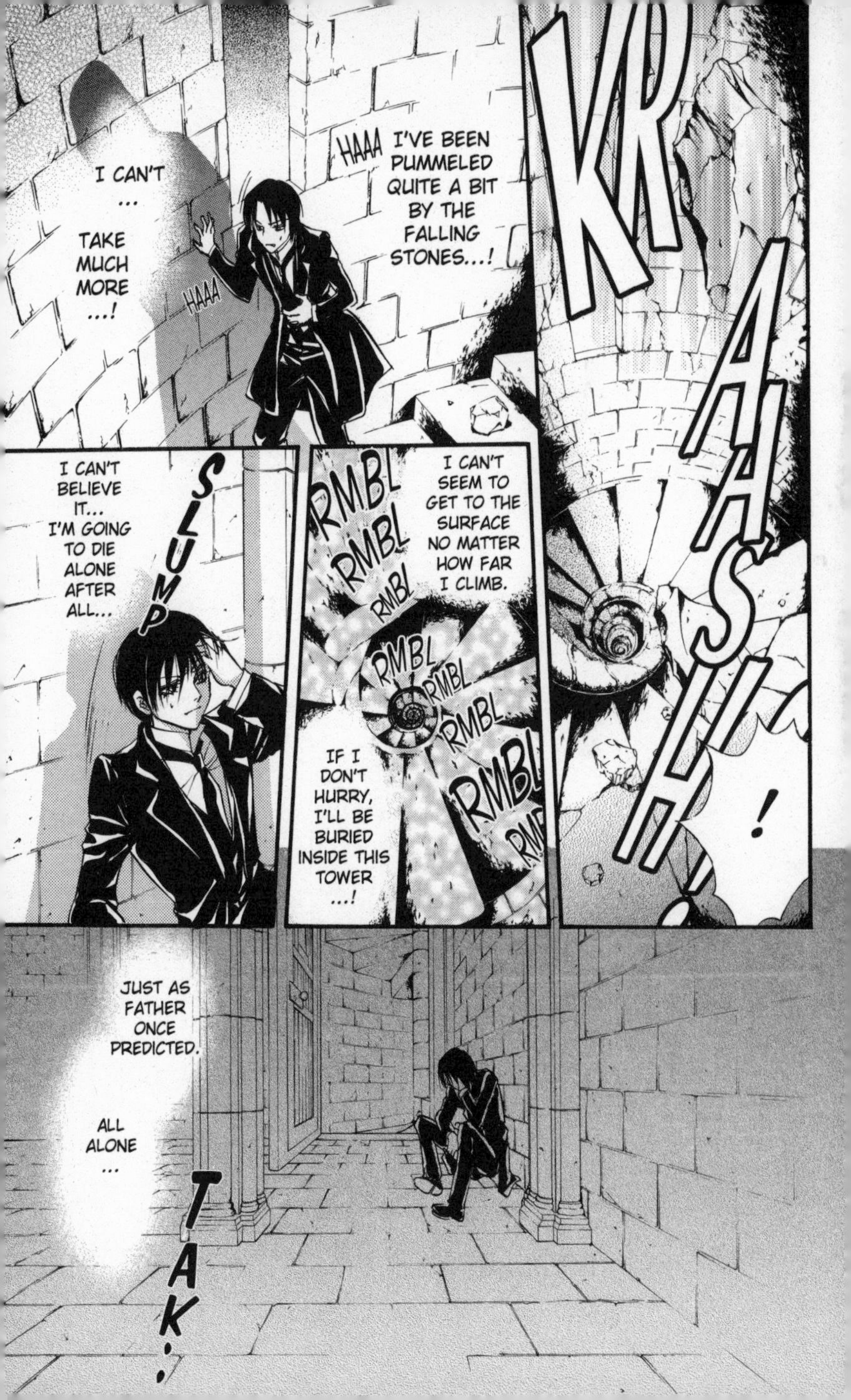

KRAASHH!
HAAA
I'VE BEEN PUMMELED QUITE A BIT BY THE FALLING STONES...!
I CAN'T ... TAKE MUCH MORE ...!
HAAA
I CAN'T SEEM TO GET TO THE SURFACE NO MATTER HOW FAR I CLIMB.
RMBL RMBL RMBL
RMBL RMBL RMBL RMBL RMBL
IF I DON'T HURRY, I'LL BE BURIED INSIDE THIS TOWER ...!
SLUMP
I CAN'T BELIEVE IT... I'M GOING TO DIE ALONE AFTER ALL...
JUST AS FATHER ONCE PREDICTED.
ALL ALONE ...
TAK.

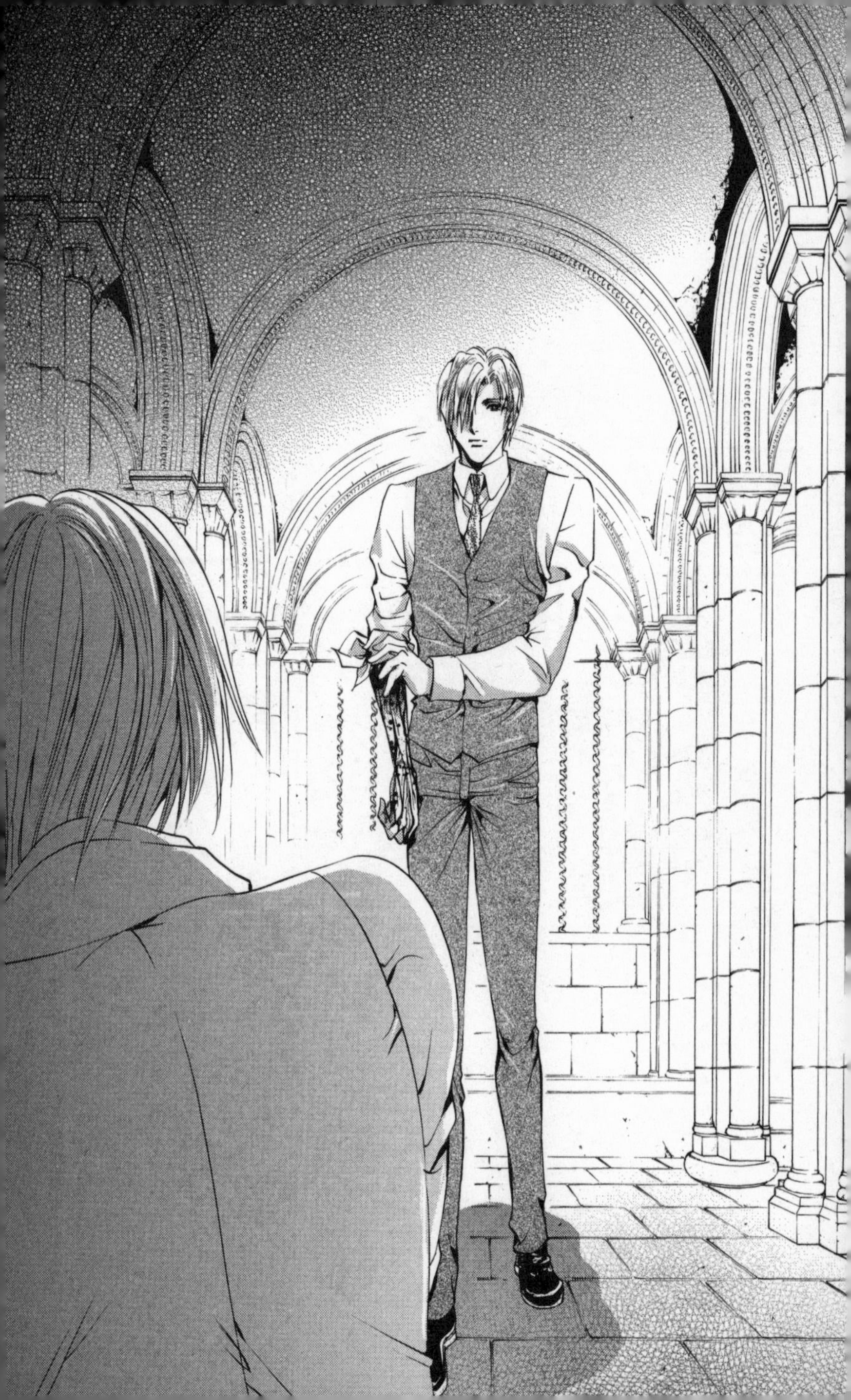

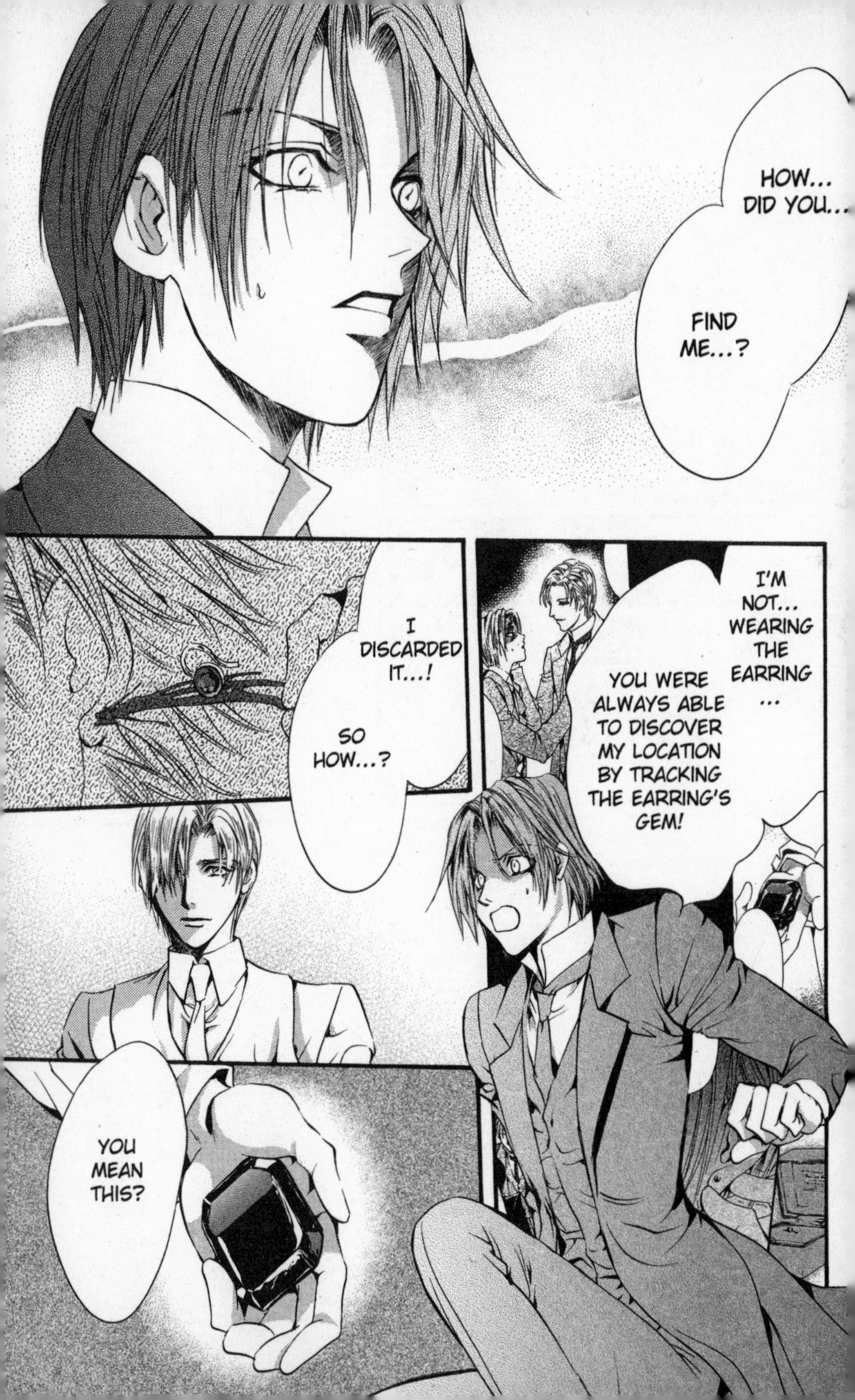
HOW... DID YOU...
FIND ME...?
I'M NOT... WEARING THE EARRING...
YOU WERE ALWAYS ABLE TO DISCOVER MY LOCATION BY TRACKING THE EARRING'S GEM!
I DISCARDED IT...!
SO HOW...?
YOU MEAN THIS?

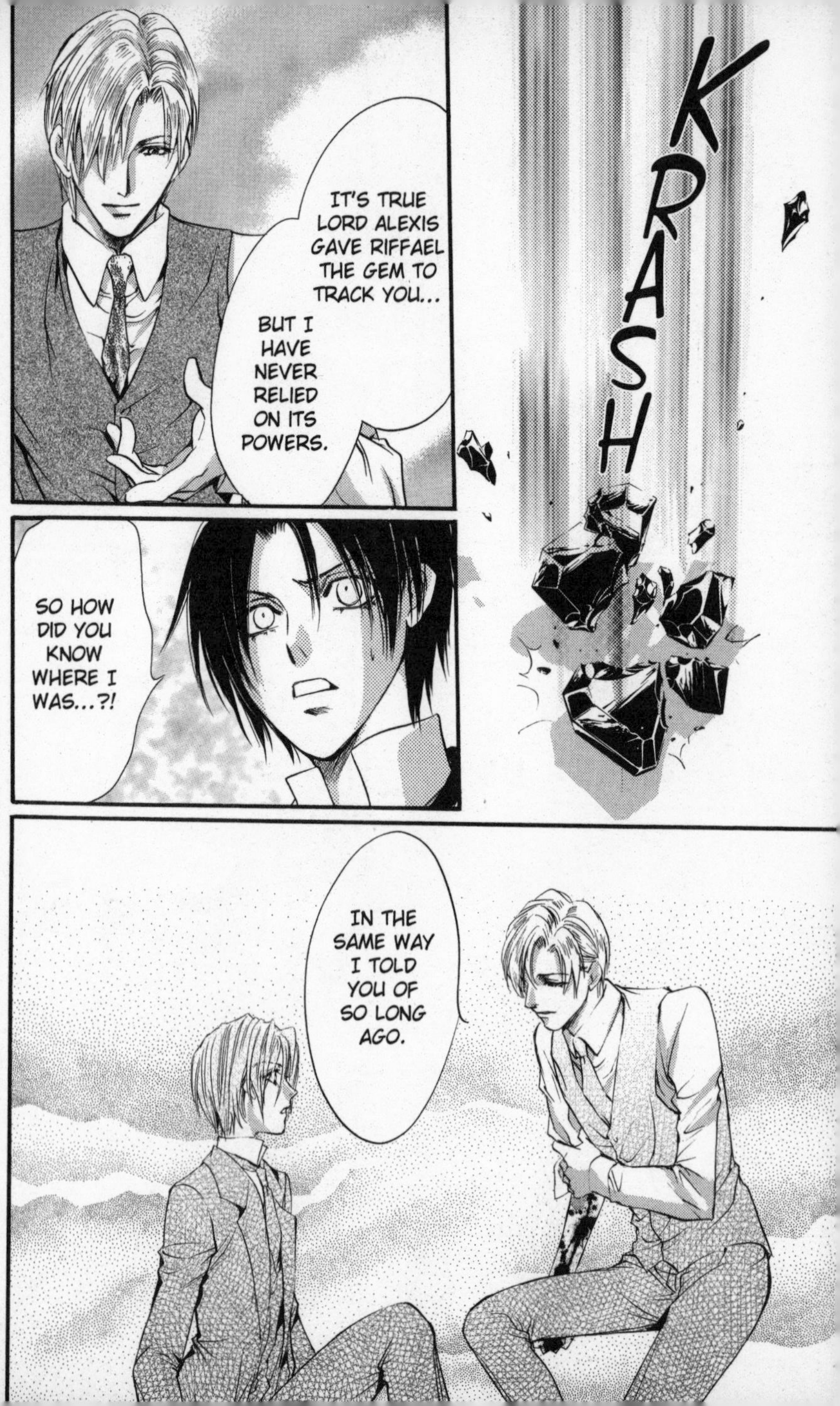
KRASH
IT'S TRUE LORD ALEXIS GAVE RIFFAEL THE GEM TO TRACK YOU...
BUT I HAVE NEVER RELIED ON ITS POWERS.
SO HOW DID YOU KNOW WHERE I WAS...?!
IN THE SAME WAY I TOLD YOU OF SO LONG AGO.

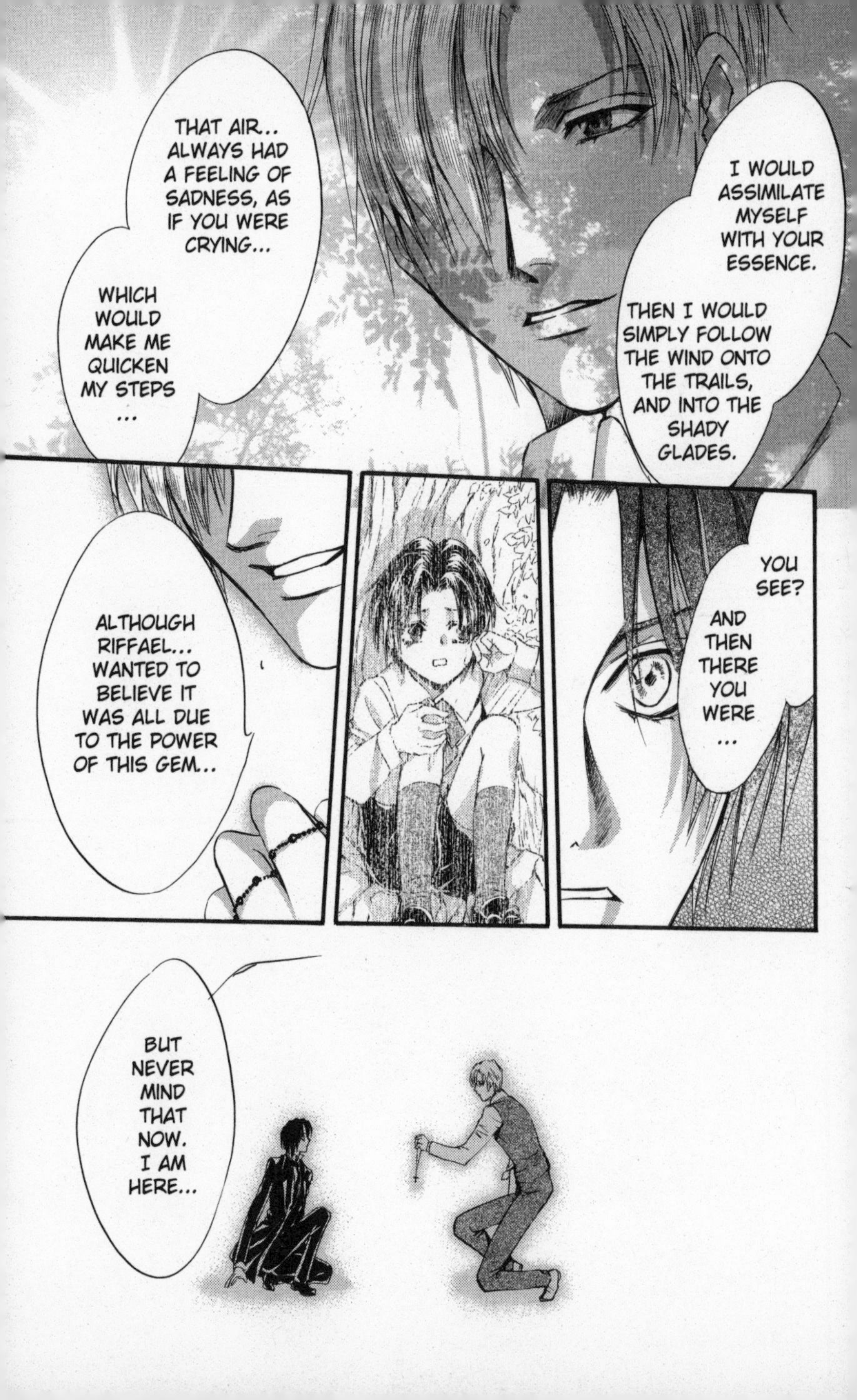
I WOULD ASSIMILATE MYSELF WITH YOUR ESSENCE.
THEN I WOULD SIMPLY FOLLOW THE WIND ONTO THE TRAILS, AND INTO THE SHADY GLADES.
THAT AIR... ALWAYS HAD A FEELING OF SADNESS, AS IF YOU WERE CRYING...
WHICH WOULD MAKE ME QUICKEN MY STEPS ...
YOU SEE?
AND THEN THERE YOU WERE ...
ALTHOUGH RIFFAEL... WANTED TO BELIEVE IT WAS ALL DUE TO THE POWER OF THIS GEM...
BUT NEVER MIND THAT NOW. I AM HERE...

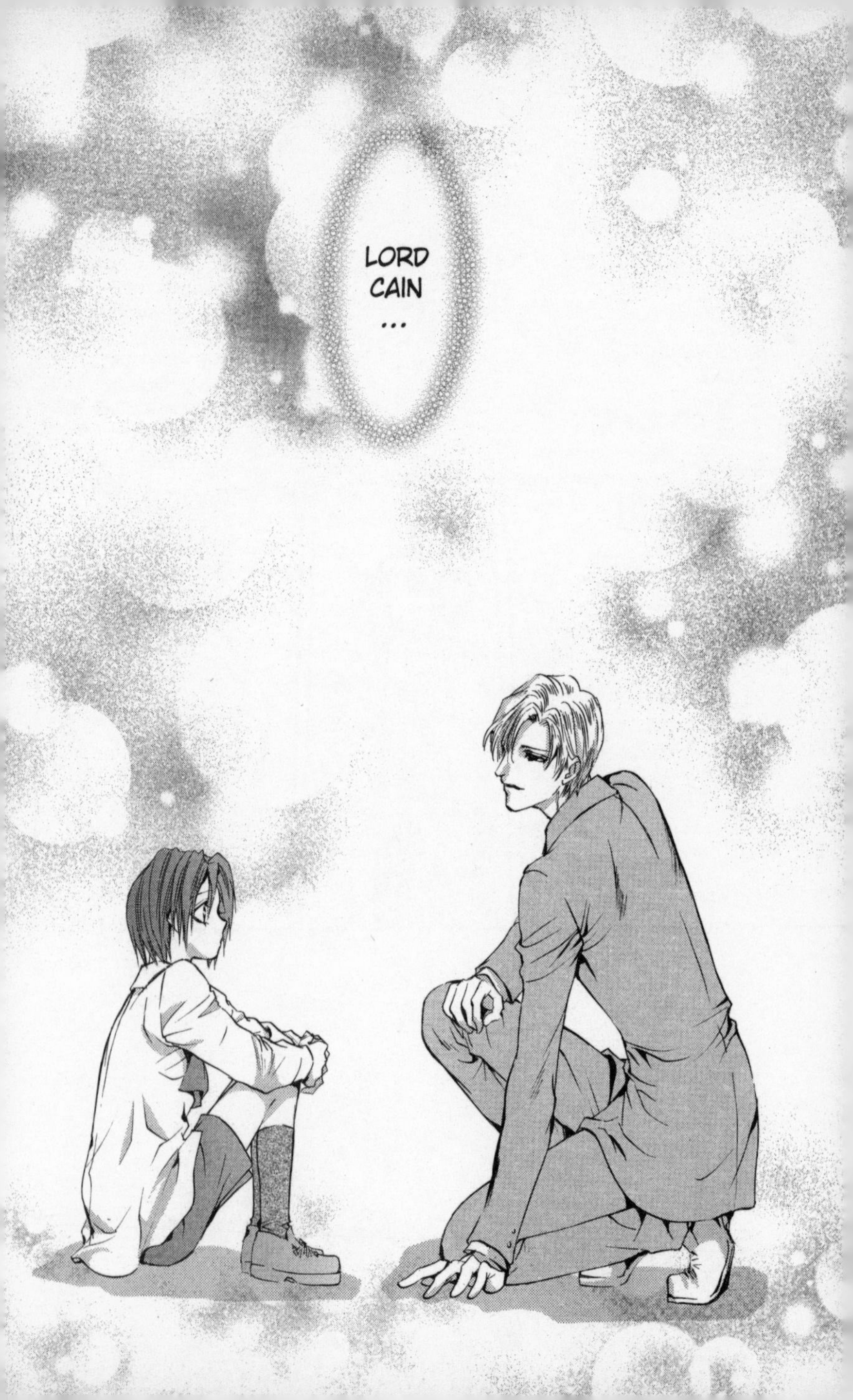
LORD CAIN ...

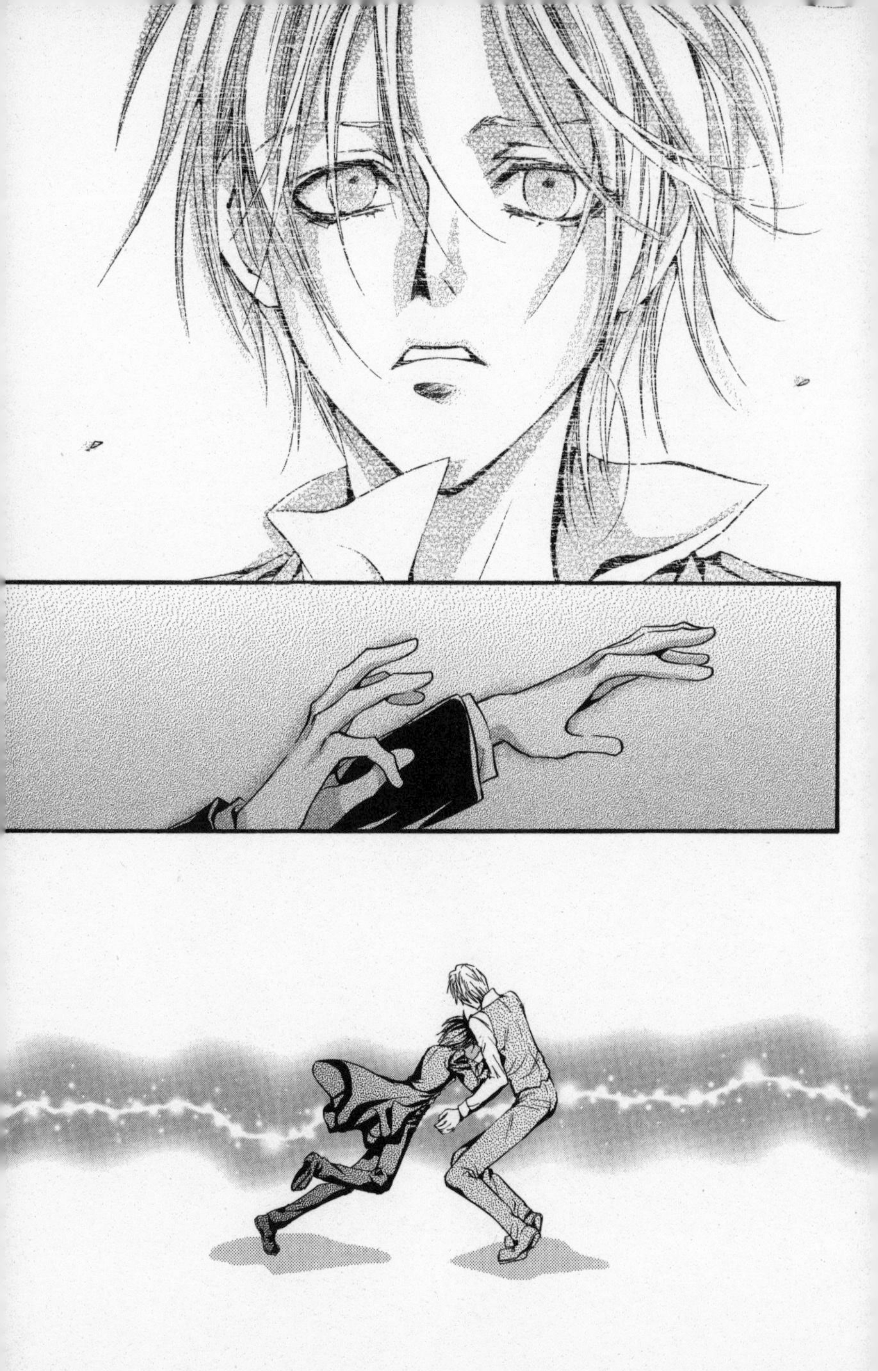

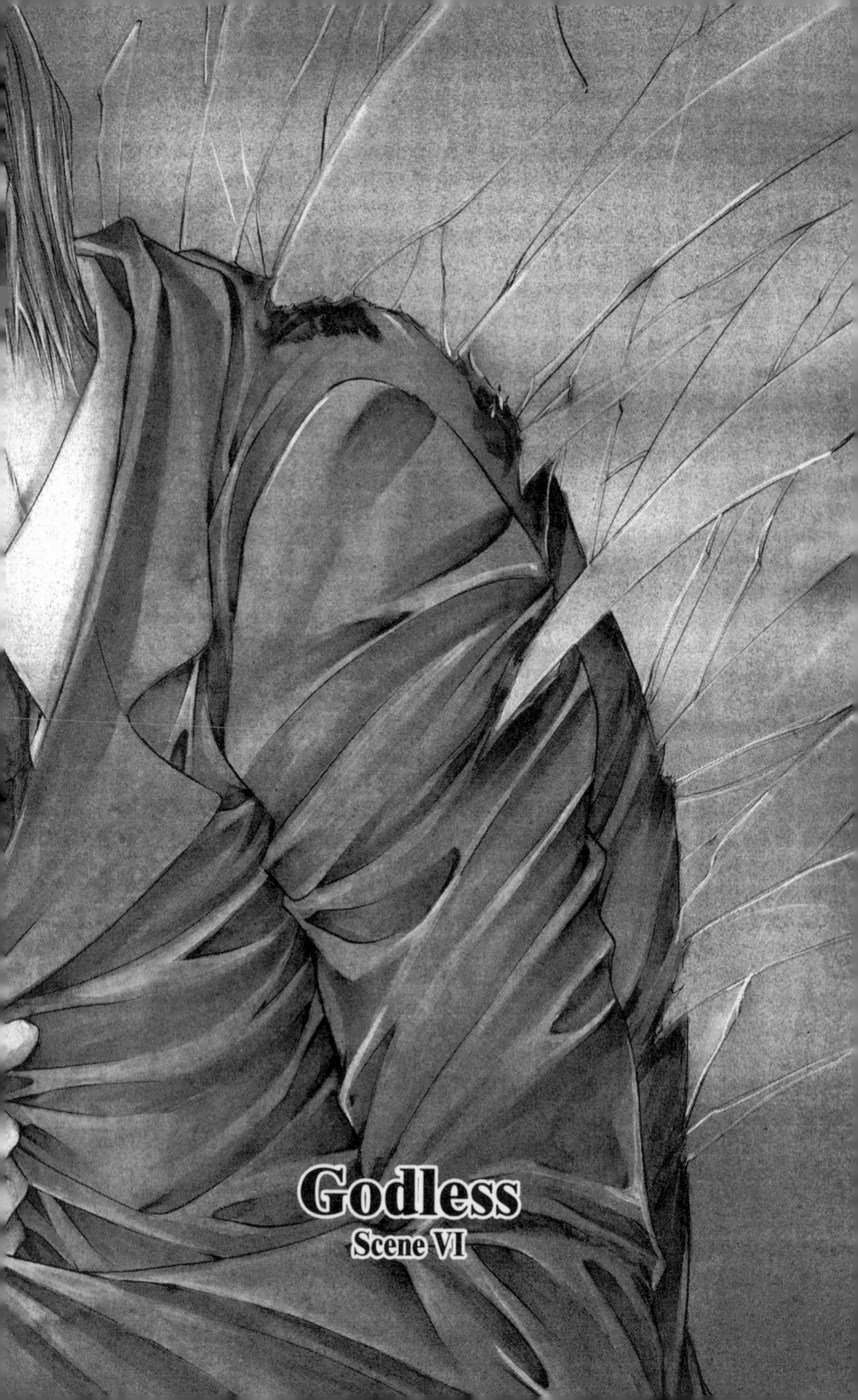
Godless
Scene VI

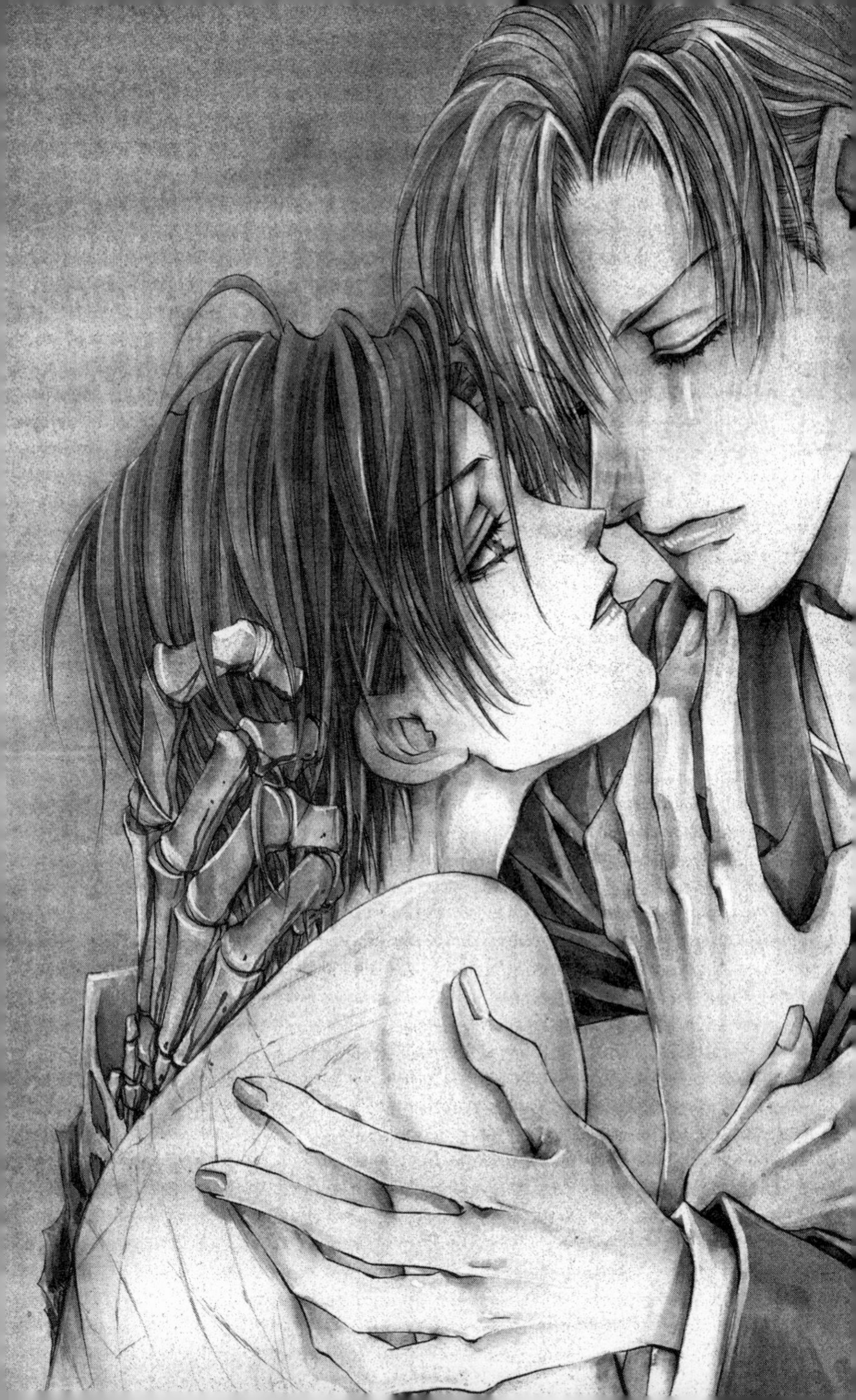

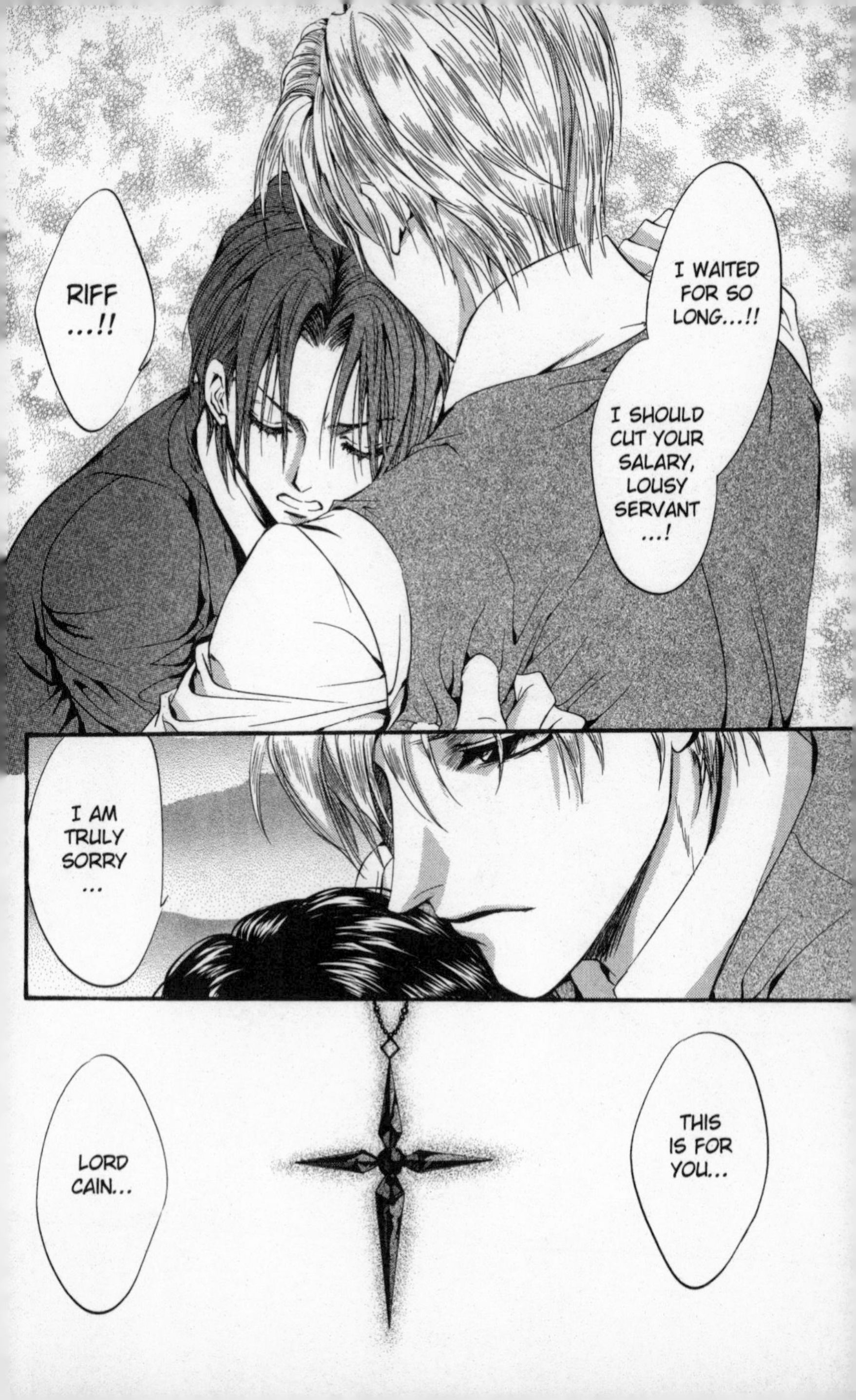
I WAITED FOR SO LONG...!!
I SHOULD CUT YOUR SALARY, LOUSY SERVANT...!
RIFF...!!
I AM TRULY SORRY...
THIS IS FOR YOU...
LORD CAIN...

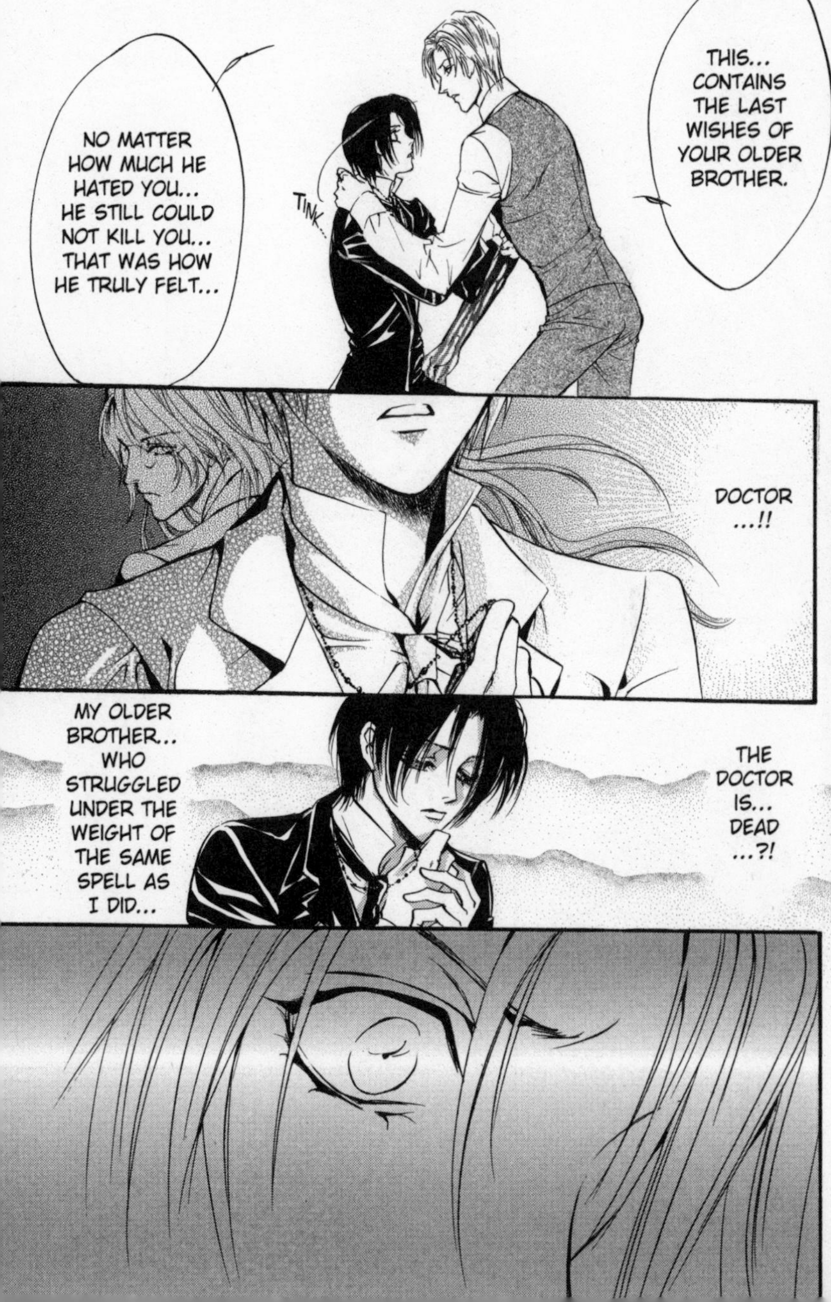
THIS... CONTAINS THE LAST WISHES OF YOUR OLDER BROTHER.
TINK...
NO MATTER HOW MUCH HE HATED YOU... HE STILL COULD NOT KILL YOU... THAT WAS HOW HE TRULY FELT...
DOCTOR ...!!
THE DOCTOR IS... DEAD ...?!
MY OLDER BROTHER... WHO STRUGGLED UNDER THE WEIGHT OF THE SAME SPELL AS I DID...

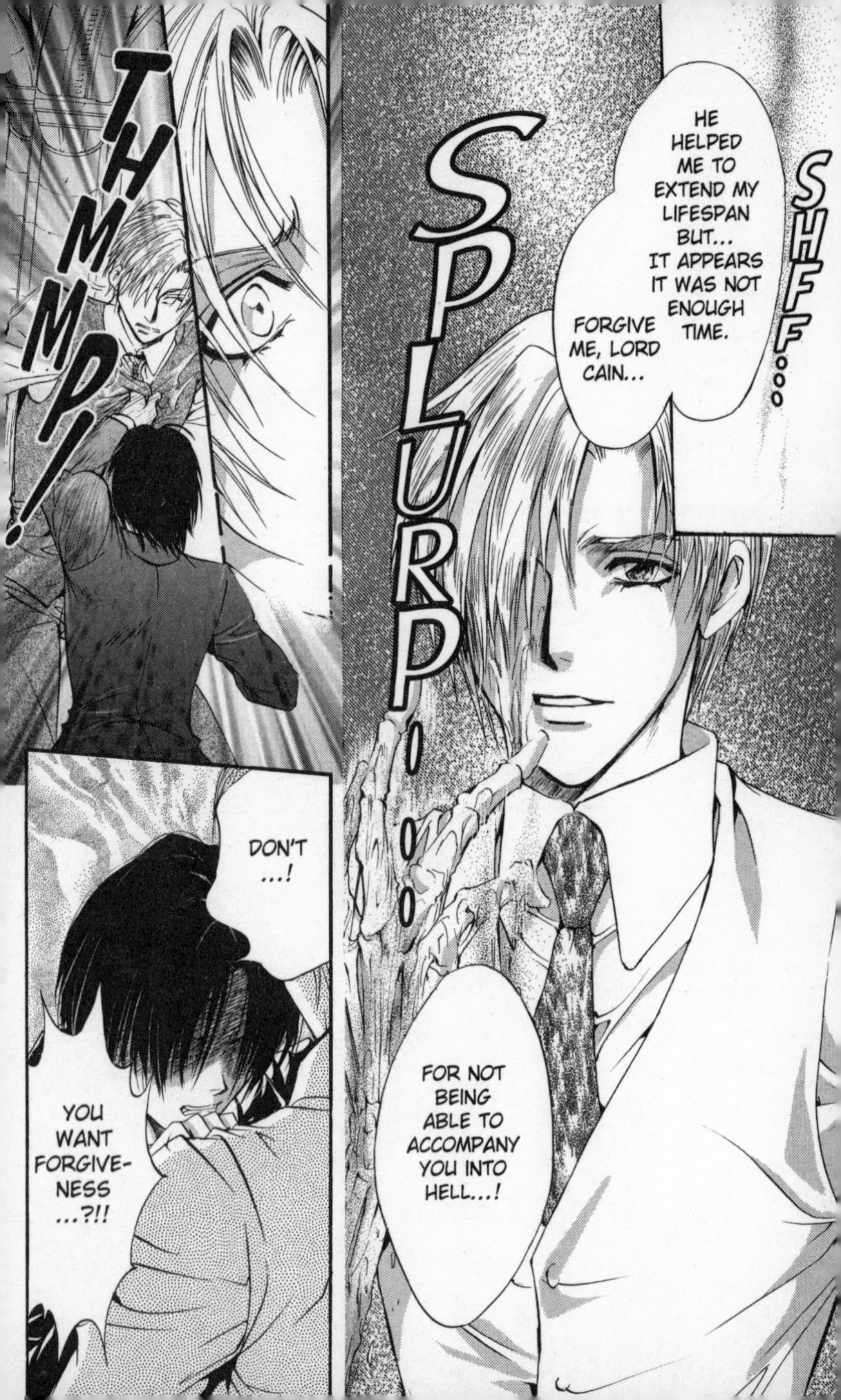
SHFF...
HE HELPED ME TO EXTEND MY LIFESPAN BUT... IT APPEARS IT WAS NOT ENOUGH TIME.
FORGIVE ME, LORD CAIN...
SPLURP...
FOR NOT BEING ABLE TO ACCOMPANY YOU INTO HELL...!
THMMP!!
DON'T ...!
YOU WANT FORGIVE-NESS ...?!!

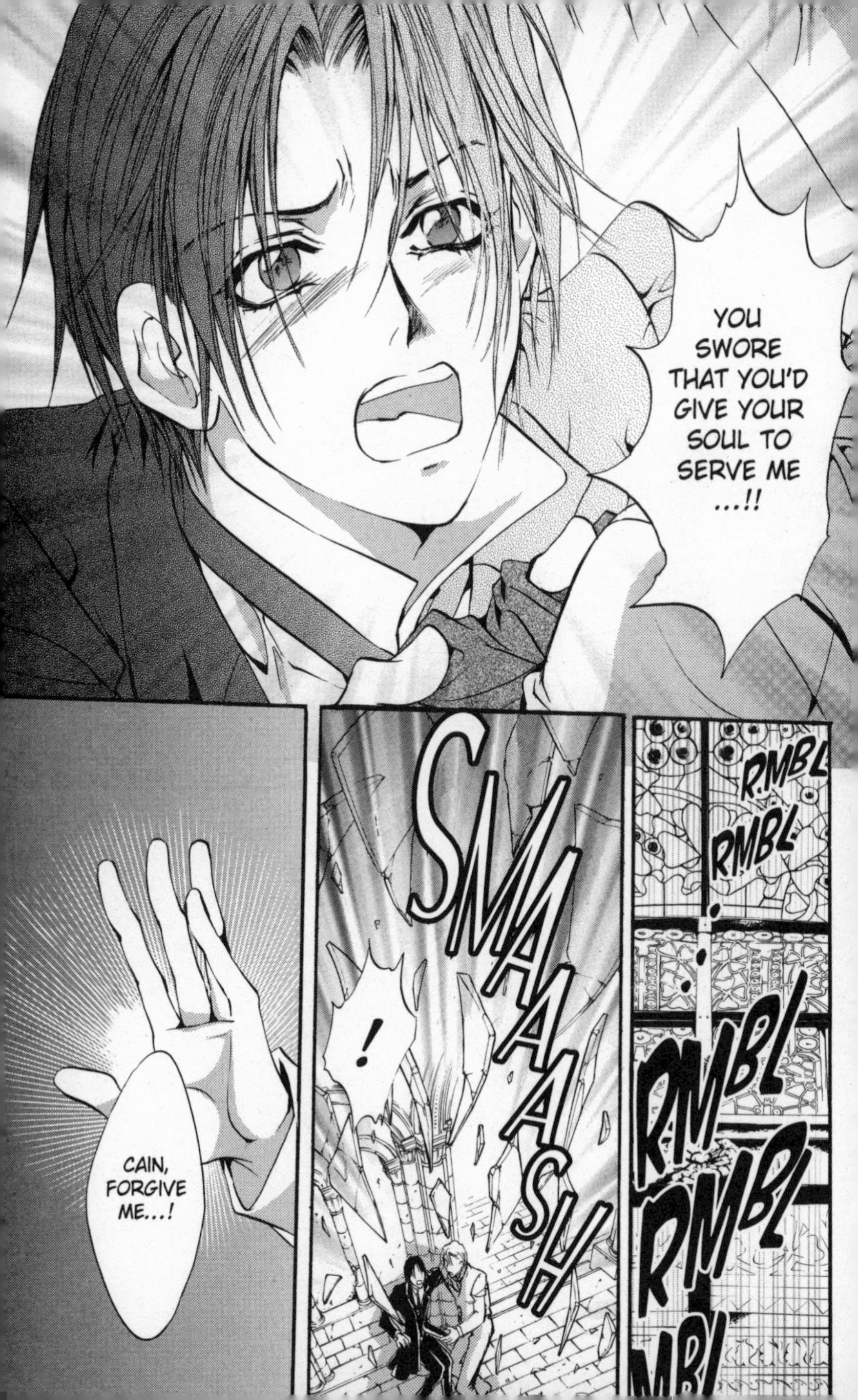
YOU SWORE THAT YOU'D GIVE YOUR SOUL TO SERVE ME ...!!
RMBL
RMBL
RMBL
RMBL
RMBL
SMAAAASH
!
CAIN, FORGIVE ME...!

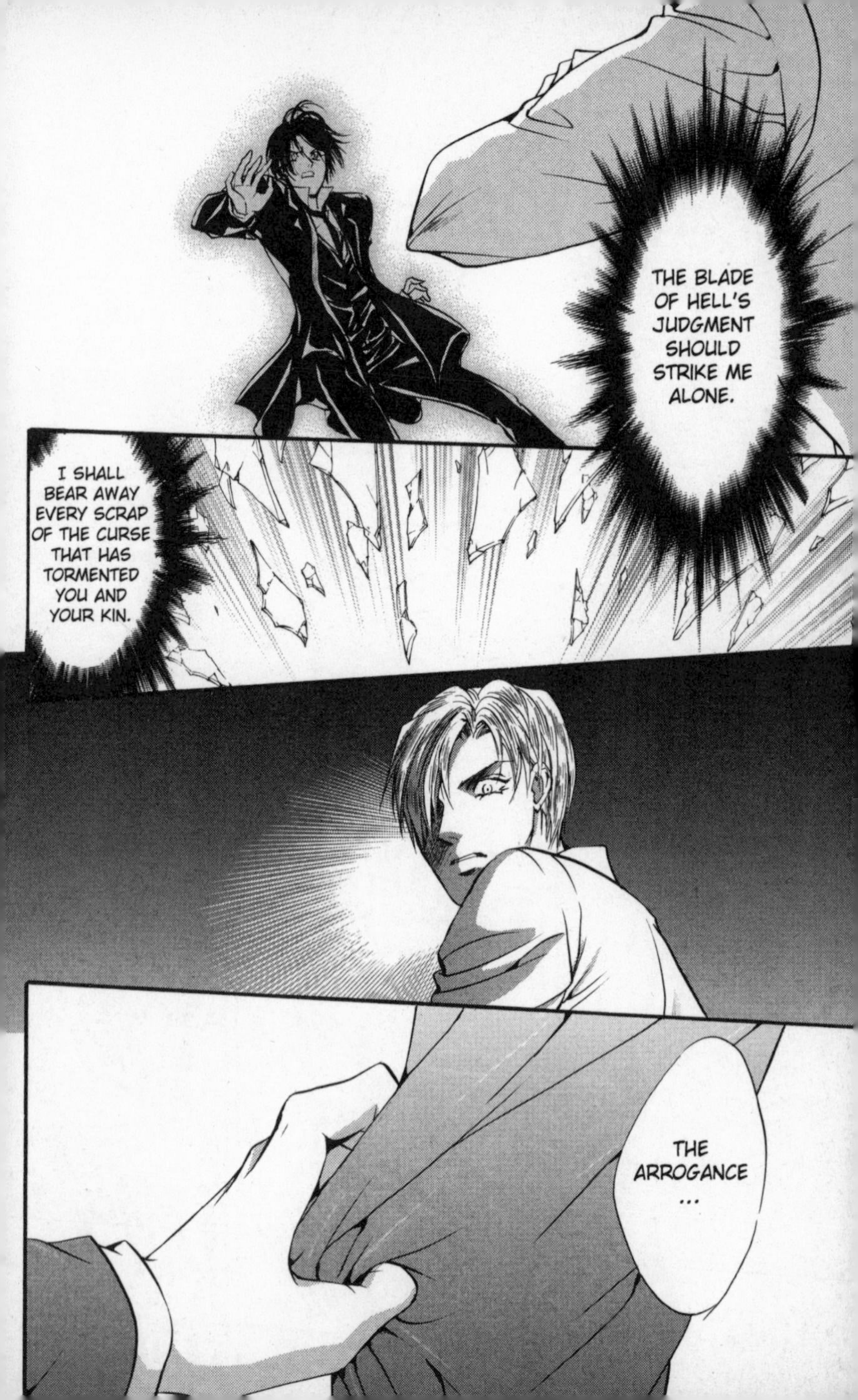
THE BLADE OF HELL'S JUDGMENT SHOULD STRIKE ME ALONE.
I SHALL BEAR AWAY EVERY SCRAP OF THE CURSE THAT HAS TORMENTED YOU AND YOUR KIN.
THE ARROGANCE...

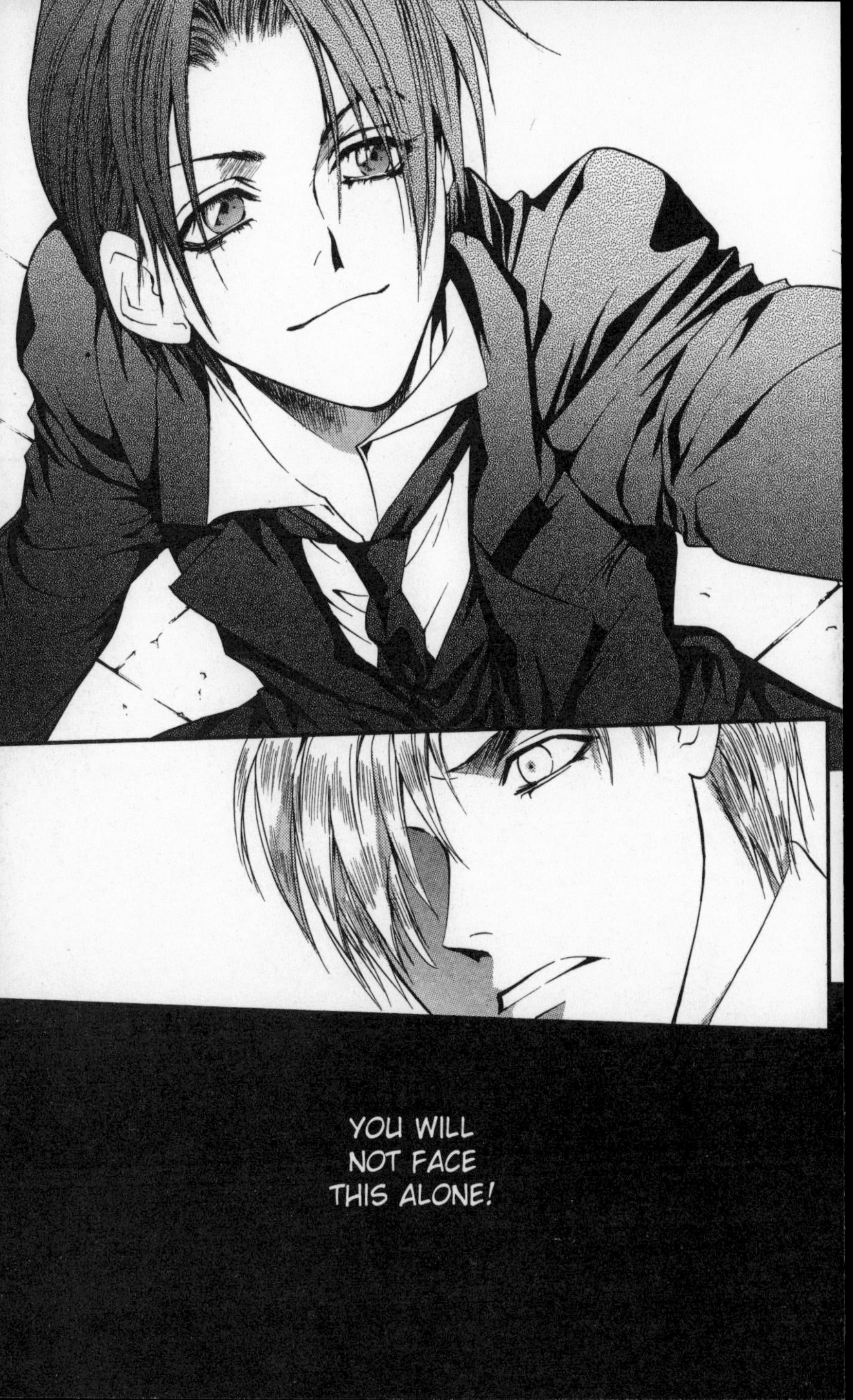
YOU WILL NOT FACE THIS ALONE!

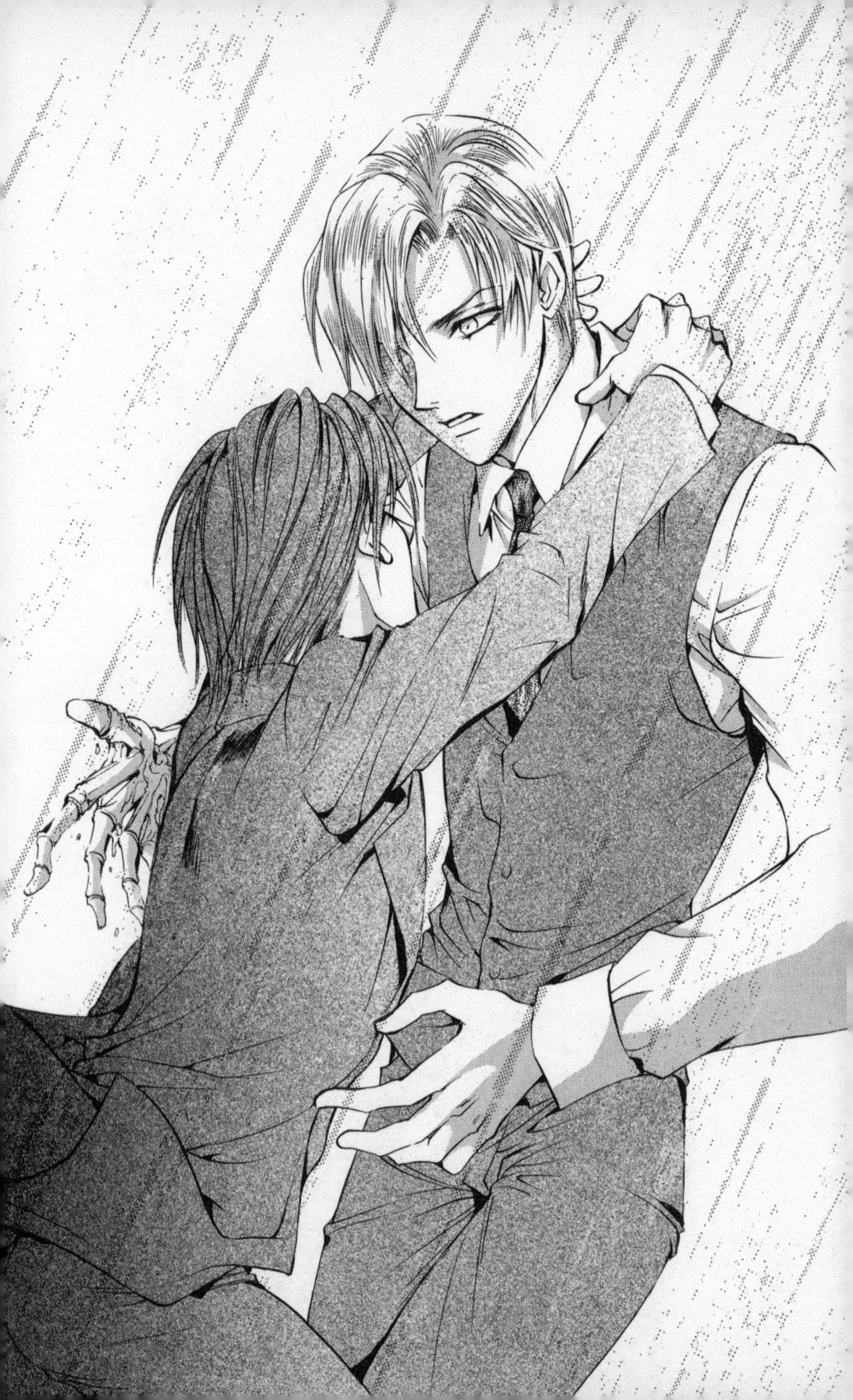

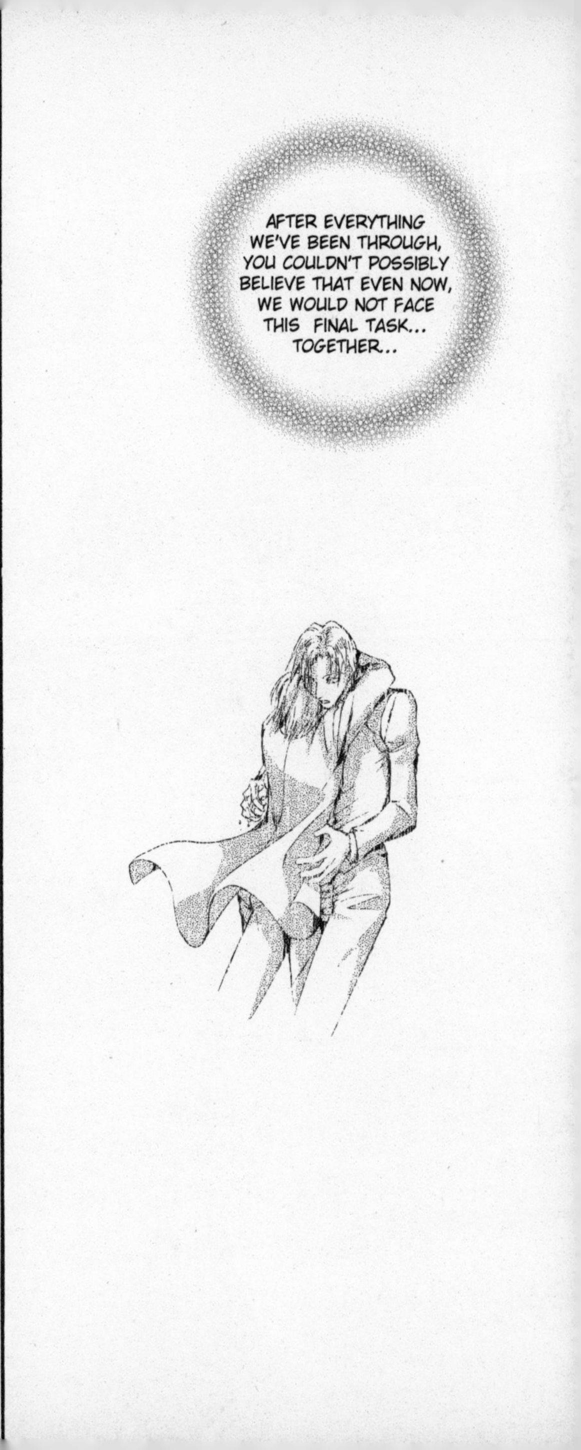
AFTER EVERYTHING WE'VE BEEN THROUGH, YOU COULDN'T POSSIBLY BELIEVE THAT EVEN NOW, WE WOULD NOT FACE THIS FINAL TASK... TOGETHER...

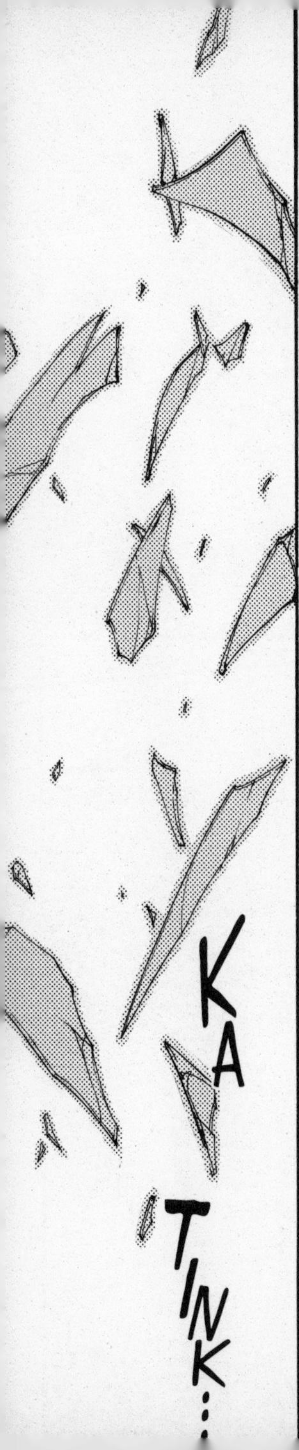
KA
TINK...

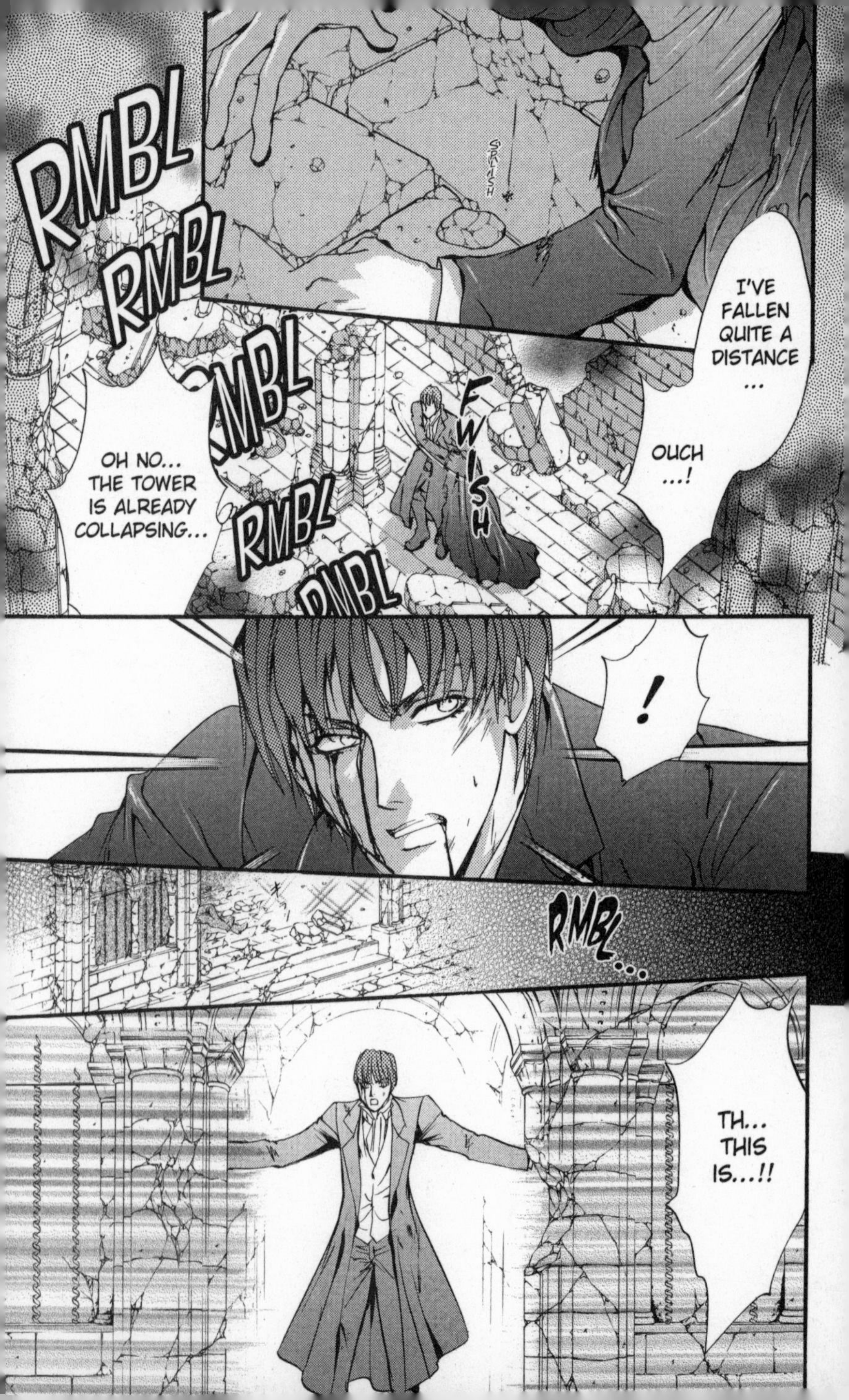
RMBL
RMBL
SPLISH
I'VE FALLEN QUITE A DISTANCE ...
OUCH ...!
RMBL
FWISH
OH NO... THE TOWER IS ALREADY COLLAPSING...
RMBL
RMBL
!
RMBL...
TH... THIS IS...!!

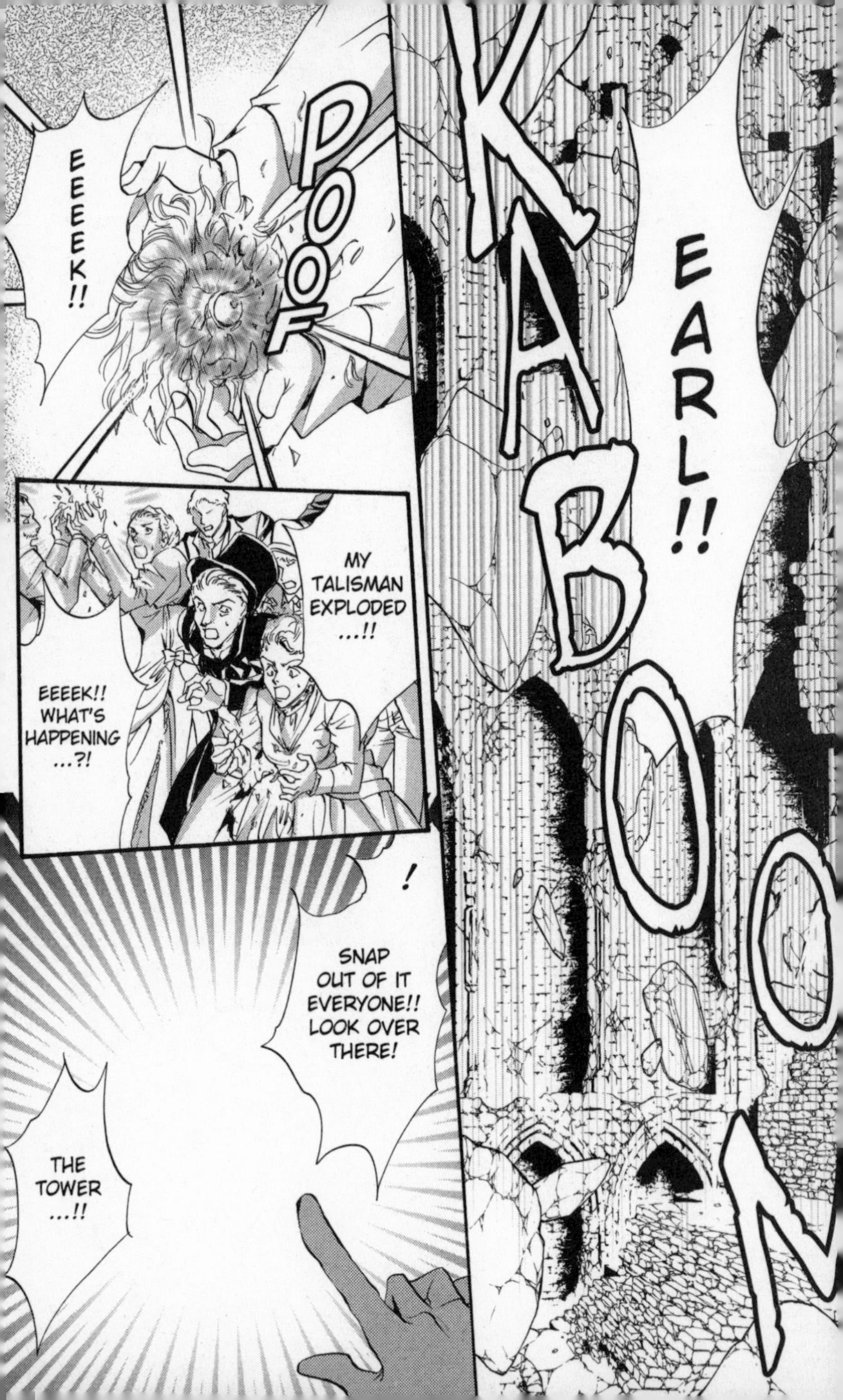
KABOOM
EARL!!
POOF
EEEEEK!!
MY TALISMAN EXPLODED ...!!
EEEEK!! WHAT'S HAPPENING ...?!
!
SNAP OUT OF IT EVERYONE!! LOOK OVER THERE!
THE TOWER ...!!

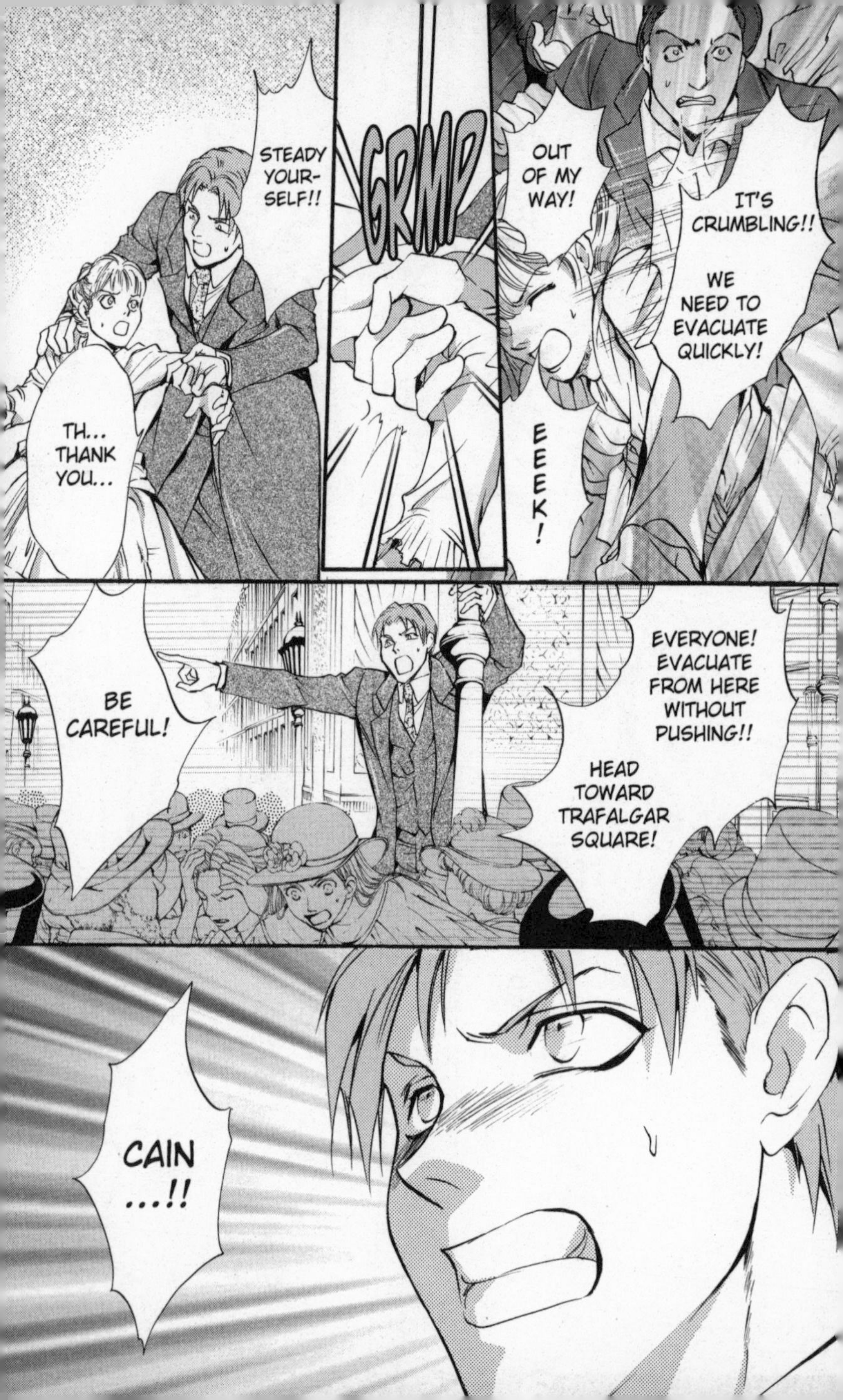
IT'S CRUMBLING!!
WE NEED TO EVACUATE QUICKLY!
OUT OF MY WAY!
EEEK!
GRMP
STEADY YOUR-SELF!!
TH... THANK YOU...
EVERYONE! EVACUATE FROM HERE WITHOUT PUSHING!!
HEAD TOWARD TRAFALGAR SQUARE!
BE CAREFUL!
CAIN ...!!

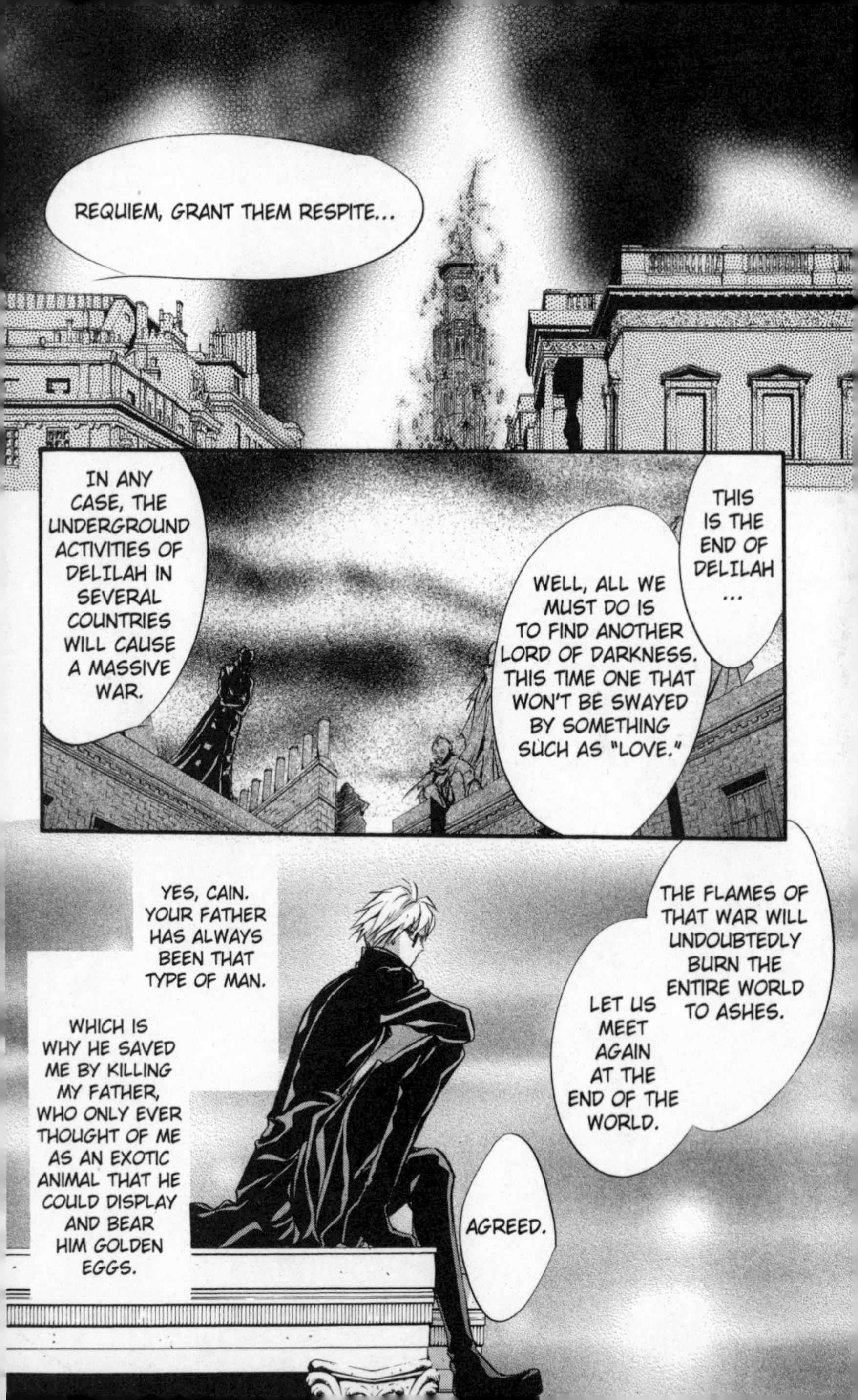
REQUIEM, GRANT THEM RESPITE...
THIS IS THE END OF DELILAH ...
WELL, ALL WE MUST DO IS TO FIND ANOTHER LORD OF DARKNESS. THIS TIME ONE THAT WON'T BE SWAYED BY SOMETHING SUCH AS "LOVE."
IN ANY CASE, THE UNDERGROUND ACTIVITIES OF DELILAH IN SEVERAL COUNTRIES WILL CAUSE A MASSIVE WAR.
THE FLAMES OF THAT WAR WILL UNDOUBTEDLY BURN THE ENTIRE WORLD TO ASHES.
LET US MEET AGAIN AT THE END OF THE WORLD.
AGREED.
YES, CAIN. YOUR FATHER HAS ALWAYS BEEN THAT TYPE OF MAN.
WHICH IS WHY HE SAVED ME BY KILLING MY FATHER, WHO ONLY EVER THOUGHT OF ME AS AN EXOTIC ANIMAL THAT HE COULD DISPLAY AND BEAR HIM GOLDEN EGGS.

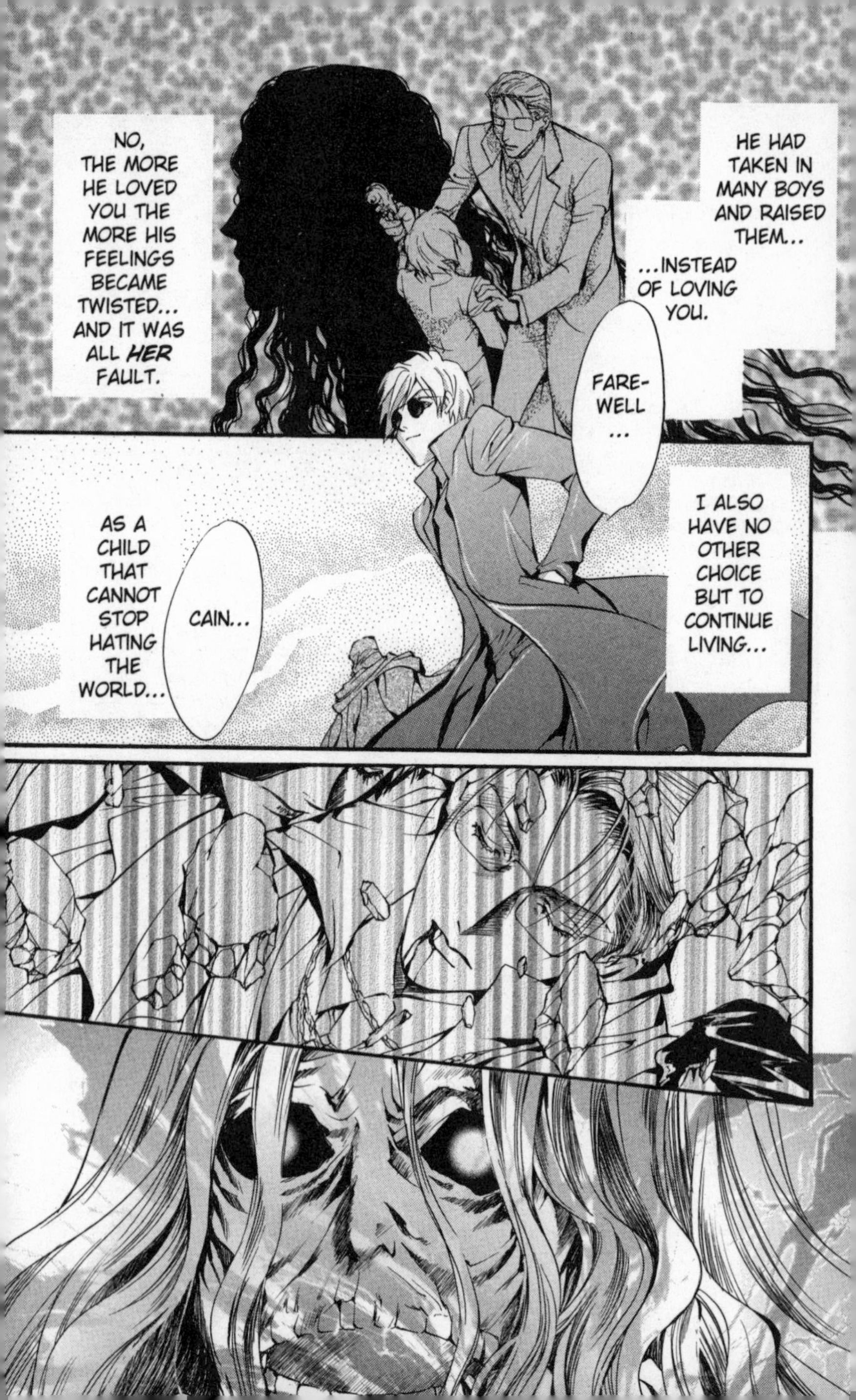
HE HAD TAKEN IN MANY BOYS AND RAISED THEM...
...INSTEAD OF LOVING YOU.
NO, THE MORE HE LOVED YOU THE MORE HIS FEELINGS BECAME TWISTED... AND IT WAS ALL *HER* FAULT.
FARE-WELL...
I ALSO HAVE NO OTHER CHOICE BUT TO CONTINUE LIVING...
CAIN...
AS A CHILD THAT CANNOT STOP HATING THE WORLD...

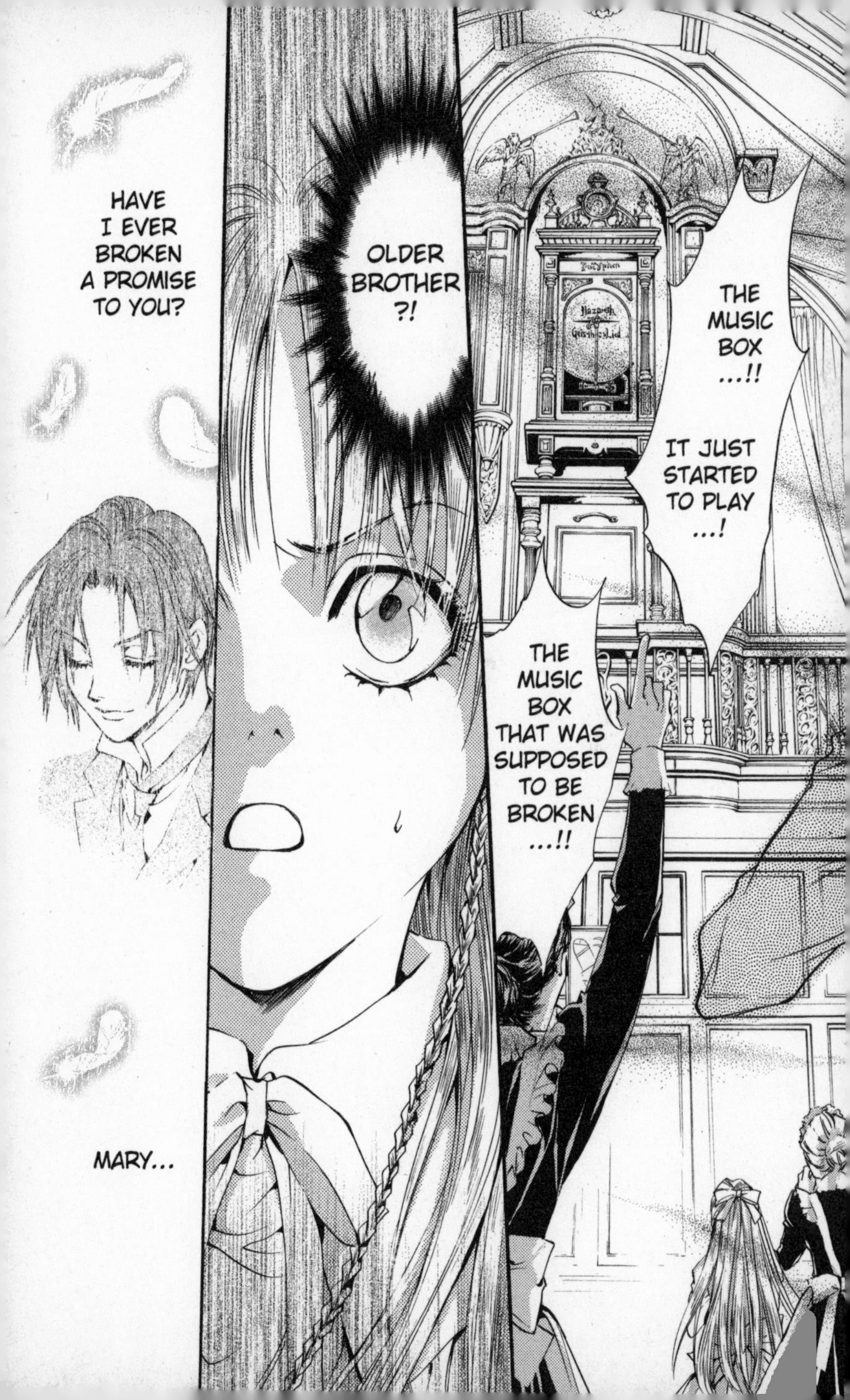
THE MUSIC BOX ...!!
IT JUST STARTED TO PLAY ...!
THE MUSIC BOX THAT WAS SUPPOSED TO BE BROKEN ...!!
OLDER BROTHER ?!
HAVE I EVER BROKEN A PROMISE TO YOU?
MARY...

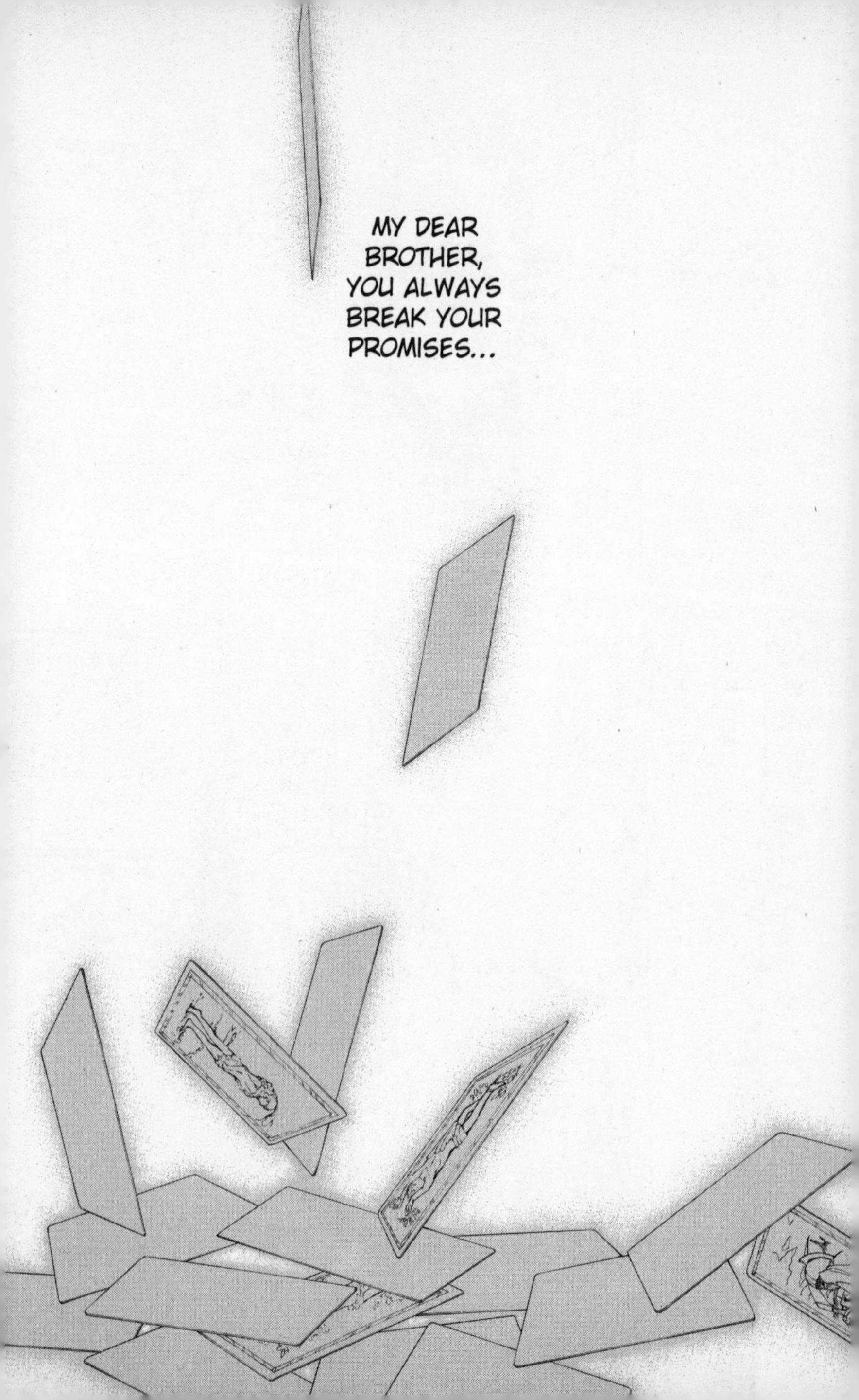
MY DEAR BROTHER, YOU ALWAYS BREAK YOUR PROMISES...

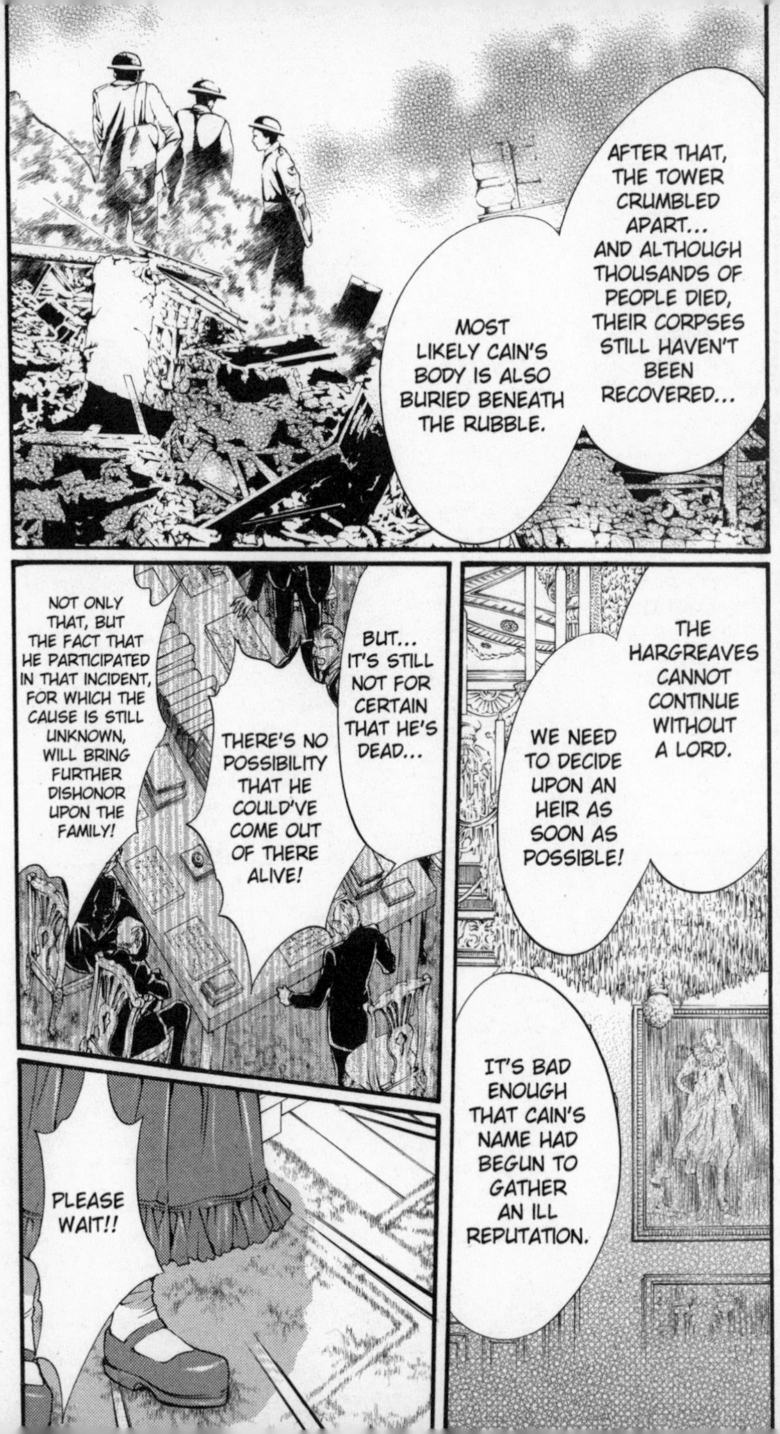
AFTER THAT, THE TOWER CRUMBLED APART... AND ALTHOUGH THOUSANDS OF PEOPLE DIED, THEIR CORPSES STILL HAVEN'T BEEN RECOVERED...
MOST LIKELY CAIN'S BODY IS ALSO BURIED BENEATH THE RUBBLE.
THE HARGREAVES CANNOT CONTINUE WITHOUT A LORD.
WE NEED TO DECIDE UPON AN HEIR AS SOON AS POSSIBLE!
IT'S BAD ENOUGH THAT CAIN'S NAME HAD BEGUN TO GATHER AN ILL REPUTATION.
BUT... IT'S STILL NOT FOR CERTAIN THAT HE'S DEAD...
THERE'S NO POSSIBILITY THAT HE COULD'VE COME OUT OF THERE ALIVE!
NOT ONLY THAT, BUT THE FACT THAT HE PARTICIPATED IN THAT INCIDENT, FOR WHICH THE CAUSE IS STILL UNKNOWN, WILL BRING FURTHER DISHONOR UPON THE FAMILY!
PLEASE WAIT!!

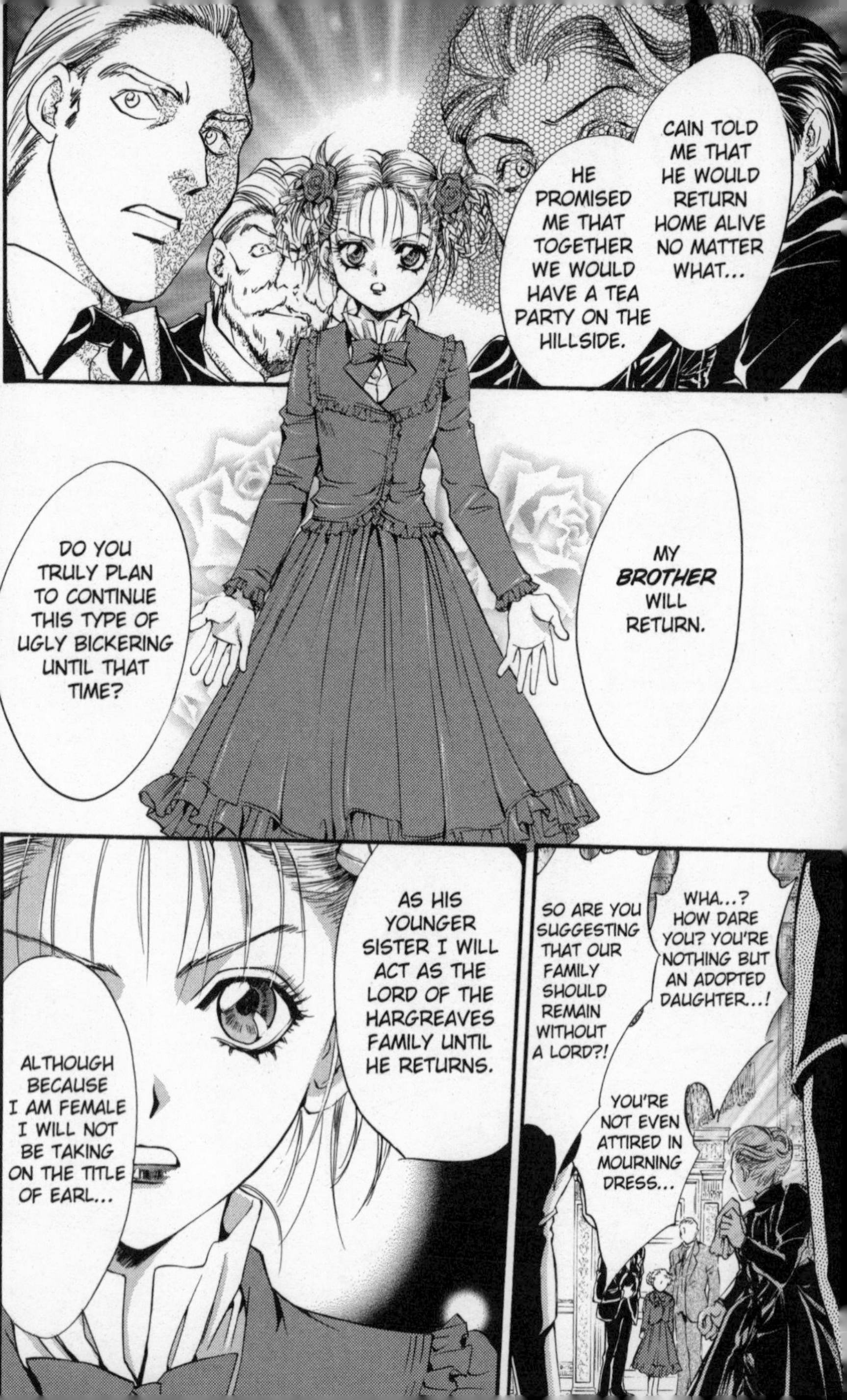
CAIN TOLD ME THAT HE WOULD RETURN HOME ALIVE NO MATTER WHAT...
HE PROMISED ME THAT TOGETHER WE WOULD HAVE A TEA PARTY ON THE HILLSIDE.
MY **BROTHER** WILL RETURN.
DO YOU TRULY PLAN TO CONTINUE THIS TYPE OF UGLY BICKERING UNTIL THAT TIME?
WHA...? HOW DARE YOU? YOU'RE NOTHING BUT AN ADOPTED DAUGHTER...!
SO ARE YOU SUGGESTING THAT OUR FAMILY SHOULD REMAIN WITHOUT A LORD?!
YOU'RE NOT EVEN ATTIRED IN MOURNING DRESS...
AS HIS YOUNGER SISTER I WILL ACT AS THE LORD OF THE HARGREAVES FAMILY UNTIL HE RETURNS.
ALTHOUGH BECAUSE I AM FEMALE I WILL NOT BE TAKING ON THE TITLE OF EARL...

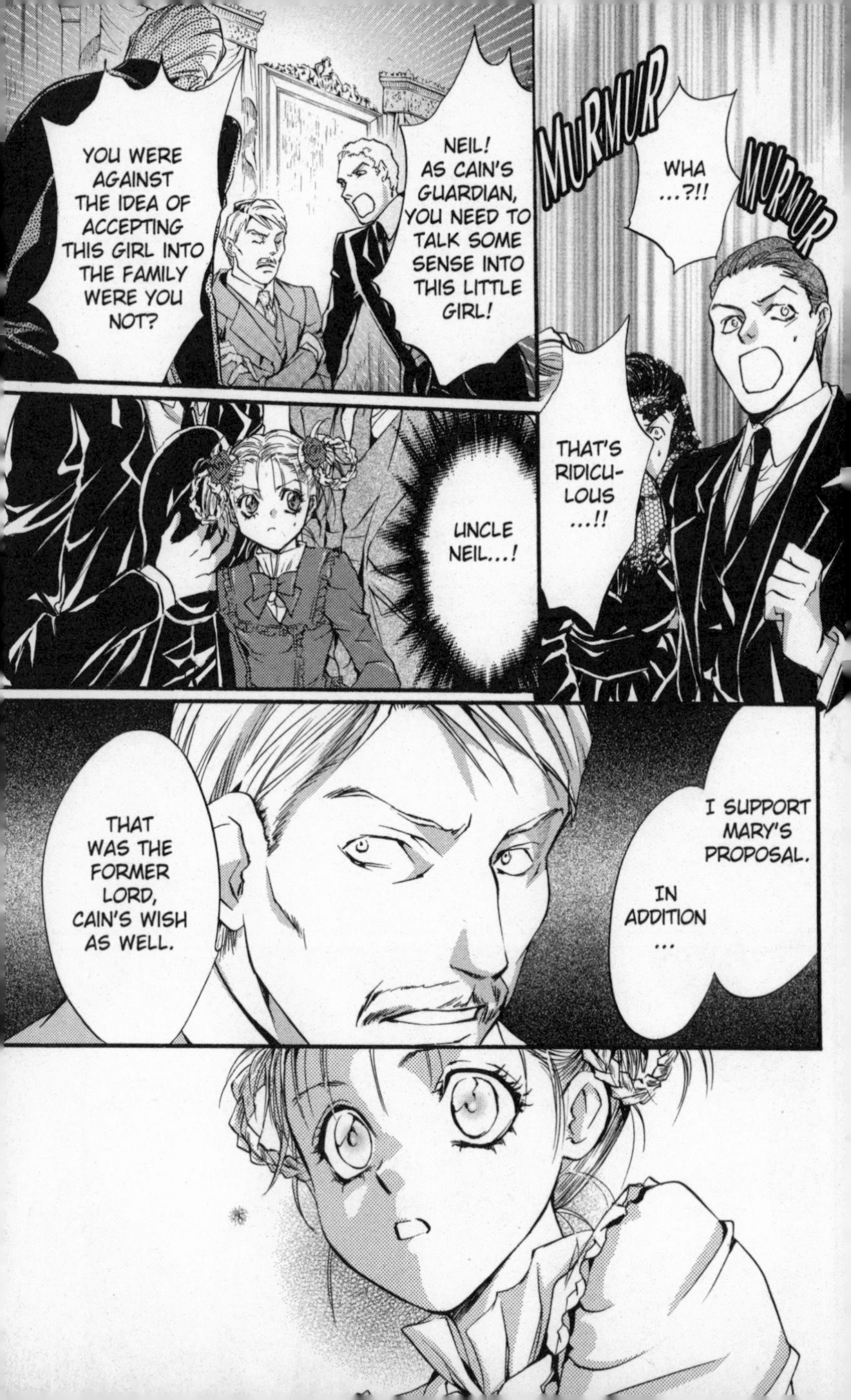
MURMUR
WHA ...?!!
MURMUR
THAT'S RIDICULOUS ...!!
NEIL! AS CAIN'S GUARDIAN, YOU NEED TO TALK SOME SENSE INTO THIS LITTLE GIRL!
YOU WERE AGAINST THE IDEA OF ACCEPTING THIS GIRL INTO THE FAMILY WERE YOU NOT?
UNCLE NEIL...!
I SUPPORT MARY'S PROPOSAL.
IN ADDITION ...
THAT WAS THE FORMER LORD, CAIN'S WISH AS WELL.

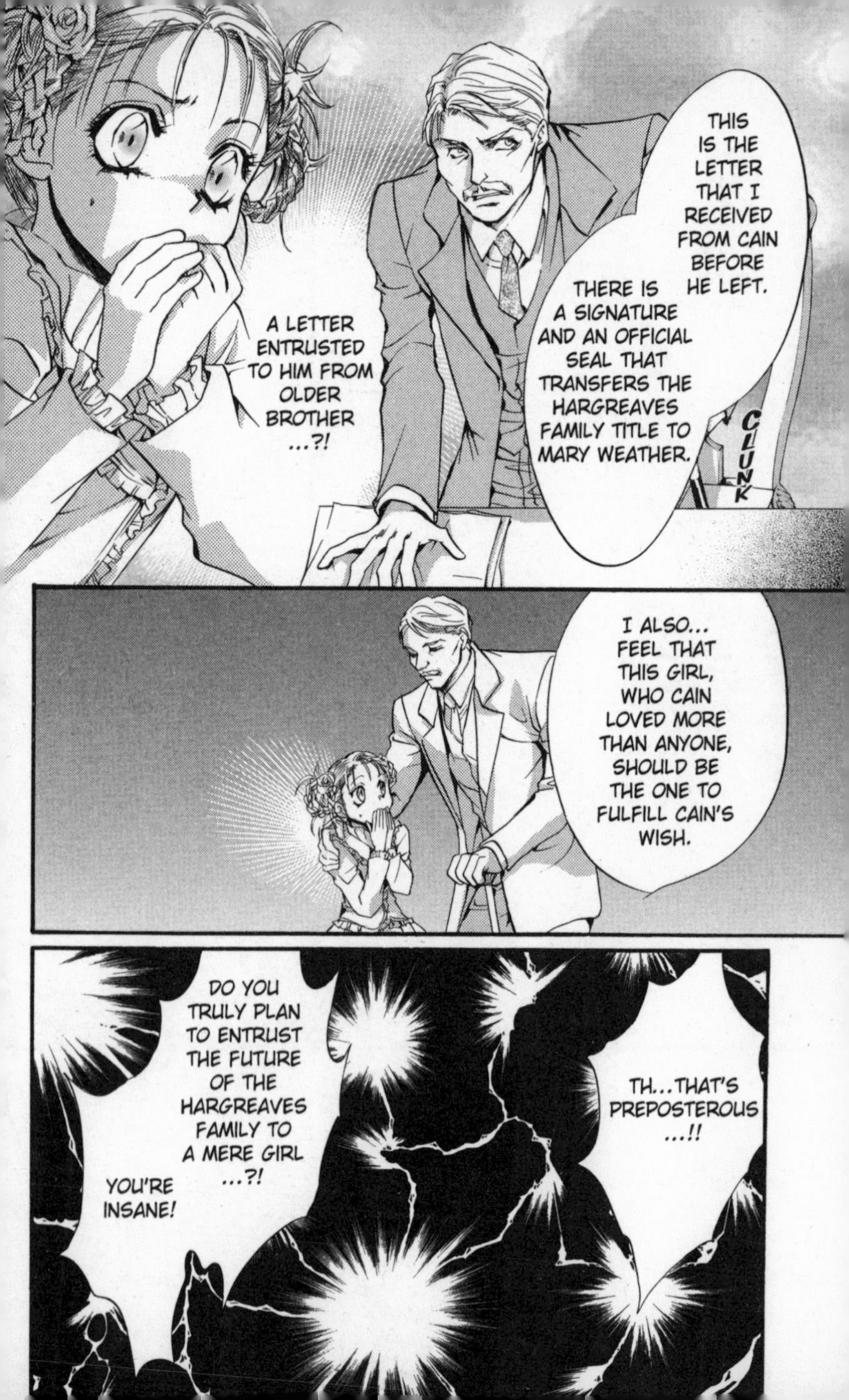
THIS IS THE LETTER THAT I RECEIVED FROM CAIN BEFORE HE LEFT.
CLUNK
THERE IS A SIGNATURE AND AN OFFICIAL SEAL THAT TRANSFERS THE HARGREAVES FAMILY TITLE TO MARY WEATHER.
A LETTER ENTRUSTED TO HIM FROM OLDER BROTHER ...?!
I ALSO... FEEL THAT THIS GIRL, WHO CAIN LOVED MORE THAN ANYONE, SHOULD BE THE ONE TO FULFILL CAIN'S WISH.
TH...THAT'S PREPOSTEROUS ...!!
DO YOU TRULY PLAN TO ENTRUST THE FUTURE OF THE HARGREAVES FAMILY TO A MERE GIRL ...?!
YOU'RE INSANE!

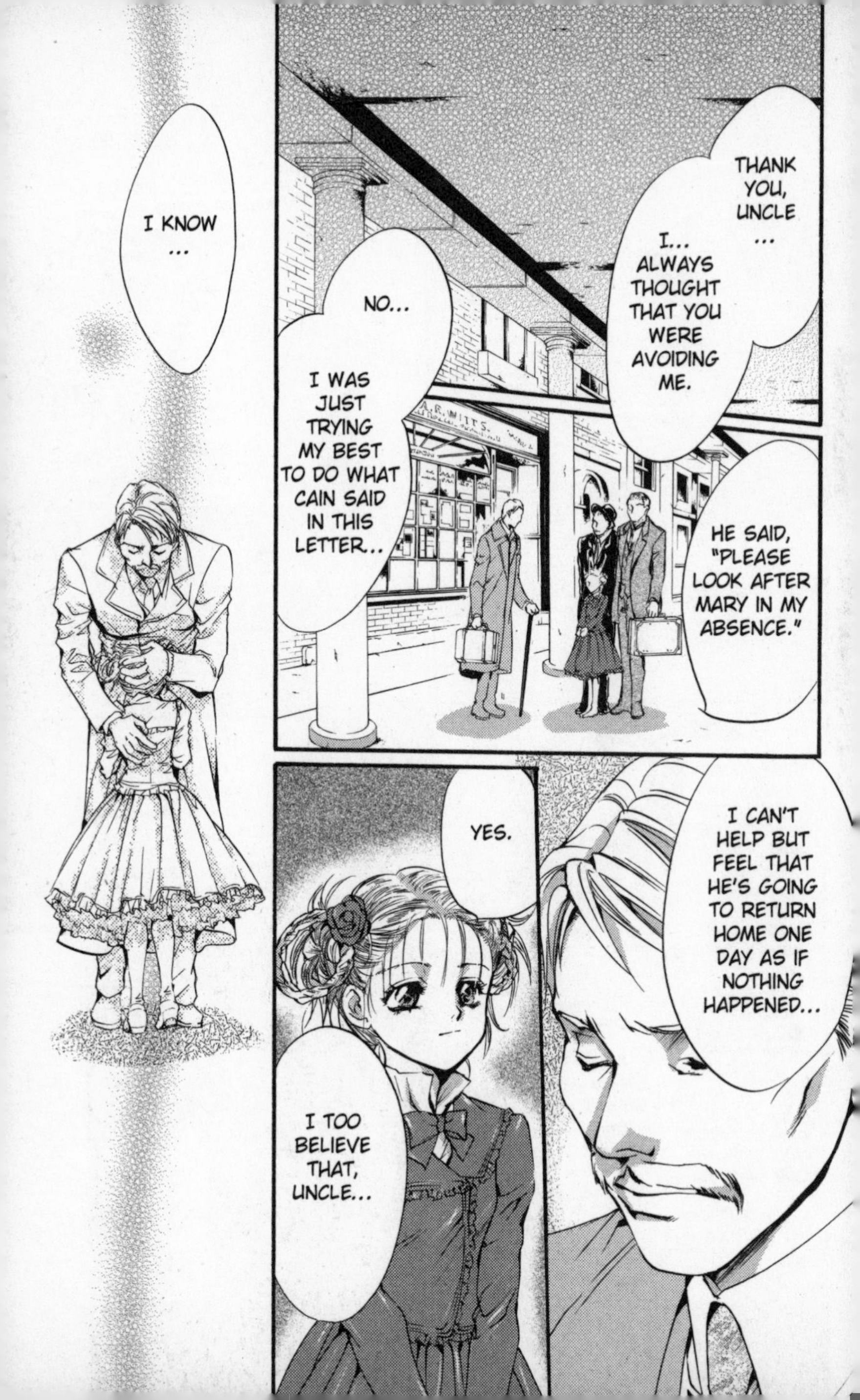
THANK YOU, UNCLE...
I... ALWAYS THOUGHT THAT YOU WERE AVOIDING ME.
NO...
I WAS JUST TRYING MY BEST TO DO WHAT CAIN SAID IN THIS LETTER...
HE SAID, "PLEASE LOOK AFTER MARY IN MY ABSENCE."
I CAN'T HELP BUT FEEL THAT HE'S GOING TO RETURN HOME ONE DAY AS IF NOTHING HAPPENED...
YES.
I TOO BELIEVE THAT, UNCLE...
I KNOW...

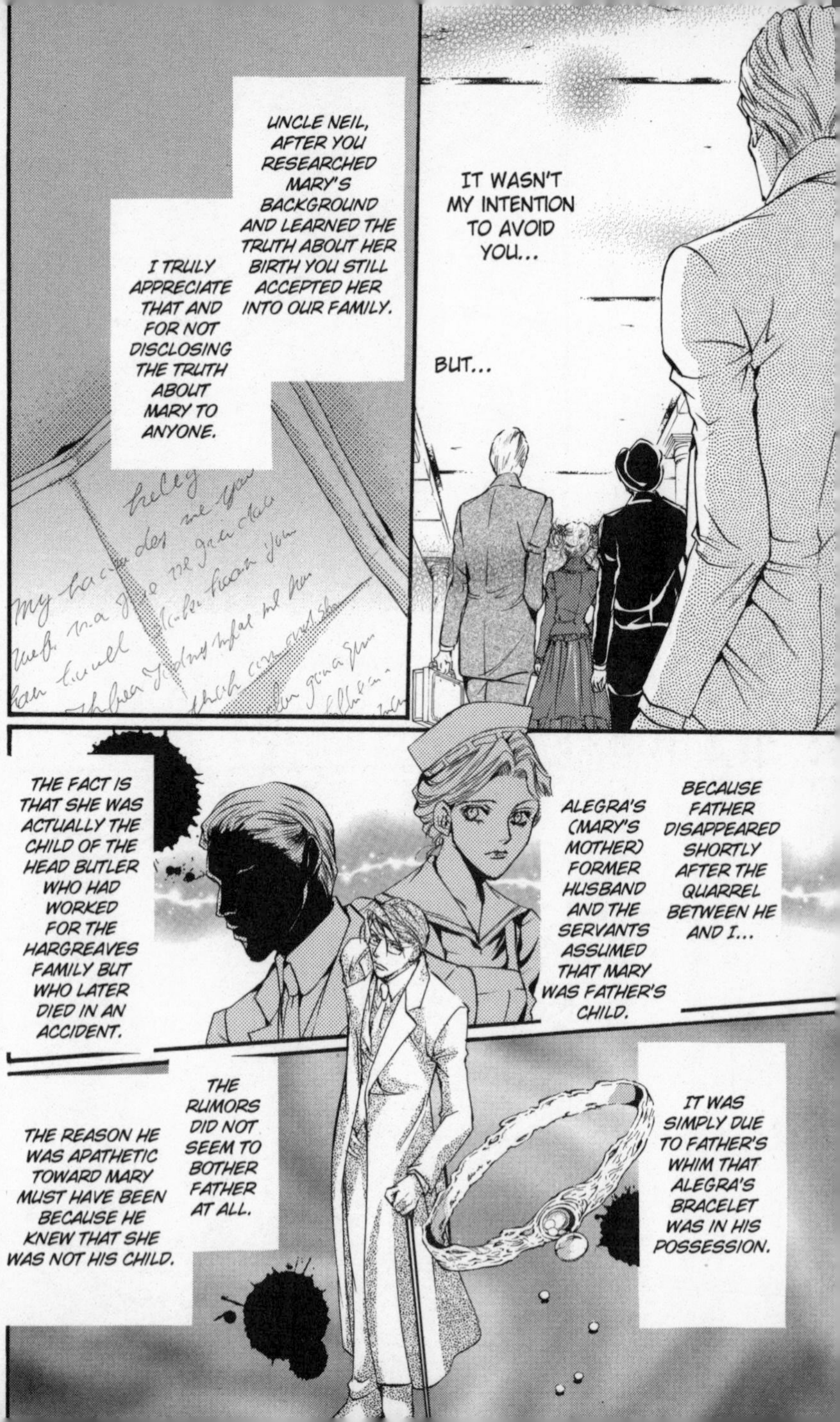
IT WASN'T MY INTENTION TO AVOID YOU...
BUT...
UNCLE NEIL, AFTER YOU RESEARCHED MARY'S BACKGROUND AND LEARNED THE TRUTH ABOUT HER BIRTH YOU STILL ACCEPTED HER INTO OUR FAMILY.
I TRULY APPRECIATE THAT AND FOR NOT DISCLOSING THE TRUTH ABOUT MARY TO ANYONE.
BECAUSE FATHER DISAPPEARED SHORTLY AFTER THE QUARREL BETWEEN HE AND I...
ALEGRA'S (MARY'S MOTHER) FORMER HUSBAND AND THE SERVANTS ASSUMED THAT MARY WAS FATHER'S CHILD.
THE FACT IS THAT SHE WAS ACTUALLY THE CHILD OF THE HEAD BUTLER WHO HAD WORKED FOR THE HARGREAVES FAMILY BUT WHO LATER DIED IN AN ACCIDENT.
IT WAS SIMPLY DUE TO FATHER'S WHIM THAT ALEGRA'S BRACELET WAS IN HIS POSSESSION.
THE RUMORS DID NOT SEEM TO BOTHER FATHER AT ALL.
THE REASON HE WAS APATHETIC TOWARD MARY MUST HAVE BEEN BECAUSE HE KNEW THAT SHE WAS NOT HIS CHILD.

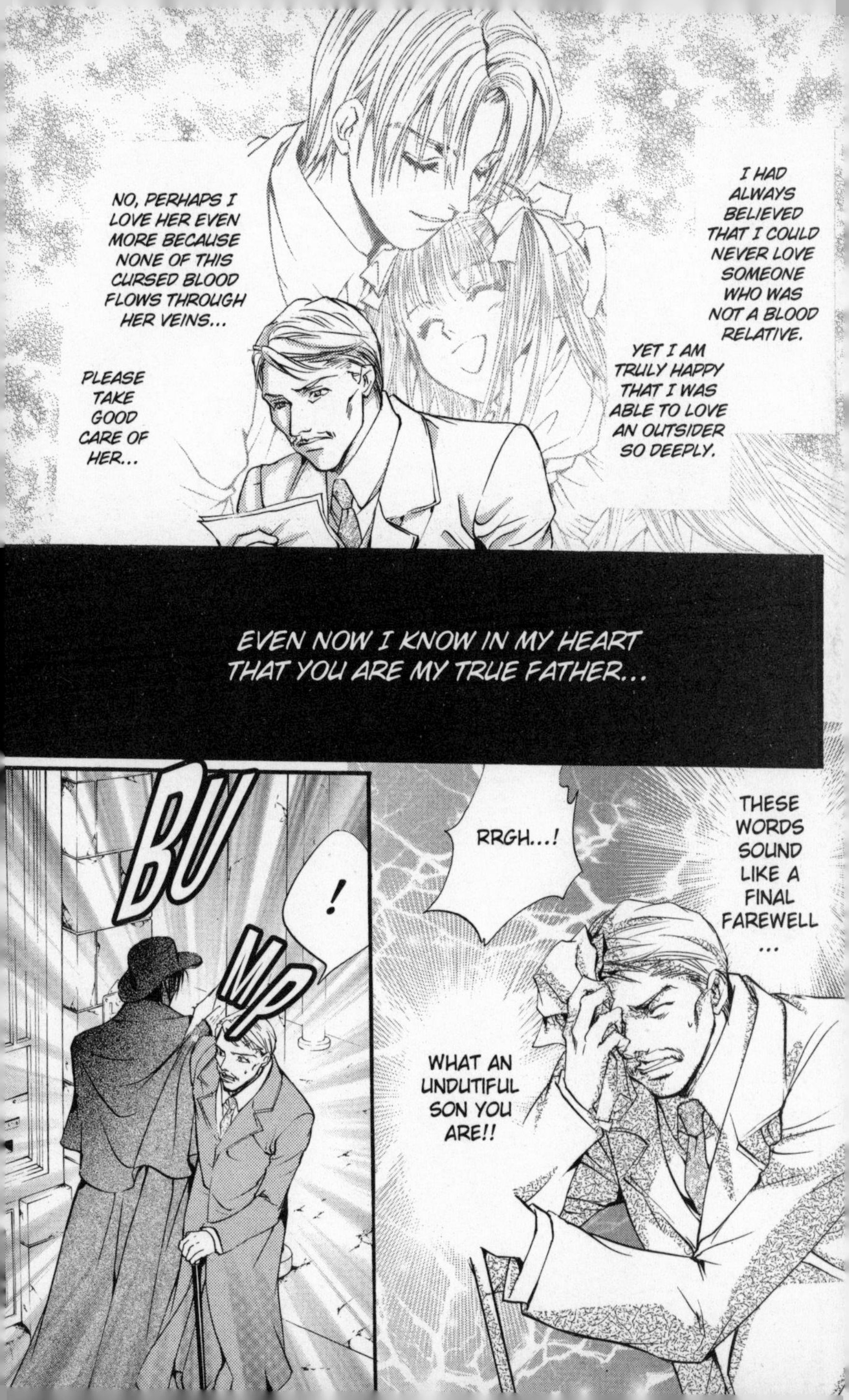
I HAD ALWAYS BELIEVED THAT I COULD NEVER LOVE SOMEONE WHO WAS NOT A BLOOD RELATIVE.
YET I AM TRULY HAPPY THAT I WAS ABLE TO LOVE AN OUTSIDER SO DEEPLY.
NO, PERHAPS I LOVE HER EVEN MORE BECAUSE NONE OF THIS CURSED BLOOD FLOWS THROUGH HER VEINS...
PLEASE TAKE GOOD CARE OF HER...
EVEN NOW I KNOW IN MY HEART THAT YOU ARE MY TRUE FATHER...
THESE WORDS SOUND LIKE A FINAL FAREWELL ...
RRGH...!
WHAT AN UNDUTIFUL SON YOU ARE!!
BUMP
!

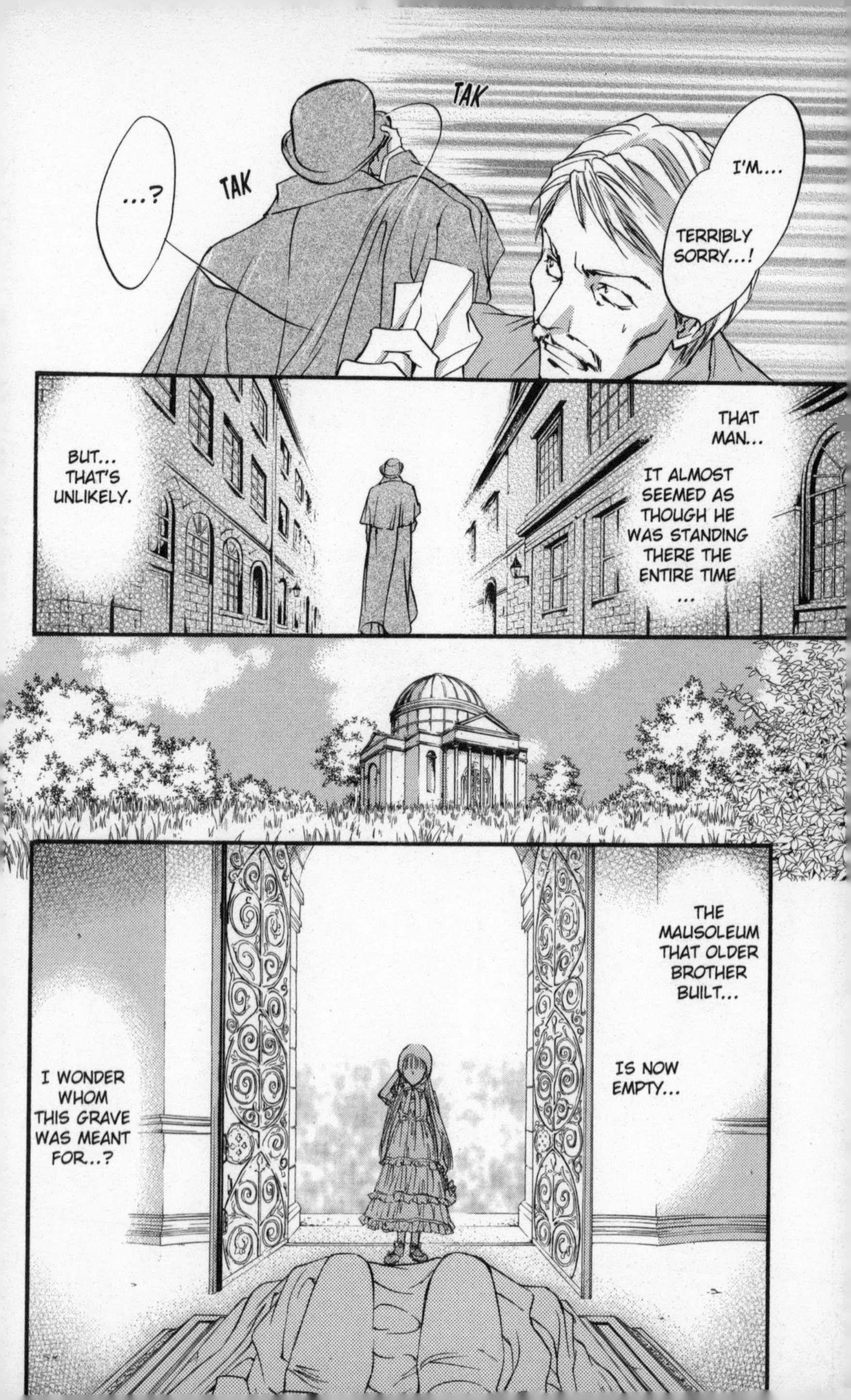
I'M...
TERRIBLY SORRY...!
TAK
TAK
...?
THAT MAN...
IT ALMOST SEEMED AS THOUGH HE WAS STANDING THERE THE ENTIRE TIME ...
BUT... THAT'S UNLIKELY.
THE MAUSOLEUM THAT OLDER BROTHER BUILT...
IS NOW EMPTY...
I WONDER WHOM THIS GRAVE WAS MEANT FOR...?

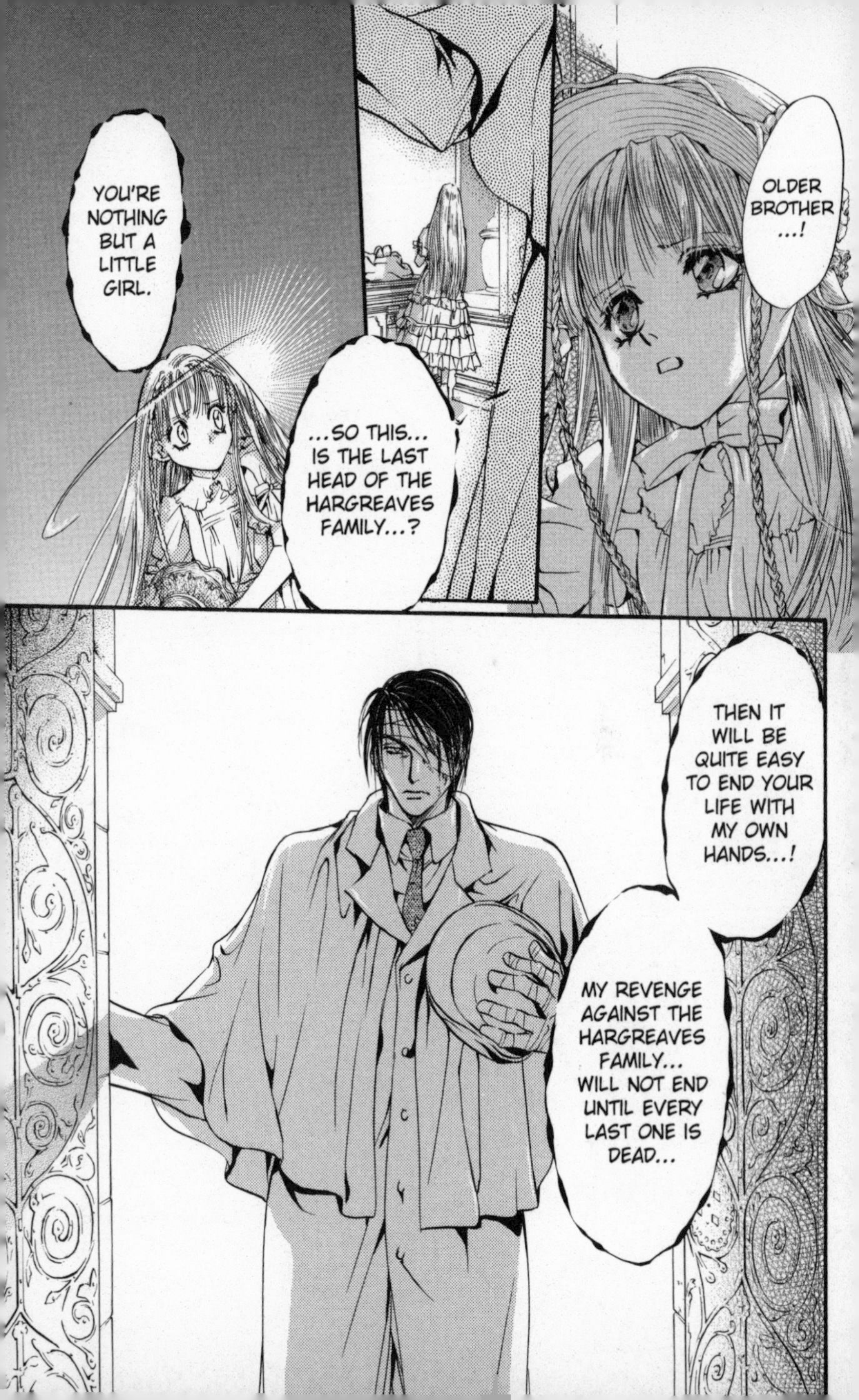
OLDER BROTHER ...!
...SO THIS... IS THE LAST HEAD OF THE HARGREAVES FAMILY...?
YOU'RE NOTHING BUT A LITTLE GIRL.
THEN IT WILL BE QUITE EASY TO END YOUR LIFE WITH MY OWN HANDS...!
MY REVENGE AGAINST THE HARGREAVES FAMILY... WILL NOT END UNTIL EVERY LAST ONE IS DEAD...

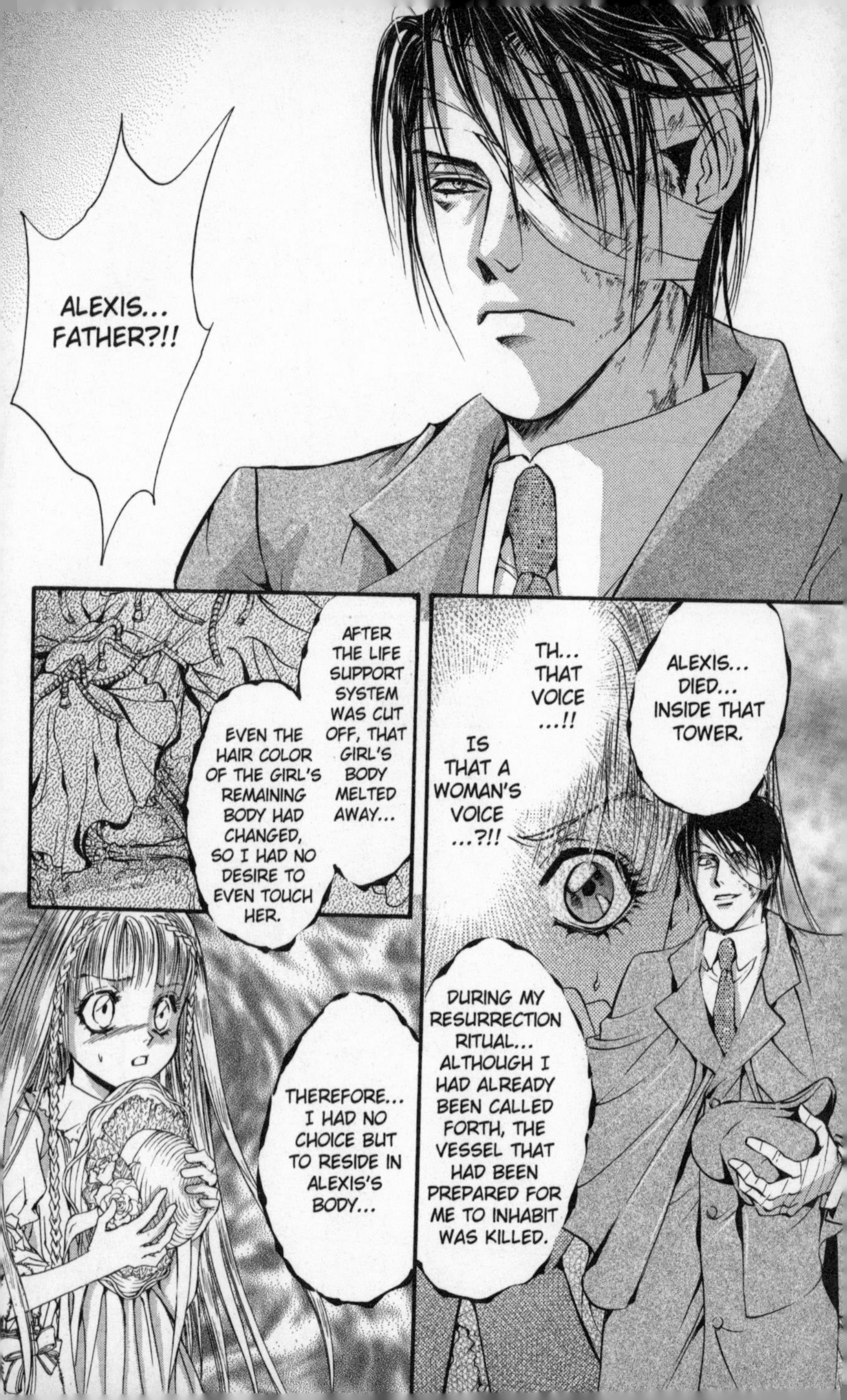
ALEXIS... FATHER?!!
ALEXIS... DIED... INSIDE THAT TOWER.
TH... THAT VOICE ...!!
IS THAT A WOMAN'S VOICE ...?!!
DURING MY RESURRECTION RITUAL... ALTHOUGH I HAD ALREADY BEEN CALLED FORTH, THE VESSEL THAT HAD BEEN PREPARED FOR ME TO INHABIT WAS KILLED.
AFTER THE LIFE SUPPORT SYSTEM WAS CUT OFF, THAT GIRL'S BODY MELTED AWAY...
EVEN THE HAIR COLOR OF THE GIRL'S REMAINING BODY HAD CHANGED, SO I HAD NO DESIRE TO EVEN TOUCH HER.
THEREFORE... I HAD NO CHOICE BUT TO RESIDE IN ALEXIS'S BODY...

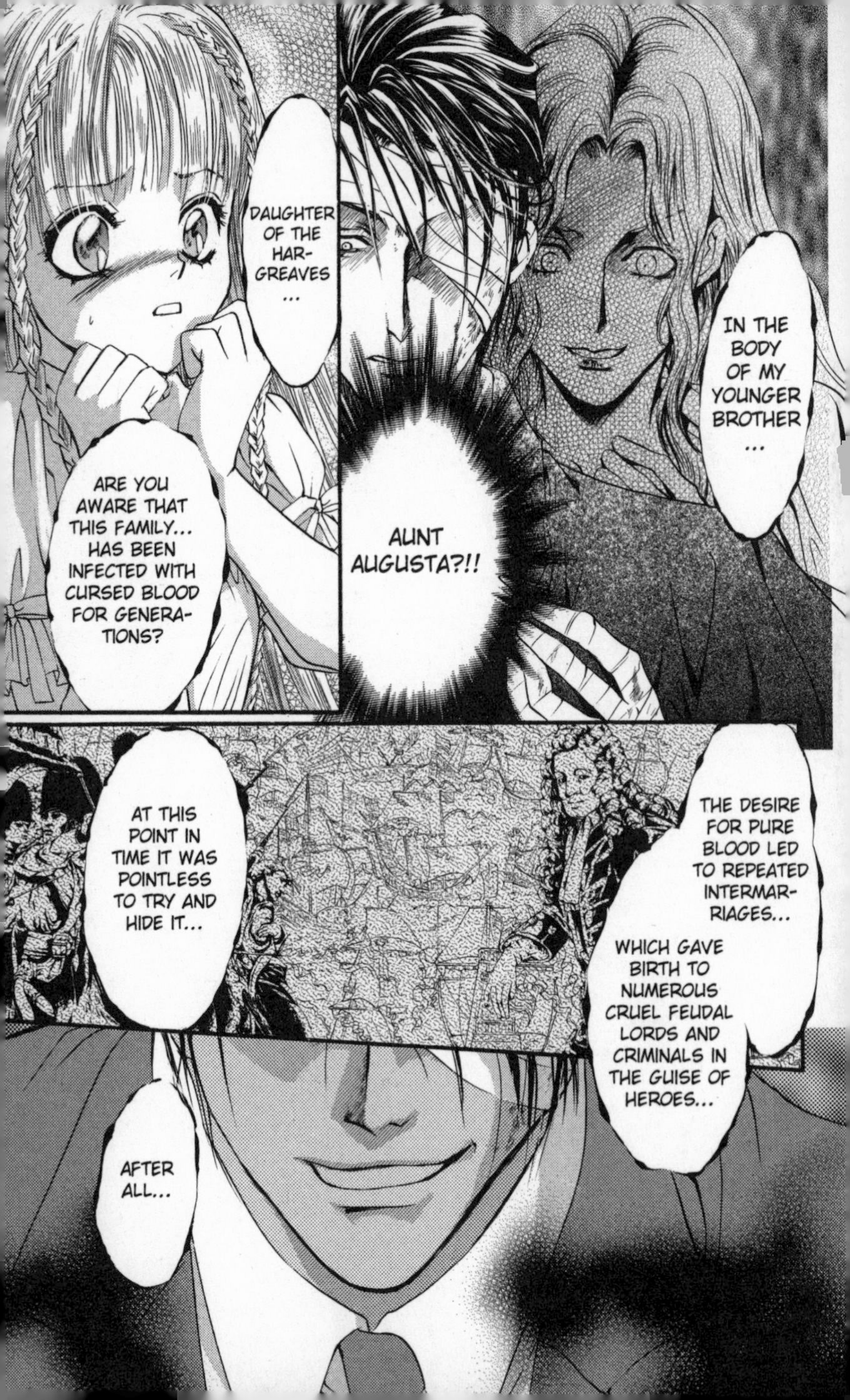
IN THE BODY OF MY YOUNGER BROTHER...
AUNT AUGUSTA?!!
DAUGHTER OF THE HAR-GREAVES...
ARE YOU AWARE THAT THIS FAMILY... HAS BEEN INFECTED WITH CURSED BLOOD FOR GENERA-TIONS?
THE DESIRE FOR PURE BLOOD LED TO REPEATED INTERMAR-RIAGES...
WHICH GAVE BIRTH TO NUMEROUS CRUEL FEUDAL LORDS AND CRIMINALS IN THE GUISE OF HEROES...
AT THIS POINT IN TIME IT WAS POINTLESS TO TRY AND HIDE IT...
AFTER ALL...

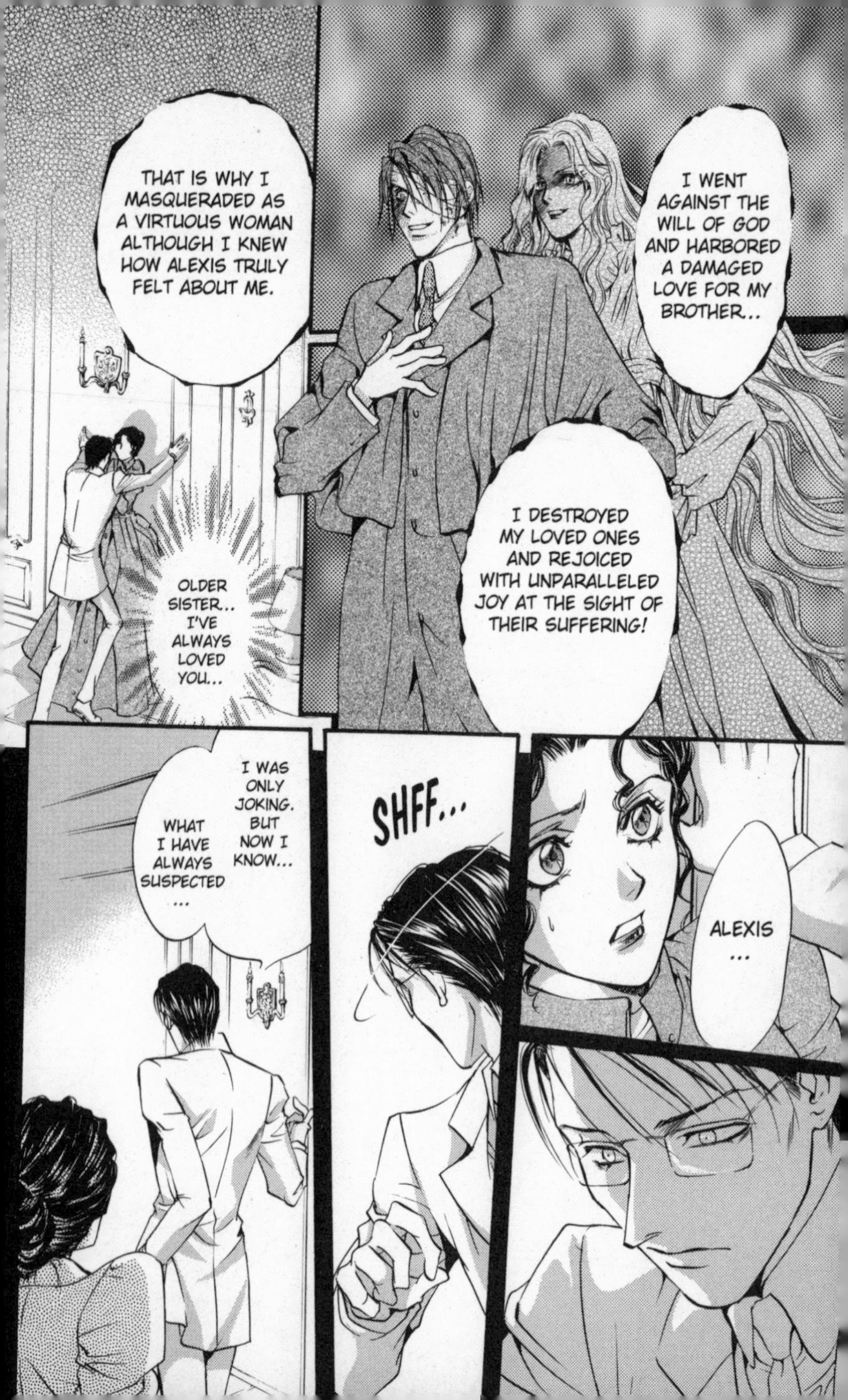
I WENT AGAINST THE WILL OF GOD AND HARBORED A DAMAGED LOVE FOR MY BROTHER...
I DESTROYED MY LOVED ONES AND REJOICED WITH UNPARALLELED JOY AT THE SIGHT OF THEIR SUFFERING!
THAT IS WHY I MASQUERADED AS A VIRTUOUS WOMAN ALTHOUGH I KNEW HOW ALEXIS TRULY FELT ABOUT ME.
OLDER SISTER... I'VE ALWAYS LOVED YOU...
ALEXIS...
SHFF...
I WAS ONLY JOKING. BUT NOW I KNOW...
WHAT I HAVE ALWAYS SUSPECTED...

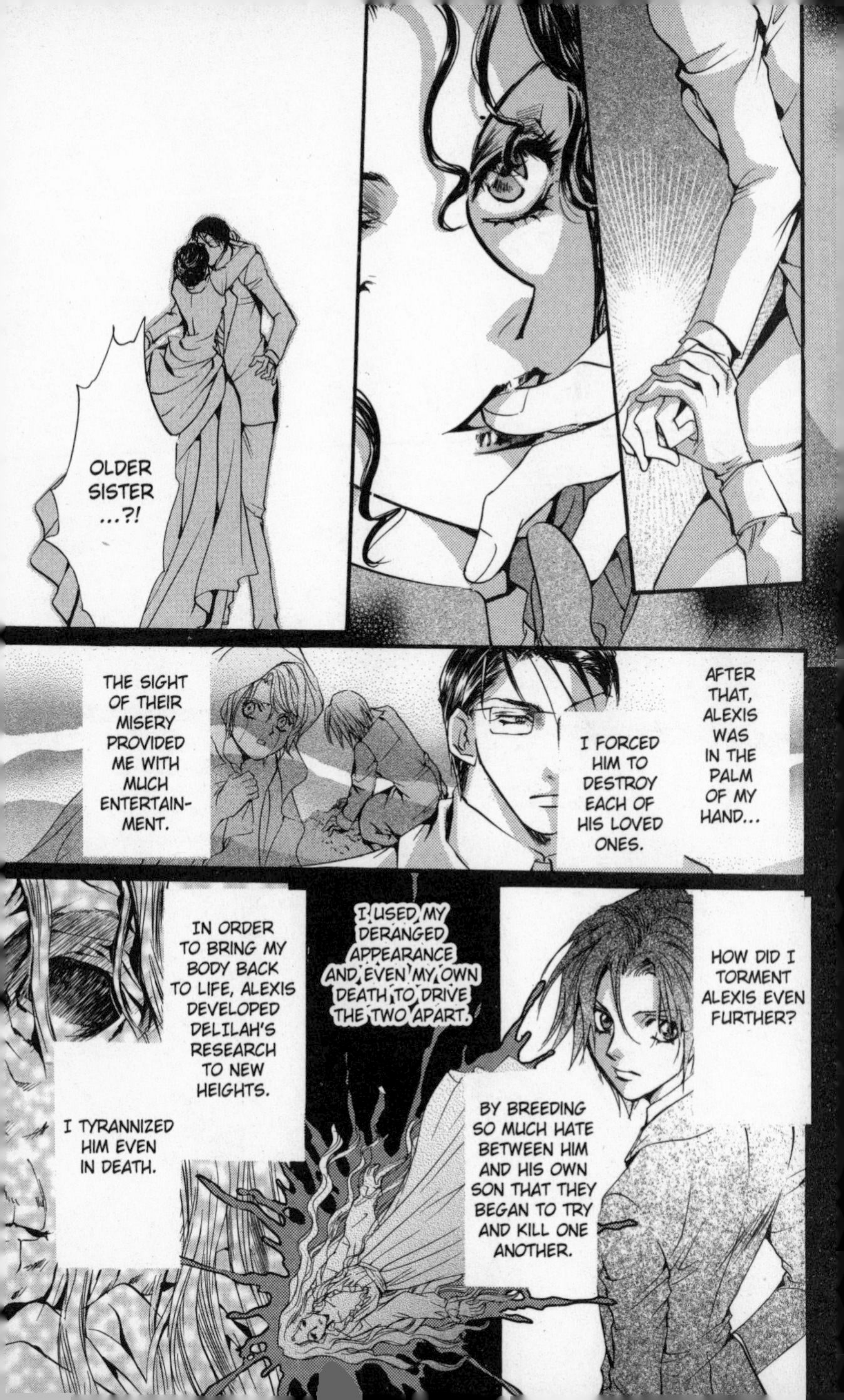
OLDER SISTER ...?!
AFTER THAT, ALEXIS WAS IN THE PALM OF MY HAND...
I FORCED HIM TO DESTROY EACH OF HIS LOVED ONES.
THE SIGHT OF THEIR MISERY PROVIDED ME WITH MUCH ENTERTAIN-MENT.
HOW DID I TORMENT ALEXIS EVEN FURTHER?
BY BREEDING SO MUCH HATE BETWEEN HIM AND HIS OWN SON THAT THEY BEGAN TO TRY AND KILL ONE ANOTHER.
I USED MY DERANGED APPEARANCE AND EVEN MY OWN DEATH TO DRIVE THE TWO APART.
IN ORDER TO BRING MY BODY BACK TO LIFE, ALEXIS DEVELOPED DELILAH'S RESEARCH TO NEW HEIGHTS.
I TYRANNIZED HIM EVEN IN DEATH.

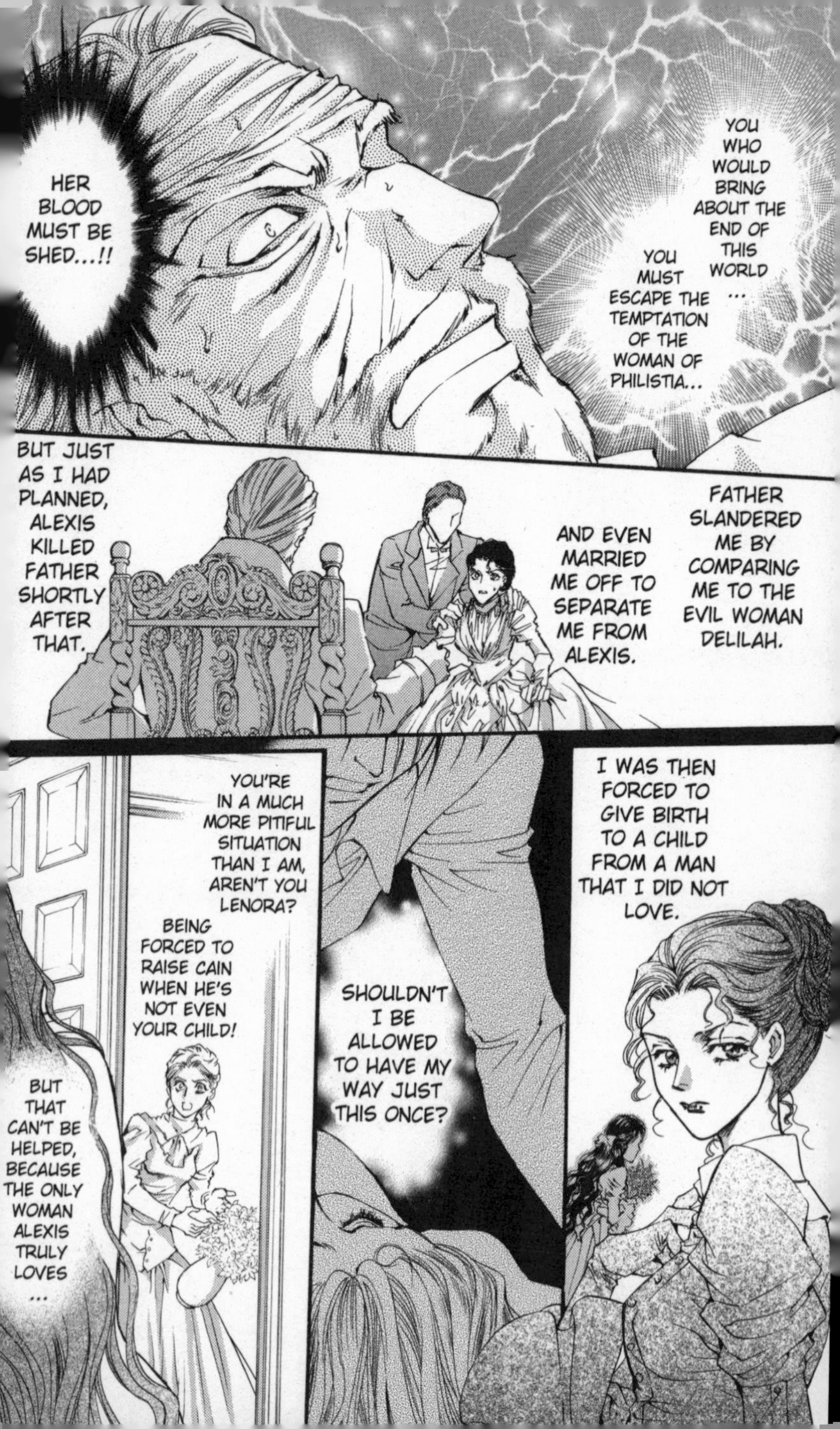
YOU WHO WOULD BRING ABOUT THE END OF THIS WORLD...
YOU MUST ESCAPE THE TEMPTATION OF THE WOMAN OF PHILISTIA...
HER BLOOD MUST BE SHED...!!
FATHER SLANDERED ME BY COMPARING ME TO THE EVIL WOMAN DELILAH.
AND EVEN MARRIED ME OFF TO SEPARATE ME FROM ALEXIS.
BUT JUST AS I HAD PLANNED, ALEXIS KILLED FATHER SHORTLY AFTER THAT.
I WAS THEN FORCED TO GIVE BIRTH TO A CHILD FROM A MAN THAT I DID NOT LOVE.
SHOULDN'T I BE ALLOWED TO HAVE MY WAY JUST THIS ONCE?
YOU'RE IN A MUCH MORE PITIFUL SITUATION THAN I AM, AREN'T YOU LENORA?
BEING FORCED TO RAISE CAIN WHEN HE'S NOT EVEN YOUR CHILD!
BUT THAT CAN'T BE HELPED, BECAUSE THE ONLY WOMAN ALEXIS TRULY LOVES...

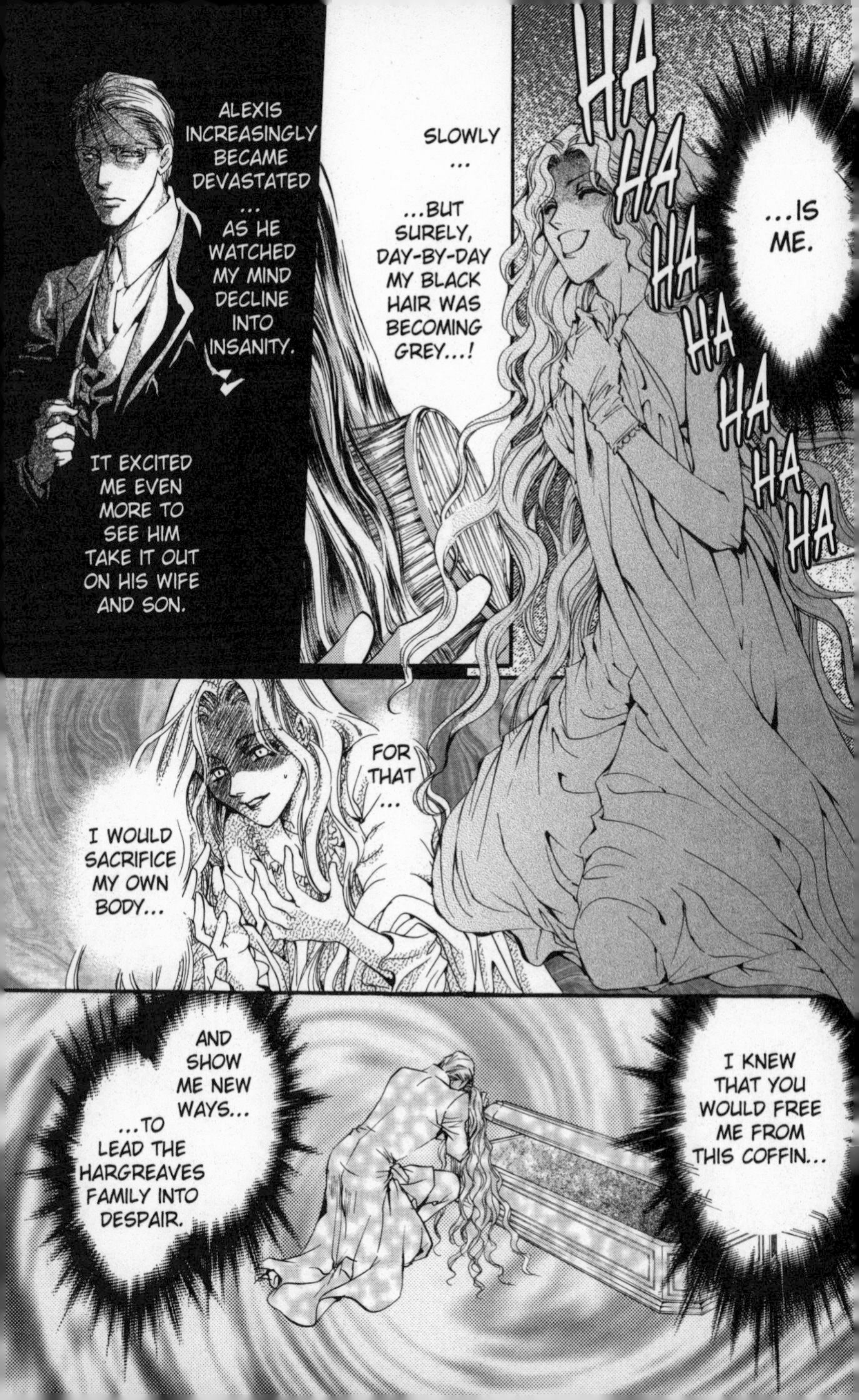

...IS ME.
HA HA HA HA HA HA HA HA
SLOWLY ...
...BUT SURELY, DAY-BY-DAY MY BLACK HAIR WAS BECOMING GREY...!
ALEXIS INCREASINGLY BECAME DEVASTATED ... AS HE WATCHED MY MIND DECLINE INTO INSANITY.
IT EXCITED ME EVEN MORE TO SEE HIM TAKE IT OUT ON HIS WIFE AND SON.
FOR THAT ...
I WOULD SACRIFICE MY OWN BODY...
I KNEW THAT YOU WOULD FREE ME FROM THIS COFFIN...
AND SHOW ME NEW WAYS...
...TO LEAD THE HARGREAVES FAMILY INTO DESPAIR.

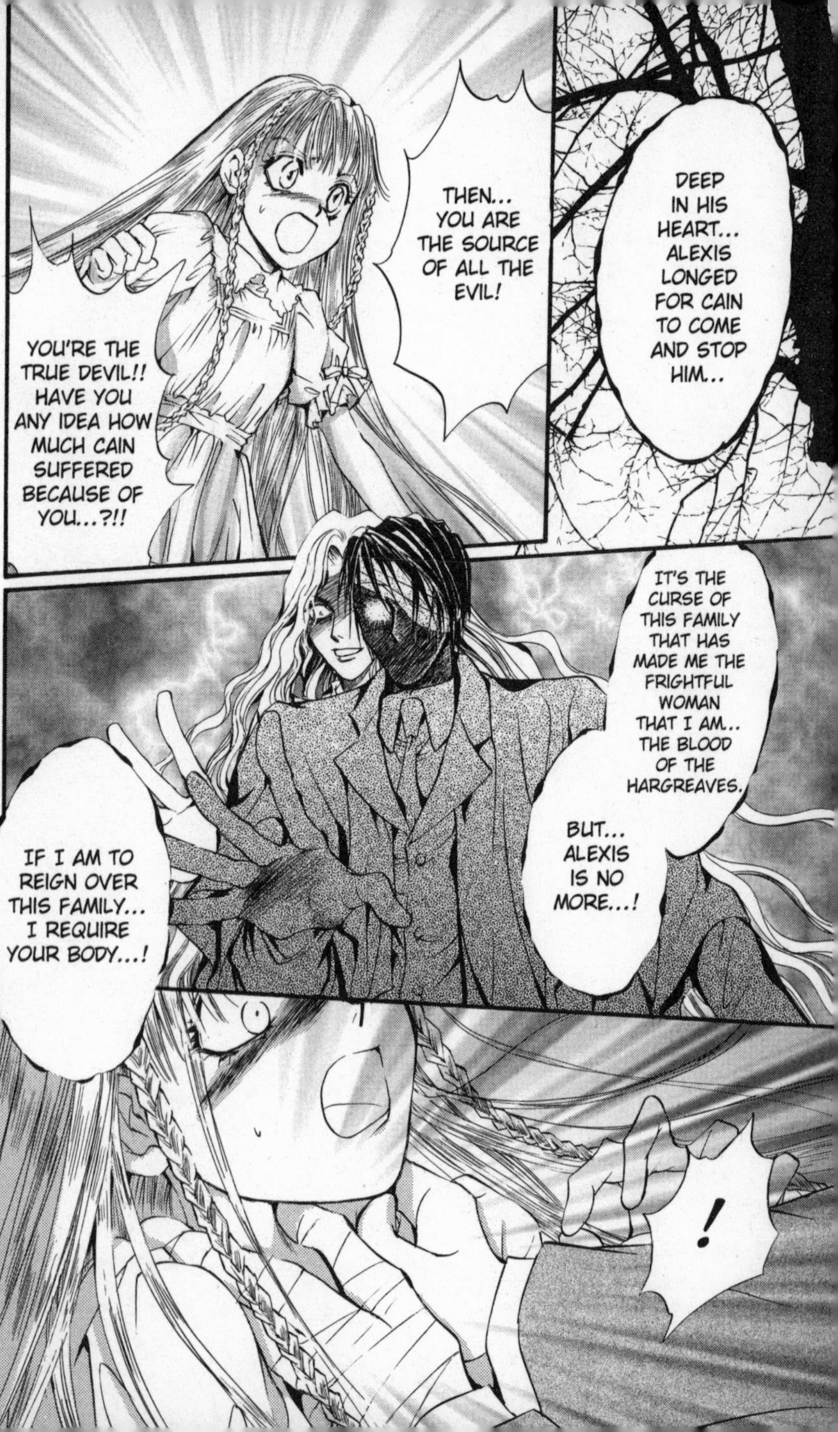
DEEP IN HIS HEART... ALEXIS LONGED FOR CAIN TO COME AND STOP HIM...
THEN... YOU ARE THE SOURCE OF ALL THE EVIL!
YOU'RE THE TRUE DEVIL!! HAVE YOU ANY IDEA HOW MUCH CAIN SUFFERED BECAUSE OF YOU...?!!
IT'S THE CURSE OF THIS FAMILY THAT HAS MADE ME THE FRIGHTFUL WOMAN THAT I AM... THE BLOOD OF THE HARGREAVES.
BUT... ALEXIS IS NO MORE...!
IF I AM TO REIGN OVER THIS FAMILY... I REQUIRE YOUR BODY...!
!

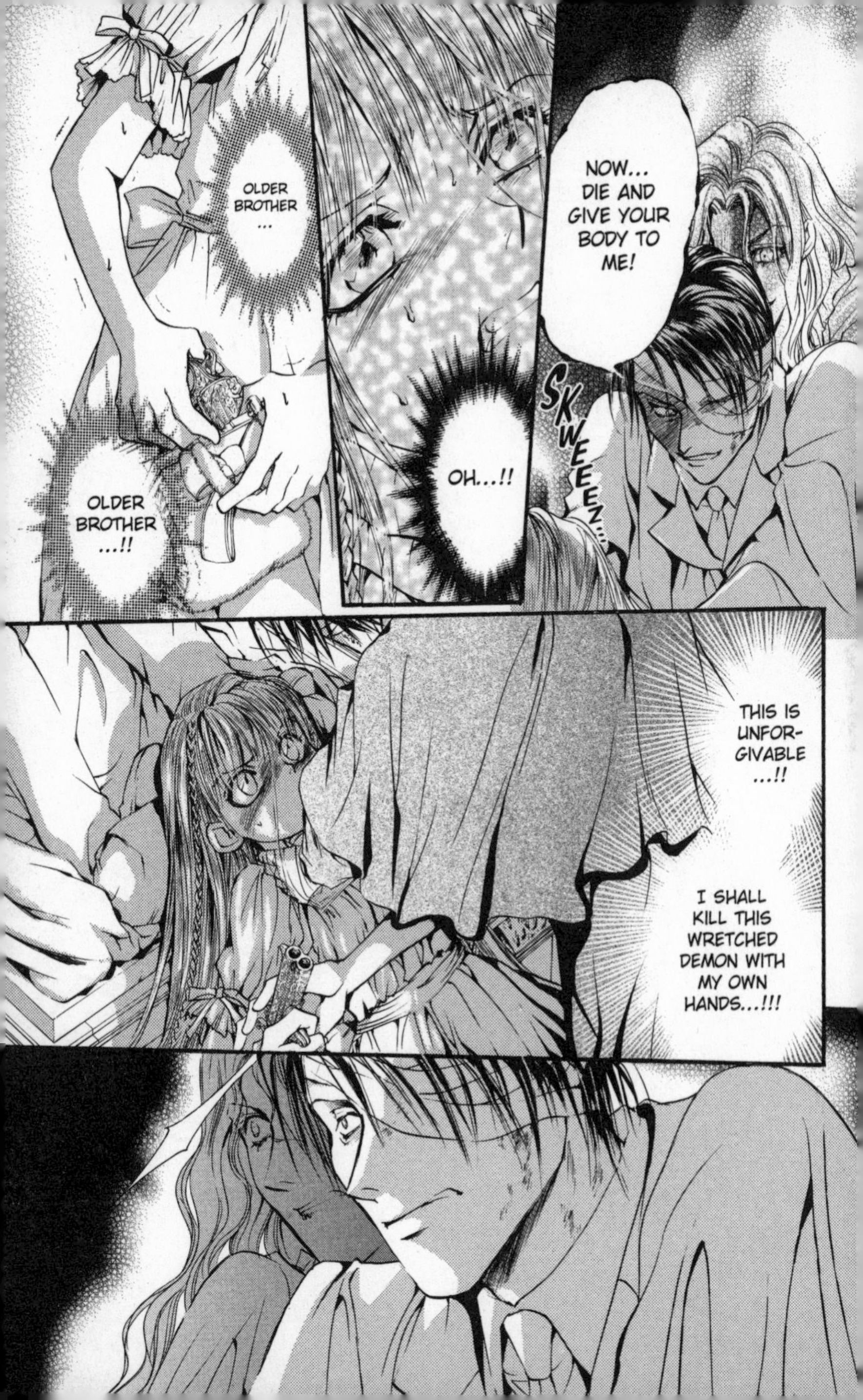
NOW... DIE AND GIVE YOUR BODY TO ME!
SKWEEEZ...
OH...!!
OLDER BROTHER...
OLDER BROTHER...!!
THIS IS UNFORGIVABLE...!!
I SHALL KILL THIS WRETCHED DEMON WITH MY OWN HANDS...!!!

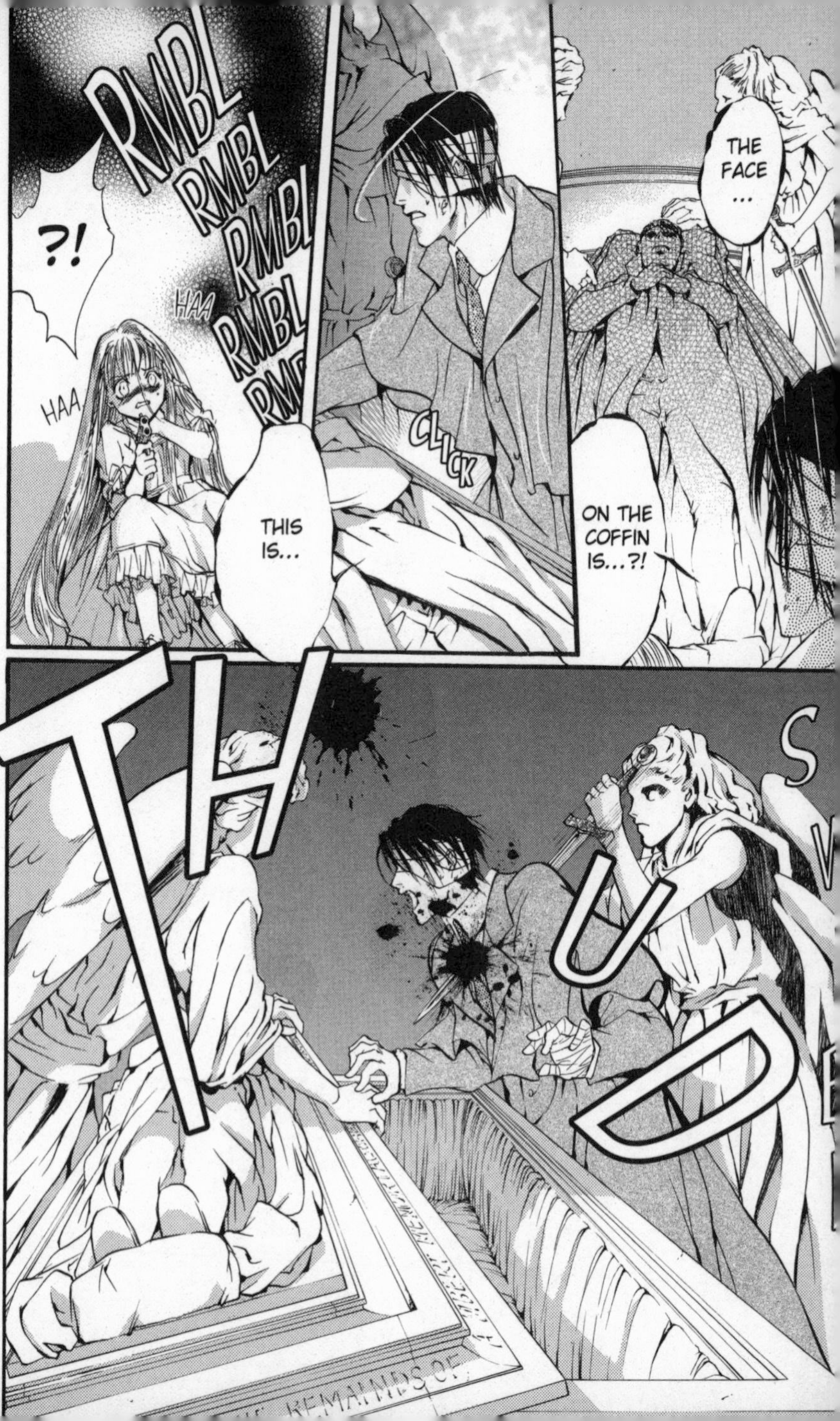
THE FACE ...
ON THE COFFIN IS...?!
CLICK
THIS IS...
RMBL RMBL RMBL RMBL RMBL
?!
HAA
HAA
THUD

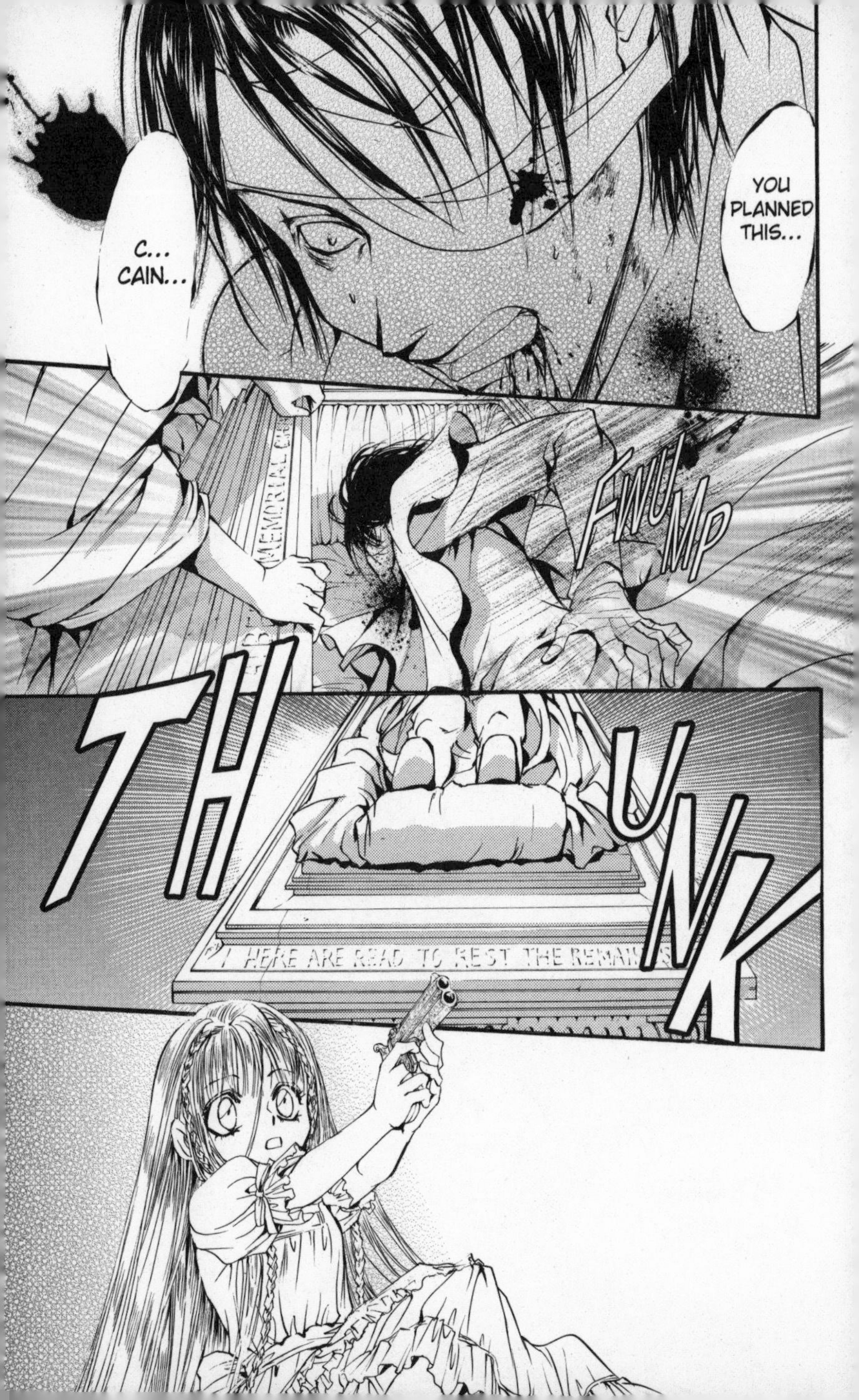
YOU PLANNED THIS...
C... CAIN...
FWUMP
THUNK

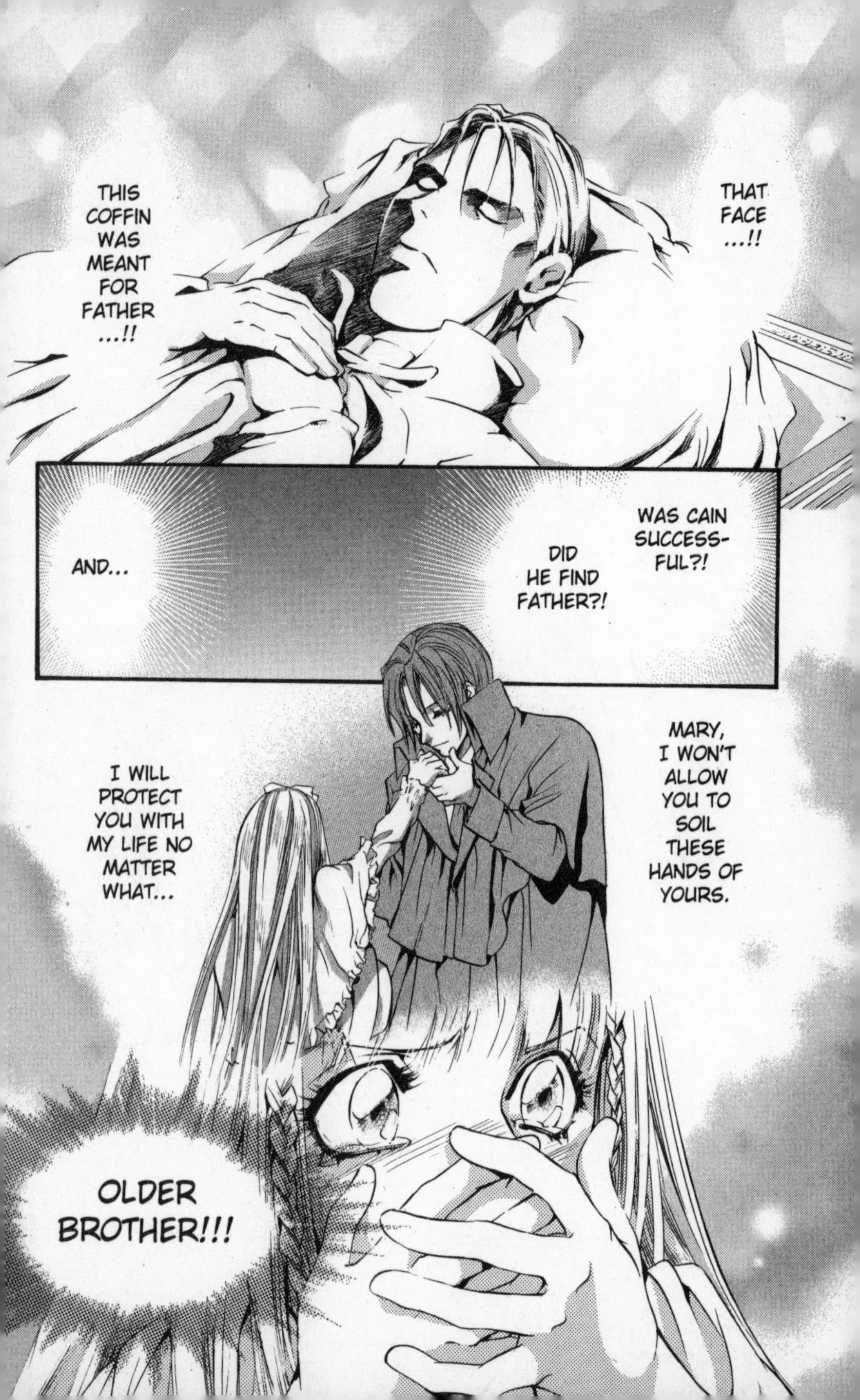
THAT FACE ...!!
THIS COFFIN WAS MEANT FOR FATHER ...!!
WAS CAIN SUCCESS-FUL?!
DID HE FIND FATHER?!
AND...
MARY, I WON'T ALLOW YOU TO SOIL THESE HANDS OF YOURS.
I WILL PROTECT YOU WITH MY LIFE NO MATTER WHAT...
OLDER BROTHER!!!

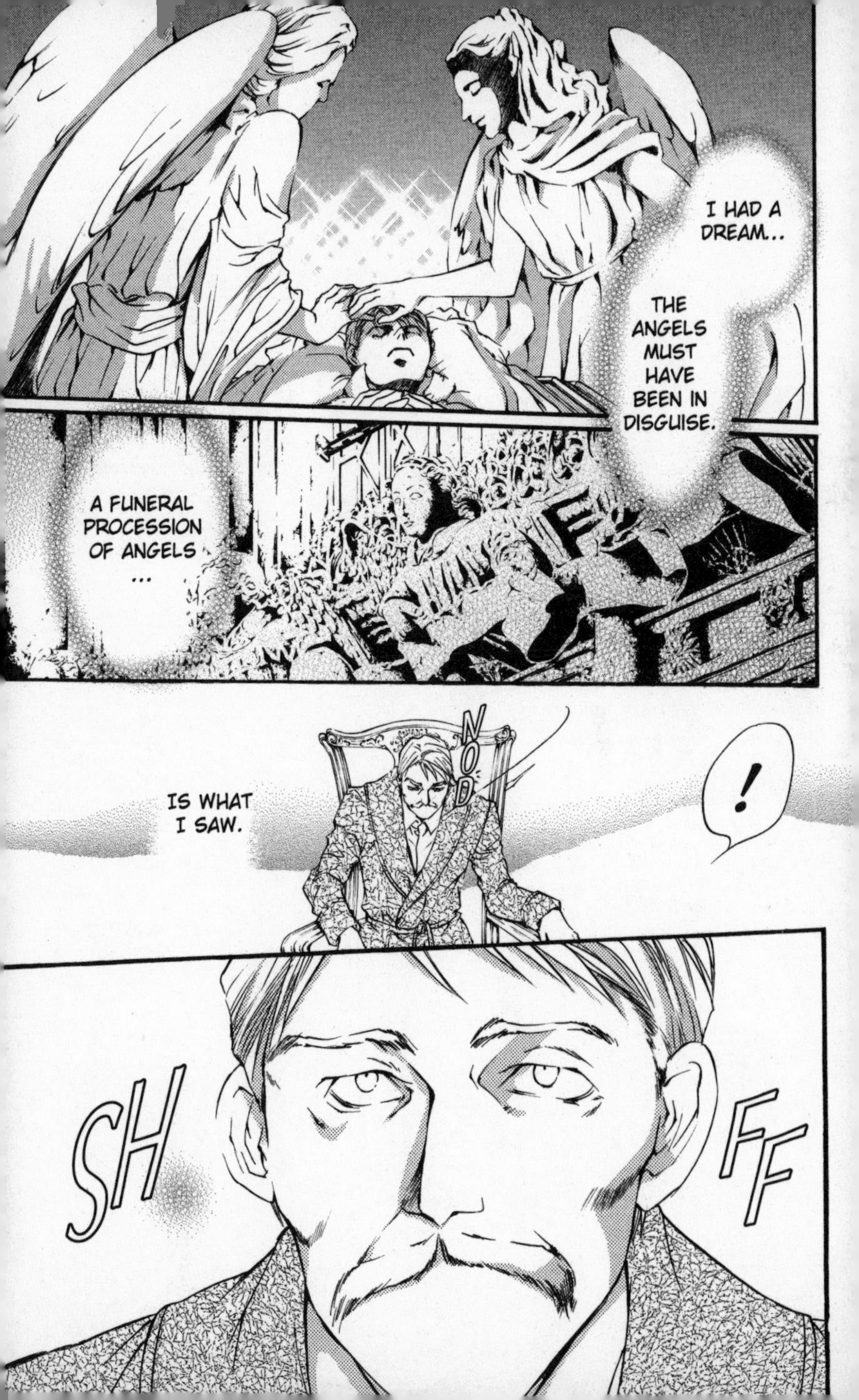
I HAD A DREAM...
THE ANGELS MUST HAVE BEEN IN DISGUISE.
A FUNERAL PROCESSION OF ANGELS ...
!
NOD
IS WHAT I SAW.
SHFF

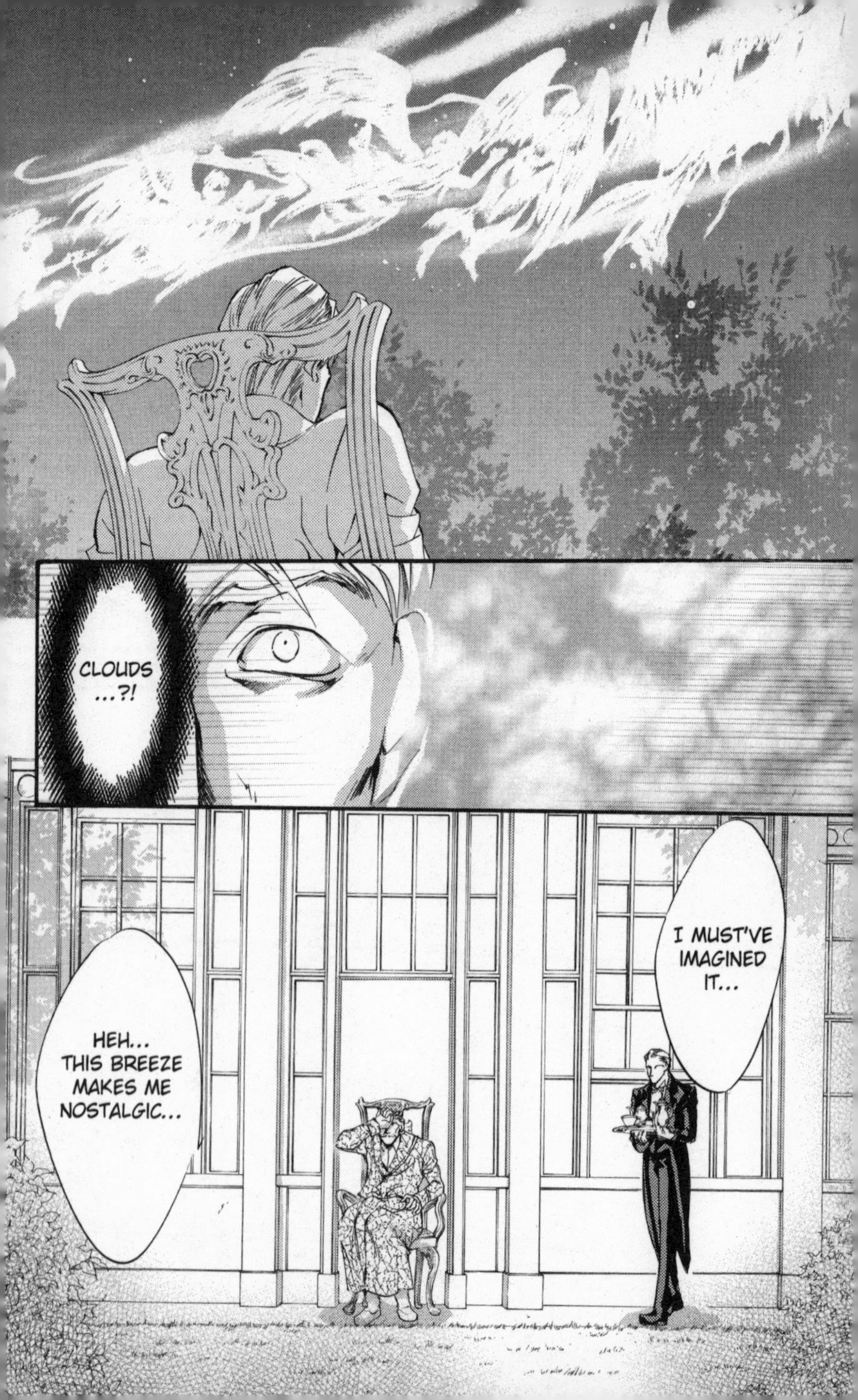
CLOUDS ...?!
I MUST'VE IMAGINED IT...
HEH... THIS BREEZE MAKES ME NOSTALGIC...

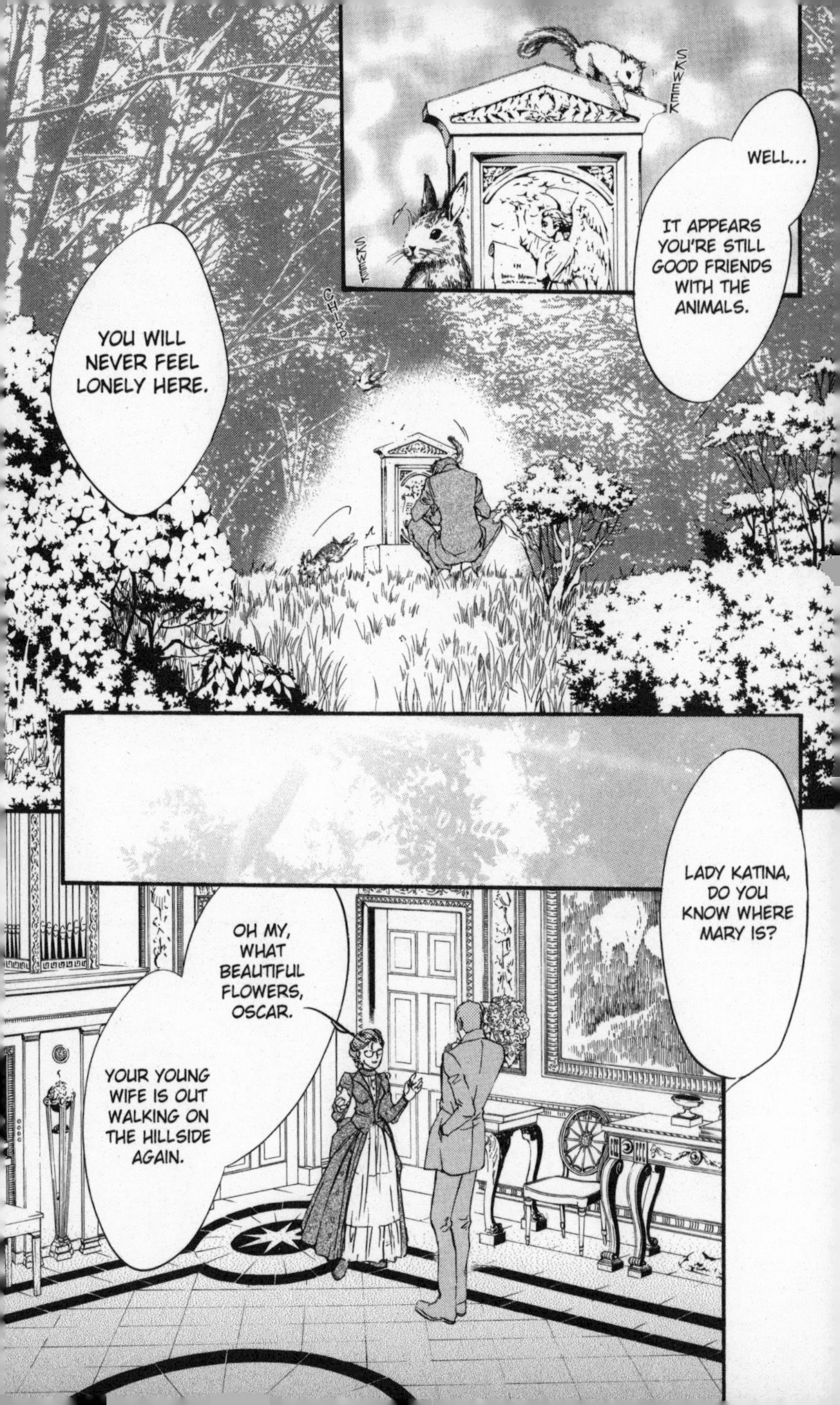
SKWEEK
SKWEEK
WELL...
IT APPEARS YOU'RE STILL GOOD FRIENDS WITH THE ANIMALS.
CHIRP
YOU WILL NEVER FEEL LONELY HERE.
LADY KATINA, DO YOU KNOW WHERE MARY IS?
OH MY, WHAT BEAUTIFUL FLOWERS, OSCAR.
YOUR YOUNG WIFE IS OUT WALKING ON THE HILLSIDE AGAIN.

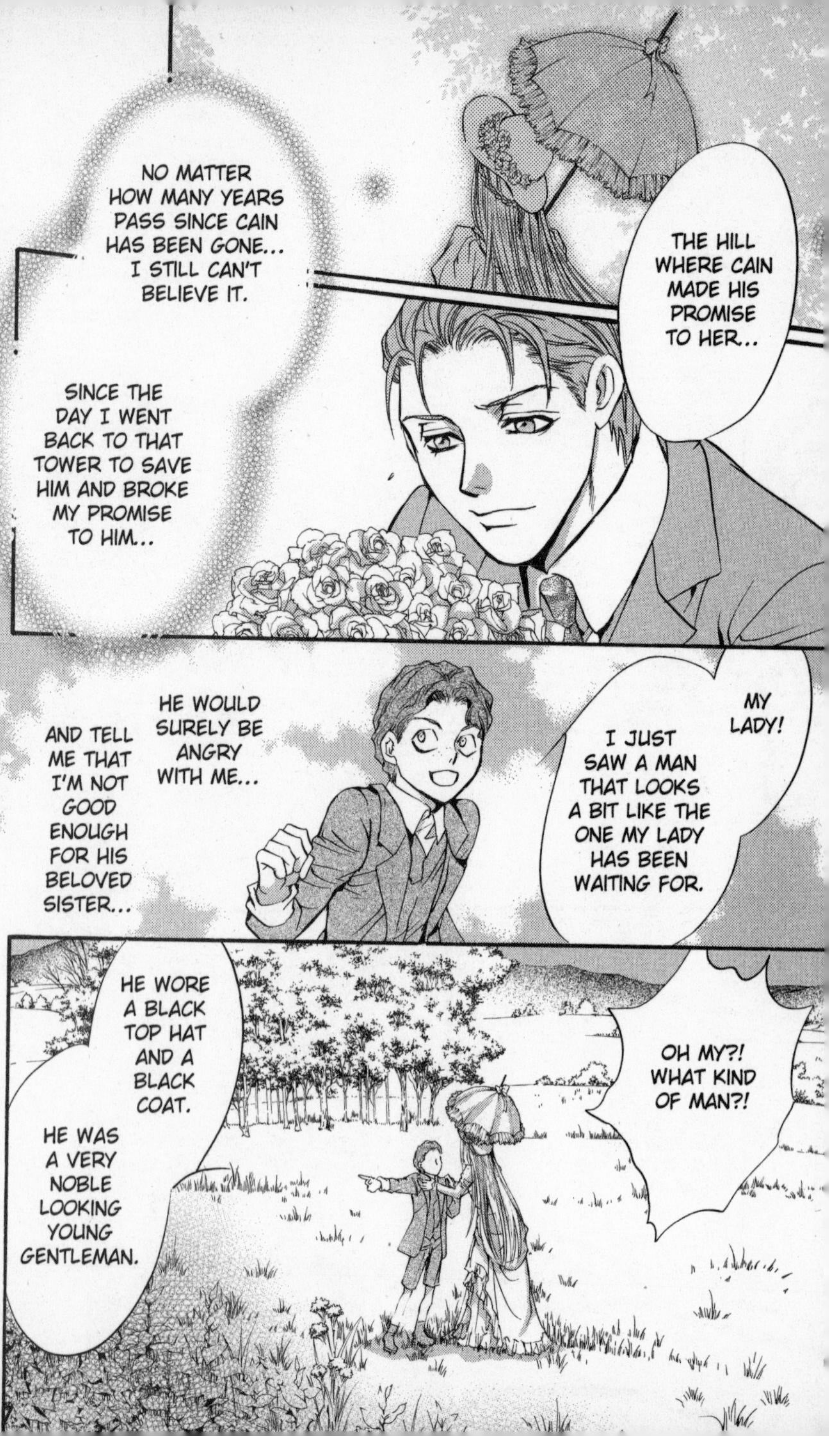
THE HILL WHERE CAIN MADE HIS PROMISE TO HER...
NO MATTER HOW MANY YEARS PASS SINCE CAIN HAS BEEN GONE... I STILL CAN'T BELIEVE IT.
SINCE THE DAY I WENT BACK TO THAT TOWER TO SAVE HIM AND BROKE MY PROMISE TO HIM...
MY LADY!
I JUST SAW A MAN THAT LOOKS A BIT LIKE THE ONE MY LADY HAS BEEN WAITING FOR.
HE WOULD SURELY BE ANGRY WITH ME...
AND TELL ME THAT I'M NOT GOOD ENOUGH FOR HIS BELOVED SISTER...
OH MY?! WHAT KIND OF MAN?!
HE WORE A BLACK TOP HAT AND A BLACK COAT.
HE WAS A VERY NOBLE LOOKING YOUNG GENTLEMAN.

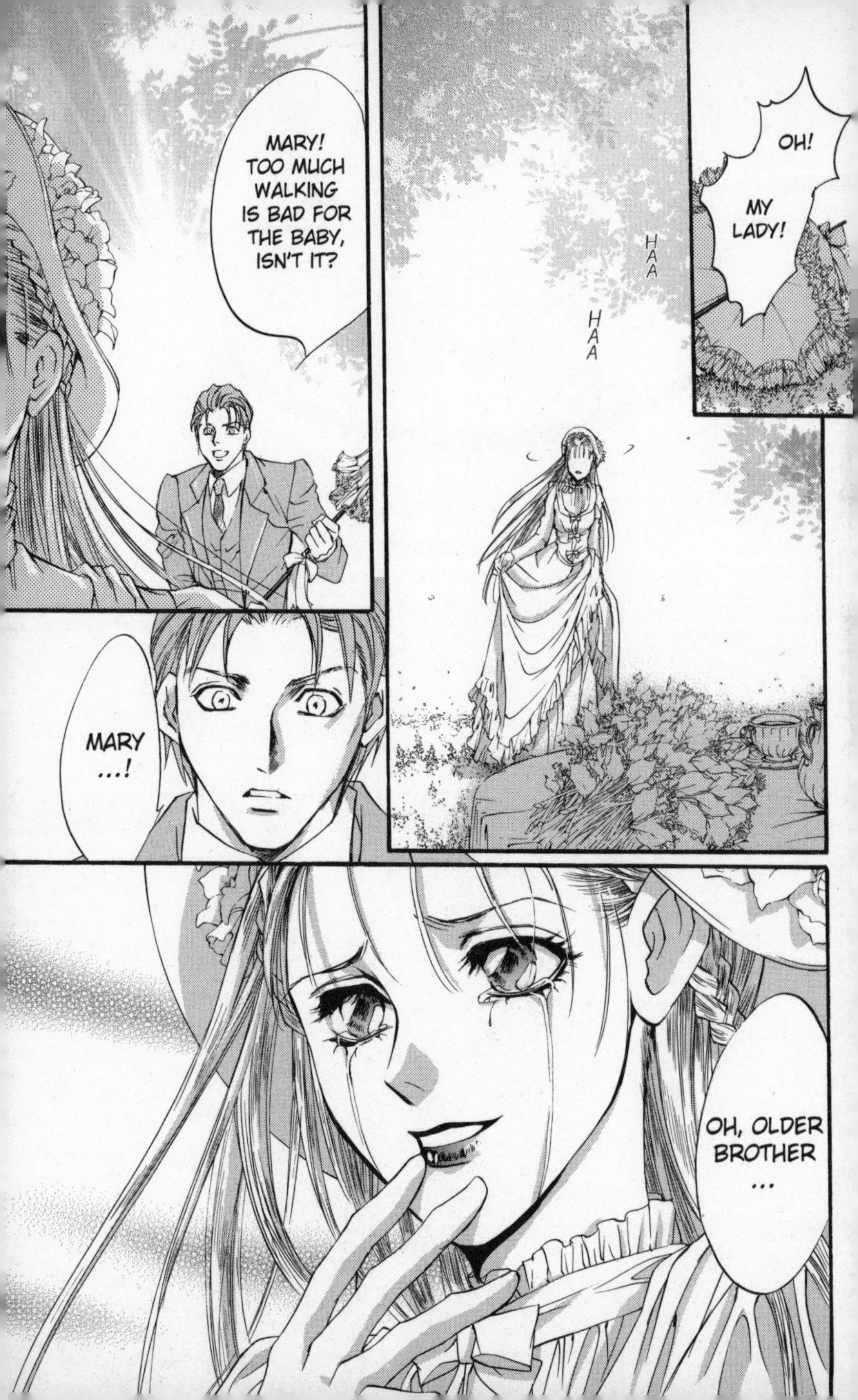
OH!
MY LADY!
HAA
HAA
MARY! TOO MUCH WALKING IS BAD FOR THE BABY, ISN'T IT?
MARY ...!
OH, OLDER BROTHER ...

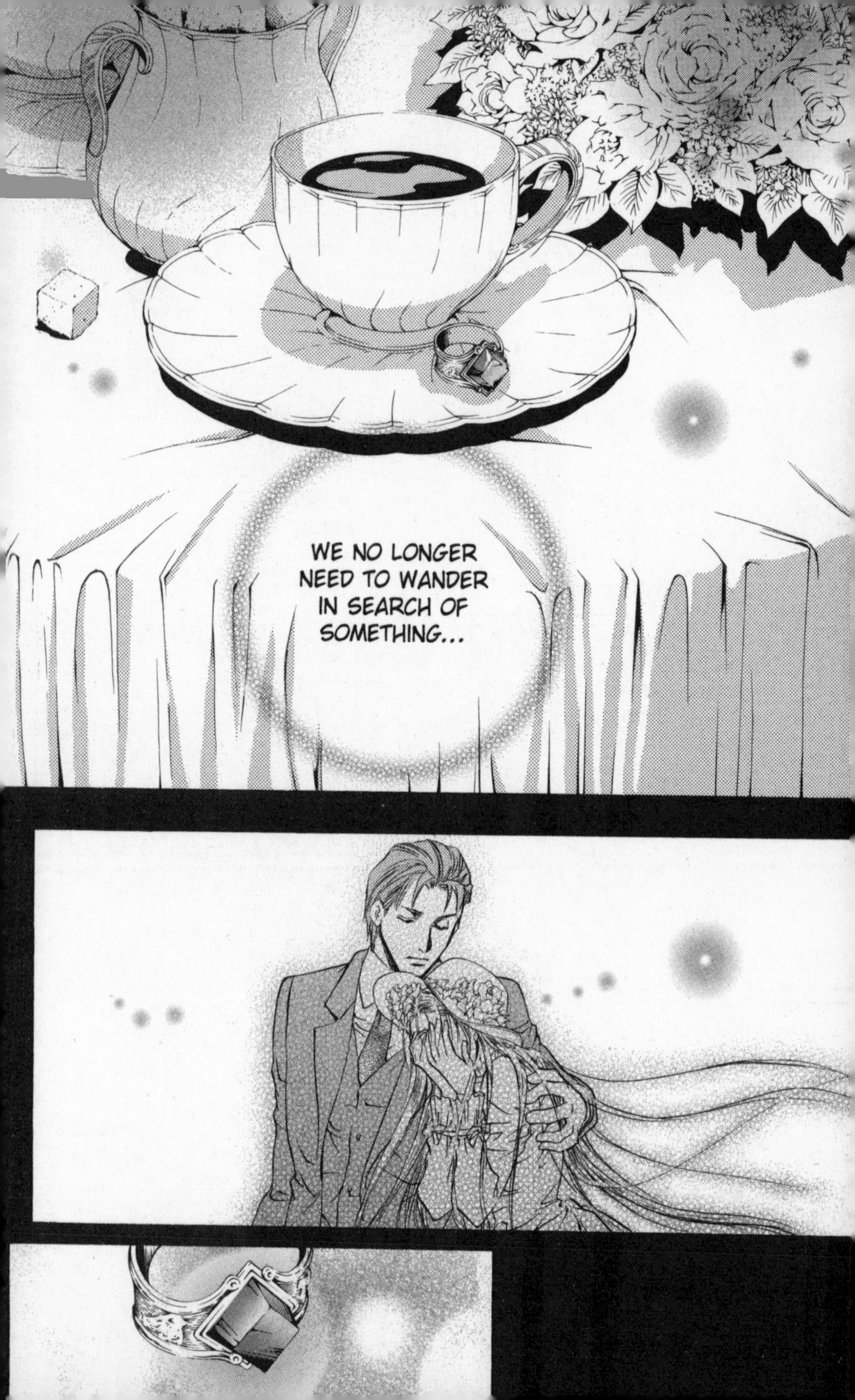
WE NO LONGER NEED TO WANDER IN SEARCH OF SOMETHING...

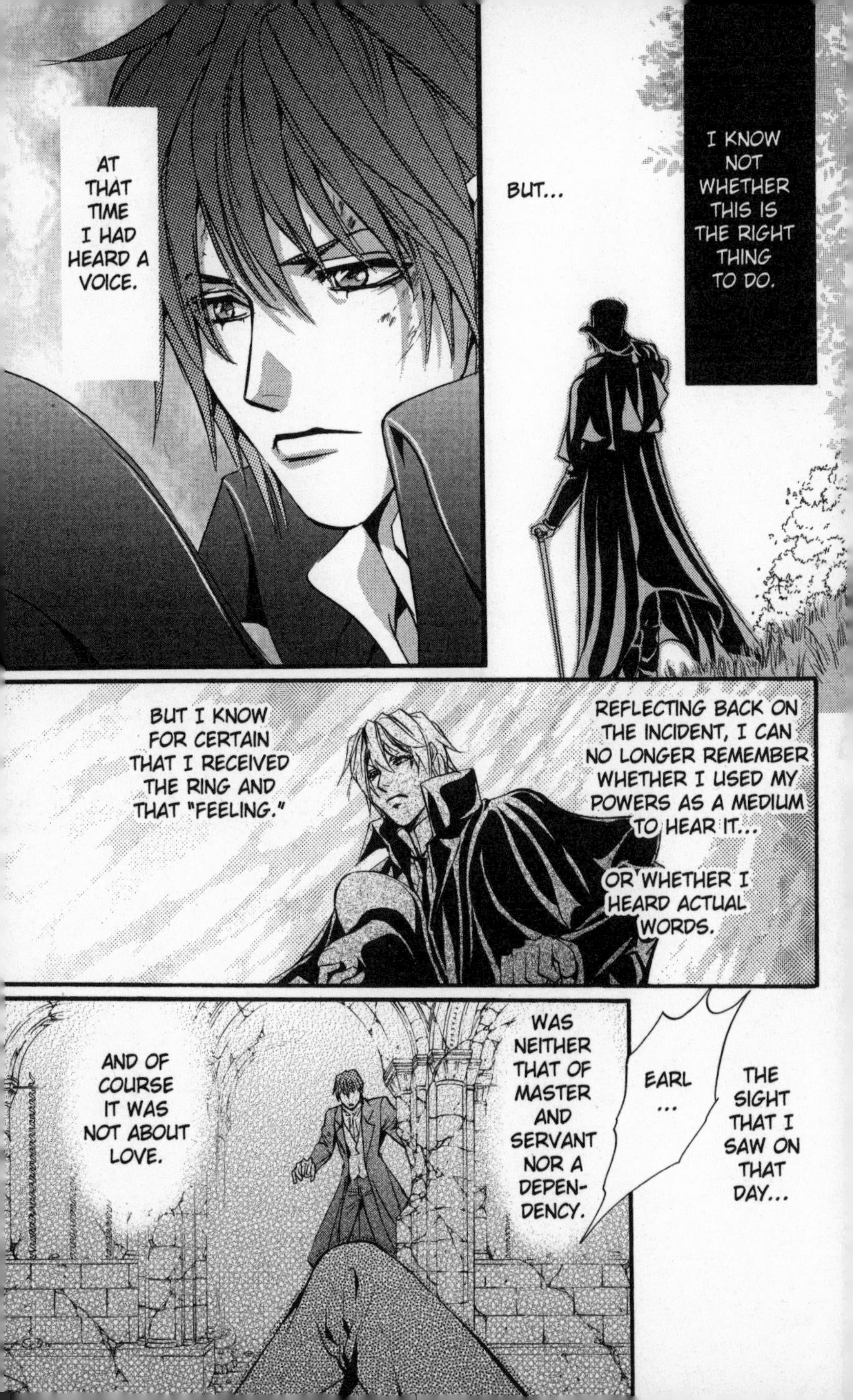
I KNOW NOT WHETHER THIS IS THE RIGHT THING TO DO.
BUT...
AT THAT TIME I HAD HEARD A VOICE.
REFLECTING BACK ON THE INCIDENT, I CAN NO LONGER REMEMBER WHETHER I USED MY POWERS AS A MEDIUM TO HEAR IT...
OR WHETHER I HEARD ACTUAL WORDS.
BUT I KNOW FOR CERTAIN THAT I RECEIVED THE RING AND THAT "FEELING."
THE SIGHT THAT I SAW ON THAT DAY...
EARL...
WAS NEITHER THAT OF MASTER AND SERVANT NOR A DEPEN-DENCY.
AND OF COURSE IT WAS NOT ABOUT LOVE.

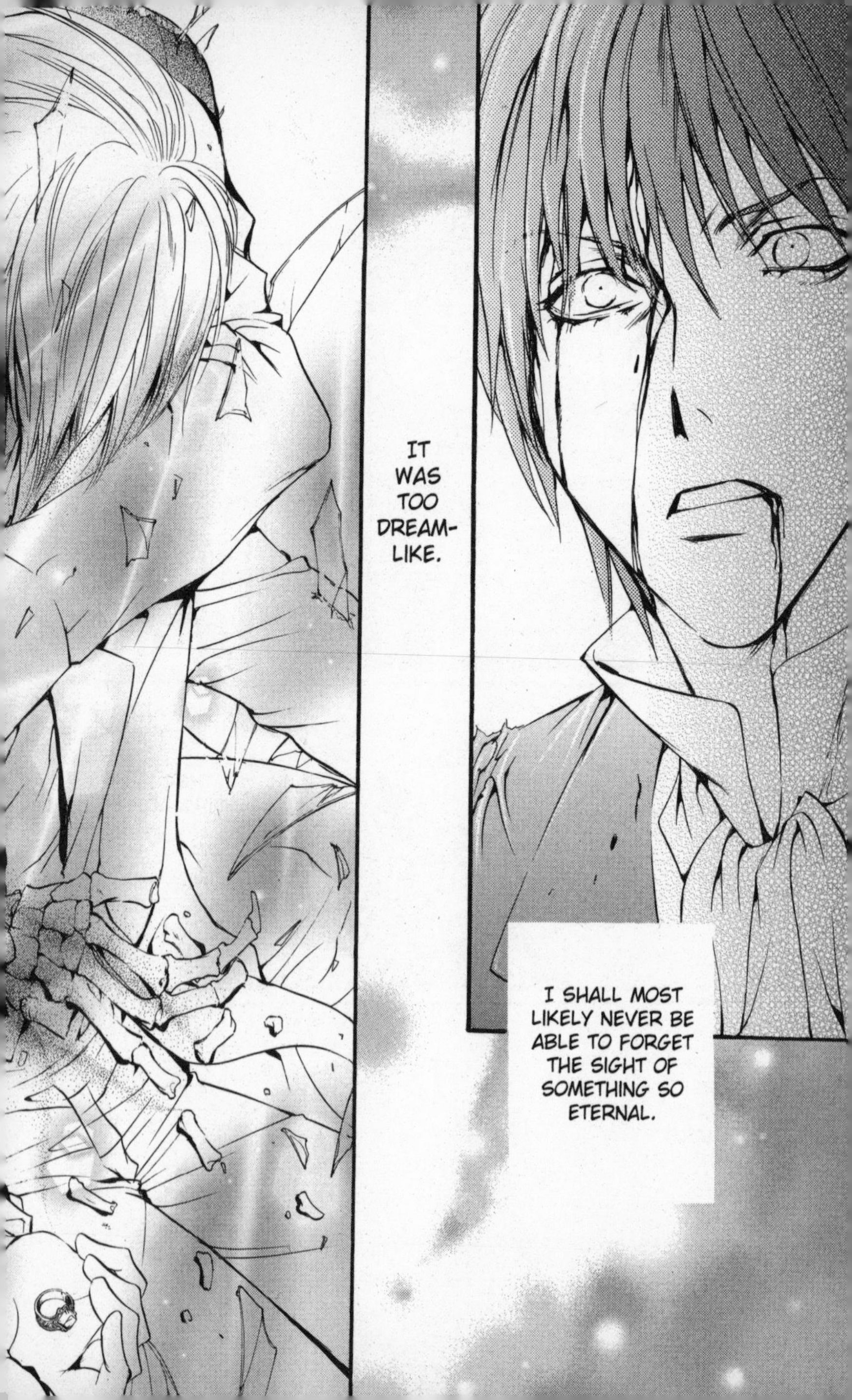
IT WAS TOO DREAM-LIKE.
I SHALL MOST LIKELY NEVER BE ABLE TO FORGET THE SIGHT OF SOMETHING SO ETERNAL.

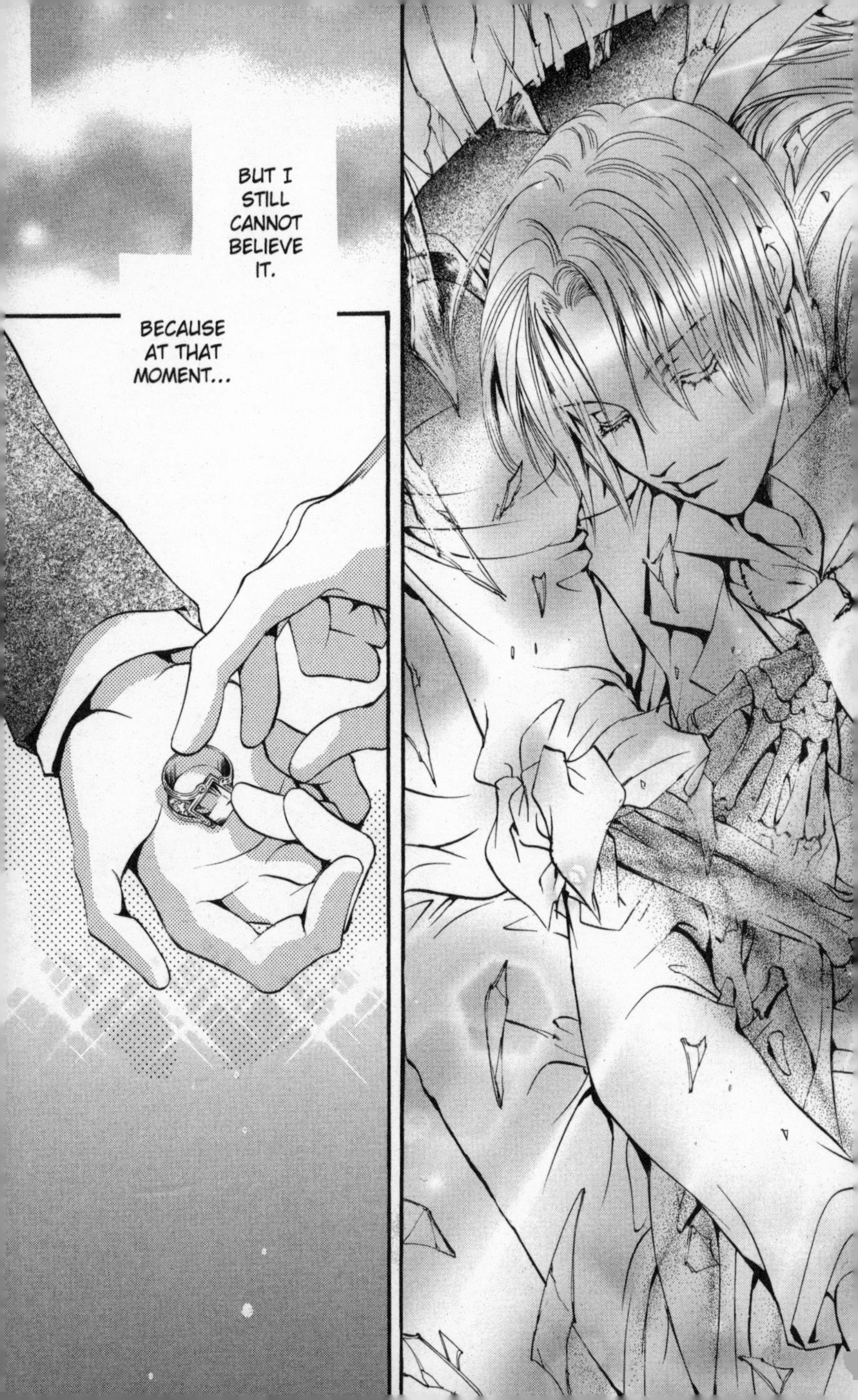
BUT I STILL CANNOT BELIEVE IT.
BECAUSE AT THAT MOMENT...

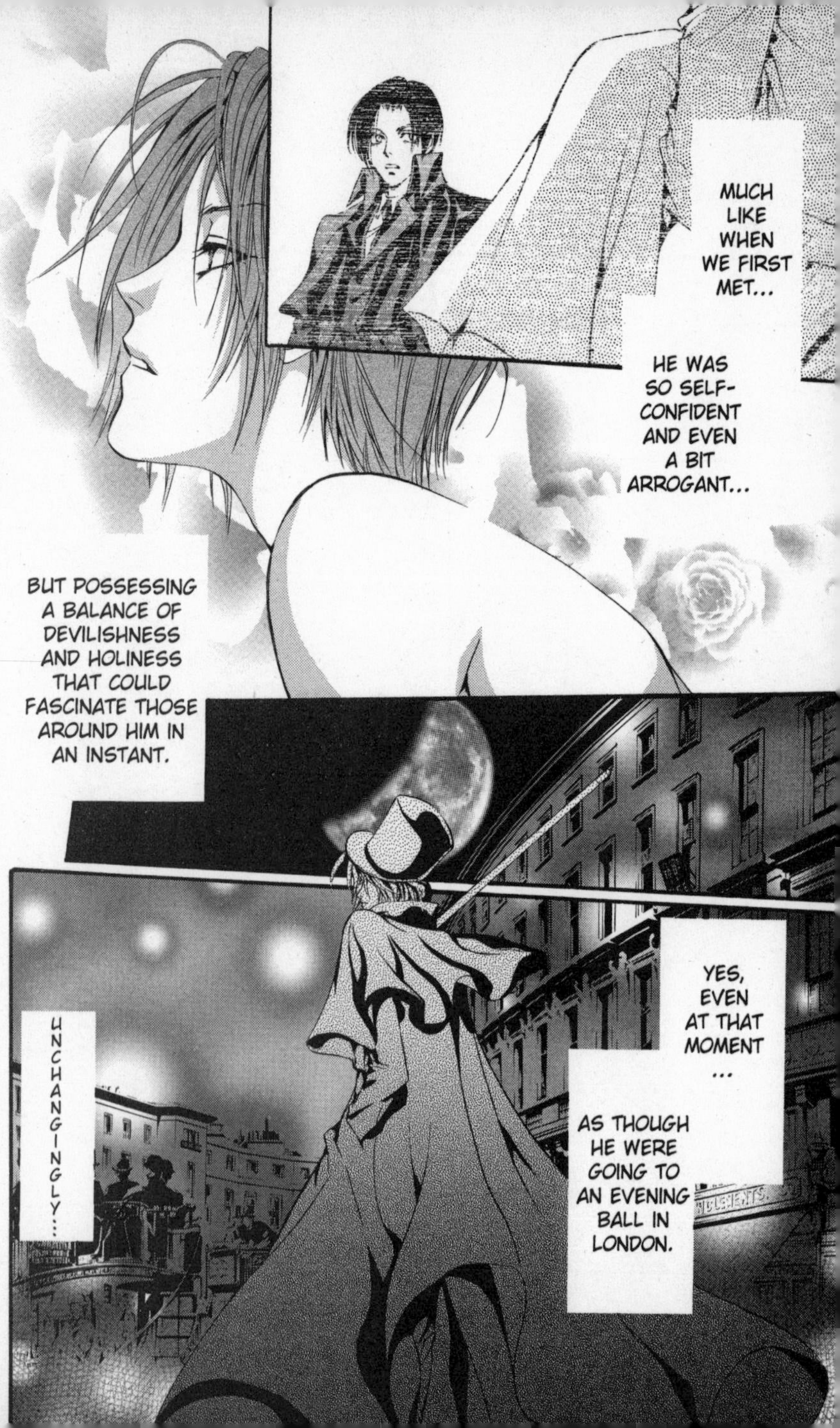
MUCH LIKE WHEN WE FIRST MET...
HE WAS SO SELF-CONFIDENT AND EVEN A BIT ARROGANT...
BUT POSSESSING A BALANCE OF DEVILISHNESS AND HOLINESS THAT COULD FASCINATE THOSE AROUND HIM IN AN INSTANT.
YES, EVEN AT THAT MOMENT ...
AS THOUGH HE WERE GOING TO AN EVENING BALL IN LONDON.
UNCHANGINGLY...

HE CONTINUES AS GRACEFULLY AS EVER...

TO SMILE.

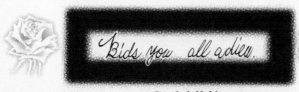

Bids you all adieu.

Godchild/The End

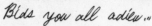

Bids you all adieu...

The phrase that graced the ending is the last line of the Mother Goose nursery rhyme "Simple Simon." It means something like "It's time to say goodbye. Farewell." I used it so it could go with the phrase "And that's all" from Mother Goose's "This Old Man". I'm just happy it wasn't more like "And Then There Were None"... Ha ha.

When the ending was published in the magazine it was 38 pages which is quite a bit more than usual.(normally it's 30pgs.) But there were certain scenes that needed to be included otherwise the story wouldn't make sense and in the comics there are even more scenes that I drew and added. For the time being this is five volumes + eight volumes... so it ends with a total of 13 volumes. It was quite a long story... It took a lot of years didn't it? At this point, I haven't considered any additional episodes or side stories. Although I have the same policy for all of my works... Well I guess I won't know until that time comes. After the series became **Godchild** I became a bit nervous because I knew that the plot was going to become much darker in the second half... The reason is that I knew I was going to use this ending. But I had also already discussed with the editorial department that the real story would start after Riff's betrayal. I also knew that from that point until the ending, the story would become very interesting. I needed to work hard. It's difficult as a writer to place the characters within all of the changing events. Plus, it was right after I realized that although there were a lot of unconventional supporting characters in my previous series **Angel Sanctuary** the readers wanted the two protagonists to have a happy ending... So I had a difficult time in deciding whether I should really have an ending like this. Some of the fans wrote to me and said that they wanted an unhappy ending but it makes sense that most people would want a happy ending. I'm that way too. But I thought there

should be a correct ending for Cain... so I knew I had to do it. Of course this is not a completely hopeless ending and I think it could also be considered happy in some ways. Like Crehador mentions, it is a situation where it's difficult to tell whether he's alive or dead... 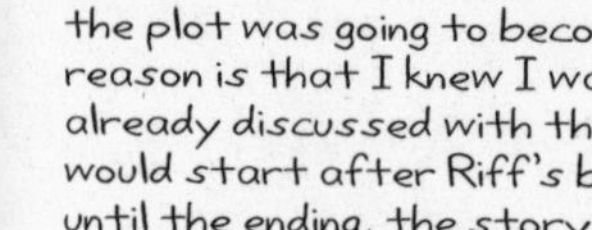
That's why there's no evidence of Cain suffering a fatal wound and there's also no sign of blood. As he's being embraced by Riff even the broken glass in the background looks like wings...

I took great pains not to reveal that Augusta was the villain. Well there probably are some amazing readers out there who knew as soon as they saw her severed head but... When I told my assistants that there was a "hidden boss character" I think it might have scared them a bit, because I had mentioned her name before in that context. But the story was still too vague, so I had to add some more pages. I had to try a lot of different things.

Right now I've been working on a few short stories but it will be some time before I do another series. But that doesn't mean that I have a lot of time. I have to deal with something new every day... and there's hardly enough time for anything. I will have to juggle three or four life-changing events until well into the coming year, but being a manga artist I am somewhat inept at these things and am in a state of panic...!! I am trying my hardest at everything by savoring the happy feeling of being helped by family and friends. I will eventually come back to you with a brand new series so please support me when that time comes! I'd like to say thank you from the bottom of my heart to all the readers who have supported the Cain series.

Well then,
see you soon. ♥
11/18/2003

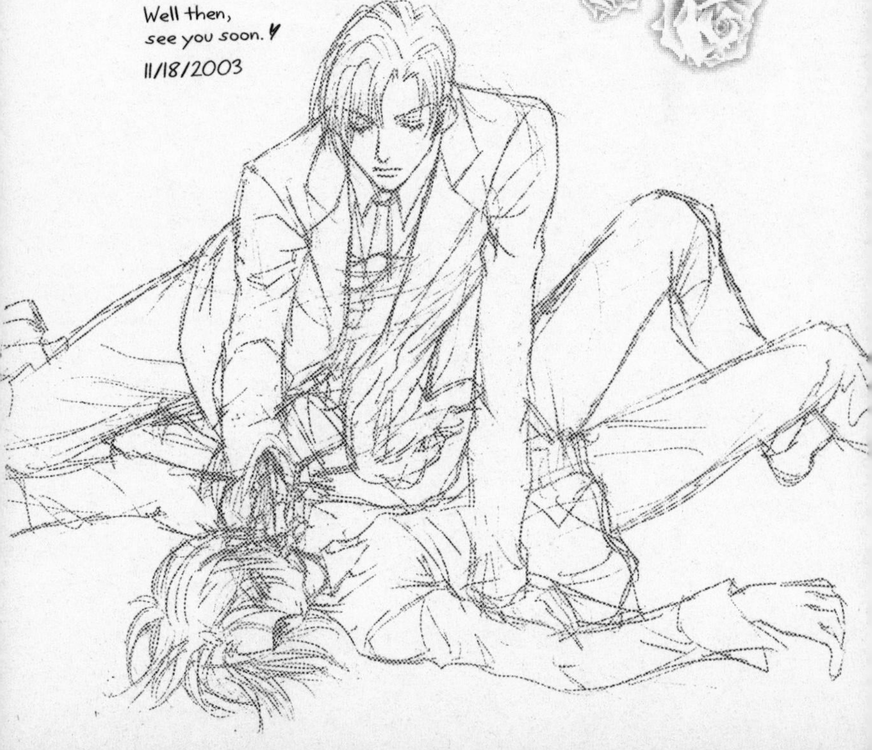

Creator: Kaori Yuki
Date of Birth: December 18
Blood Type: B
Major Works: *Angel Sanctuary*
and *The Cain Saga*

K aori Yuki was born in Tokyo and started drawing at a very early age. Following her debut work *Natsufuku no Erie* (Ellie in Summer Clothes) in the Japanese magazine *Bessatsu Hana to Yume* (1987), she wrote a compelling series of short stories: *Zankoku na Douwatachi* (Cruel Fairy Tales), *Neji* (Screw), and *Sareki Ôkoku* (Gravel Kingdom).

As proven by her best-selling series *Angel Sanctuary* and *The Cain Saga*, her celebrated body of work has etched an indelible mark on the gothic comics genre. She likes mysteries and British films, and is a fan of the movie *Dead Poets Society* and the show *Twin Peaks*.

Read Kaori Yuki's entire Earl Cain Series

Series 1: *The Cain Saga*: Forgotten Juliet
Series 2: *The Cain Saga*: The Sound of a Boy Hatching
Series 3: *The Cain Saga*: Kafka
Series 4: *The Cain Saga*: The Seal of the Red Ram, Volumes 1 & 2
Series 5: *Godchild*, Volumes 1-8

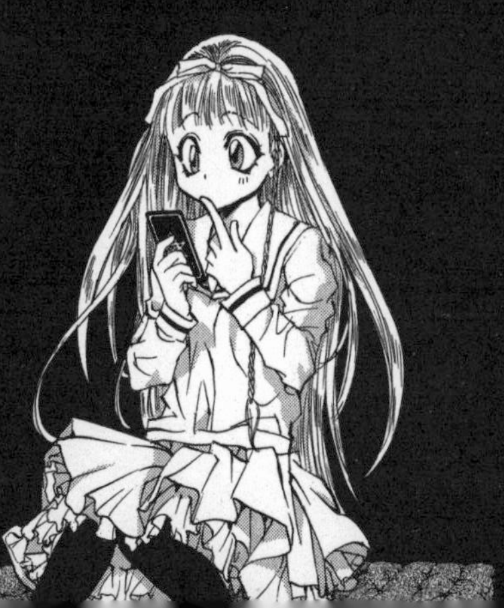

GODCHILD, vol. 8
The Shojo Beat Manga Edition

STORY & ART BY **KAORI YUKI**

Translation/Akira Watanabe
Touch-up Art & Lettering/James Gaubatz
Design/Courtney Utt
Editor/Joel Enos

Editor in Chief, Books/Alvin Lu
Editor in Chief, Magazines/Marc Weidenbaum
VP of Publishing Licensing/Rika Inouye
VP of Sales/Gonzalo Ferreyra
Sr. VP of Marketing/Liza Coppola
Publisher/Hyoe Narita

Printed in Canada

Published by VIZ Media, LLC
P.O. Box 77010
San Francisco, CA 94107

Shojo Beat Manga Edition
10 9 8 7 6 5 4 3 2 1
First printing, February 2008

store.viz.com

Kaori Yuki's latest epic is here!

Fairy Cube

Special Preview!

IAN

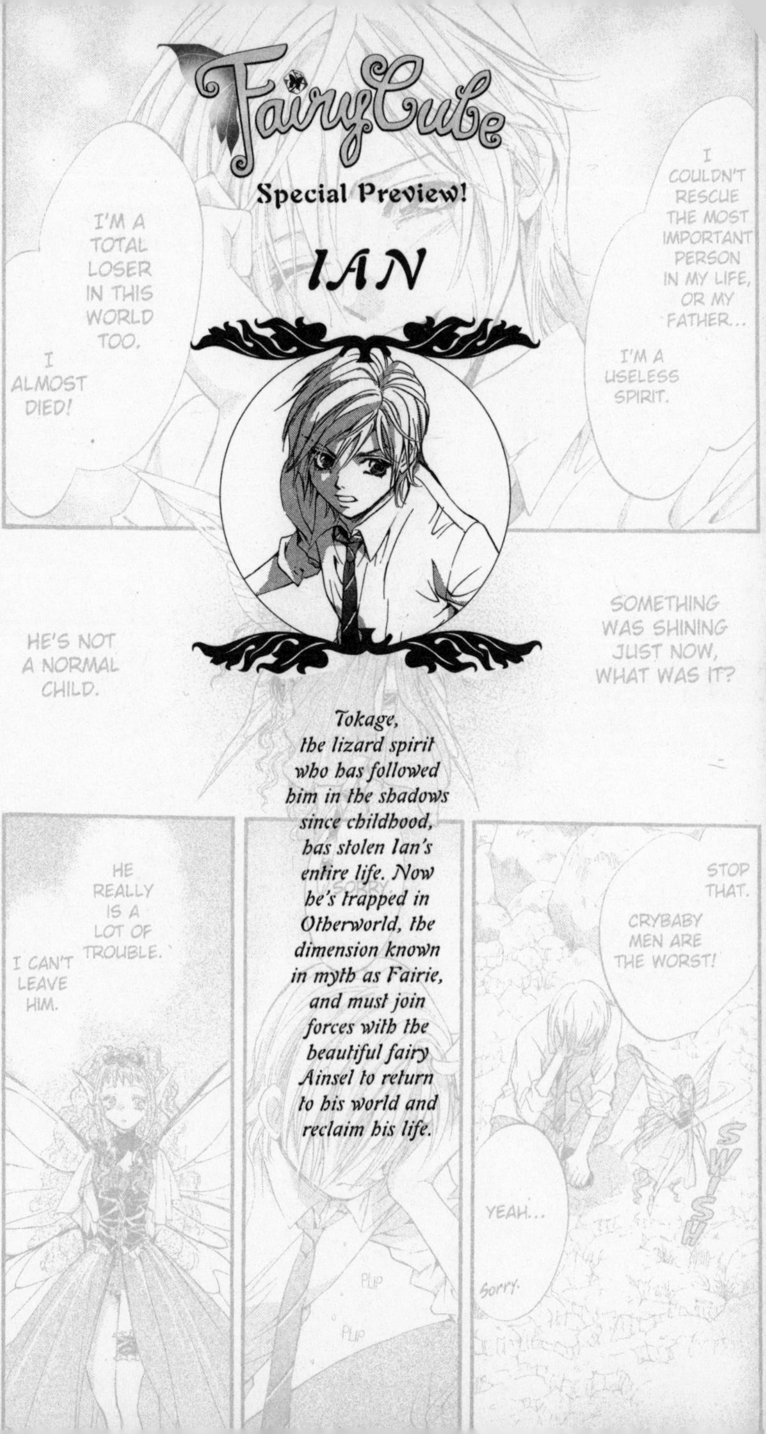
I COULDN'T RESCUE THE MOST IMPORTANT PERSON IN MY LIFE, OR MY FATHER...
I'M A USELESS SPIRIT.
I'M A TOTAL LOSER IN THIS WORLD TOO.
I ALMOST DIED!
SOMETHING WAS SHINING JUST NOW, WHAT WAS IT?
HE'S NOT A NORMAL CHILD.
STOP THAT.
CRYBABY MEN ARE THE WORST!
SWISH
YEAH...
Sorry.
SORRY.
PLIP
PLIP
HE REALLY IS A LOT OF TROUBLE.
I CAN'T LEAVE HIM.

Tokage, the lizard spirit who has followed him in the shadows since childhood, has stolen Ian's entire life. Now he's trapped in Otherworld, the dimension known in myth as Fairie, and must join forces with the beautiful fairy Ainsel to return to his world and reclaim his life.

Fairy Cube

Special Preview!

RIN

Rin shares Ian's ability to see spirits. But she can't see that Tokage is posing as Ian. She's at risk of falling in love with a lizard spirit disguised as her soul mate while Ian is trapped in Otherworld!

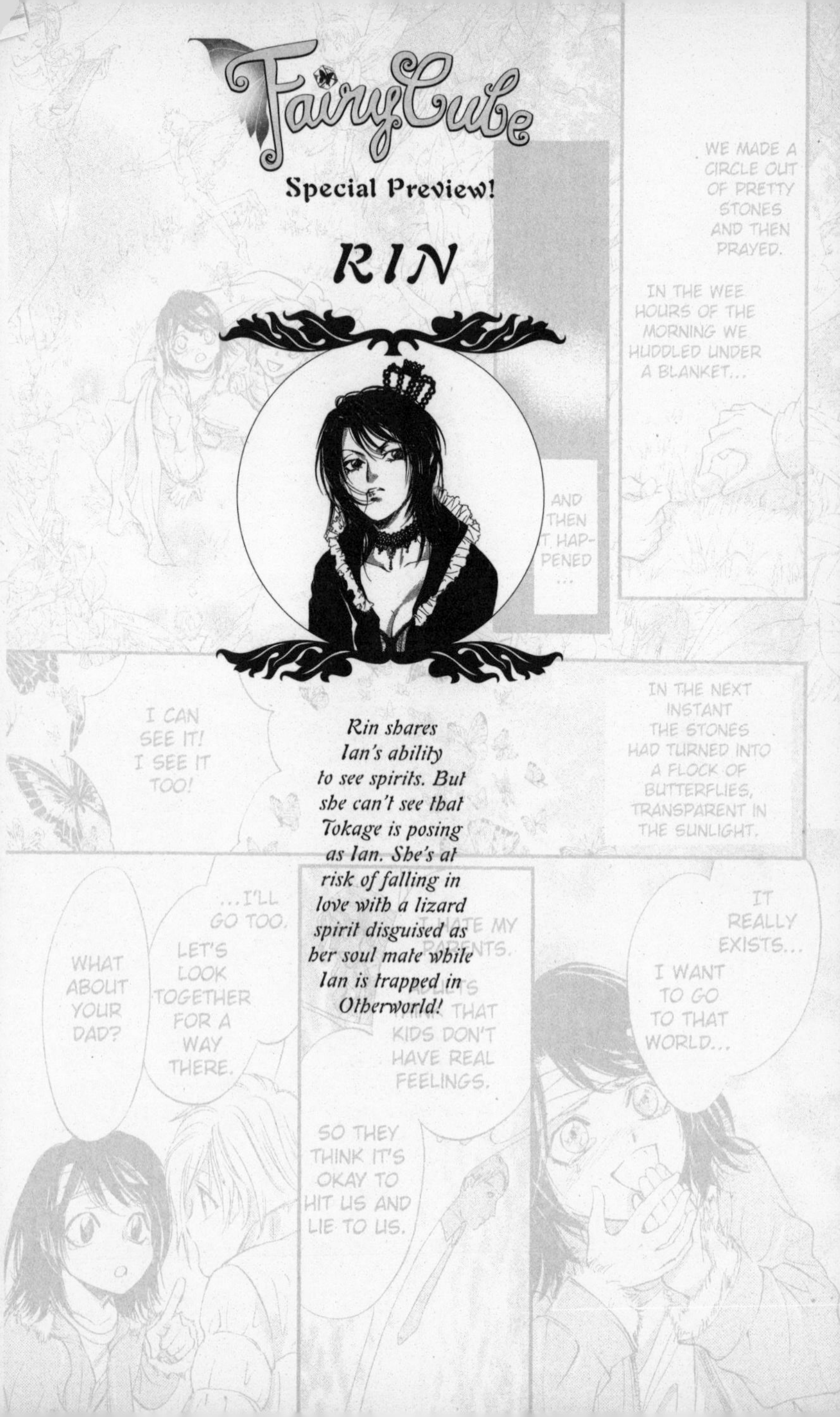
WE MADE A CIRCLE OUT OF PRETTY STONES AND THEN PRAYED.
IN THE WEE HOURS OF THE MORNING WE HUDDLED UNDER A BLANKET...
AND THEN IT HAPPENED...
IN THE NEXT INSTANT THE STONES HAD TURNED INTO A FLOCK OF BUTTERFLIES, TRANSPARENT IN THE SUNLIGHT.
I CAN SEE IT! I SEE IT TOO!
IT REALLY EXISTS...
I WANT TO GO TO THAT WORLD...
I HATE MY PARENTS.
THAT KIDS DON'T HAVE REAL FEELINGS.
SO THEY THINK IT'S OKAY TO HIT US AND LIE TO US.
...I'LL GO TOO.
LET'S LOOK TOGETHER FOR A WAY THERE.
WHAT ABOUT YOUR DAD?